American Democracy: Promise and Betrayal

Fifth Edition

DEAN DARRIS

Cover Art: Courtesy of EyeWire/Getty Images

Copyright © 2009 by Pearson Custom Publishing
All rights reserved.

Permission in writing must be obtained from the publisher before any part of this work may be reproduced or transmitted in any form or by any means, electronic or mechanical, including photocopying and recording, or by any information storage or retrieval system.

All trademarks, service marks, registered trademarks, and registered service marks are the property of their respective owners and are used herein for identification purposes only.

All views, opinions, and language expressed in this book are solely those of the author or other contributors and are not to be attributed to any staff or officers of Pearson Education.

Printed in the United States of America

10 9 8 7 6 5 4 3 2 1

2009480004

**Pearson
Custom Publishing**
is a division of

PEARSON

www.pearsonhighered.com

ISBN 10: 0-558-38533-8
ISBN 13: 978-0-558-38533-0

Contents

Preface .... *v*

SECTION I: GETTING STARTED

CHAPTER 1
Introduction: Promise and Betrayal 3

CHAPTER 2
Constitutional Contemplation: *E Pluribus Unum*
(From Many, One) 13

SECTION II: POLITICAL PROCESSES

CHAPTER 3
Public Opinion and Political Polls:
Permission or Submission? 37

CHAPTER 4
Political Parties, Ideologies, and the American
Political Spectrum: Tweedledee & Tweedledum 49

CHAPTER 5
The Media: Through the Looking Glass 77

CHAPTER 6
Economic Policy: The Divine Command 103

Chapter 7
Foreign Policy: Minding the Empire 129

SECTION III: NATIONAL INSTITUTIONS
Chapter 8
The Article I Branch: The Congress 167

Chapter 9
The Article II Branch: The Presidency 185

Chapter 10
The Article III Branch: The Federal Judiciary 209

SECTION IV: WHERE DO WE GO FROM HERE?
Chapter 11
Representation: We the People 229

Chapter 12
Remedies: Justice for All 245

Appendix
The Declaration of Independence 261
The Articles of Confederation 265
The Federalist No. 10 272
The Federalist No. 51 279
The Constitution of the United States 283
Amendments to the Constitution 294

Glossary 305
Index 315
About the Author 331

Preface

When first published in 1997, *American Democracy: Promise and Betrayal,* predicted a rather bleak future for our constitutional democracy. It warned of an impending financial crisis and an emerging foreign policy quagmire. Four editions later, much of what the text predicted has become our present political reality. America is now involved in two very hot wars, while the economy is in its worst shape since the Great Depression. No longer is there a debate over the health of America's democracy, what matters now is how to fix it. There is no time for "I told you so," we have too much important work to do to restore America's democracy. So, as you read the book, keep in mind that by doing so you have already taken the first step in becoming part of the solution. That is, we must understand that there is no such thing as an "uninformed voter" or "uninformed citizen." Upon closer inspection, what we really have in such a case are "uninformed individuals." The concept "voter" or "citizen" implies that someone is already politically informed, which makes their vote and citizenship meaningful because they know what they are doing and why, period. In short, an uninformed voter or citizen is an oxymoron, while the term "informed" voter or citizen is a redundancy. So, we can assert with scientific certainty that America's future will be as bright as its citizens, who must become better educated in all things political if they are to improve their futures. That is why the book's subtitle could read, "A Citizen's Guide to Better Government," since that is its purpose and challenge. By committing ourselves to an intellectual engagement with the text, we begin the process of taking our roles as citizens more seriously. And by taking our roles as citizens more seriously, we lessen the likely hood that we'll lose the democracy that has been entrusted to us. Moreover, only through a thorough understanding of America's political system can we begin to rebuild our society on more hopeful grounds. That is what is at stake. It is with this mission statement that I present the fifth edition of my small contribution to America's political revival.

Like the fourth edition, *American Democracy: Promise and Betrayal* examines the orthodox subjects of American politics. Unlike most American government texts, however, it does so with a critical perspective derived from the values inherent in classical republicanism, a philosophy which puts a concern for the common good at the center of its political theory. Yet the book is hardly what most would consider conservative. In fact it may seem almost radical in its analysis of present political reality. This apparent paradox says as much about modern conservative thought as it does about the public's alienation from the very principles which gave rise to self-government in America. In short, this book will disappoint any reader looking for a celebration of contemporary politics, while rewarding the reader searching for an academic text which places ethics at the core of its political analysis.

The book's format has remained relatively unchanged to keep it reader friendly for both students and teachers alike. Besides the usual clarifications and corrections that alone justify a new edition, the chapter on the media has been revised to account for the Internet's effect on the mainstream media and the political system. The entire book has been revised to account for the 2008 elections and their effect on America's political system. The chapter on economics has been updated so as to better explain the present state of our economy. The so-called "War on Terror" is addressed as well throughout the book, but particularly in chapter seven. Moreover, each chapter ends with some "final thoughts" that point to a new way forward. And the book concludes with a new chapter eleven that introduces four steps to better government followed by chapter twelve that provides the foundational solutions that are required if we want a "more perfect union." In fact, the entire book is an attempt to provide real solutions to America's political problems, and it should be read with this in mind. This systemic approach helps each reader understand that foreign and domestic policies are interconnected and cannot be comprehended in isolation. For example, the economy is as much a result of foreign policy as it is about economics, and foreign policy is closely linked to economics.

One thing which has not changed from one edition to the next is the spirit which permeates the work, a spirit descended from America's founding principles and brilliantly echoed by Lincoln at Gettysburg more than a century ago: "It is for us the living...to be here dedicated to the great task remaining before us...that government of the people, by the people, and for the people, shall not perish from the earth." To this end, this book is dedicated to Lincoln's belief that the preservation of self-government rests upon a commitment to civic education on the part of Americans. With this in mind, I have attempted to provide a text which inspires the heart as much as the mind. A book which challenges students to take seriously their citizenship as a way not only to improve their lives but as a way to honor those whose bloody sacrifice granted them their liberty. To refuse this challenge constitutes a betrayal of America's most sacred promise—the promise that those who, in Lincoln's words, "gave the last full measure of devotion . . . shall not have died in vain."

In attempting to realize this purpose, I am indebted to a host of talented individuals who were more than generous in committing their expertise to the project. Therefore, I would like to thank the following people for their tremendous help in completing this book, without which it would not have been possible. Before doing so, however, allow me to present the obligatory (though no less sincere) disclaimer releasing them of all responsibility for whatever deficiencies my book might contain, while sharing with them whatever kudos it might receive.

That being said, I would first like to acknowledge the tremendous support I received throughout the writing process from the people of Pearson Publishing in general and Kelly Ross in particular. In spite of the book's less than friendly view of corporations, the people of Pearson Publishing consistently went above and beyond their professional duties in working with me to produce the best book possible, and for this I am eternally grateful. I would also like to extend my sincerest appreciation to the following: To my mentor, Craig Carr of Portland State University, for whatever analytic ability I might now possess, and for proving first-rate scholarship and superior teaching are not mutually exclusive; to my dissertation advisor, Ken Fishell of Berne University, whose suggestions made the book much more professional, as well as to Colin Brock of Oxford University and Marilyn Nelson of the University of New York for agreeing to be readers and whose enthusiasm for the project was a great source of inspiration. Special thanks goes to Tom Woodhouse of Riverland Community College, whose historical expertise and intellectual support proved to be invaluable. Moreover, I want to recognize the efforts of numerous former students whose help with the book was essential. I would like to express my heartfelt appreciation to my wife, Tara, for her long hours of proofreading the text in addition to her intellectual guidance that ensured my pedagogic and political aim remained true throughout the book.

Again, thanks to you all.

Section I

Getting Started

CHAPTER 1
Introduction: Promise and Betrayal

"Liberty cannot be preserved without a general knowledge among the people . . . Let us dare to read, think, speak, and write."
—*John Adams*

"Knowledge is in every country the surest basis of public happiness."
—*George Washington*

"Upon the subject of education . . . I can only say that I view it as the most important subject which we as a people may be engaged in."
—*Abraham Lincoln*

INTRODUCTION

The American struggle for **democracy** has always had a split personality because it has taken place in two separate arenas, one philosophical, the other practical. It is my thesis that this struggle has been successful on only one of these fronts (the philosophical) but has had only limited success on the other (the practical). That is to say, although democracy may no longer require much defense in the realm of ideas, it is, however, in dire need of support in the realm of governmental practice.[1] As American citizens it is time for us to comprehend this simple truth: *It is one thing for a political system to profess allegiance to democratic ideals, yet it is an entirely different matter for it to govern democratically.*[2] In short, actions will always speak louder than words when measuring a political system's democratic reality. For this reason, it would behoove us to review briefly democracy's history and theoretical deficiencies so as to better understand why this ideal has failed to translate into the actuality of governmental policy.

Today, democracy is clearly the brightest star within the constellation of political thought. To say this was not always the case is to put it mildly. Not long ago most philosophers considered democracy to be at best a silly political theory, or at worst a dangerous form of political association. Moreover, history has never failed to lend credence to the philosopher's logic as democratic governments were not only rare players on history's stage, they also played poorly in their scant appearances. So poorly in fact, James Madison, when commenting on their history, wrote that democratic societies tend to be "as short in their lives as they are violent in their deaths."[3] To be sure, democracy would flicker to life from time to time, be it in the guise of an Athenian city-state or in the deeds of a revolutionary Hebrew prophet.

Nevertheless, democracy would eventually recede into the far reaches of human consciousness due, it seems, to its own inadequacies. Hence, for the vast majority of the human time-line, democracy has been denigrated by both philosophy as well as history; by intellect as well as experience; by thought as well as action.

Political philosophers tended to dismiss democracy as a governing ideal because it rested its legitimacy and longevity on what most scholars thought was very shaky ground indeed—the political wisdom of the common person. Plato, for example, argued democracies inevitably fail because nature does not equip the majority of people with the intellectual and moral sophistication to manage the rigors of statesmanship as required by democracy.[4] He believed nature intended for the vast majority of persons to do no more than provide for the material needs of the community, while those few individuals who happened to be blessed with superior intelligence should cover the task of governing. Hence, Plato believed democracy was evil because it inverted the natural order by forcing individuals designed primarily to work with their bodies into the role of citizens charged with exercising their minds. For this reason, he believed allowing the majority to govern would be as inappropriate as permitting children to choose their own diet; as foolish as practicing medicine via **popular opinion**; and as dangerous as setting sail aboard a ship which lacks an experienced pilot yet is stocked with an ignorant crew eager to run her aground. Aristotle, while not sharing the depths of Plato's democratic pessimism, feared democracy's tendency to degenerate from a polity in which all citizens govern with a view to the common good into an environment where the people behave less like citizens and more like a mob; a situation so perverse that individuals spend more time competing against each other for private gain than they do working together for public renewal.[5] Aristotle not only believed such a life would prove intrinsically unsatisfactory to the virtuous citizen, he also believed it spelled doom for a democratic society by severing the ties of friendship which provide the only lasting bonds of political association.

The Greeks were not alone in their philosophical suspicion of democracy. Such 19th century philosophers as Alexis de Tocqueville and John Stuart Mill also found democracy less than perfect as a governing ideal.[6] Both de Tocqueville and Mill thought democratic societies are prone to collapsing under the weight of their own equality. Although each gave their theory the unique stamp of their own personality, both worried that excellence would suffer at the hands of mediocrity, which grows ever more powerful in the egalitarian soil of democracy. Moreover, they believed the democratic instinct to settle for the lowest common denominator in public affairs (to assuage the egalitarian sentiments of so-called political equals) creates a condition in which the intellectually lazy are soon enamored with the simplistic "wisdom" of popular opinion. Within such an environment, they feared the mediocre majority, so enslaved by their own narrowing minds, would not hesitate to compel conformity upon those unwilling to see the light.

It seems then, both history and philosophy speak very clearly on this point: If democracy is ever to be more than a vacuous ideal in the American governing experience, then we, the contemporary Americans, *must do no less than prove most political history and philosophy wrong.* It is no stretch to conceive of the present American political system as only the most recent experiment in the (so far) sad history of democratic self-government. Therefore, given the immensity of our task, how do we help push the democratic ideal into the realm of governmental policy? The first step is to resist the urge to ignore democracy's theoretical inadequacies and historical failures, and instead confront them head on with open minds and courageous hearts. If we do, we cannot help but see why our professed democratic government has not lived up to its moral promise. It has failed to become an actuality for the very reason so many philosophers dismissed democracy to begin with—too many "ordinary" Americans have proven uninterested in cultivating within themselves the wisdom to govern wisely. **In short, our American experiment in self-government has not lived up to its potential because too few of us take seriously our role as citizens.**

In the movie *Saving Private Ryan,* the character played by Tom Hanks, (Captain Miller), whispers to Private Ryan with his dying words, "earn this." This fictional scene superbly captures the duty which is incumbent on all contemporary American citizens: We have an obligation to earn the privileges of citizenship granted to us by the bloody sacrifice of others. We can begin earning these privileges by improving our understanding of what it takes to be a citizen. Be aware, however, the practice of responsible citizenship does not come naturally. We cannot fool ourselves into thinking governing a community is easy just because so many of us received citizenship merely by being born. There is no genetic propensity to govern wisely. In addition to being born, wise citizenship also requires that we educate ourselves in both the practices of our institutions as well as in the principles of democratic philosophy. To this end, this book contains what I believe to be the information necessary to practice responsible citizenship (think of it as an owner's manual for American government). For pedagogic purposes, the book is divided into four primary sections beginning with the section titled, "Getting Started," which includes this introduction as well as a chapter on the history and theory behind the U.S. Constitution. The chapter on the Constitution will help set the stage for all further chapters by helping us grasp the basic principles of the American political system. From there, the book proceeds as follows:

The second section, "Political Processes," contains chapters 3–7, and begins with a chapter discussing the merits and deficiencies of elections and public opinion polls as governing tools in the American political system. To this end, Chapter 3 will first examine the evolution of elections while addressing the issue of America's low voter turnout. We will then look at both how public opinion polls help our politicians stay in touch by voicing the concerns of the working majority, while also being used to manipulate the public into accepting whatever policies the political class[7] deems appropriate. The fourth chapter examines three interrelated topics (political parties, ideologies and the political spectrum) which constitute much of the bedrock of the American political system. In doing so, we will first analyze the present menu of political choice, asking such basic questions as: Who are the major political parties? Why these two? Are there any others? From there we will attempt to comprehend two of the most ubiquitous and nebulous concepts in the American political landscape—"conservative" and "liberal." It will be argued these two concepts are as little understood as they are overused by most Americans. Next, we will attempt to graphically articulate the American ideological universe by devising our own political spectrum.

This will be followed by Chapter 5, which details the condition of the modern media and its effect on our democratic culture. In doing so, we will first analyze how the media is limited as a democratic vehicle by both the nature of television and its own ignorance. Following this, we will discuss the question of whether the media is either liberally or conservatively biased, arguing along the way, it may in fact be both. Also, the chapter will discuss the rise of the Internet and what it may mean for our democracy. In Chapter 6 we will examine the apparent complexities of economic policy by discussing monetary, fiscal, and trade policy and their effect on working families. To this end, we will examine how the Federal Reserve Systems' anti-inflationary policies serve a specific political purpose. In addition, we will examine how the political class has set up one of the largest transfers of wealth in the history of democratic government by authorizing fiscal policies which constantly endorse deficit spending. Lastly, we will articulate the essentials of America's trade policy, exposing both the inadequacies of free trade and the present state of the American economy. The section will conclude with Chapter 7 which will discuss some of the history of American foreign policy; a history in which, it will be argued, much of our blood and treasure have been spent supporting policies of dubious merit at best. In doing so, we will examine some of the main actors who determine American foreign policy as well as how they go about implementing it.

Section III will consist of three chapters covering the institutional apparatus of the federal government.[8] Chapter 8 will discuss Congress, focusing on its constitutional duty as well as its contemporary practice. Next, Chapter 9 will discuss the executive branch, paying particular attention to the presidency, while also briefly detailing the federal bureaucracy. We will end this section with Chapter 10 which will analyze that most mysterious of branches—the federal judiciary.

The last section, Section IV, will begin with Chapter 11, which will center on political representation, or the lack thereof, for working families. This will entail examining how the privileged few[9] dominate our political system through campaign financing, the information industry and various other political tricks of the trade. Chapter 12 will conclude this section and the book by offering some remedies to help enhance the democratic nature of the American political system.

Now that I have outlined what this book is, let me stress what it is not: First, it is not partisan. There is no Democratic Party or Republican Party bias; I am an equal opportunity critic—and there is plenty of blame to go around for all members of the political class, regardless of their particular political persuasion. It is not motivated by any specific ideology, be it conservative, liberal, communistic, capitalistic, or what have you. To be sure, every author brings a bias to the table, and I am no exception to this rule; my bias is, simply stated, democratic justice. That is, I need no political label to help me see the obvious injustice of a system which promotes the interests of the fortunate few at the expense of the working majority. This non-ideological approach granted me the freedom to draw from various sources all over the political spectrum. I have quoted and cited liberals and conservatives; mainstream advocates and radicals; Ralph Nader and Patrick Buchanan; William Greider and Kevin Phillips. In short, I chose information which according to fact and logic best promoted the common good, rather than information which supported a particular political dogma.

And, lastly, this book is not a substitute for your own self-respect. This may seem like a strange comment from a political scientist, but it is in essence the main obstacle to democratic justice. For this reason, the duty to begin respecting oneself constitutes the fundamental task of the contemporary citizen and is at least as important as all the political knowledge one can acquire. None of us will ever be granted equal concern and respect from our government, no matter how much academic knowledge we gain concerning it, until we, the working Americans, *start believing we are in fact worthy of it*. Most of us have heard the cliché about how absolute power tends to corrupt people absolutely,[10] but too few of us have thought about its corollary, which is, powerlessness tends to corrupt people as well. We have become so disenfranchised by the political class we have begun to internalize their belief in our worthlessness. Our self-disrespect is so prevalent we have accepted our present social reality as the fullest expression of democratic potential; we have allowed a few select families (Clinton, Bush, Rockefeller, Kennedy, ring a bell?) to ordain themselves as the new nobility all in the name of American freedom; in short, we presuppose that democracy entails a political culture in which the lives of the working majority simply are not as worthy as the lives of the fortunate few.

This apparent lack of respect for ourselves is nothing new in the struggle for democracy, it has always plagued any attempt to improve the lives of the vast majority of citizens. It reminds me of a scene which took place right before the bloodiest battle in the history of American freedom, Gettysburg. The commanding officer of the Union Army's 20th Maine regiment, Colonel Chamberlain (who was, by the way, a professor who secretly joined the Union Army), was attempting to persuade some disgruntled war veterans why the cause was worth the constant death struggle the Civil War had become (eventually costing 620,000 American lives, which is more than the total of all other American wars combined).[11] Here is what he said:

> This is free ground. All the way from here to the Pacific Ocean. No man has to bow. No man born to royalty. Here we judge you by what you do, not by what your father was. Here you can be something. Here's a place to build a home. It isn't the land [we're fighting for]—there's always more land. It's the idea that we all have value, you and me, we're worth something more than the dirt. I never saw

dirt I'd die for, but I'm not asking you to come join us and fight for dirt. What we're all fighting for, in the end, is each other.[12]

This book is dedicated to all those who have taken these words to heart, that we all have value, and have demanded our government do the same. As you read the following chapters I will be asking each of you to do likewise—take these words to heart and politically act on them. But be aware, our contemporary battle for the realization of our own value requires we open our minds to the truth of governmental injustice and our own intellectual laziness. If you are up to the task, we would welcome the company, for, as Chamberlain asserted, we are, in the end, indeed fighting for each other.

NOTES

1. The evidence for this assertion can be found in many recent economic studies comparing wealth disparities between American economic classes as well as generations.

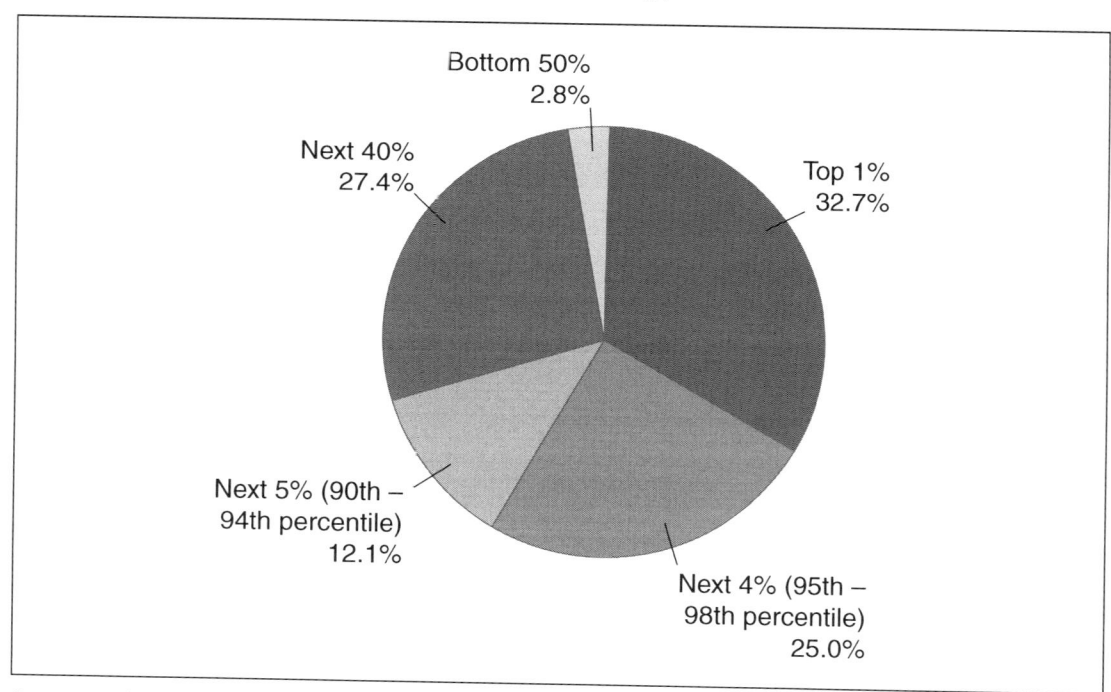

Figure 1: Distribution of US Wealth Ownership, 2001

- Top 1% — 32.7%
- Next 4% (95th – 98th percentile) — 25.0%
- Next 5% (90th – 94th percentile) — 12.1%
- Next 40% — 27.4%
- Bottom 50% — 2.8%

Source: Arthur B. Kinnickell, "A Rolling Tide: Changes in the Distribution of Wealth in the U.S. 1989–2001," Table 10. (Levy Economics Institute: November 2003)

Figure 2: Change in Average Household Net Worth, 1983–98

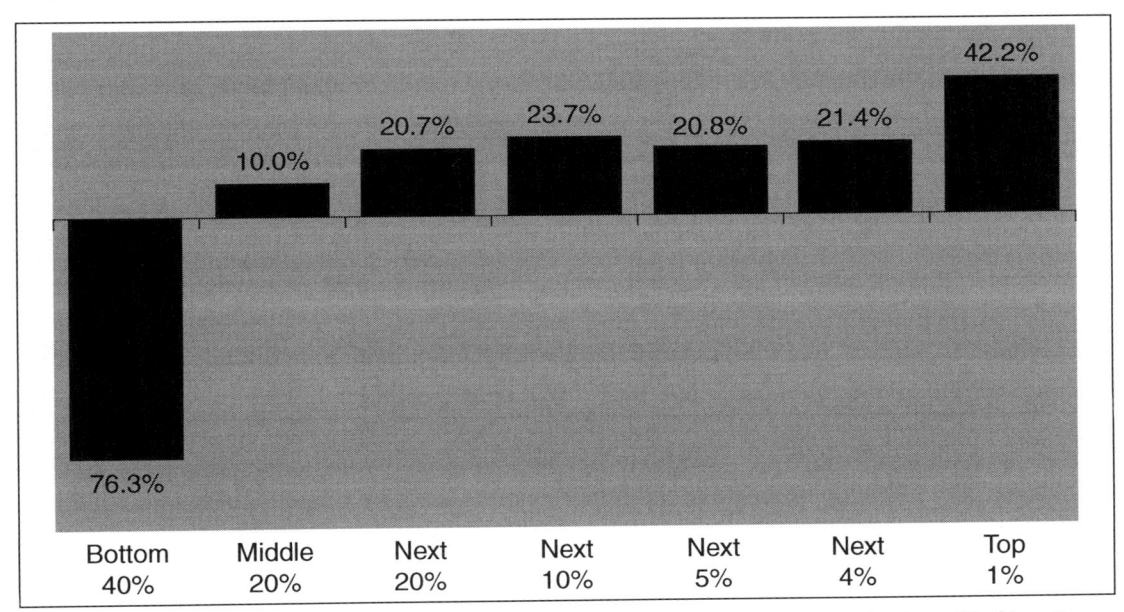

Bottom 40%	Middle 20%	Next 20%	Next 10%	Next 5%	Next 4%	Top 1%
-76.3%	10.0%	20.7%	23.7%	20.8%	21.4%	42.2%

Source: Edward N. Wolff, "Recent Trends in Wealth Ownership 1983–1998," Levy Institute Working Paper No. 300, Table 3. (Levy Economics Institute: April 2000)

Figure 3: Percentage Share of Household Wealth Held by Top 1%, 1922–98

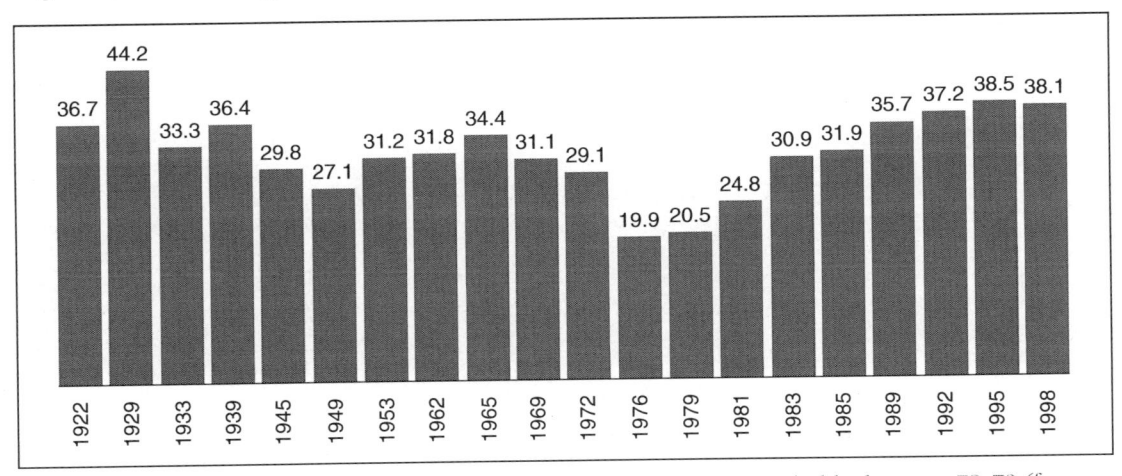

Year	Share
1922	36.7
1929	44.2
1933	33.3
1939	36.4
1945	29.8
1949	27.1
1953	31.2
1962	31.8
1965	34.4
1969	31.1
1972	29.1
1976	19.9
1979	20.5
1981	24.8
1983	30.9
1985	31.9
1989	35.7
1992	37.2
1995	38.5
1998	38.1

Source: Edward N. Wolff, *Top Heavy* (New Press: 1996), New Series Households data, pp. 78–79 (for years 1922–89) and "Recent Trends in Wealth Ownership 1983–1998," Levy Institute Working Paper No. 300, Table 2. (Levy Economics Institute: April 2000)

Figure 4: Share of Total Ownership of Stocks, Mutual Funds, and Retirement Accounts, 1998

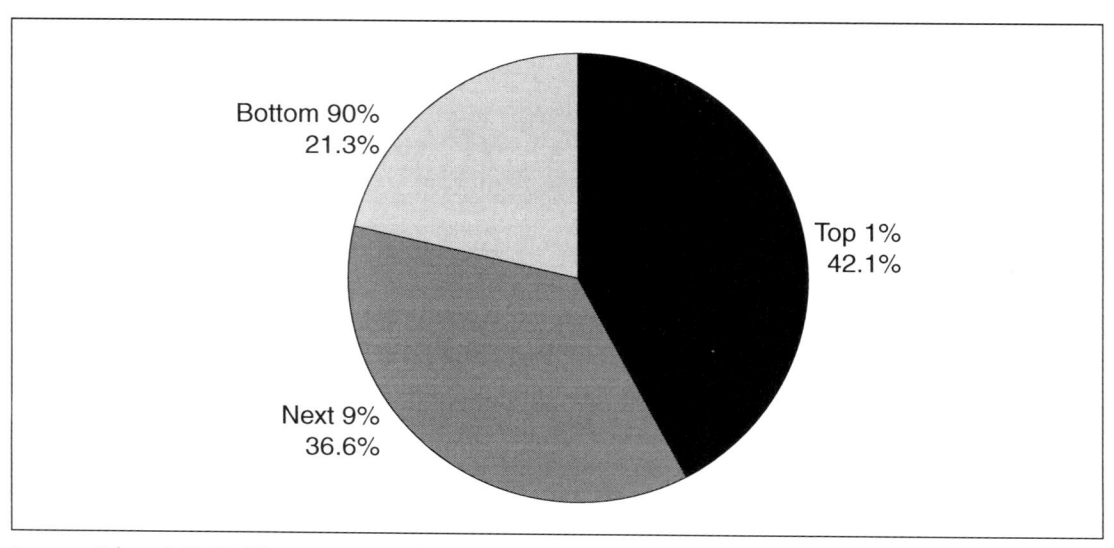

- Top 1%: 42.1%
- Next 9%: 36.6%
- Bottom 90%: 21.3%

Source: Edward N. Wolff, "Recent Trends in Wealth Ownership 1983–1998," Levy Institute Working Paper No. 300, Table 6. (Levy Economics Institute: April 2000)

The much more questionable claim is not whether economic policy is skewed in favor of the fortunate few (it clearly is), but rather, is it appropriate to use *economic* figures to determine the *political* health of the American community? I think it is appropriate for three interrelated reasons: One, economics give us a tangible and quantifiable measure of who benefits and who does not via the American political system; two, it can be reasonably inferred that if the few are receiving more than their fair share of economic benefits from the political system, then they must also be receiving more of its social benefits as well; and, three, it helps prove my thesis that democracy has only triumphed in the realm of rhetoric (ideal) and yet is nowhere near realized in the realm of actual political practice.

2. The democratic character of a political system is best determined by focusing on whose interests that system serves, rather than, as is too often the case, by highlighting who theoretically rules. That is, democracy is best defined as a political system which, in the words of the Utilitarians, promotes "the greatest happiness for the greatest number," and not one in which the few manipulate the many into endorsing policies which are detrimental to the majority. To be sure, it will trouble some thinkers that governmental policy ought to be reduced to a mere majoritarian ethic. However, such concerns are essentially suspicions of democracy as a governing ideal rather than, strictly speaking, disagreements over its definition.

3. *The Federalist*, No.10

4. See Plato, *Republic, Statesman,* and *Laws* (Chicago: Encyclopaedia Britannica, Inc., 1952); or for an excellent analysis of Plato's political philosophy see, Irving M. Zeitlin, *Plato's Vision* (New Jersey: Prentice Hall, 1993).

5. See Aristotle, *Politics* (Chicago: Encyclopaedia Britannica, Inc., 1952) Book III.

6. See in particular, Alexis de Tocqueville, *Democracy in America* (New York: Vintage Books, 1958), and John Stuart Mill, *On Liberty* (Chicago: Encyclopaedia Britannica, Inc., 1952).

7. The term "political class" must be taken to mean any person who has national political influence. That is, the political class includes anyone who can and does actually affect federal policy, and

who depends on the federal government favoring the economic elite for his or her privileged social position. This includes, but is not limited to, all federal politicians, top-level bureaucrats, advisors, and staff members, as well as major media personalities and executives, top-level members of the banking and finance community, and, many "ivy" league intellectuals.

8. The interested reader should be aware of a slight methodological difference between these two primary sections (processes and institutions). While the perspective of both sections is descriptive as well as normative, each section, nonetheless, has a different accent. The section covering processes accents the normative perspective, while the section on institutions accents the descriptive stance. This was necessary for both pedagogic as well as scientific reasons. That is, since institutions deal primarily with means and not ends, I covered them in more of a descriptive sense (e.g., how does Congress work? What role in the legislative process does the president play? How does the Supreme Court decide what cases to hear?). And since processes deal essentially with ends, I was compelled to take a more normative stance. Or, to put it another way, processes by their very nature concern normative issues (e.g., political parties are organizations advocating for what *ought* to be America's public philosophy; economic and foreign policy deals with what we *ought* to do; the media is also a normative endeavor since they make a judgment concerning what it is the public *ought* to know; and so forth), and, therefore, require a more explicit normative stance when evaluating them.

9. For a general account of who the privileged few are, see John J. Harrigan, *Empty Dreams, Empty Pockets* (New York: MacMillan Publishing Company, 1993), pp. 5–16. Harrigan describes the privileged few as the top 5% of wage earners (those who earn more than $98,963 annually are temporarily "rich," while those with wealth of at least $3.3 million are permanently rich). More specifically, the "privileged few" refers to, in the words of Kevin Phillips, the "100,000 American families in the top tenth of one percent [who enjoyed] by far and away the greatest wealth and income gains in the 1980s." Their privilege does not extend merely to the sphere of economics; it also reaches to the heart of the political. As the political class learned long ago, "challenging America's richest 100,000 families is not good for campaign contributions." In short, the privileged few are those select individuals mentioned above who exercise nearly hegemonic control in America. See, *Arrogant Capital: Washington, Wall Street, and the Frustration of American Politics* (Boston: Little, Brown & Company, 1994), pp. 207–210.

10. Lord Acton, quoted in George Seldes, ed., *The Great Thoughts* (New York: Ballantine Books, 1985), p. 3.

11. For excellent historical accounts of the Civil War see, James M. McPherson, *Battle Cry of Freedom: The Civil War Era* (New York: Oxford University Press, 1988); Shelby Foote's three volume set, *The Civil War: A Narrative* (New York: Vintage Books, 1958); and, the nine volume video series by Ken Burns, *The Civil War*, Time-Life Video, 1990.

12. Michael Shaara, *The Killer Angels* (New York: Random House, 1974), p. 3.

Chapter 2
Constitutional Contemplation: *E Pluribus Unum* (From Many, One)

We the People of the United States, in Order to form a more perfect union, establish Justice, insure domestic Tranquility, provide for the common defence, promote the general Welfare, and secure the Blessings of Liberty to ourselves and our Posterity, do ordain and establish this Constitution for the United States of America.

INTRODUCTION

Correctly perhaps, most Americans and many others view the **Constitution** as one of the most important documents in the history of political association. It (along with the ***Declaration of Independence***) has become, so to speak, the bible of our civic religion; a document so sacrosanct, tourists will wait in line for hours just to view it in hushed reverence. And, unfortunately, much like the Bible, the Constitution is more often quoted by Americans in support of a particular political interest than read (if at all) for intellectual and moral guidance. It seems respect for the Constitution is based more on a general ignorance about it than from any knowledge pertaining to it; more on symbolism than substance; more on familiarity than understanding; more on tradition than inquiry. In other words, most Americans honor the Constitution because it is mysterious and they have been told to do so. Nonetheless, whereas respect based on mystery is necessary to religious practice (after all, it deals with metaphysical uncertainties) it is deadly in politics. In politics mere faith in political symbols will deliver not political salvation but only oppression, since politics, unlike religion, concerns itself not with a Supreme Being, but with beings just like ourselves.

This chapter will not attempt to convince the reader his or her allegiance to the Constitution is misplaced, but rather provide him or her with the intellectual grounds for securing it. In doing so, this chapter will dispel much of the mystery surrounding the Constitution while (it is hoped) still fostering the respect most Americans have toward it by replacing their ignorance with knowledge, their faith with deliberation, and, most of all, their blind acceptance with an appreciation for the monumental task of creating a political blue print for self-government that has become a beacon for liberty everywhere. That is to say, although the document is undoubtedly the result of human intellect rather than, as some have suggested, divine inspiration, it is, nonetheless, a remarkable document for its very humanity. It is a document that attempts to secure a durable framework of self-government for successive generations of Americans while, at the same time, being flexible enough so that each generation may alter it as they see fit. It is a document forged as much by political experience as theoretical precision; as much by low motives (greed, bigotry) as by high ones (rejection of **monarchy**, a concern for self-government); as much by self-interest as public virtue. In a word, the Constitution is American.

We will begin our inquiry by briefly reviewing the historical context surrounding the drafting of the Constitution. In doing so, we will examine some of the primary political motives that led to its formulation and structure. Following this, we will discuss the four most important theoretical principles underpinning the Constitution. To this end, we will analyze what these concepts mean and where in the Constitution they are articulated. Next, we will briefly trace the history of some selected **amendments** to the Constitution to help illustrate its flexible and republican character. We will conclude with a very brief discussion on what this all means for us, the contemporary Americans.

A LITTLE HISTORY: THE FIRST AMERICAN CONSTITUTION—THE ARTICLES OF CONFEDERATION

On June 12, 1776, as the thirteen colonies prepared for war with England (at the time, the world's greatest superpower) the Continental Congress appointed a committee composed of representatives from each colony to write a constitution for a new central government. This would prove to be no easy task since they would not be designing a government for a nation as we understand it, but rather for thirteen quasi-independent countries. That is, to the vast majority of Americans their homeland, or country if you will, was their state of, say, Virginia, New Jersey, or Rhode Island, and not any larger political unit. To be sure, the thirteen colonies did see themselves as connected by culture and combat, however, they were more wartime allies than political family. Given this reality, it is not surprising the constitution they eventually created, called *The **Articles of Confederation***, declared that the colonies had agreed to only a "league of friendship" in which "each state retains its sovereignty, freedom, and independence."[1] In short, the articles created a political relationship between the newly free states which was very similar to the relationship that exists today between countries in the **United Nations**; all member countries agree to meet and discuss international (or, in the states' case, continental) problems without sacrificing any national independence. Hence, the first principle of this new government was state equality and independence. For this reason, each state was granted one vote regardless of size or population and the powers of the newly created **Congress** were very limited (similar to the UN General Assembly).[2] For example, not only did the *Articles* deny Congress the power to tax altogether, they also required Congress to receive the consent of at least nine state representatives to pass any law; furthermore, it took unanimous agreement among all thirteen states to amend the *Articles*. Needless to say, this made it very difficult for the newly created central government to exercise any control over the much more popular (and powerful) state governments; which was exactly what colonial America wanted.

In any event, this loose confederation of states created by the *Articles* worked about as well as could have been expected during the war given the general distrust among the people of even the hint of centralized authority. It must be remembered that the colonists were engaged in a bloody death struggle to ward off the oppressive rule of a distant central government, and, hence, they were in no mood to create another powerful central authority. Therefore, for better or for worse, the *Articles* were as much centralized power as the colonists were going to stand—at least during the Revolution. Almost immediately after the end of the war, however, sentiment among the wealthiest and most powerful Americans began to turn against the *Articles*.[3] Those who were wealthy enough to be engaged in interstate commerce felt frustrated by the lack of any regulatory authority under the *Articles* in the area of business, or commerce. They began demanding something be done concerning the lack of consistency in the rules regulating trade matters between the thirteen states to allow for an easier transfer of goods and services between state borders.[4]

Now, before we proceed further with our constitutional discussion, let me take this opportunity to expose one of the great myths of the American **economy**, past and present: Nothing could be further from the truth than the myth that business wants a "deregulated" economy. Business interests, more than anyone, depend upon a thoroughly regulated economy for their economic life. How would any interstate (or, in present terms, international) businessperson expect to run a profitable venture if the commercial rules are different everywhere they transact business? Imagine the following scenario: Suppose that you have been asked to purchase 100 gallons of gas from a Texas oil company for your company's auto fleet in Oregon. After negotiations, you agreed to buy 100 gallons of gas for 100 dollars, and so you send the check. Now, imagine your shock when you receive in return for your 100 dollars a shipment of gasoline that could barely fill a thermos! Wanting to get to the bottom of this, you call the oil company and ask what happened to your order and are informed that Texas considers an Oregon dollar only worth about half a Texas dollar since Texas is, after all, bigger than Oregon. While not agreeing at all with the exchange rate (but wanting to cut your losses), you respond you still should have received fifty gallons of gas and not a mere thermos worth. To your chagrin, the Texan exclaims, "that's what y'all got, fifty gallons, you see in Texas a gallon is about equal to a thimble, what's it like in Oregon?" Welcome to a deregulated economy.

Though an extreme example, this is what those engaged in interstate or international commerce face. This is why it is much more accurate to say business wants a thorough and uniform regulated economy *in their favor*, than to ever claim business wants a deregulated economy. This is also why it is accurate to view our present Constitution, in part, as the first North American Free Trade Agreement. And, this is why, in present times, you repeatedly hear corporate spokespersons exclaiming the virtues of "**free trade**," as they extend it throughout the globe. What first applied only to the thirteen American states now applies to all of America, Mexico and Canada (**NAFTA**), as well as Central America (CAFTA). And, lastly, this is why so-called free trade agreements consist of hundreds of pages of regulations—their purpose is not to free the economy but to regulate it so business transactions are predictable and profitable. In any event, the need for a uniform commercial rule was one of the main motivations for the wealthy Americans' rejection of the *Articles*.

The other main motivation (if not *the* motivation)[5] for revamping the *Articles of Confederation* was the **Founders'** fear of the emerging democratic feelings growing in America.[6] It is now time to dispel one of the great myths of American political history: The present day Constitution was not written to promote democracy, as so many Americans seem to believe, but rather to frustrate it. I know this may be difficult for some of us to believe today, so immersed as we are in our democratic times, but it is vital that we do if we are to understand our own Constitution. Hence, the *Articles of Confederation* were found wanting, at least among the wealthy class, because while they prevented the reemergence of monarchy, they nonetheless, created a political system which tilted too far in the direction of democracy. Or, as Benjamin Rush, a colonial elite, put it, "In our opposition to monarchy, we forgot that the temple of tyranny has two doors;"[7] and, to the elites, the second door to tyranny was democracy. As numerous scholars have noted, according to members of the political elite at the time:

> "Democracy" was still an epithet in the eighteen century, commonly used disparagingly, because it evoked much the same emotional response that [communism] did in the twentieth. To gentlemen educated in the Greek and Roman classics, democracy was inevitably associated with mob rule and demagoguery.[8]

Why did the political elites of the revolutionary generation fear democracy? In short, because they feared that the same spirit of equality which overthrew the crown would be extended to the estates of the wealthy. In other words, the Founders feared they would lose their privileged status and wealth to the majority of American citizens who were, by and large, poor farmers. This is why one Founder referred to democracy as "the worst of all political evils," while Madison himself warned of "the danger of the leveling spirit" while writing, "[h]ence it is that such democracies have ever been spectacles of turbulence and contention; have ever been incompatible with personal security or the rights of property; and have in general been as short in their lives as they are violent in their deaths,"[9] and Hamilton wrote, "[a]ll communities divide themselves into the few and the many. The first are the rich and the well-born, the other the mass of the people [and] . . . they seldom judge or determine right."[10]

Into this hotbed of contempt for (and fear of) the common person came the proverbial straw that broke the elite's camel's back—the so-called "**Shays' Rebellion**." To early

American elites nothing illustrated the deficiencies of the *Articles* more than their inability to muster a national force capable of putting down uprisings among the common people. So, when in the late fall of 1786, a retired revolutionary war Captain, by the name of Daniel Shays (a farmer who had gone bankrupt after the Revolution), led a revolt of several hundred men against the Massachusetts courts trying to foreclose on their farms, nothing could stop the critics of the *Articles* from demanding that they be strengthened. As one historian has written: "[T]he reaction of eastern conservatives verged on hysteria. This was just the sort of radicalism that they had long feared. . . . Even in distant Virginia, Washington, informed by his Massachusetts friend Henry Knox that the rebels were "**levelers**" who aimed to redistribute property, shivered in apprehension."[11] Hence, the elites were now convinced that the *Articles* not only made it difficult to make money, given the commercial irregularities between states, they made it near impossible to keep the money they already possessed from the clutches of the rural poor. From all of this came a call from the most privileged Americans for a convention charged with "the sole and express purpose of revising the *Articles of Confederation*."

THE SECOND CONSTITUTION—THE U.S. CONSTITUTION

The second constitutional convention was scheduled to start May 14, 1787 (though due to difficulty in travel and other contingencies, it would not officially begin until May 25), with the expressed purpose of strengthening the *Articles of Confederation* in an effort to balance the government between the extremes (in the eyes of the Founders) of a government by kings (monarchy) and a political system of mob rule (democracy).[12] Yet in their effort to revise the *Articles,* the Founders instead replaced them with an entirely new social contract—our present day Constitution. To be sure, not all persons of the elite class agreed with the need to amend the *Articles*. For example, such note worthy citizens as Virginians, Patrick Henry, who declared he "smelt a rat," and Richard Henry Lee refused to attend. The state of Rhode Island was so suspicious of the proceedings they refused to even send a delegation to the convention. Other notables who were conspicuous by their absences were the famous Massachusetts pair of Sam Adams and John Hancock, neither of whom were chosen as delegates; another famous New Englander, John Adams, could not attend as he was in London; and, lastly, Thomas Jefferson, the primary author of the *Declaration of Independence,* was also unable to attend since he was in Paris engaged, like John Adams, in diplomatic affairs.

Nonetheless, there was no shortage of American celebrity or intellect at the convention; which led Jefferson, with his customary hyperbole, to declare the convention an, "assembly of demi-Gods." There was, among others, James Madison from Virginia, who would emerge from the convention as the chief author and intellectual guiding force behind the Constitution; also present was the author of the Virginia Declaration of Rights, George Mason; from Pennsylvania there was the impressive threesome of Robert Morris, Gouverneur Morris, and James Wilson; from New York came Alexander Hamilton, a staunch supporter of a strong national government; from Delaware came

John Dickinson, who supported a stronger national government since independence; South Carolina provided the impressive pair of John Rutledge and Charles Cotesworth Pinckney; and, lastly, also attending were two authentic American heroes, one from Virginia and the other from Pennsylvania, whose very presence lent the proceedings legitimacy—George Washington and Benjamin Franklin, respectively.

After electing Washington president of the convention, the next order of business was agreeing to conduct the proceedings in secret to allow the necessary deliberations to take place absent public scrutiny. From there, the delegates began building, not a monarchy, not a democracy, but rather a republic. All the Founders believed that the best form of government was one that mediated between the centralized authority of a king (monarchy) and the chaotic anarchy of mob rule (democracy), which they called, **republicanism**. Though a very complex concept, republicanism can best be simplified as a system of government in which, "a scheme of representation takes place,"[13] rather than direct democratic elections, and where the rule of law supersedes the whims of either kings or democratic majorities. There is, of course, more to the concept (which will be discussed in detail below), but, suffice it to say at this point, all the delegates agreed, whatever the eventual form this new government they were creating was to take, it must fundamentally rest on the republican concepts of representation and the rule of law.

There were other areas of broad consensus. First and foremost was agreement on the need to strengthen America's national defense against enemies both foreign and domestic. Hence, the Constitution that eventually emerged from the convention would not only grant Congress the power to, "declare war," "raise and support armies," and, "provide and maintain a navy," it would also declare that Congress may, "provide for calling forth the militia to . . . *suppress insurrections* and repel invasions [italics added]."[14] This new federal, or national, power would be quickly exercised as soon as the Constitution was ratified when, under the direct orders of President Washington, Alexander Hamilton (then the Secretary of the Treasury) led a federal army larger than the one Washington led at Yorktown during the Revolution[15] to put down an uprising of farmers in Pennsylvania; this whole affair has come down to us today as the "Whiskey Rebellion."[16] What caused the farmers to rebel was a newly enacted excise tax on whiskey which fell disproportionately hard on farming Americans. Whiskey was the main commodity of farmers since they could only ship their wheat to eastern markets by turning it into liquor, otherwise it would spoil along the way. When the troops arrived in Pennsylvania the farmers dispersed with a clear understanding that this new government would not tolerate uprisings among working Americans—just as Hamilton had planned.[17] In addition to allowing the new federal Congress to raise and support a military establishment, the Constitution would also create an executive "commander in chief," namely the president, so as to remove command and control of the armed forces from the states and place it under the auspices of the national government.[18]

The next area of general agreement was over the need to provide a uniform interstate commercial system. That is, the Founders (as mentioned earlier) shared a belief in the need to bring some consistency to their commercial dealings between states; in short, they wanted a free trade agreement. Hence, the first half of Article One, Section Eight, of the Constitution, would end up reading like a model free trade agreement. It would stipulate that Congress shall have power "to regulate commerce . . . among the several states," and, "to coin money, regulate the value thereof . . . and fix the standard of weights and measures." If you are wondering what this has to do with making it easier to conduct interstate commerce, recall our earlier hypothetical example of purchasing gas interstate where neither the value of a dollar was regulated nor the size of a gallon was fixed. Furthermore, the Constitution would allow Congress to "provide for the punishment of counterfeiting" and lastly to make sure "all duties, imposts and excises shall be uniform throughout the United States."

The Founders also agreed that the Constitution must secure the creditor against the debtor; or, in other words, since they were mostly wealthy and, therefore, lenders of money, they wanted to make sure they would be paid back.[19] This was arguably their greatest concern over democracy—its tendency toward, in the vernacular of the times, "leveling."[20] That is to say, in a democracy the majority rule, and the majority in any community are persons who owe money rather than lend it. Think about it. How many of you issue your own credit cards? Why not? They are an excellent source of income since you do not actually have to work to make money; you need only have people pay you interest for borrowing yours. The reason, of course, none of you are in the credit card business is because you do not have the money necessary to lend; which is also why so many of you use credit cards to begin with. Now, imagine a democratic town hall where the citizens of a community have gathered to discuss the issues that are important to them; first and foremost among them is the damn bills that arrive every month. It seems there is just not enough money to make ends meet, so one student of democracy submits the following proposal to a vote: "All in favor of eliminating our credit card debts this month say, yes." And, lo and behold, it passes unanimously. This is democracy, and this is also why the wealthy throughout history have feared it. To review: If in a democracy the majority rule, and the majority always owe the wealthy money (Who do you think has lent you that money to begin with?), then the majority have the right to vote their bills away, since they, in a democracy, rule.

Not willing to tolerate this kind of nonsense, the Founders made certain the Constitution would spell out the limits of democratic action. Hence, in Article One, Section Ten, the Constitution declares that "no state shall . . . pass any . . . law impairing the obligation of contracts." What does this have to do with voting your bills away? Well, what is a bill but a contract? And, as such, it stipulates that you will borrow 'X' amount while paying pay back 'X' plus interest at some future date. Or, in other words, a bill is a contractual obligation. And, when you vote to ignore your bills, you have quite clearly interfered with an obligation. So, in short, the Constitution makes illegal the type of vote mentioned above. Moreover, you cannot simply escape your debts by moving to another state either, as so many colonial Americans did. Article Four, Section One, of the Constitution, states: "Full faith and credit shall be given in each state to the public acts, records, and judicial proceedings of every other state." What could this legal jargon possibly mean? Simply, it means if you owe money in one state you owe it in another.[21] That is, Americans could no longer escape their debts by moving to another state—now the government, the national government, would come after you. And, lastly, to make certain bankruptcy proceedings (which will become much more prevalent as individuals are no longer able to vote away or run from their debts) favor the creditor over the debtor, the Constitution grants Congress the authority to make, "uniform laws on the subject of bankruptcies throughout the United States."[22] This, of course, not only guarantees consistency, it also helps ensure payment.

Therefore, we can see four general areas of agreement the delegates shared going into the convention: A belief in republican government; a desire to strengthen the national defense; a commitment to a uniform interstate commerce system; and, a strong inclination to secure the creditor against the debtor. In the next section we will examine the areas of disagreement rather than consensus.

Even though there was general agreement concerning the broad outline of this new government, the convention was, nevertheless, hardly conflict free. The largest area of disagreement arose over the question of representation in the new federal Congress. The question as to how to ensure the proper representation for each state in Congress was of prime importance to the Founders as representation was (and is) the backbone of the republican theory they all adhered to. Delegates from the larger states believed the new Congress should reflect their state's population superiority, whereas, delegates from the smaller states argued it should respect the principle of state equality embedded in the *Articles*.[23] Each side to the debate proposed a plan which called for a system of representation coinciding with their particular bias; the big states supported the so-called "Virginia Plan," which proposed a legislative assembly based on population (the more people a state has, the more representatives), while the small states endorsed the so-called "New Jersey" plan, which called for one based on state equality (each state receives the same amount of representatives). In the end, they compromised by agreeing to the "**Connecticut Compromise**," so named because it was introduced by Roger Sherman of Connecticut.[24] His plan called for a bicameral legislative assembly, or Congress, in which one house is based on population (the **House of Representatives**) and the other rests on state equality (the **Senate**). Hence, today, for example, the Senate is composed of 100 Senators, with each state receiving two representatives regardless of population, while the House has 435 members, allotted according to population (for example, California has 53 representatives compared to Oregon's 5).[25]

Another area of considerable disagreement resulted from the fact that some states permitted slavery while others did not. And, again, this conflict centered on the issue of representation. Simply put, the question was, should slave states be allowed to count slaves for population purposes in Congress, even though they failed to count them as persons in their communities? To the non-slave states, allowing slave states to count slaves verged on hypocrisy, since these states would get their political cake and could eat it, too. That is, slave states in essence would be allowed to treat African-Americans as slaves for economic purposes, while, at the same time, counting them as free individuals for political advantage. The delegates settled the issue, once again, via compromise; it seems slaves would count as three-fifths of a person.[26] In addition, the question of slavery also created some controversy regarding the importation of slaves and the "problem" (or, from the perspective of the slave, solution) of runaway slaves. In true compromising fashion, the non-slave states agreed to guarantee the return of runaway slaves[27] in return for the slave states granting Congress the authority to stop the importation of slaves as of 1808.[28]

There were other areas of disagreement, of course, ranging from, for example, the question of how to elect the president,[29] to taxation, to who should control navigation and other commercial details,[30] but all proved amenable to political compromise. So, on September 17, 1787, thirty-nine of forty-two delegates present signed the Constitution of the United States and submitted it to the states for ratification. (The Constitution would become law only after it was accepted by nine of thirteen state ratification conventions and not by the mere signing of it by the delegates, regardless of the number.) The three delegates[31] who refused to sign did so because they wanted a **bill of rights** added to the Constitution—and they eventually got their wish. It quickly became apparent the Constitution would not be ratified (accepted) by the required number of states unless it came equipped with a bill of rights. Jefferson himself, upon learning the proposed Constitution lacked a bill of rights, wrote, "a bill of rights is what people are entitled to against every government on earth, general or particular, and what no just government should refuse."[32]

Now, before we begin discussing the reasons why the Founders failed to supplement the Constitution with a bill of rights, we first must dispel another myth of the American community: *The Bill of Rights was not, as is so often explained in high school, enacted to allow individuals free speech, press, religion, and so forth; the primary reason for it was to protect the states from the newly created federal government.*[33] I know this may seem shocking at first, so let me offer a mind experiment to help you believe it. Think back to our earlier analogy between the United States and the United Nations (UN) in which we imagined the thirteen colonies being countries in the UN rather than states in our union. Now, imagine the UN (or, at colonial times, the new federal government) declaring that all countries (or states) must practice only the UN approved religion of Islam. Do you think this would fly in America? Me neither. I would guess that most Americans would respond something like this: "Absolutely not, here in America we'll believe as we like, thank you very much. And, while we're at it, we need to design an international bill of rights preventing the UN from dictating to us, or anyone else, for that matter, what to believe, say or write." Well, this is exactly how the states felt—they would decide for themselves how much religious freedom (if any)[34] to grant their citizens, as well as if there would be free speech, press and so forth. So, for this reason they decided to limit the power of this new central government by listing exactly what it could not do—we call these restrictions the Bill of Rights. Or, as one scholar on the matter has written:

> [Jefferson wanted a bill of rights as] a legal check against the *national* government—he was not worried about the states since they had their own Bill of Rights. . . . The central government, however, was a different matter, and there is simply no doubt whatever that the overriding reason for the . . . Bill of Rights was to place demonstrably far-reaching restraints on the fledgling central government [italics original] . . .[35]

In any event, the reason the Founders failed to provide a bill of rights originally was because they believed it would be unwise politically and philosophically.[36] First, they believed it would be foolish tactically since it would provide the opponents of ratification with something more to criticize; that is, they reasoned the more they included, regardless of its merit, the more there would be for critics to scrutinize and complain about. Second, and much more importantly, they (particularly Madison) thought it would be unsound to include a bill of rights since they could theoretically do as much to limit liberty as protect it. As one scholar has written:

> [Madison believed that,] adding [a bill of rights] could prove a danger . . . because to enumerate essential rights could not be safe unless it was complete. Any list of rights might inadvertently omit a vital claim, and its omission could become grounds for an insistence that the government could act on matters that were never meant to be included in its province.[37]

In short, Madison feared that if we listed in a bill of rights the freedoms of, say, X, Y, and Z, then we have implied that we are not free to do P, Q, R, and so on. Or, in other words, just because we may desire freedom of speech (X), press (Y), and religion (Z) at one moment in time, we may also someday want the right to an abortion (P), privacy (Q), or, what have you (R); but, since these were not listed in 1787, there simply would be no constitutional protection in these areas. As a matter of fact, Madison, once realizing it was useless to resist a bill of rights, quickly added the Ninth Amendment to prevent this very occurrence.[38] Nevertheless, with the addition of the Bill of Rights (the first ten amendments to the Constitution) enough states ratified the Constitution to have produced a uniquely American spectacle—a bloodless revolution. That is to say, when the states ratified the Constitution what they had done, in effect, was to overthrow, albeit peacefully, one government (under the *Articles*), and replaced it with a wholly new one—our present federal establishment. So, what began as an attempt to simply strengthen the *Articles of Confederation* led the early Americans to replace their national government, yet again, for one they found more suitable—I am sure there is a lesson for us in there somewhere.

A LITTLE POLITICAL PHILOSOPHY—THE THEORETICAL PRINCIPLES EMBEDDED IN THE CONSTITUTION

Although the Constitution most assuredly bubbled out of the unique historical experiences and political realities of the American colonial generation, nonetheless, it is the product of centuries of political thought. The Founders were experts in both ancient Greek and Roman political philosophy, as well as the so-called Enlightenment theories of the 17th Century, and they wisely took advantage of this expertise in developing the American Constitution. In doing so, they incorporated the four following political ideals into the fabric of the Constitution—republicanism, government by social contract, **natural rights**, and **federalism**. We will now turn our attention to analyzing each of these political principles in more detail below.

Republicanism

As mentioned earlier in the chapter, republicanism was the main ingredient of the American constitutional recipe. Republicanism demands that a government respect the four following principles in its political system—representation; rule-of-law; separation of powers; and a "balanced" or "mixed" legislature.[39]

Representation—For a government to qualify as republican it must be representative in nature. That is, it cannot contain any semblance of monarchy (rule by kings). Hence, Article One, Sections 9 and 10, specifically prohibits both state and national legislatures from granting any "title of nobility." This respect for representation explains the Constitution's requirement that all federal[40] and state[41] representatives be beholden to the people in which they govern. In short, republicanism requires a political system that rests on the consent of the governed. This demand for representation not only led to our American revolution, it has also spurred a world wide trend toward more and more responsive governments that continues today. It is important to note that republicanism does not necessarily require a democratic political system (which the Founders feared), but only a representative one. Nonetheless, republicanism tends to push a political system in that direction. This has certainly been the case in America; what began as a republican revolution in 18th century America had germinated into a full-fledged democratic revolution in the 20th century. In any event, representation is the first principle of republican government.

Rule of Law—Republicanism also requires a government to respect the rule of law.[42] Traditionally, republican theorists advocated the rule of law as a way of preventing kings from ruling arbitrarily. That is, republican theory resisted monarchical government because in such a political system the citizenry were at the mercy of the king's mood—if the king had a bad day so did the peasants. That is, ideally[43] republican theory stipulates that no matter who you happen to be, rich or poor, black or white, male or female, you must still obey the law. In addition to this, the Founders also believed the rule of law would protect individuals from (in their words) the "tyranny of the majority."[44] That is, they believed the rule of law would ensure that no minority group (in their day, this meant the wealthy; today it has a more racial connotation) would be sacrificed to the ignorant whims of the majority. We have already discussed, for example, the constitutional prohibition regarding democratic interference with "the obligation of contracts," but the Constitution also disallows any *"**ex post facto**"* laws or any "**bill of attainder**" from being enacted.[45] An *ex post facto* law is any law written after the fact. The Constitution prohibits *ex post facto* laws to prevent a government from holding anyone accountable for an act that was not illegal at the time it was performed.[46] This was to ensure that government could not investigate the previous activities of, say, a political critic, and then make those activities illegal at some future date just to silence him or her. A bill of attainder is a legislative conviction; or, in other words, voting someone into jail without a trial.[47] Bills of attainder were prohibited to prevent Congress from convicting their rivals by mere vote, which would in no way respect the rule of law.

In addition, the Fifth Amendment to the Constitution promises "due process"[48] in all criminal proceedings, as well as granting any person the right to refuse to "testify against himself." These protections not only ensured a fair trial they also forever abolished trials-by-ordeal as a way to convict a defendant. That is, it was no longer legal to torture someone until they confessed as a way to secure conviction. The Fifth Amendment also guarantees "just compensation" any time government practices its right to eminent domain (the government's authority to take your property at any time). Please note, it does not prevent government from taking your property, but it does ensure payment—something very few citizens could count on from a national government prior to the growth of republicanism. Further evidence of the Constitution's respect for the rule of law is its prohibition against "unreasonable searches and seizures," in addition to requiring "probable cause" whenever a government exercises its police power.[49] Lastly, the general respect Americans accord the Constitution (a legal document, after all) is itself a monument to America's republican character since without respect for the law, there would simply be no grounds for respecting the Constitution.

Separation of Powers—Republicanism assumes that government is a necessary evil, both conducive and destructive of the good life; too little political authority and there is nothing to prevent encroachments from one citizen on another, too much political power and the government itself preys upon the citizenry. According to republicanism the remedy for this paradox is the principle of separation of powers. Following the political philosopher Montesquieu,[50] the Founders created a system of checks and balances within the federal governing apparatus which they believed would allow the government enough authority to govern without ever letting it become too powerful.[51] In short, the Founders believed the way to check the awesome political power inherent in any government is to divide its functions so that no one person or institution controlled them all. Hence, the Constitution creates three branches of government in which each branch has a specific and limited duty independent of the other two.[52] The first branch of government, Congress, can make law but can neither enforce nor interpret it, these duties are reserved for the Executive branch (the presidency and bureaucracies) and the Judicial branch (the federal courts) respectively. In this way republican theory solves the governing paradox by using the power of the federal government to check and limit itself.

Mixed or Balanced Government—Another tenet of the republican faith is its belief in a "balanced" or "mixed" government. The Founders were much aware that the chief cause of most political turmoil, be it crime, revolution, or war, is that some people are rich and many more are poor. Hence, Madison wrote, "the most common and durable source of factions [conflict] has been the various and unequal distribution of property.

Those who hold and those who are without property have ever formed distinct interests in society."[53] In political theory there are, in essence, two possible approaches one can take to prevent society from crumbling due to inequities of wealth. One approach is to distribute wealth more equally as suggested by Plato,[54] the historical Jesus Christ,[55] and Karl Marx,[56] for example. This, they argue, eliminates conflict caused by unequal distribution of wealth by removing its cause. The other approach is not to distribute property more equally but to make sure all economic classes are represented in government. In this way conflict becomes institutionalized and expresses itself peacefully rather than violently. That is, by granting the rich and middle class a place in the political system, conflict over material distribution takes place in a peaceful manner *within the governing process* instead of violently out in the streets. Granted, this does not eliminate conflicts generated by economic conditions, but it does allow conflicts to be resolved in a peaceful and orderly fashion via the political process.

Needless to say, the Founders chose the second route. For this reason the Constitution creates a "mixed" or "balanced" government in which those who have property and those who do not are each granted an institution to represent their particular interests. Hence, the House of Representatives was designed to represent the so-called middle class, while the Senate was intended to protect the interests of the wealthy.[57] To ensure this bias the Constitution originally allowed the "people"[58] to vote only for members of the House of Representatives, whereas, the Senate was elected by the State Legislators (who were more affluent than the general voting body).[59] In addition, the Constitution stipulates that only the House may originate, "all bills raising revenue" (tax laws) since historically most taxes were paid by the middle class.[60] Furthermore, the Constitution grants only the House the power to impeach (charge someone with a political crime),[61] while only the Senate may convict.[62] This meant the middle class would be capable of voicing their displeasure via impeachment (rather than with a musket) but would be prevented from actually removing anyone from office. The class bias of the Senate is also evident by the fact that the Constitution allows only the Senate to confirm executive appointments or ratify treaties, which are very important to the wealthy since they have much at stake in regulatory and international policy. In short, the Founders' respect for republican theory led them to construct a Constitution rife with mixed or balanced elements.

The Social Contract Theory of Government

The Constitution is also a product of the **social contract theory** of government. The Founders were deep believers in the philosophy of John Locke[63] who proposed a system of government based on the contractual consent of the governed.[64] Locke argued that all monarchical governments were flawed since they rested on the belief that kings were superior to all others—the so-called "Divine Right of Kings." Locke reasoned that since all persons are equally created by God, then all persons are, therefore, naturally equal. Or, to put it another way, Locke believed we are all equal because we are all equally the product of God's labor. And since we were all created equal (sound familiar?), Locke declared that no person owes any other person obedience. (The only exception is one's parents who Locke believed held a natural authority over their children until about the age of 16 since they also helped create them.) Moreover, since no individual owes any other individual obedience, then it stands to reason that all political relationships are, therefore, artificial (man made) arrangements requiring the consent of the governed to be legitimate and not oppressive. Hence, political authority is only legitimate if it is derived from a political contract that explicitly details the scope and limits of political power and has been freely consented to by a majority of citizens. And, of course, our Constitution is just this contract.

Natural Rights

In addition to adhering to Locke's notion of government by social contract, the Founders were also staunch believers in his notion of natural rights. Locke believed individuals came equipped with "certain inalienable rights"[65] which government, if it was to be legitimate, must not abridge. He thought these natural rights consisted of life, liberty, and property.[66] His reasoning went like this: All people are the product of God investing His labor into the earth, therefore, all of us are God's property since He has invested Himself into each of us. Moreover, to kill a person (that is, deny them life) is to destroy God's property, and to deny a person their liberty, by illegally imprisoning them, is to steal God's property (that is, to use God's property against His wishes). Hence, as God's property we have a natural (that is, prior to any social arrangements) right to life and liberty. Furthermore, since we have the potential to invest our labor into the earth, we can also acquire a property right. In other words, we may remove raw material from the common (public) domain and, by investing our labor into it, transform it into personal (private) property. Therefore, according to Locke, each individual comes equipped with natural rights to life, liberty, and property, just as much as they are equipped with hearts and lungs, arms and legs.

Given their allegiance to Locke, it is no coincidence that the Founders believed all governments must respect a persons life, liberty and property—and they wrote the Constitution to ensure it. For example, the Fifth Amendment to the Constitution states, "no person shall be . . . deprived of life, liberty or property, without due process of law," revealing the Constitution's respect for both the rule of law and natural rights. The Fifth Amendment also declares, "nor shall private property be taken for public use, without just compensation." As mentioned earlier, this may not prevent government from taking your property, but it does ensure it will compensate you. In other words, the Constitution prevents the government from simply taking an individual's property and instead commands it to exchange one form of property (real estate) for another (money). Of course the notion of rights has grown much beyond the scope of 18th century "natural" rights and now encompasses such "civil" rights as speech, press, and religion, as well as such political rights as "voting"[67] and "equal protection"[68] of the laws.[69] In short, our contemporary commitment (obsession?) to a world awash in political rights owes its existence to the Founders' belief in a system of natural rights.

Federalism

The last important constitutional ideal we will analyze is the only one with a uniquely American ancestry—federalism. That is, the concept federalism was invented by the Founders to address the unique characteristics of the newly independent American colonies.[70] Remember from our earlier discussion that most all Americans were much more beholden to their state (which was the word they used for country) than they were to any continental government. For this reason the Founders had to create a theoretical concept that would both respect each state's independence while also allowing for some political uniformity between the several states. Federalism, they believed, would accomplish this task. So, borrowing from a book devoted to the subject, we will define federalism as the mode of political organization that unites separate polities within an overarching political system by distributing power among general and constituent governments in a manner designed to protect the existence and authority of both.[71] Or, in other words, federalism is a system of government in which political power is shared between local governments (states) and a national government (federal). To be sure, originally it was never intended for the national (federal) government to be equal, not to mention superior, to the states in either power or influence. That is, it never dawned on the vast majority of colonial Americans that the major governmental player in their lives would be the federal (national) government instead of their state governments. As a matter of fact, most all southerners during the Civil War believed this was the real issue behind what they called the "War Between the States," and, hence, to them slavery was simply an excuse the "federals" used to exercise their power. Nevertheless, any notion of state supremacy (not to mention, equality) met its death along with hundreds of thousands of Americans on the battle fields of the Civil War. Furthermore, regardless of which is more powerful, the states or the national government, (now the national government dwarfs the states in governing authority), the end result of federalism is that the American political system contains 51 independent and unique governments (one federal government and fifty state governments). Arguably, the best expression of federalism in the Constitution is the very structure of Congress which was, after all, predicated on the prior existence of states coupled with the fact that Senators technically represent simply the state (and not the people) in which they were elected. Moreover, the Constitution also required *state* ratification[72] for it to become the "supreme law of the land,"[73] while explicitly protecting the states from federal encroachment via the 10th Amendment which reads: "The powers not delegated to the United States by the Constitution, nor prohibited by it to the States, are reserved to the States respectively, or to the people."

THE AMENDMENTS—A NATION REDEFINES ITSELF

The Constitution has been amended (that is, changed) 27 times since its inception in 1789. The first ten amendments, as noted earlier, are collectively referred to as the Bill of Rights and were included to appease the states and thereby ensure ratification of the

Constitution. In short and in order, they cover the right to free speech, press and religion (1st Amendment); the right to bear arms (2nd Amendment); they forbid government from housing soldiers in private homes during peace time (3rd Amendment); they prohibit unreasonable search and seizure (4th Amendment); they guarantee due process in legal proceedings (5th Amendment); they ensure the right to a public and speedy trial (6th Amendment); they limit suits in common law (7th Amendment); they outlaw cruel and unusual punishments (8th Amendment); they protect rights that are not presently included in the Constitution (9th Amendment); and, lastly, they ensure a federal system of government (10th Amendment).

Like the Bill of Rights, the remaining 17 amendments are also the product of American political history and are best understood in that light. For example, the 12th Amendment was a direct response to the electoral confusion generated by the presidential election of 1800. In that election, even though Jefferson and his apparent running mate, Aaron Burr, beat their federalist opponents, members of the **electoral college** failed to identify which candidate (Jefferson or Burr) was to be president and which was to be vice-president. So, Burr theoretically had in fact tied Jefferson for president since no elector had noted who was their presidential preference (even though it was widely understood at the time that Jefferson was the presidential candidate). According to the Constitution, if there is a tie in the electoral college (as there was in this case), then the House (with each state casting one vote) shall select from the top five candidates the president of the United States.[74] Hence, the election was thrown into the House. After numerous attempts to declare a winner, the House finally selected Jefferson president when Alexander Hamilton persuaded an undecided representative to cast his vote in Jefferson's favor. As it turned out, Hamilton's persuasion not only cost Burr the presidency, it also ended up costing Hamilton his life. That is, as many of us have heard, Burr, upset at Hamilton for what he believed to be a betrayal, shot and killed him in a duel.[75] Nonetheless, the 12th Amendment was ratified in 1804 to prevent such an electoral mess from ever occurring again by requiring all presidential electors to spell out in writing who it was they were voting for as president and vice-president respectively.

Even better examples of history pushing constitutional change are the 13th, 14th, and 15th Amendments, or the so-called Civil War Amendments. They are collectively referred to as the Civil War Amendments because they emerged from our nation's bloodiest conflict—the Civil War. Hence, the 13th Amendment reinforces the results of the battlefield and outlaws slavery; the 14th Amendment guarantees ex-slaves citizenship, "due process" and "equal protection"; and, the 15th Amendment forbids states from preventing African-American males the vote because of race.[76] Another good example of history serving as the catalyst to constitutional change would be the 17th Amendment, ratified in 1903, which removed the authority to elect Senators from state legislative bodies and granted it to the voting public. The 17th Amendment is the result of numerous turn-of-the-century governmental reform movements which wanted to make government less the servant of corporate authority (what they called "trusts") and more responsive to the public at large (sound familiar?). Also, the 18th and 21st Amendments bubbled out of our nation's fascination with (or is it addiction to?) alcohol. The 18th Amendment outlawed or prohibited (hence, historians usually refer to this era as "prohibition") the manufacture or consumption of alcohol in the United States, while the 21st Amendment repealed the 18th Amendment. The 18th Amendment was removed from the Constitution because the public realized there was little wisdom in limiting the supply of any given intoxicant when there is an extremely high demand for it. In other words, rather than providing peace and tranquility such a policy usually just drives the users into the arms of the criminal element and thereby increases both crime and violence (I wonder if there is a lesson in here for us contemporary Americans?).

Other examples are the 19th Amendment, ratified in 1920, which was the result of decades (if not centuries) of women advocating for political equality; hence, it no longer allowed governments in America to deny women the vote simply because they are not male. Or, the 26th Amendment, ratified in 1971, which lowered the constitutional minimum voting age to eighteen instead of the previous twenty-one. This, of course, was in response to the sorry fact eighteen-year-old American men could die in Vietnam but not vote in America. In short, the Amendments to the Constitution, taken as a whole, are very much like a road map of American political history; they may not describe everything in detail, but they certainly outline America's major historical events and general social trends, and in so doing they highlight an important constitutional truth: *Not only did the Founders provide in the Constitution a mechanism for political change,*[77] *they, in fact, encouraged it.* For as Madison himself said:

> If there be a principle that ought not be questioned within the United States, it is that every man has a right to abolish an old government and establish a new one. This principle is not only recorded in every public archive, written in every American heart, and sealed with the blood of a host of American martyrs, but is the only lawful tenure by which the United States hold their existence as a nation.[78]

Or, as the *Declaration of Independence* sums up so nicely: "Governments are instituted among men, deriving their just powers from the consent of the governed. That whenever any form of government becomes destructive . . . it is the right of the people to alter or to abolish it." There is simply no more important point to emphasize in this chapter—*as Americans we have both the right (are allowed) and the duty (are required) to constantly rethink what it is we want from government and then act accordingly.* In other words, the Founders, who were keenly aware that any political community requires constant upkeep and innovation to remain healthy and vibrant, provided in the Constitution the means to adapt the political system to the needs of each American generation. Hence, the Constitution stipulates that if we, the people, want to alter our political system in part or abolish it altogether, all we need to do is follow one of four simple procedures outlined in the Constitution and it is done. For example, if you think Congress is not fulfilling its representative duties, then reform it or eliminate it altogether. If you do not see much justice in our criminal law system, then change it. If you want to eliminate the influence of special interest money from your elections, then just do it (my apologies to Nike). That is, the Constitution (if it is anything), is simply a blue print for self-government; however, this requires that we, the contemporary Americans, must be politically energetic and informed enough to make it happen. In short, if we, the American people, want self-government, then we must be willing to govern ourselves.

FINAL THOUGHTS

As we have seen, the Constitution is a unique blend of theory and practice, mixing the highest motives with the meanest, all in an effort to produce a framework for self-government. To this end, the Founders incorporated the best theoretical principles of the day, both borrowed (republicanism and natural rights) and their own (federalism), to address the very real practical problems of governing a political community that was already geographically larger than the homeland of the empire they had recently defeated; but, in the end, only we, the present day Americans, can secure this victory. Therefore, in conclusion, we are left with the following important question: Has the Founders' constitutional experiment in self-government succeeded? Well, the answer to this question may, surprisingly, lie more in our hearts than in their deeds. That is, the answer to this question may depend less on reviewing constitutional history than it does on rethinking our present political morality. Or, to put another way, it seems, rather than wondering if *they were* successful, we should be asking ourselves what it is *we are doing presently* to make America a better place for all. In short, the Constitution, like America, is a work in progress—and, just like America, the Constitution will be whatever we make it.

NOTES

1. *Articles of Confederation*.
2. The UN General Assembly is not enabled to pass binding resolutions. Only the UN Security Council has that power. Additionally, of the Security Council's 15 members the 5 permanent members have absolute veto power.
3. Norman K. Risjord, *Jefferson's America: 1760–1815* (Madison: Madison House, 1991), p. 140.
4. Ibid., p. 154.
5. Michael Parenti, *Democracy for the Few* (New York: St. Martin's Press, 1988), p. 56.
6. This was hardly paranoia since in 1789 the French democrats led a bloody revolution against the minority ruling class.
7. Norman K. Risjord, *Jefferson's America: 1760–1815*, p. 155.
8. Ibid., p. 132.
9. *The Federalist Papers* #10.
10. Michael Parenti, *Democracy for the Few* (New York: St. Martin's Press, 1988), p. 58.
11. Norman K. Risjord, *Jefferson's America: 1760–1815*, pp. 153–154.
12. Ibid, p. 154–158.
13. *The Federalist Papers* #10.
14. U.S. Constitution, Article I, Section 8.
15. Edward S. Greenberg & Benjamin I. Page, *The Struggle for Democracy* (New York: Harper Collins College Publishers, 1995), p. 429.
16. For an excellent discussion, see Norman K. Risjord, *Jefferson's America: 1760–1815*, pp. 223–225.
17. In fact the rebellion was much more widespread than is commonly believed. For a full discussion see Ibid., p. 224.
18. U.S. Constitution, Article II.

19. See for an excellent discussion on this point, Michael Parenti, *Democracy for the Few,* and David Hellinger & Dennis R. Judd, *The Democratic Facade,* 2nd ed. (Belmont, CA: Wadsworth Publishing Company, 1994).
20. Norman K. Risjord, *Jefferson's America: 1760–1815,* p. 154.
21. Edward F. Cooke, *A Detailed Analysis of the Constitution* (Lanham, Md.: Rowman & Littlefield Publishing, Inc., 1995), p. 102.
22. U.S. Constitution, Article I, Section 8.
23. Edward F. Cooke, *A Detailed Analysis of the Constitution,* pp. 9–10.
24. Norman K. Risjord, *Jefferson's America: 1760–1815,* pp. 163–164.
25. The House of Representatives has been limited by federal statute to 435 members. Since there has been no enlargement of House membership for over 75 years, population increases, decreases, and/or shifts are accommodated either by reshaping congressional districts or by eliminating a district in one state so it can be awarded to another more populous state. Each state, however, is constitutionally required to have at least one district and representative.
26. U.S. Constitution, Article I, Section 2.
27. U.S. Constitution, Article IV, Section 2.
28. U.S. Constitution, Article I, Section 9.
29. Norman K. Risjord, *Jefferson's America: 1760–1815* , p. 163.
30. Edward F. Cooke, *A Detailed Analysis of the Constitution,* p. 10.
31. Elbridge Gerry (N.Y.), George Mason (V.A.), and Edmund Randolph (V.A.) refused to sanction the document with their names. Randolph eventually supported the ratification of the Constitution but the other two bitterly opposed ratification.
32. Lance Banning, *Jefferson and Madison: Three Conversations from the Founding* (Madison: Madison House, 1995), pp. 5–6.
33. As Chief Justice of the United States Supreme Court John Marshall wrote: "We are of the opinion that the [Bill of Rights] is intended solely as a limitation on the exercise of power by the government of the United States, and is not applicable to the legislation of the States." *Barron v. The Mayor and City of Baltimore, 7 Pet. (32 U.S.) 243, 8 L.Ed. 672 (1833)*; see also Henry J. Abraham, *Freedom and the Court: Civil Rights and Liberties in the United States* (New York: Oxford University Press, 1988), p. 39.
34. Some states, like the Commonwealth of Massachusetts, sanctioned a state religion and severely limited other religious practices.
35. Lance Banning, *Jefferson and Madison: Three Conversations from the Founding,* pp. 5–6.
36. Ibid., Chapter 1, especially pp. 6–9.
37. Ibid., p. 8.
38. Ninth Amendment to the U.S. Constitution: The enumeration in the Constitution of certain rights shall not be construed to deny or disparage others retained by the people. James Madison, from a speech during the debates on the Bill of Rights in the First Congress: "It has been objected also against a bill of rights, that, by enumerating particular exceptions to the grant of power, it would disparage those rights which were not placed in that enumeration; and it might follow by implication, that those rights which were not singled out, were intended to be assigned into the hands of the General Government, and were consequently insecure. This is one of the most plausible arguments I have ever heard urged against the admission of a bill of rights into this system; but, I conceive, that it may be guarded against. I have attempted it, as gentlemen may see by turning to the [Ninth Amendment]."
39. David Miller, ed., *The Blackwell Encyclopaedia of Political Thought* (Cambridge: Blackwell Publishers, 1993), pp. 433–436.
40. U.S. Constitution, Article I, Section 2.
41. U.S. Constitution, Article IV, Section 4.
42. David Miller, ed., *The Blackwell Encyclopaedia of Political Thought,* p. 458.
43. In reality, our legal system is much more, in the words of William Greider, a "grand bazaar" than a body of laws describing immutable principles of justice. If you can afford a lobbyist or hefty

campaign donations you can buy access to the system or have industry cronies placed in positions of regulatory control.
44. For an excellent discussion on this concept see, F.E.L. Priestly, ed., *The Collected Works of John Stuart Mill: On Liberty* (Toronto: University of Toronto Press, 1963).
45. U.S. Constitution, Article I, sections 9 and 10.
46. Edward F. Cooke, *A Detailed Analysis of the Constitution*, p. 71.
47. Ibid., p. 71–73; and Laurence H. Tribe, *American Constitutional Law* (Mineola, NY: The Foundation Press, Inc., 1978), pp. 184–5, 230n, 474–477, 482n, 484–501.
48. See also the U.S. Constitution, 14th Amendment.
49. U.S. Constitution, 4th Amendment.
50. In 1748, Charles de Secondat, Baron de Montesquieu, released his work of two decades *Esprit des Lois Spirit of the Laws* (Chicago: Encyclopaedia Britannica, Inc., 1952) in which he outlined a remedy for the dilemma of scale and proposed his version of the tripartite system of dividing the power of central government between a judicial, legislative, and executive branch. For a discussion of the problems of scale in republican governments, see Niccolo Machiavelli's *The Discourses* (Chicago: Encyclopaedia Britannica, Inc., 1952).
51. *The Federalist Papers* #51.
52. However, technically it is an over-simplification to state that the institutions of government have separated powers. While it is true that the three national governing institutions themselves are wholly separate from one another it is also quite true that they share power: the president can veto legislation and appoint Supreme Court and federal justices; the Congress can appoint minor Executive branch officers and enlarge or diminish the federal judiciary, and the Senate can refuse to ratify treaties and refuse to consent to Supreme Court and federal judicial nominees; the Supreme Court can review laws passed by Congress and signed by the president as well as the actions of both branches such as congressional investigations and Executive arbitrary actions. These are only a few of the many oversight duties and shared powers each branch possesses.
53. *The Federalist Papers* #10.
54. See Plato, *Republic* (Chicago: Encyclopaedia Britannica, Inc., 1952).
55. John D. Crossan, *The Historical Jesus: The Life of a Mediterranean Jewish Peasant* (New York: Harper Collins, 1992).
56. See the *Communist Manifesto* in, D. Mclellan, ed., *Karl Marx, Selected Writings* (Oxford: Oxford University Press, 1977).
57. Norman K. Risjord, *Jefferson's America: 1760–1815*, p. 133; see also, Marcus Boggs, ed., *Political Ideologies and the Democratic Ideal* (New York: Harper Collins College Publishers, 1995), p. 36–39.
58. Although the original Constitution does not specify voting rights (though most states restricted the franchise to white, propertied, male citizens) it did classify "personhood" for census taking, taxation, and representation purposes. Article I, Section 2, clause 3: "Representative and direct Taxes shall be appointed among the several States which may be included within this union, according to their respective numbers, which shall be determined by adding to the whole number of free persons, including those bound to Service for a Term of Years, and excluding Indians not taxed, three-fifths of all other Persons . . . " Section 1 of the 14th Amendment changed the status of "personhood" to "[a]ll persons born or naturalized in the United States and subject to the jurisdiction thereof . . . " Section 2 of the 14th Amendment established voting rights for all male citizens who are 21 years-of-age or older. Subsequent amendments have refined voting rights further.
59. This was changed by the 17th Amendment.
60. U.S. Constitution, Article I, Section 7.
61. U.S. Constitution, Article I, Section 2.
62. U.S. Constitution, Article I, Section 3.
63. John Locke, *Two Treaties of Government* (Cambridge: Cambridge University Press, 1970).
64. The idea of a government by social contract most likely appeared first in Thomas Hobbes, *Leviathan*, (Harmondsworth: Penguin, 1968).

65. *The Declaration of Independence.*
66. John Locke, *Two Treaties of Government,* ch. 5.
67. U.S. Constitution, 15th, 17th, 19th, 23rd, 24th, & 26th Amendments.
68. U.S. Constitution, 14th Amendment.
69. These catagories of rights come from Samuel Bowles & Herbert Gints, *Democracy & Capitalism: Property, Community, and the Contradictions of Modern Social Thought* (New York: Harper Collins Publisher, 1987), pp. 215n, 23.
70. Daniel Elazar, *American Federalism: A View from the States* (New York: Harper & Row, Publishers, 1984), p. 3.
71. Ibid., p. 2.
72. U.S. Constitution, Article VII.
73. U.S. Constitution, Article VI.
74. U.S. Constitution, Article II. Later the Constitution changed the number to the top 3 candidates.
75. Actually, Jefferson's election was only one of several political disputes between Hamilton and Burr which led to the duel.
76. The 15th Amendment, strictly speaking, does not grant African-Americans the right to vote. What it does do is eliminate color as a grounds for denying the franchise to otherwise eligible voters.
77. U.S. Constitution, Article V.
78. Lance Banning, Jefferson and Madison: *Three Conversations from the Founding,* p. 43.

Section II

Political Processes

CHAPTER 3
Public Opinion and Political Polls: Permission or Submission?

"Effective government cannot be conducted by [politicians] who . . . ask themselves first and last not what is the truth and which is the right and necessary course but, 'What does the Gallup Poll say?'"

—*Walter Lippmann*

"When the people is master of the vote it becomes master of the government."

—*Aristotle*

"The ballot is stronger than the bullet."

—*Abraham Lincoln*

"Public opinion wins wars."

—*Dwight D. Eisenhower*

INTRODUCTION

This chapter will focus on the concept **public opinion** and its articulation via elections and public opinion polls. In doing so, we will first define the concept public opinion and then briefly review the distinction between public opinion and popular opinion. From there, we will discuss the purpose and history of both elections and political polls in the American political system. We will conclude by reviewing some of the democratic pitfalls of using polls to project public opinion.

Defining the concept "public opinion" is more difficult than most of us would believe. Like many concepts in the American political vocabulary, it is more often used as a weapon to win a political debate than it is examined in an attempt to improve our political understanding. This is why the authors of a book on American public opinion have written, "Public opinion is notoriously difficult to define. There are scores if not hundreds of variations on a definition."[1] Nonetheless, most political scientists agree that the opinion which matters to political scholars is not the opinions of, say, the tennis-playing public or the literary public, but the opinions of the political public. And who constitutes this political public? The political public is made up of any person or groups of persons (American citizens, interested foreign agents, and most directly, citizens who are qualified to vote, for example) who have some business or connection to the government. That is, "what members of the 'public' in public opinion have in common is a connection to government."[2] Therefore, we will define public opinion as the preference of the adult population on matters of relevance to government.[3] Now that we have defined the concept public opinion, we will, to provide some context to our discussion, turn our attention to the distinction between popular opinion and public opinion.

Most members of the political elite of the revolutionary generation, though aware government could not simply ignore the concerns of the "people," believed the opinions of the many were simply too politically ignorant to be of much use to the ruling class.[4] Hence, they tended to distinguish between what the people want (what some political scientists label "popular opinion") and what the people really need (what some political scientists refer to as "public opinion"[5]). As one Founder, Alexander Hamilton, wrote, "the voice of the people has been said to be the voice of God; and however generally this maxim has been quoted and believed, it is not true in fact. The people are turbulent and changing; they seldom judge or determine right."[6] As contemporary proof of this, they could point to such popular ideas as the desire to "make government more like business" or the popular support for the "War on Terror." In each case, it can reasonably be argued that both of these ideas are not only counter to the interests of the majority of citizens, they are, indeed, destructive of much that the majority would consider conducive to the good life. For example, making government more like business has led to the virtual bankruptcy of big business and government alike. Moreover, this popular desire to remake government in the image of corporate America has neither improved people's individual economies nor increased their individual freedom. Instead, it has delivered them lower wages, a more thoroughly polluted environment, and increased the corporate authority over their lives—hardly the policies most Americans would find beneficial. Additionally, the public's desire to fight the "War on Terror" has done little to make them safer, while it has placed an immense burden on the military families duty-bound to fight it, overcrowded our prisons, bankrupted our government's abilities to address other social concerns (health care and education, for example), and turned America into the world's leader in imprisoning its own people. Again, this can hardly be what the majority intended.[7]

Modern proponents of this distinction between popular and public opinion tend to view the relationship between the government and the citizen under a doctor-patient model. Advocates of this view believe that just as doctors must sometimes prescribe a remedy their patients might not believe is in their medical interest (for example, less rest not more for the perpetually lazy), political experts must also impose policy which, no matter how unpopular, is necessary for the community's political health. To be sure, not everyone agrees that political wisdom is the sole monopoly of the political establishment; such a belief, they argue, reeks of paternalism.[8] In other words, they see those proposing a distinction between popular and public opinion as endorsing a political relationship which better reflects a parent-child model than a patient-doctor one. As contemporary proof of the wisdom of the public, they could point to such popular and wise choices as the public's growing dissatisfaction with both major political parties, its growing resistance to increasing troop levels in Afghanistan, or the popular rejection of so-called free trade, for instance. An excellent defense of the wisdom of the people was a CNN/Opinion Research Group poll conducted on October 21, 2008. It revealed that 75% of Americans believe "things are going badly," and an equal number expressed that they "were angry about the way things are going." Moreover, the same poll showed that two-thirds of the respondents "were scared" about the political situation.

It is, however, the opinion of this author that the entire debate over the public and popular opinion dichotomy is simply beside the point. The question is not whether the people are enlightened enough to rule, or whether the government is treating us like children, but rather what matters is the degree of public virtue in whomever governs, be it the people at large or their selected representatives. In other words, the best insurance against bad government, regardless of who is in charge, is to instill in the ruler(s), through education, the virtue of ruling in the public good no matter how popular or unpopular this may be in the short run. For if political history has taught us anything, it is that in the long run the best guarantee of a government's success, stability and popularity is simply to govern the community wisely. Nonetheless, for better or for worse, it is now a contemporary political reality that government's adherence (no matter how cosmetic) to public opinion provides it with the only moral authority which justifies its demand for obedience. Or, to put it another way, the belief government is ruling in accordance with public opinion has now replaced the people's devotion to kings as the main source of legitimacy for the exercise of political power. We will now turn our attention to the two dominant means for voicing the public's opinion—elections and public opinion polls.

PUBLIC OPINION AND ELECTIONS

The history of public opinion and its influence over governmental policy mirrors the evolution of democratic government. Prior to the advent of democracy (or at least the superficial belief in democracy's value as a governing system) the ruling class could not have cared less what the opinion of the peasant class was one way or the other; it simply did not matter. The nobility would do what it thought necessary regardless of the concerns of the public at large. Yet with the growth of the democratic impulse, there arose a corresponding demand that government begin to reflect the values and concerns of the majority in its institutional policies. It is no coincidence that as the democratic spirit began to spread throughout the European and American communities their governments began to take on a more representative character. Hence, originally the American Constitution not only forbade Congress or any state legislature to grant titles of nobility, it also allowed wealthy, white, males to vote for federal representatives (though not Senators) as long as they were otherwise qualified to vote for members of their most numerous state legislatures. Now, this may not sound very democratic to the modern ear, but at the time it was revolutionary—allowing someone other than a person of noble birth to have any say over political policy was a radical idea indeed.

Furthermore, as the notion of political equality caught on in America, more and more members of the community demanded the electoral privilege themselves. Hence, the Constitution was amended numerous times during the 19th and 20th centuries in an attempt to do just that. For example, in 1870, the Constitution was amended to prevent state governments from denying African-American males the vote on account of race;[9] qualified voters (adult males) were granted the privilege of voting for senators in 1913 (senators were previously elected by state legislatures);[10] in 1920, women, who were otherwise qualified, were now granted the authority to exercise their democratic privilege;[11] in 1961, citizens of Washington DC were allowed to take part in a presidential election for the first time;[12] in 1964, the Constitution was amended to prevent state governments from charging citizens to vote, thus allowing the poor more access to the electoral mechanisms;[13] and, in 1971, in response to the **Vietnam War**, the Constitution was amended to reflect the common sense notion that if 18-year-olds were old enough to die for their government in Southeast Asia, then they were certainly old enough to vote for it here in America.[14] That is, what started in the late 17th century as a rejection of the monarchical privilege had, by the late 20th century, evolved into a full scale democratic revolution, and with this evolution came the demand for more thorough access to the ballot box for all members of the community.

And, yet, as this democratic revolution took hold in America there arose a corresponding enigma: As the law granted more and more members of the community the privilege of voting, less and less of them actually voted in practice. America now ranks near the bottom of all democratic countries when it comes to voter participation; in fact, the United States ranks twenty-seventh out of the twenty-eight democratic countries when it comes to voter turnout.[15] For example, only 59% of eligible voters exercised their privilege in the 2008 federal elections. Political scientists have spent enormous intellectual energy trying to explain this apparent anomaly, and have offered the following possible explanations:

A Cumbersome Registration Process. The United States is one of the very few democratic countries which require their citizens to register prior to voting (Australia, New Zealand, and France are the others, and each has a significantly higher turnout than America, by the way).[16] Proponents of this view believe registration places an undue burden on the electoral process thereby reducing voter turnout.

The Frequency of Elections. Some political scientists insist the reason there is such a low voter turnout in America is because there is simply too much of a good thing. That is, they believe the government (either intentionally or not) overloads the electoral schedule in such a way as to render the sacred act of voting into a mundane and bothersome chore.

Apathy on the Part of the Public. Some political scientists blame our low voter turnout on the public's indifference to all things political. They believe if people really cared then they would take the time to exercise their democratic responsibility.

No Real Party Competition. Still other political scientists put the majority of blame on the lack of a clear political choice between the parties, which, they argue, turns elections into nothing more than coronations for the political class.

It is the opinion of this author that all of these are indeed factors in explaining the low voter turnout in America, but I would stress the last two factors as paramount. It seems to me that as long as the political class remains indifferent to the concerns of the middle class,[17] then it stands to reason the people will become apathetic toward government in return. Also, this desire on the part of politicians of both parties to serve their corporate sponsors would explain why the people feel there is little difference between the major parties when it comes to governmental policy. It is, however, also the opinion of this author that the proper remedy to the political class's indifference is not to register our apathy by failing to vote, but by registering our disgust by voting for somebody else. In short, if we, the American people, want democracy to work for us and our communities, then we need to do the democratic work required to make it happen.

PUBLIC OPINION AND POLLS

Another means for the government to gauge public opinion is through public opinion polls. As mentioned earlier, the notion that the governing elite should even care what the people think is a relatively recent notion in the history of political thought. Nonetheless, as the democratic spirit was diffused throughout the American community, public opinion polls developed alongside elections as another vehicle to register the wishes of the public at large. The first poll appeared in the *Harrisburg Pennsylvanian,* in 1824, incorrectly predicting Andrew Jackson would defeat John Quincy Adams and Henry Clay for the presidency.[18] These early polls were referred to as "**straw polls**," meaning they were far from scientific and consisted primarily of man-on-the-street interviews or simple mail-in ballots. It was not until 1896 that straw polling became serious business—with an emphasis on business. That is, they were used more to stimulate advertising revenue than to accurately reflect public opinion. As two experts in public opinion wrote:

> The polls were of major importance to their sponsors as a promotional gimmick. They created interest in the publication. Also, those publishers using mail-out ballots usually included a special subscription offer along with the ballot. By all indications, the scheme worked remarkably well to boost circulation.[19]

As polls became more common in the American political landscape, public frustration over their inaccuracies began to grow as well.[20] In response to this frustration, three men (Archibald Crossley, Elmo Roper, and George Gallup) began developing more scientific polling techniques which proved, in the presidential election of 1936, to be much more accurate than the previous magazine based straw polls. This scientific polling method accurately predicted the outcome of FDR's landslide victory in 1936, whereas most of the straw polls predicted that FDR would lose big; thus ended the era of straw polls. Of course not all was smooth sailing for these new scientific polls for each mistakenly predicted Thomas Dewey would defeat Harry Truman in the presidential election of 1948; a faulty polling technique, known as "quota samples," caused the error, and was quickly replaced by the much more accurate "probability samples."[21] Since then, political polls have become second only to elections as the primary tool for government and the **media** to ascertain the political opinion of the public. Yet this new tool not only provided a way for the people to register their opinion to government, polls also provided the political class with a new device in which to manipulate the people in return. Or, as two political scientists have written about the relatively recent increase in the use of polls to gauge (or create) public opinion, "Change is not neutral. New innovations benefit some at the expense of others."[22] Therefore, the rest of this chapter will be dedicated to explaining how polls can just as easily be used to manipulate public opinion as they can to articulate it.

THE PROBLEM WITH POLLS

Before we begin analyzing polls in particular, let us first remind ourselves of the importance of polls to our political system in general. Polls (like elections) serve the fundamental purpose of justifying the use of absolute governmental power. Therefore as long as government can demonstrate that the public, through the use of public opinion polls, is behind whatever policy it intends to implement, or has already implemented, its actions are considered democratic and, therefore, legitimate. Hence, we, the American people, should be no more tolerant of manipulated polls than we would be if the government, or any other powerful group, were to manipulate elections, since both are the main means of registering democratic opinion. The following are some ways in which polls (either intentionally or not) can be used more to distort public opinion than to accurately reflect it.

Polls Equalize and Homogenize Opinion. Polls are indifferent to the diversity of persons; each person in a polling sample is reduced to a mere numerical respondent, rather than accounted for as a full-fledged human being with unique life experiences or point of view. For example, the question as to whether racism is a problem in the United States will vary depending upon the race of the person asked. Very few whites have experienced racism so they are much less likely to think racism is a contemporary problem (except, of course, when it comes to affirmative action when things tend to reverse). The same could be said of sexism; men and women will generally have very different views concerning the gravity of the problem. Or, for instance, when it comes to economic issues polls tend to treat the wealthy and the working class the same, as if each group is similarly economically situated. And, arguably most disturbing, is how polls, regardless of the issue, weigh the opinion of the informed citizen equally with that of the ignoramus. When was the last time a medical survey was done in which polls equated the opinions of idiots with the opinions of doctors? Lastly, polls also equalize the intensity of all given opinion regardless of the actual level of interest within each respondent. So, a person who is, at best, casually interested in a subject is equated with any and all persons who may be much more intensely interested in the issue. Think about it. Would it be fair to equate, say, the Rockefellers' opinion with your own concerning the tax burden on the middle class? Yet this is exactly what occurs when polls homogenize and equalize opinion between those who are either informed or affected with those who are neither.

Polls Can Be Easily Manipulated. It should come as no surprise to students of politics that any well-funded group (government and otherwise) can use polls as a way to generate apparent popular support for their position on any given political question. Imagine hypothetically,[23] for example, we have been paid to provide popular support for the Obama Administration's national healthcare plan. Now, knowing our client wants support for his plan, how could we word a question to manufacture it? Suppose we asked this question: Do you agree the Obama Administration should do something about the health care *crisis*? This would probably be much more effective in generating popular support than if we had asked this question: Do you approve of the Obama Administration's attempt to *socialize* the American health care industry? Notice how by changing the wording of the question we are able to manipulate the public into supporting whatever particular political position our clients are in favor of. Let us try the same exercise for abortion. If we were employed to manufacture support for, say, the pro-choice position, we might want to frame our abortion question this way: Do you agree an *adult woman* rather than the government should have *control over her own body*? Now, if we were employed by a pro-life group, we could always ask the question this way: Do you agree there should be legal limits on a *girl's ability to abort her unborn baby*? In each case, it is not the public's opinion we are really after, what we are after is a paycheck from whomever retained us, and if that requires us to manipulate public opinion, so be it.

A deadly example of public opinion experts manipulating the public occurred when Americans were convinced to risk their lives defending a corrupt monarchy in Kuwait. The Kuwait wealthy spent over $10.8 million dollars employing an American public relations firm, by the name of Hill & Knowlton (H&K), to help convince Americans (with an assist by George H. Bush and Congress) to do their fighting for them. In doing so, they discovered American "focus groups" responded much more favorably to the theme of "Saddam as enemy" than they did to any attempt to make Kuwait out as a democratic victim. So, H&K began flooding America with stories (both true and untrue) of Iraqi atrocities in Kuwait to stir up war fever in America—and it worked. One such example was when Congress began holding heavily covered committee meetings where apparent witnesses to Iraqi cruelty were allowed to testify before the American people. One woman testified to witnessing Iraqi soldiers pulling newborn babies out of their incubators in a Kuwait City hospital. Later, it was revealed by an international human rights group that not only was the story untrue, but the woman was actually the daughter of the Kuwait ambassador to the United States and was paid to fabricate the story.[24] Nonetheless, at the time, this type of public opinion generated the necessary public support (via the polls) to justify the government's action in protecting the corporate wealth of the oil industry.

President Clinton helped "move the polls" during his legally challenged terms in office by conveniently bombing Sudan or Iraq whenever it seemed to have the most effect on his approval polls.

More recently, public opinion was manipulated by the entire Bush administration when they constantly repeated such non-sense as Saddam Hussein's regime had WMD and had connections with the 9/11 hijackers so as to push popular opinion in favor of going to war in 2003. One such example is then Secretary of State, Colin Powell's factually pathetic presentation to the United Nations Security Council regarding Hussein's WMD "stockpiles." Or President Bush's claim that Iraq had tried to buy enriched uranium from Niger, even though the administration knew it was untrue but still used it in the Bush's 2003 "State of the Union" address.

Polls Allow the Government and Their Corporate Masters to Set the Agenda of Political Debate. In any given political discussion the most important question is the one not asked. Or, to put it another way, the job of the ruling class is to control the parameters of debate to ensure that only those issues that are favorable to them are open for discussion or examination. And, there is no better mechanism for controlling the limits of political debates than popular opinion polls. Why? Well, as one political scientist has argued, polls tend to "domesticate" the public by socializing them into thinking the only way to register their democratic opinion is to wait for government to ask them questions, rather than the more traditional notion that democratic government should be ready to answer theirs.[25] This is why political scientists have written, "modern opinion polls have changed the character of public opinion from an assertion to a response."[26] That is, polls have replaced such conventional democratic activities as voting, writing representatives, protesting, and (most important) deciding for ourselves what is of importance and demanding that government act accordingly. Instead, we, the American people, are being reduced to a herd of passive receptors obediently waiting for the political elite to provide us with the "appropriate" questions and, almost as often, with the appropriate answers.

Polls Tend to Promote a Hypocritical Public. One of the least recognized problems with polls is how they tend to foster a political community of self-deceivers. Polls, in other words, do not require people to "walk the walk," all polls demand is one talk a good talk. For example, during any given sex scandal, polls consistently show the vast majority of Americans are sick of the whole thing and wish to move on to more important issues. Yet the media finds these very same Americans flock to any program or magazine which covers the scandal in detail. Moreover, if these media outlets would lessen their coverage their ratings or readership would suffer accordingly. In addition, polls show a significant majority supports term limits for politicians, and, yet, these are the very same Americans who reelect their politicians at a 90% clip. These are also the same Americans who, polls demonstrate, desire "less government," but, God forbid, let a natural disaster strike their community and they become instant advocates for "big government." Another very serious result of saying one thing while doing another is when Americans express their opinion in favor of going to war. Many who are in favor of war in the abstract, never seem to find the courage to actually fight the war in reality. In short, these people don't put their bodies where their mouths are. Veterans refer to such hypocritical people as either "POGS" or "Armchair Rangers"; that is, POGS and Armchair Rangers love to watch the war from the comfort of their living rooms, but can't seem to get themselves to the local Armed Forces recruiting center. It seems if government has a moral responsibility to reflect the public's views in its policy, then the public has a corresponding moral obligation to be honest about these views.

Polls Foster an Isolated Public. Another rarely discussed political deficiency of polls is their inherent isolating quality. Polls single each respondent out and demand they think in an isolated and independent fashion. On its face, this may seem like a positive characteristic of polls. After all, should not everyone think and decide for themselves? Well, of course they should, but since when does thinking for yourself entail thinking *by* yourself? Imagine, for instance, having to make an important medical decision about a family member's health. Would you want to make such a decision in a social vacuum, without the input of, say, your doctor, family members or other significant persons (teachers, clergy, friends, or others in a similar situation, for example)? Now, imagine a community whose system of government is predicated on the notion that policy will be set according to its collective wisdom, that, nevertheless, decides most of its public issue in a private and isolated fashion. Does this make any sense? How are members of this community supposed to articulate wise public policy if they never have an opportunity to deliberate with other members of their community prior to deciding it? Two experts in public opinion have written that prior to public opinion polls, "public opinion was once largely a group phenomenon," hence, community members, "would consult with the leaders of various advocacy groups, such as farmers or organized labor. . . . Opinion polls have undermined [this] ability."[27] That is, it seems just as foolish to voice your opinion on economic, trade, or **foreign policy** without the advice of your neighbors and community leaders, as it would be to attempt to prescribe yourself medication without first consulting a medical expert. One political theorist has gone so far as to argue that the primary purpose of democratic education should be to facilitate a, "citizenry in action, capable of thinking as a 'we' in the name of public goods," and to do so, we must, through public discourse, not private contemplation, help, "inform their discretion and enlarge their political experience."[28] Unfortunately, none of this is possible with public opinion polls, since polls, by definition, are asocial and, therefore, apolitical. In short, public opinion polls have the effect of making public opinion, private opinion; or, to put it another way, polls tend to remove the public from public opinion.

Public Opinion Polls Help Deintellectualize Politics. Lastly, polls tend to promote the "dumbing down" of political thought in America by reducing political inquiry to a poll watching exercise. During the next election, for instance, notice how often the media's so called political coverage (as well as most casual conversations about politics) consists solely of commentary about the polls. There was no better example of polls dumbing down political debate in America than the poll asking Americans which presidential candidate they would rather have babysit their kids or choose the toppings for their pizza.[29] Unfortunately, this poll-centered understanding of politics has even affected (or should I say, infected?) the practice of political science. More and more political scientists are, simply stated, polling experts with very little understanding of the intricacies of political scholarship. This quantitative bias is, frankly speaking, ignorant of the complexities inherent in the study of the political; the act of governing wisely, in short, is much more complex than the mere counting of heads, be it in the guise of a poll or an election. The sincere scholar of politics must deal with what occurs after elections and before polls, namely the complex conceptual and factual phenomenon which constitutes the political universe, ranging from the study of governmental processes to the examination of ideology, from the study of political history to exploring the intellectual high ground of political theory. Think about it. How does a pollster, recording what some of us already think, improve our understanding of any given political issue? What is missing in the polling process is an educational aspect concerning the issue, because lacking public discourse we never learn what others think and why. In other words, we cannot reduce the practice, nor the academic study, of democracy to a bean counting exercise if we intend on improving our communities—no matter what the polls say.

FINAL THOUGHTS

The social impulse to a more democratic government has been constant and unbending in the American political experience, but, at the same time, it has brought with it new problems and unforeseen dangers. The job of the democratic citizen, in part, is to recognize not all that politically glitters is, therefore, democratic gold. That is to say, just because someone asks your opinion on a political issue doesn't necessarily mean your government is more democratic than one which does not. The best measure of a government's democratic nature is not simply if it does or does not ask for the public's opinion, the best measure of a government's commitment to democracy is what it does with the answers. Maybe what we need to do is require pollsters to issue the following "Miranda" warning before asking any citizen a question: Democratic citizen, you have the right to remain silent, but if you fail to exercise this right, what you say can, and will, be used against you.

NOTES

1. Robert S. Erikson and Kent L. Tedin, *American Public Opinion: Its Origins, Content, and Impact*, 5th ed. (Boston: Allyn and Bacon, 1995), p. 6.
2. Ibid., p. 6.
3. Ibid., p. 7.
4. William Lyons, John M. Scheb II and Lilliard E. Richardson Jr., *American Democracy: Politics and Political Culture* (Minneapolis: West Publishing Company, 1995), p. 164; see also, Erikson and Tedin, *American Public Opinion*, p. 2.

5. Thomas Patterson, *The American Democracy,* 2nd ed. (New York: McGraw-Hill, 1994), pp. 209–210. The interested reader may want to examine, Robert Nisbet, "Public Opinion versus Popular Opinion," *Public Interest* 41 (1975): 167.
6. Erikson and Tedin, *American Public Opinion,* p. 2.
7. See chapter 6 (on economic policy) of this text for further clarification.
8. For an excellent discussion on paternalism see John Stuart Mill, *On Liberty* (New York: Penguin Books, 1985).
9. See the 15th Amendment of the U.S. Constitution.
10. See the 17th Amendment of the U.S. Constitution.
11. See the 19th Amendment of the U.S. Constitution.
12. See the 23rd Amendment of the U.S. Constitution.
13. See the 24th Amendment of the U.S. Constitution.
14. See the 26th Amendment of the Constitution.
15. Robert L. Lineberry, George C. Edwards III and Martin P. Wattenberg, *Government In America: People, Politics, and Policy,* 6th ed. (New York: HarperCollins, 1994), p. 316.
16. Patterson, *The American Democracy,* p. 239.
17. See the following chapters of this book for further analyses.
18. Erikson and Tedin, *American Public Opinion,* p. 8.
19. Ibid., pp. 8–9.
20. See for example, the 1936 election between FDR and Alf Landon. Ibid., p. 10.
21. Ibid., p. 10.
22. Ibid., p. 12.
23. For actual examples, see Ibid., p. 41.
24. For full details see Daniel Hellinger and Dennis R. Judd, *The Democratic Facade,* 2nd ed. (Belmont, CA.: Wadsworth Publishing Company, 1994), pp. 74–79.
25. Benjamin Ginsberg, *The Consequences of Consent: Elections, Citizen Control and Popular Acquiescence* (Reading, MA: Addison, 1987).
26. Erikson and Tedin, *American Public Opinion,* p. 14.
27. Ibid., p. 13.
28. Benjamin Barber, *The Conquest of Politics: Liberal Philosophy in Democratic Times* (New Jersey: Princeton University Press, 1988), p. 211.
29. Mike Royko, "Remember that Clinton is a Member of the TV Generation," *The Oregonian* (May 5, 1996), p. B9.

CHAPTER 4
Political Parties, Ideologies, and the American Political Spectrum: Tweedledee and Tweedledum

"All political parties die at last of swallowing their own lies."
—John Arbuthnot

"Political parties . . . [are] designed to make lies sound truthful and murder respectable, and to give an appearance of solidity to pure wind."
—George Orwell

"All political parties . . . are at bottom only questions of might."
—August Bebel

"Ignorance maketh most men go into a party, and shame keepeth them from getting out of it."
—George Savile

INTRODUCTION

This chapter will focus on three interrelated topics (Political Parties, Political Ideologies, and the **Political Spectrum**) and their effect on the American political system. We will begin our analysis with a brief discussion on the purpose of political parties in general. From there, we will briefly review the history of political parties in America. Following that, we will identify the essential characteristics of the two major political parties, the Democrats and Republicans, and some of the lesser-known political parties. While doing so, we will also examine American political ideologies, paying close attention to the terms "**liberal**" and "**conservative**." We will conclude with a graphic analysis of the American political spectrum.

POLITICAL PARTIES

Before we begin discussing political parties in particular (for instance, the Democrats or Republicans) we first need to define what the concept of "**political party**" means in general. Political parties, whatever their particular persuasion, exist only to capture governing power by winning elections. That is, the primary purpose of a political party is to take advantage of the fact that in America the government is available to any citizen who meets some very minimal constitutional conditions and can garner more votes than anyone else. There is no hereditary test; you need not be the son or daughter of a king. There is no religious test. There is no racial test. Again, all that is required is that you receive more votes than anyone else. Political parties are very much aware of this truth, and attempt to take advantage of it by organizing and capturing a majority of votes. And two political parties in particular have been very successful in doing so—the Democrats and Republicans.

But before we examine the contemporary Democratic and Republican Parties it would behoove us to review briefly the history of political parties in America.[1] During the nation's colonial period political parties were unwelcome, as it was believed parties were detrimental to the public good. In the words of the founding generation, parties constituted "factions" which were divisive and self-serving, rendering the common good vulnerable to partisan needs. President Washington constantly warned of the dangers of the divisive nature of parties during his two terms of office. Yet the very real political differences that permeated his administrations proved to be too great to prevent the emergence of two distinct political camps—one focused around the person of John Adams and one whose intellectual force originated in Thomas Jefferson. These two camps evolved into the first American political parties, Adam's Federalist Party and Jefferson's Democratic-Republican Party.

Simply put, the Federalists favored federal power and commercial interests, while the Democratic-Republicans supported the interests of farmers and wanted political power located in the hands of states and local communities. The Federalist Party proved to be short-lived, finding its political death in the elections of 1800, as the vast majority of Americans, being farmers, resented the aristocratic and commercial leanings of the Federalists and were angered by the Federalists' suspicions of democracy. By the 1820s, however, the Democratic-Republicans had been captured by business interests and began to advocate for essentially Federalist programs, especially those supporting manufacturers and their desire for a stronger federal government. This meant the ideas of the rural majority, especially those not engaged in commercial farming, became poorly represented by what was left of Jefferson's Party.

Such an abandonment of their rural core might not have proved fatal for the Democratic-Republicans had it not coincided with the expansion of the franchise. As mentioned in the previous chapter, the vast majority of Americans were originally excluded from the voting booth due to race, sex, or lack of wealth. Perhaps half of all white males could not vote, let alone women and blacks. By the 1830s, however, property qualifications were removed in most states resulting in the enfranchisement of most white males. This increase in eligible voters, bringing with them their lower income interests to the political arena, spelled doom for the Democratic-Republican Party, as it had existed since the 1820s. With this change in the political landscape came a fragmenting of the party into two new political parties, one representing noncommercial farmers, many cotton growers, urban workers and favoring state power, and another favoring commercial interests and federal authority. The first, under the leadership of Andrew Jackson, became known as the Democratic Party. The second became the short-lived Whig Party.

By the 1850s the political disagreements that would lead to the nation's bloodiest struggle, the Civil War, were becoming the bane of both parties. While the issues of immigration, **tariffs**, and most of all, slavery, absorbed the nation's attention, both parties avoided taking a strong stand on these issues in hopes of not alienating either their southern or northern membership. As a result, new political parties formed around these seemingly unaddressed concerns, draining away members from each of the established parties. The newly formed Know-Nothing Party supported restrictions on immigration and the political influence of immigrants, while the newly formed Republican Party focused on preventing the expansion of slavery. As the issue of slavery was dividing the nation on sectional grounds, southerners in favor of slavery, northerners more and more opposed to its expansion, if not its outright existence, the Democratic Party could no longer remain a unified party and split along sectional lines. Moreover, by 1860 the issue of slavery had become so pervasive it rendered the Whig and Know-Nothing Parties irrelevant, while ordaining the Republicans as the Democrat's chief opposition. With the election of the first Republican president, Abraham Lincoln, the political system proved incapable of managing the deep divide within the American community. The Republican Party, under Lincoln's leadership, became the party of the union North as it made war against the Democratic Party of the southern cause. It seems a political reality that some political disagreements are so profound they are only amenable on the battlefield; such was the case regarding southern and northern division, especially over the issue of slavery.

The Civil War had a lasting affect on political parties. White southerners would continue to vote strongly Democratic into the 1970s, whereas, the most northern states tended to vote strongly Republican during the same time period. Moreover, after the Civil War the parties enjoyed differences in support among ethnic, class, and religious groups. Roman Catholics, the urban working-class, Irish, and non-evangelical Protestants generally voted Democratic while northern farmers and evangelical Protestants voted Republican. In general, throughout the remainder of the nineteenth century, both major parties remained closely balanced in their public appeal. During this period, the parties differed mainly on industrial policy; with the Republicans favoring federal, state and local aid to business while the Democrats supported limiting aid to business to state and local enterprises only.

In this closely balanced environment, third party movements flourished in both variety and influence. For example, the Greenback Party supported a more inflationary

monetary policy to ease the burden on debtors, and the temperance parties favored the prohibition of alcohol. The largest third party movements were the Socialist and Populist Parties. At the end of the nineteenth-century, economic conditions were so dire for the American rural and urban working poor it was inevitable that political organizations would arise in an attempt to address their grievances—for the urban factory worker it was the Socialists, for the rural poor it was the Populists. The Socialist Party reached its peak in the 1912 election where its presidential candidate received six percent of the popular vote. The Socialist Party's strong advocacy for economic justice proved too radical for the establishment (and much of ordinary America) so the government crippled the party with police harassment and economic suppression. This governmental campaign proved so successful the Socialist Party has not fully recovered from it even today. On the other hand, the Populist Party was not so much intentionally targeted as it was co-opted by the establishment politics. That is to say, the Democrats rendered the Populist Party moot by absorbing some of the Populist's policies into their own platform for the election of 1896. In the presidential election of 1892, the Populists received almost nine percent of the vote by advocating for government aid to farmers and nationalization of the railroads. The Democrats simply co-opted the cosmetics of the Populist's platform for the next election (while secretly rendering the platform much more acceptable to establishment interests) thereby convincing the public that the Populist platform was redundant at best. Such a maneuver is not uncommon in politics; both major parties did the same to Perot's third party challenge by co-opting his demand for a balanced federal budget.

Major parties co-opting the ideas of reformers is not always detrimental and can actually serve to improve the political system. The so-called progressive era from 1900 to 1916 serves as an example. During this period, reformers working within the two-party system convinced both major parties to use the power of the government to regulate the economy in such a manner as to curb the industrial elite's exploitation of the environment and the public at large. To be sure, the progressive era was replete with reform minded third party advocates; nonetheless, many more reformers affected real change by working within the two-party system.

In any event, between 1896 and 1932 the Republican Party dominated national politics. However, its refusal to address the economic calamity known as the **Great Depression** (1929–1930s) put an end to its electoral success. The Democratic Party, under the leadership of Franklin D. Roosevelt, introduced what became known as the "**New Deal**" to help mitigate the depression's effect on ordinary Americans. FDR's so-called alphabet soup programs put the power of the government behind the needs of the working American through various work projects, labor organizations, and most notably, the creation of social security insurance. The Democrats would come to dominate the national scene well into the 1960s, as they became identified as the party of the middle class. However, the Democratic Party was showing serious signs of political overreach. With the growth of the civil rights movement, Democrats, as generally the majority party, assumed the lead in the desegregation policies of the federal government. Yet the more the party attempted to include racial and other minority groups within its membership the more it drove out its conservative members. For the first time since the Civil War period, Republicans began winning elections in the South as the Democratic Party was increasingly seen as the party of civil rights. Democrats were also losing the vote of northern working class white males, who tended to be socially conservative, as the Democrats became identified in the popular conscience as the party of the liberal left. All of this culminated in what has come to be known as the Reagan Revolution of the 1980s. America, it seemed, had taken a collective turn to the Right and was rejecting all things liberal, particularly liberal-Democratic "tax and spend" programs. Throughout the 1980s, the Republicans were very successful playing up their traditionally close relationship with corporate and other elite establishment interests. By the 1990s, the Democrats, in hopes of improving their electoral success, introduced a "new kind of Democrat." This new version was to prove to be more "conservative" and corporate friendly and would be personified by Bill Clinton, who helped realign the national Democratic Party so it appeared very much like the Republican Party it purportedly opposed.

This has led to one of the most controversial issues of contemporary American politics: Is there a meaningful difference between the two major parties? Those who contend there is, point to the hyper-partisan nature of present American Politics. For example, David Broder of the *Washington Post* reported:

> "*Congressional Quarterly* reported that 2005 was one of the most partisan years since it began its record keeping. It found that the parties took opposing stands on 328 of 669 roll calls in the House and 229 of 366 in the Senate . . . In the House, the subjects that provoked disagreements included immigration rules, stem-cell research, surveillance and interrogation policies, arms sales to China, the Central American Free Trade Agreement, the Endangered Species Act, energy and the intervention in the Terry Schiavo case. In the Senate, the parties split on class-action lawsuits, bankruptcy protection, Central American Free Trade Agreement, The Patriot Act, the budget, defense appropriations, energy and the nomination of John Bolton to the United Nations."[2]

As the evidence shows, the Democratic and Republican Parties do have their differences. Democrats are more likely to be pro-choice when it comes to abortion, whereas, Republicans are more likely to be pro-life. Democrats tend to give more weight to environmental concerns than do Republicans. Republicans are more likely to support industry over labor than their Democratic counterparts. Democrats are more likely to endorse a social safety net, or welfare, than are Republicans. Of course there is some overlap between the two parties, with some Republicans and Democrats holding similar positions on each of these issues. Where one finds the most striking difference between the two parties is among the far edges of both political parties; what is referred to as being "far left" for Democrats and "far right" for Republicans (we will discuss the difference between "right" and "left" later in the chapter).

On the other hand, many critics of the two party system argue that, generally speaking, the disagreements between the two parties seem to be a case where there is distinction with little difference. According to critics of the two party system, Republicans and Democrats narrow the focus of debate so that there will be disagreement, while at the same time, keeping their disputes within a very limited range of political possibilities. In philosophical terms, when it comes to actually governing, the two parties differ more over a matter of degree than of kind. In other words, their policy positions are in general agreement over the substance of an issue, while differing, if at all, only over the small details of an issue. A good example of this was the foreign policy debates during the presidential election of 2008. The two major party candidates, Barack Obama and John McCain, agreed that the "War on Terror" would continue, while every other political party called for its immediate halt and the return home of America's troops. Nonetheless, both candidates vociferously debated which war was the "right" war to increase America's military commitment, while never advocating for a diplomatic and political resolution for both conflicts. McCain wanted to increase troop levels in Iraq, while Obama strenuously objected while calling for a large increase of American combat troops in Afghanistan.

So, rather than having a substantive debate regarding peace or war—a difference of kind—they simply agreed to disagree over which war was the best one to escalate America's commitment—a difference of degree. Another example is the debate regarding so-called free trade. Although Democrats recently have been more vocal in their support for tougher labor and environmental standards within America's so-called free trade agreements (as have many Republicans) they refuse to endorse an American worker friendly rejection of free trade and its attendant institutions like the World Trade Organization. For example, as Obama was campaigning against free trade policies that have hurt the American worker, he sent a private message to Canada telling them not to take Obama's comments seriously, as they were "more reflective of political maneuvering than policy."[3]

To be sure, the devil is often said to be in the details, but it is also true that debates over the "big picture" are necessary for a healthy democracy. For example, which of the two major parties opposed the bailouts of the financial sector? Which of the two major parties want to decriminalize marijuana use and end the so-called war on drugs? Which of the two parties endorse **proportional representation** and public financing of campaigns? Which of the two parties opposed the invasion of Afghanistan or Iraq? Which of the two parties opposed bank deregulation, and advocated for true reform like community investment banks and mandating low interest loans for low-income individuals? Why has neither major party proposed **legislation** to revamp the American legal process in family courts so as to allow for meaningful access and legal representation for working Americans? Why did neither party oppose the giveaway of our public airwaves to private companies under the guise of telecommunications deregulation? Which party supports a major reduction in current defense spending?

Moreover, even when one looks into the details of a supposed policy dispute between the two major parties, one finds the details dovetailing into a profoundly similar policy. For example, candidate Obama campaigned against President Bush's legally dubious "anti-terrorism" policies. However, once elected, President Obama began endorsing those very same policies that he had so adamantly denounced on the campaign trail. As *The New York Times* reported:

> "In little-noticed confirmation testimony recently, Obama [officials] endorsed continuing the CIA's program of transferring prisoners to other countries without legal rights and indefinitely detaining suspects without trials even if they were arrested far away from a war zone. The Obama administration has also embraced the Bush legal team's arguments that a lawsuit by former CIA detainees should be shut down based on the "state secrets" doctrine. It has also left the door open to resuming military commission trials . . . "It was literally just Bush redux," said Margaret Satterthwaite, a faculty director at the Human Rights Center at the New York University Law School. "Exactly the same legal arguments that we saw the Bush administration present to the court" . . . . The Obama administration's recent policy moves have attracted praise from outspoken defenders of the Bush administration. Last Friday, *The Wall Street Journal's* editorial page argued that "it seems that the Bush administration's anti-terror architecture is gaining new legitimacy" as Obama's team embraces aspects of Bush's counter terrorism approach. Anthony Romero, executive director of the ACLU said the sequence of "disappointing" recent events heightens concerns that Obama might end up carrying forward "some of the most problematic policies of the Bush presidency." Obama has clashed with civil libertarians before. Last July, he voted as a senator to authorize eavesdropping on some phone calls and e-mails without a warrant."[4]

This morphing of the two major parties at the national level so infuriated the late Democratic **pundit**, Molly Ivins, that she wrote of the possibility of Hillary Clinton gaining the Democratic nomination for president,

> I'd like to make it clear to the people who run the Democratic Party that I will not support Hillary Clinton for president. Enough. Enough triangulation, calculation and equivocation . . . Sen. Clinton is apparently incapable of taking a clear stand on the war in Iraq, and that alone is enough to disqualify her . . . Look at this war, from the lies that led us into it, to the lies [the Republicans] continue to dump on us daily . . . I've said it before: War brings out the patriotic bullies. Do not sit there cowering and pretending the only way to win is as Republican-lite. If the Washington based [Democratic] Party can't get up and fight, we'll find someone who can.[5]

Today, many political analysts on the left and the right, as well as a growing number of "average" Americans,[6] now believe there is no substantive difference between these two parties when it comes to the important political issues facing Americans today.[7] This is known in political circles as the Tweedledee and Tweedledum view of the political parties.[8] According to this view the two parties are now so concerned with pleasing their wealthy contributors they will avoid confronting any issue which may displease their corporate sponsors. As Ralph Nader has said, "Washington is corporate-occupied territory, and the two parties are ferociously competing to see who's going to go to the White House and take orders from their corporate paymasters . . . "[9] For example, the Democrats, who traditionally relied on organized labor as a centerpiece of their core constituency, have become, like the Republicans, so beholden to corporate interests, that a union leader declared when asked his union's political affiliation, "we have no permanent party and no permanent candidates."[10] In addition, William Greider, a so-called liberal critic has written, "the major political parties . . . have instead gravitated toward another source of power—the elite interests that dominate government."[11] And, from the so-called Right, Kevin Phillips has written:

> Democrats . . . found themselves drawn as collaborators into what were basically conservative rescriptions of the U.S. economic policy: the tax overhauls of 1981 and 1986, the Social Security tax exemption of 1983, the Gramm-Rudman budget reform, the 1989 Republican-Democratic deal over increased congressional pay (both sides agreed not to attack each other for pay-raise support), the 1990 bipartisan budget . . . and so on . . . leading Democratic politicians had abandoned their "little guy" moorings to join in what were essentially "establishment" economics. [This] inhibited Democrats from developing either an opposition mind-set or an effective critique of the 1980s political economy. Belaboring what many of their own senior congressional leaders had joined in shaping wasn't easy.[12]

Bolstered by more recent data, Pulitzer Prize winning *New York Times* journalist David Cay Johnston, author of the best-selling book on America's tax system, *Perfectly Legal*, has argued that:

> "Both Democrats and Republicans are responsible for transforming the nation's tax system from its progressive roots into one that favors the super-rich . . . 'Bill Clinton gave the richest people in America a bigger tax cut than George Bush,' . . . [I]n the past decade, Presidents Clinton and Bush enacted huge tax cuts skewed toward the rich . . . As a result, the United States now has a tax system that requires the richest 400 people in the country—people who make an average of $176 million a year—to pay only 17 cents in taxes for every dollar they take in . . . [t]hat is barely more than the 15 cents paid by the average U.S. taxpayer and is the same rate paid by families earning $100,000 to $200,000 . . . 'That's not a progressive system . . . We have a tax system where the burden rises until you reach the political donor class, and then it falls . . . Tax systems that are not progressive are commonly found in societies that are dictatorial, oligarchical or feudal.'"[13]

CNN commentator and author Lou Dobbs has written that there is a bipartisan political war being waged on the middle class:

> It's now a war being prosecuted by both political parties. Neither party in Congress is looking out for the interests of the middle class. "The middle-class working family interests are not being guarded on Capitol Hill," says Illinois Democratic Sen. Dick Durbin . . . "They are, unfortunately, victims of what has become a tidal wave of pro-business legislation, which has been unfair to a lot of families that are struggling to get along." Durbin acknowledges that too many in his party are now under the sway of the all-powerful political influence of corporate America . . . Abraham Lincoln declared that a government "of the people, by the people, for the people shall not perish from the Earth," but the 21st century has so far seen it certainly diminishing. Unless one political party (and let's hope both) finds the courage to resist corporate interests and put working men and women first, our middle class will be among the loneliest people in a faded nation.[14]

In other words, according to the Tweedledee and Tweedledum view of politics, both parties, at the national level, are now in agreement that it is corporate interests that are, and ought to be, the primary concern of the political class (this is not surprising, since the leadership of both national parties are themselves wealthy corporate shareholders).[15] For example, both parties support so-called "free trade"; both favor a large **military-industrial complex**; both support a tax code that shifts the tax burden to the working class; and both favor the interests of industry over environmental concerns. The populist political and media critic Michael Moore summed up this idea nicely when he stated: "No one denies that the richest 1% of Americans deserve political representation, but why do they get two political parties while the rest of us don't even get one?"[16] To further support this contention, former Democratic Vice-President Al Gore stated, "let us not avoid unpleasant truths. Both parties have shortchanged America's ideals."[17]

Of course the national parties and the mainstream media continue to bemoan the partisan divide that has enveloped Washington recently. But this partisan environment may be more about party allegiance than about real policy differences. That is, members of both parties are always appearing to be engaged in some heated and passionate political debate, yet under closer scrutiny, the issues under discussion usually turn out to be relatively unimportant to the leadership of both major parties. Nonetheless, they do this to draw public attention away from their similarities. So, the parties, by focusing their political debates on social issues which mean nothing in the long run to corporate interests, give the appearance of a real difference and, hence, of a real electoral choice. For instance, how often is the debate between the two parties focused on such cultural issues such as gay marriage, flag burning, school prayer, and even abortion. None of these issues will affect the wealthy or their friends in the political class; they will always be able to sleep with whomever they please, procure an abortion if need be, pray when they want, and burn whatever they like. And when they do disagree on economic issues, the disagreements are so trivial they are rendered all but meaningless. This is why both parties will make such a big deal over the fact that one believes the financial bailout should be $1.3 trillion dollars while the other argues it should be $1.5 trillion dollars, or that we should begin removing troops from Iraq while debating if America should leave a "residual force" of either 50,000 troops or 30,000 troops behind to continue to fight and die in Iraq.[18] This similarity between the two parties may account for the reason why so many Americans are frustrated—no matter which party they vote for, nothing ever seems to change.

At this point in the discussion, defenders of the status quo usually begin defending the integrity of the American two-party system by stressing the very real ideological differences between the two parties. They will argue, to understand the differences between the two parties you must look past their agreement on specific policies and focus instead on the fact Democrats tend to be more "liberal" while Republicans tend to be much more "conservative." Of course, this begs the question: What does it mean to be conservative or liberal? Most Americans who use either one of these terms have only a vague notion, at best, what one or the other term actually means, so the issue tends to degenerate into a debate more over fashion than philosophical principles. In other words, if you wear sandals and tie-dye you're a liberal, and if you look like a member of the *Wall Street Journal*'s editorial board you're a conservative. How one appears may be important as far as the fashion police are concerned, but it has nothing to do with determining the appropriate principles one should adopt as a governing formula. Therefore, to obtain a better sense of what the words *liberal* and *conservative* entail, we will need to examine not only where these concepts came from and what they originally meant, but also, how their definitions have changed and what effect this has had on contemporary American politics. It will be argued their meanings have become so mangled and mutated in the present climate of political debate they have come to mean whatever anyone wants them to mean.

The term *conservative* came from the idea that the main purpose of government should be, simply put, to conserve the past.[19] As the authors of a book on political ideologies have written, "all conservatives share a desire to conserve or preserve something—usually the traditional or customary way of life of their societies."[20] At the core of conservative political theory is the belief that since each of us exists for only a fraction of any community's history, it is an act of incredible ignorance (as well as arrogance) to think any one of us could improve on the political principles of a community, since these principles are the result of generations of political practice. That is, why would any mere individual think they could suddenly improve on centuries of trial-and-error practical experience? Therefore, the best philosophy for any government is to use the wisdom of the past to regulate and monitor the present, while also helping to guide the future. And, where do we find the wisdom of the past when we live in the present? It is to be found in the political traditions of your community, since tradition is essentially the past made present. This is why you rarely find a student standing in front of the blackboard facing the other students on the first day of class. The reason for this is because students know it is the instructor who traditionally stands or sits at the front of the class. Or, does anyone else find it irritating to visit someone's house for, say, Thanksgiving dinner, only to find them serving halibut, or some other equally nontraditional meal? Don't they know we always have turkey on Thanksgiving? If any of this seems familiar to you, then you have experienced what one political theorist called the "conservative disposition."[21] Furthermore, conservatives argue, since this disposition (to prefer the things we know to those things we don't) constitutes a governing principle of human psychology, then it should also constitute a governing principle of our political philosophy.

The term *liberal* emerged from the philosophical movement of the 17th and 18th centuries that historians usually refer to as either, "The Enlightenment," or "the Age of Reason." This was the European movement that promoted the idea that individuals could best understand and improve their world by employing the rational tools of science rather than relying on the metaphysics of religious faith. Hence, the term liberal was coined to refer to the notion that individuals, by exercising their reason, could thereby liberate themselves from the institutional authority of both the church and the state. As one author stated in a book devoted to the subject, "in general, liberals have been rationalists," consequently, they, "have advocated separation of church and state," while the idea of liberty from institutional authority also, "made an especial appeal to the rising [merchant class], resentful of the restraints on its economic activities and of the privileges enjoyed by the nobility."[22] Ironically, liberal skepticism of institutional authority may have been as much a product of religious debate as it was of scientific inquiry. It is no coincidence political liberalism follows on the heels of what could be called "religious liberalism," in the form of the 16th century Protestant Reformation. Members of the Protestant movement, after all, earned their name by protesting the institutional authority of the Catholic Church. Therefore, the first "liberals" were the Protestants and the emerging Capitalists, who were rejecting the crown's institutional authority over the economy, what they called "mercantilism."[23] This, of course, illustrates one of the great ironies of modern politics: The first liberals, the Capitalists and the so-called Religious Right, now constitute what most Americans consider the hard core conservatives.

Now that we have examined the historical and philosophical underpinnings of the terms liberal and conservative, compare the above discussion on conservatism and liberalism with the following definitions found in a few contemporary texts on American government. First, the definitions of conservatism:

Greenberg & Page:
Those who favor private enterprise and oppose government regulations or spending; the term sometimes refers to those who favor military strength or enforcement of traditional social values.[24]

O'Connor & Sabato:
Those who advocate streamlined government, a business sector free from governmental regulation, a return to traditional social values, and a priority on military needs over social needs.[25]

Patterson:
Those who emphasize the marketplace as the means of distributing economic benefits but look to government to uphold traditional social values.[26]

Do these definitions square with the previous discussion? More importantly, do they make any sense in and of themselves? I think the answer to both questions is a resounding no. Here is why: Notice all three of the textbook definitions include at least two of the three following issues as central to the conservative faith:

1. Support of the free market;

2. Support for a strong military establishment; and,

3. Support for traditional family values.

Now, ask yourself, how does supporting either a free market or a strong defense establishment conserve America's traditions? First, as American political history makes clear, America was founded on the principle that there should never be a large standing army, or, in other words, a strong defense establishment.[27] So, how does suddenly defending one constitute a conservative ideal? One may think having a large military is a good thing, and it may be, but it is hardly conservative. Second, how can supporting a free market be conducive to conservatism? Capitalism, by definition, is itself the very antithesis of conservatism. One of the basic principles of a free market economy is that you must constantly innovate (that is, change) or die. As one political scientist so nicely put it: "There is nothing less conservative than capitalism, so itchy for the new. It expends, in order to expand; it razes, to rebuild; it destroys, to employ. Whatever merits it may have, conservatism is not among them."[28] And, if the free market is in fact conservative, like so many of its advocates preach, then why do they keep telling Americans they should be ready to change careers at least six times in the *new* global economy? Or, why is it they say, given the realities of the market, never again expect lifetime employment, secure pensions, or any of the other traditional benefits of working full-time in America? Again, one may think these things are beneficial or necessary, but they cannot be defended by conservatives.

In addition, it is a blatant contradiction to support both a free market and a strong defense establishment and since the first principle of capitalism is the belief in economic *individualism* that contradicts the notion of *collective* defense. That is, free market economics preaches that each individual is solely responsible for their own economic successes and failures, while the military is predicated on the idea we should all help each other maintain and protect our property. It seems what the proponents of this view of conservatism are really supporting, in the name of free markets and strong militaries, is the belief that the working person should only defend the rich man's wealth, not share it. By the way, how many middle class taxpayers owned an oil well in Iraq? Since few, if any, did, then why did the taxpayer pick up the expense of securing all that Iraqi oil?

Of course, the third tenet, supporting traditional family values, is indeed a conservative principle; nonetheless, there is no way one can support it while also supporting a free market. For example, why is it those who most often preach the virtues of the stay-at-home mom, are the very same people who refuse to pay a father enough so the mother can afford to? And, of course, they argue the reason they cannot afford to pay either parent enough is because (you guessed it) the dictates of the free market. In other words, how can any American practice family values, when very few of us can afford a family? Is it any wonder our political situation is the mess it is with thinking like this? Could it be one of the reasons (if not the reason) America's political situation is such a mess, is because so few of us think deeply about the meaning or ramifications of the political labels we adopt prior to accepting them?

Unfortunately, the story is no better when it comes to defining the liberal philosophy. To demonstrate the incoherence and nebulous quality of what constitutes contemporary liberalism, we will need to analyze closely the three textbook definitions below:

O'Connor & Sabato:

> *Those who advocate an active government, support social welfare programs and expanded individual rights and liberties, tolerate social change and diversity, and oppose "excessive" military spending and involvement.*[29]

Patterson:

Those who favor activist government as an instrument of economic security and equitable redistribution of resources but reject the notion that government should favor a particular set of social values.[30]

Lineberry, Edwards & Wattenberg:

*A **political ideology** whose advocates prefer an active government in dealing with human needs, support individual rights and liberties, and place a priority on social needs over military needs.*[31]

Given these typical textbook definitions, we can identify the three following characteristics as the core of the liberal doctrine:

1. The belief in an activist government to address social needs;

2. The belief in social toleration and diversity; and,

3. The favoring of social needs over military needs.

Taking the first issue, an activist government to address social needs, ask yourself the following two questions: First, how does endorsing an activist government square with the historical meaning of liberalism? It seems patently false to argue that by increasing institutional authority (activist government) one can somehow liberate oneself from that very same institutional authority. Second, how does this vague definition in any way differentiate liberals from conservatives? That is, they both want an activist government addressing social needs. For example, conservatives, as noted earlier, want an activist government addressing the social needs of economic freedom (government promoting a free market), of personal and community safety (a strong defense establishment), and social morality (a government that endorses a set of strong family values). Which, of course, shows that tenet number three (favoring social needs over military needs) is itself a fallacy, since physical safety is one of the primary social needs of any given political community. That is, social interaction of any kind depends first and foremost on people feeling physically safe so they may socially interact in a positive manner. And while we are at it, what constitutes a "social need" anyway? Economic freedom? Traditional family values? High speed Internet? In short, what do these feel-good slogans really mean in detail?

In addition, what does it mean to believe in social toleration and diversity? If it is true so-called liberals are more tolerant than so-called conservatives, then why do liberals seem so reluctant to tolerate those they disagree with? For example, a colleague, who prides himself on being "liberal," once defended a diversity plan with the comment, "this way we can deal with the jerks in the Religious Right." Now, that was mighty tolerant of him. Or, why is it liberals, who boast of being so tolerant, are always the first to boycott comedians they find intolerable, or impose speech codes on ideas they reject, and so forth. It seems, for the liberal, toleration is a one-way street. That is, liberals are no more or less tolerant than the conservative; they just seem to tolerate different things. To be sure, one may believe one's views are more tolerable, that is one's right, but one cannot do so while claiming to be more tolerant. It seems more accurate to say liberals are more intolerant of the intolerant than are conservatives, rather than arguing liberals are more tolerant.

Lastly, what does it mean to value social diversity? Diversity is defined in *Webster's II: The New Riverside University Dictionary* as: "The fact or quality of being diverse: Difference. A point or respect in which things differ." Now, if we take this concept literally, then does this mean we should welcome the Nazis to the community table, since they do indeed differ from (thank God) most Americans? Or, how about rapists? Murderers? Of course, supporters of diversity will respond, "that's not what we mean by diversity." But, such a response would be self-defeating, since it would prove that the person making such a comment values neither toleration nor diversity. Why? Well, because they would be demonstrating their intolerance for any definition of diversity that did not conform to their own, which, of course, eliminates any diversity of thought concerning the issue. This may also explain why so many so-called "diversity plans" have a monolithic quality which seems to do less to endorse social diversity than they do to impose social uniformity. Such is the sorry state of ideological debate in America today.

WHY ONLY TWO POLITICAL PARTIES?

Whether one believes there is or is not any difference between the two parties, ideological or otherwise, the question which still begs to be asked is: Why has America's political system evolved into a two-party system? The most common explanations for the American two-party system are: One, an electoral system based on **single-member districts**; two, popular acceptance of the two party system; three, the media; four, the role of money in campaign financing; and, five, the ability of Democrats and Republicans to be whatever the electorate want them to be. We will now examine each of these factors in more detail below.

1. An Electoral System Based on Single-member Districts Unlike most democratic nations, America's electoral system is based on a winner-take-all single-member district plan. That is, in America voting areas are divided into districts in which the candidate with the most votes thereby represents the entire district, hence, the term "single-member" districts. So, for example, imagine we have four candidates for an electoral district—a Democrat, a Republican, a Libertarian, and a Socialist. Furthermore, suppose during an election each candidate received one vote, except, say, the Republican candidate who got two votes; with our single-member electoral system, the Republican, even though she got only one more vote, would represent the entire district. In most other democratic governments the results would have been different because they use a proportional plan instead of our single-member system for electing representatives. Hence, in our example above, they would have voted for a party and divided the electoral district in proportion to the vote; therefore, the Republicans would have been rewarded

40% of the seats since they received 40% of the vote, while the Democrats, Libertarians, and Socialists would have received their proportional 20% of the seats. This proportional method of electing representatives allows for much more party competition because minor parties can garner some political power without actually beating the major parties. In other words, with our winner-take-all electoral system there is very little incentive for a minor party to go to the expense of running a high cost campaign, since only one party stands a chance of winning any election. This, of course, helps maintain the Democrats' and Republicans' monopoly on our representative system.

2. Popular Acceptance of the Two Party System The Democrats and Republicans also share the advantage human nature accords them—most people will go with what they know, voting for the parties they are familiar with regardless of their specific policies. That is, apparently most Americans simply accept the political status quo as the limit of democratic possibility since no matter how displeased they are with the two dominant parties it never dawns on them to vote for somebody else. To be sure, it does not help that the two dominant parties reinforce the people's conservative nature by espousing the Democratic and Republican **propaganda** that, "a vote for a third party is a wasted vote."

This propaganda has been so effective that it requires me to address its fallaciousness before going further. Most people buy this propaganda because they think the only purpose of voting is to pick the winner, even if this means that they personally lose because of the two parties' failure to represent these same voters. What one must remember is that a vote *for* a third party is also a vote *against* the two major parties. Or at least that part of each major party that refuse to represent working Americans while doing the bidding of their corporate masters. If Americans ever want to fix the political system they must stop voting for (enabling) the two parties that have caused the problems. Keep in mind that a vote for the two major parties is essentially a vote for the status quo; that is, it is a vote to keep things they way they are. So, if even ten percent of Americans voted for any other party but the two major parties that would be a certified ten percent vote against the status quo. Moreover, say ten percent of the electorate voted Libertarian in the next election. What these few courageous voters would have done is drastically empowered the more conservative members of the Republican Party, or its "far right" members (Ron Paul, for example) at the expense of the corporate Republicans, thereby having a greater impact than just voting Republican—hardly a wasted vote. Now, say ten percent of the voters in the next election voted for The **Green Party**. What these brave voters have done is greatly enhanced the influence of true progressives in the Democratic Party (like Dennis Kucinich, for instance) at the expense of those Democrats who are the Republican-light members of their party. So, again, these few voters carry more weight than those who simply vote for the "lesser of two evils," which is hardly a wasted vote.

One last thing: These brave Americans who refused to conform to what the major parties instruct them to do, will actually be starting the process of America's political revival. How? Well, the two major parties aren't concerned with those who vote for them, after all, these voters have shown that they will put up with whatever these two parties do, so there is no need to appease them; however, these other voters are asking for real and substantial change, so they must be accounted for before they become twenty percent of the voters, and then thirty percent, and then forty percent . . . So, the two parties would have to act fast to address these few voters' concerns so that their actions don't start spreading to more and more voters because pretty soon people will start realizing that the only wasted vote is one you don't believe in. So, it seems that a vote for a third party is most assuredly a wasted vote, if you happen to be a Democrat or Republican candidate; on the other hand, it most assuredly is not, if you happen to be an American citizen. By the way, which one are you?

3. The Media The mainstream media helps promote and maintain the dominance of the two major political parties in two fundamental ways. First, the media makes money by selling advertising, and there are no better customers than the Democrats and Republicans. The next time you find yourself getting nauseous over the constant flood of political advertising you encounter, stop and think about the tremendous amount of money these irritating political commercials must be generating for the media and you will immediately understand why the media is in no hurry to break from the status quo. That is, the reason the media helps reinforce the dominance of the two major political parties has less to do with some political conspiracy than it does with the realities of the advertising business. For instance, would you, as an advertising executive, want to upset two of your best customers and risk losing those important accounts by running an advertisement for the Libertarians? In short, as long as the two major parties keep buying large blocks of advertising from the media they will continue to dominate the menu of political choice.

The second way in which the media cements our two-party system is by its awareness that Americans love nothing more than to hear about the lives of the rich and famous. There is a slew of programs running throughout the day on network television devoted solely to reporting what the "beautiful" people are doing, and there are no larger celebrities than the leaders of the Democratic and Republican Parties. This is why Obama cannot go to Starbucks or go bowling without the paparazzi swamping him under. Think about it. When was the last time anyone filmed the leader of the Socialist Party having a cheeseburger? Of course, these two factors become self reinforcing: The more advertising the Democrats and Republicans buy the more famous they become, hence, the more the media will follow them around, which makes them more famous and more likely to win elections, so they will be able to afford more advertising, which makes them more famous which means the media will follow them. . . . I think you get the idea.

4. The Role of Money in Campaign Financing There is an old political slogan that goes something like this, "campaign money flows to the winners." Those who can afford to contribute huge sums of money to political campaigns want to make sure their money is well spent, so they contribute to the parties and candidates who have the best chance of winning, who, of course, are the Democrats and Republicans. As one CEO remarked when asked if he expected special favors not available to most Americans from the candidates he had heavily invested in, "darn right I do!" This is the reason president Obama, while saying he still supports "a robust system" of public financing, decided to opt out of the taxpayer-funded structure for the general election campaign of 2008. He was the first candidate to have done so since the public funding process was enacted after the Watergate scandal more than 30 years ago.[32]

Obama refused because he understood the dynamics of corporate campaign financing. The corporate elite, though aware they would be granted a privileged place in either party's administration, still knew their money would be better spent on Obama, since he was more likely to win the coming election than any Republican candidate. Obama refused to participate in the public funding of his campaign so he could ignore the limits that system puts on campaign contributions so he could rake in his corporate bounty. And, just like the media, this process of campaign money flowing to the winners becomes self-perpetuating; the more elections the Democrats and Republicans win the more money they attract, which, of course, makes them more likely to win, which attracts more campaign contributions which makes it more likely they will win.

5. The Democrats' and Republicans' Ability to Be Whatever the People Want Them to Be One political scientist suggested the reason the Republicans and Democrats dominate the American electoral system is because they tend to be much more "pragmatic" than their minor party competitors.[33] What he was referring to is the ability of professional politicians to be whatever any particular audience wants them to be. This is the oldest politician's trick known to democratic government—be and say whatever the present audience requires of you to secure their vote come election time. For example, former president Bush stated he was personally "pro-life" but his wife originally identified herself as "pro-choice"; this, of course, allowed them to placate all sides of the abortion debate while allowing them to stay above the fray. Clinton, like all professional politicians, was a master at this technique. When Clinton talked to a so-called conservative and rural audience he sounded like a character from the *Beverly Hillbillies*, invoking phrases like, "that dog won't hunt," or, "my mamma once told me," and so forth; whereas, when he was in front of a so-called professional audience he suddenly sounded like a Yale educated policy wonk, peppering his speeches with the appropriate techno speak required of such an animal.

President Obama has taken a page right out of the Clinton's playbook of political semantics when explaining his policy positions. For example, in the early months of his administration, Obama told his administration to stop referring to the "war in Iraq," and instead, he instructed them to refer to it as an "Overseas Operational Contingency," that way he could try to convince America that the Iraq war was over so he could increase troops in Afghanistan. Another example of this "pragmatic" approach to politics was the Obama's campaign team's promise of "change we can believe in." It seems the change they had in mind was replacing the Bush family and their cronies with a staff made up of Bill Clinton's old cronies—some change.

This "pragmatic" approach to politics allows politicians to support the idea of affirmative action while, at the same time, opposing quotas; or to agree we should end welfare as we know it, while also arguing we should not remove the safety net for the neediest Americans; or to support curtailing immigration in one speech, while reminding another audience we are a nation of immigrants; or to advocate in favor of free trade at one campaign stop, while promising to do something about the job situation at another. In short, politicians from the two major parties have no problem saying one thing to one audience and the very opposite to another; what most of us would call lying, but what politicians refer to as good political strategy.

In conclusion, we can list all of these factors, ranging from single-member districts to campaign financing to the media, as legitimate explanations for why the Democrats and Republicans dominate the American political system, but, in doing so, we must never forget the central cause of their dominance reduces down to our refusal to vote for any other party. It seems we have met the enemy and it is us.

SOME OTHER POLITICAL PARTIES

As mentioned earlier, the Democrats and Republicans are not the only electoral choices available to Americans. In this section we will briefly identify and articulate some other lesser-known political parties.

The Libertarians

The Libertarians are members of a twentieth-century political movement that believes the core principle of American political philosophy is, and ought to be, liberty—particularly economic liberty as articulated by free market orthodoxy. Hence, Libertarians believe the only legitimate purpose of government is to promote free market policies.[34] However, they are not anarchists (those who refuse to accept any form of government as legitimate) but believe in a minimal government whose primary function is to provide a police force necessary to protect each citizen's private property. Most Libertarians, for instance, want to legalize drugs and prostitution, as these activities constitute free and consensual economic transactions. If people want to buy drugs, or a blonde, it is nobody's business except those involved in the economic exchange. Also, Libertarians oppose public financing for such things as public education, roads, or food and drug testing. If you want an education pay for it yourself; if you want a transportation system then buy one; and, if any given product harms you in any way, then next time avoid it. In short, Libertarians preach liberty, even if the consequences of liberty may be difficult for those involved. Freedom, they argue, is not easy, but essential; any other governing system that does not promote freedom as its core principle is, by definition, unjust and illegitimate.

Following this principle, Libertarians believe that if government takes a citizen's money for any reason other than to protect that citizen's property, then that government is no different than a criminal organization; both, they argue, are organized crime syndicates which force Americans to hand over their hard earned money to finance the operations of an unjust regime. In other words, to the Libertarian, no matter who takes your money, be it government or an individual, it is still wrong if they take your money to support themselves and not to facilitate free market operations. Again, the primary function of government, according to the Libertarian, is to protect private property, not to make it easier for government to redistribute it. For this reason, Libertarians question the entire federal establishment. What does the federal government actually do, they ask, other than take your money in the form of taxes and then give it to someone else? How does this differ from being robbed? In addition, they wonder why Americans allow the government to determine who can be a carpenter. Or who can be a dentist or lawyer. If a person happens to be a lousy homebuilder, tooth mechanic, or legal advisor, word-of-mouth advertising will take care of this problem much more efficiently than any government bureaucrat. In short, the Libertarians believe that if you fear their political program, then it is not really their specific policies you find unacceptable, it is freedom you find terrifying.

The Socialists

Socialism is a philosophical tradition that dates at least as far back as the Greeks and has included such disparate thinkers as Plato, Jesus Christ, and Karl Marx.[35] Though each of these thinkers had radically different visions of socialism, they all, nonetheless, believed (as all socialists must) that people are inherently social and are, therefore, dependent on each other for human happiness.[36] Given this philosophical premise, socialists tend to support political policies that promote social and economic equality because such policies will promote what most scholars refer to as the "socialist intent."[37] The purpose (intent) of the socialist's political program must be to free people from the bonds of poverty and oppression so each person is able to realize their full human potential in an environment of equality. This intent, they argue, is the only purpose that justifies the exercise of governmental authority over any individual's life. Hence, Socialists are diametrically opposed to Libertarians when it comes to economic policy.

To realize this socialist intent, the American Socialist Party[38] promotes the following specific political policies: They believe there should be a strong progressive tax code (the more you earn, the larger percentage of income tax you should pay); they believe we should "socialize," that is, publicly own, all large industry, (health care, energy, auto industry, sports, education, etc.); socialists advocate for a major decrease in "defense" spending; and, they believe in promoting the withering away of any social caste systems which do more to divide Americans than they do to bring us together (boss and employee, for example). Much of the criticism of socialism is usually based less on the idea of treating people as equals, than with the practical problem of doing so. That is, most people dismiss socialism, not because they find its ideas of equality repugnant, but because they believe it is an unrealistic and impractical political philosophy. In response, Socialists point to the socialist success stories all around us. For example, the family (by the way, if people are not socialist, then why do parents take care of their kids, since it is not cost effective to do so?), or public colleges which allow individuals to pursue an education at the fraction of the cost of private colleges, or, for that matter, the police and fire departments, which maintain the public's safety. All of these are "socialized" agencies the Socialist believes help to make our lives better than they would be without them; all the Socialist wants to do is extend this idea to all other areas of corporate economic life. The Socialist Party, on the other hand, would not interfere with the workings of small family owned businesses; they are only concerned with liberating people from oppression, and are not concerned with eliminating private property altogether.

The Reform Party (Perot's Party)

The **Reform Party** is an attempt to find political middle ground between the two major political parties in the American political system. Or, better said, the Reform Party is an attempt to fill the political gap left by the Democrats' recent and Republicans' traditional refusal to represent the interests of middle class Americans in the political arena. In doing so, they tend to agree partly with the Republicans and partly with the traditional Democrats. Hence, the Reform Party is dedicated to a social program modeled after the Republicans and an economic program more like the traditional Democratic Party.[39] That is, they tend to preach the virtues of traditional family values (like Republicans), while at the same time, pursuing an economic program dedicated to job training, balancing the budget, and resisting "free trade" policies.

The Green Party

The Green Party (also known as the Pacific Party in Oregon) endorses a political platform that resembles the Socialist Party in that it calls for stronger governmental action in the areas of labor, consumer, and environmental protection. The Green Party, in the words of its best-known advocate, Ralph Nader, wants to stop the "corporate dismantling of our democracy."[40] To do so, they endorse such specific actions as limiting corporate campaign contributions and granting free media time to all candidates in hopes of lessening the corporate stranglehold on political information. In addition, they endorse balancing the budget by eliminating special tax breaks for the wealthy, ending corporate welfare, and reducing defense spending much below present levels. And lastly, the Green Party supports proportional democracy to help improve the representative character of the American political system.

The Constitution Party

The **Constitution Party** supports a political platform, which calls for a legal system based on "biblical foundations" as well as repealing the 16th Amendment that would abolish the Internal Revenue Service and all federal income taxes, coupled with a social philosophy more in-line with the Religious Right.[41]

Therefore, if any of you desire change, then you have encountered some other political parties that will deliver exactly that, change. Of course, none of you are limited to selecting only among these choices, as there are at least a dozen more political parties to choose from.[42] Under our Constitution, you are free to create and disband, join and leave, political parties whenever you see fit—that is your right as an American, and your duty as a citizen.

THE AMERICAN POLITICAL SPECTRUM: PUTTING IT ALL TOGETHER

Now that we have identified and examined some American political parties, it is time to place them accordingly on the ideological map of the American political system. This will allow us to graphically comprehend both their place in the American ideological universe and their political relationship to each other. Yet, before we begin doing so, let me make clear that this model of the American political spectrum is at best an ideal and simplified representation of American ideologies. The fact that our model will be a simplification of political ideologies in America, however, will in no way affect the academic merit of such a model. All academic models suffer from the same deficiency, be it a map of the world in a geography class, a model of the universe in a physics class, or a time line in a history class; none of these are, in the strict sense, an accurate rendition of the reality they attempt to conceptualize. Nonetheless, scientists from all disciplines attempt to construct simplified models as a way to better grasp the reality of whatever particular phenomenon they study. For example, the world is much larger in reality than any globe which represents it; the universe would never fit within any text which attempted to contain it; and no historian knows exactly when any given world event occurred. For instance, did the American Revolution begin at Lexington and Concord, or with the signing of the *Declaration of Independence*? Or, was it after the publication of Thomas Paine's *Common Sense*? Or, could it have occurred at different times for different people, as they came to recognize the ramifications of their own rebellion? In other words, the following political spectrum is simply an academic tool of political science designed to further our inquiry into the American political system and its attendant ideologies.

The Political Spectrum[43]

Notice we have drawn two parallel lines and have labeled one "economic beliefs," and the other "social beliefs" (Figure 1).

Economic Beliefs
L ←—————————→ R
Social Beliefs

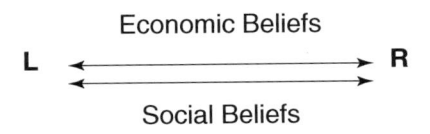

Figure 1

Next, to help better illustrate the American political spectrum, we have tilted or rotated the "social beliefs" line 90 degrees so it now stands vertical (Figure 2). Hence, what was once left-of-center has become up and what was once right-of-center has become down. For this reason, we have identified the line moving up from the intersection of both lines as "L" and the line moving down from center "R."

```
              Social Beliefs
                   ↑
              ╱ ─ ─ L
             ╱    Economic
            ╱     Beliefs
        L ←─┴─────────┼─────────→ R
             ╲       ╱
              ╲     ╱
               R   ╱
                  ↓
              Social Beliefs
```

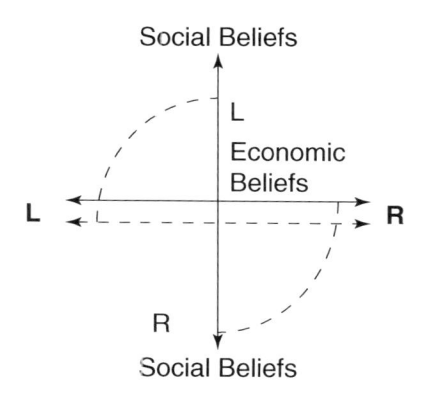

Figure 2

Please note that these lines represent a continuum. That is, the farther one moves down the social line the more one believes government should be pursuing a fundamentalist Christian political program. The opposite is true as well; the farther up one moves on the social line the more one demands a thorough separation of church and state. Also, note that when most Americans use the terms "conservative" or "liberal" to describe their social perspective, what they are really referring to is how far up (left-of-center) or down (right-of-center) on the social line one would place oneself. That is, the farther down one moves from center, the more conservative that person is, and the farther up one moves from center, the more liberal that person is. The horizontal line labeled "economic beliefs" reflects one's position regarding the distribution of property. The farther right one traces the line from the point they intersect, the more one will notice an emphasis on resisting any sharing of private property; whereas, as we move left from the intersection there is an increasing commitment to redistributing private property from those who have it, to those who do not. And, again this represents a continuum—the farther right or left, the more adamant one is on whether government should or should not redistribute property. We may now begin placing various political parties on our political spectrum.

Political Parties and the Political Spectrum

Now that we have discussed the political spectrum, Figure 3 shows where some of the political parties fit on our political spectrum.

Libertarians. The Libertarians are placed on the upper right hand corner of the graph because they believe government should concentrate on facilitating pure market economics, which requires a political program that imposes strong support for private property rights and intolerance for welfare programs that use the taxing powers of the state to redistribute property from those that have it to those that do not. They are also placed on the upper right hand corner because they believe that there should be a complete separation of church and state.

Socialists. The Socialists are placed in the far left hand corner directly across from the Libertarians because they believe—in direct opposition to the Libertarian Party—one of

```
                        SOCIAL BELIEFS
       SOCIALISTS              ↑ L      LIBERTARIANS

              PACIFIC GREEN
              PARTY
              (SECULAR
              POPULISTS)
   L ←─────────────────────────┼─────────────────────────→ R
   ECONOMIC BELIEFS                     ECONOMIC BELIEFS

              BUCHANAN'S
              PLATFORM
              (CHRISTIAN
              POPULISTS)
                                          THE CONSTITUTION
       CHRISTIAN COMMUNISM      ▼ R       PARTY
                        SOCIAL BELIEFS
```

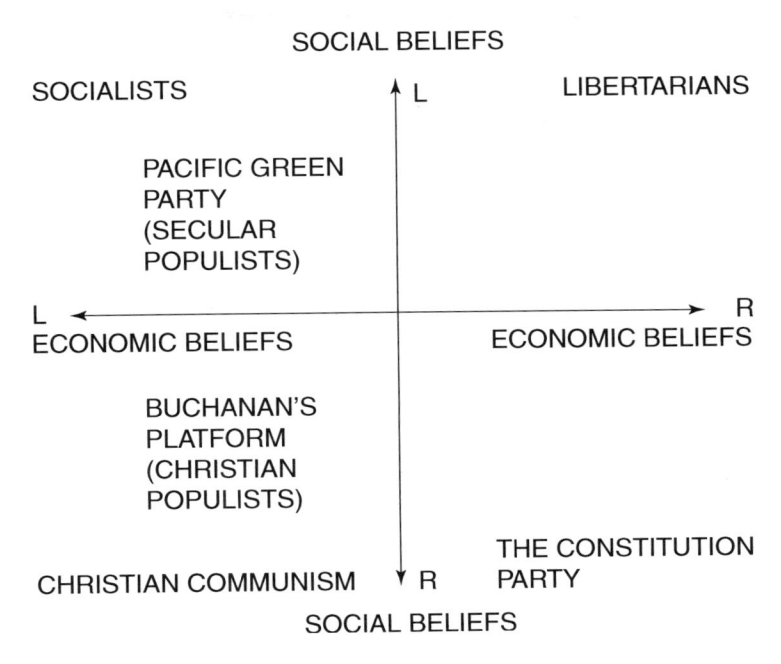

Figure 3

the primary purposes of government is to redistribute property from the wealthy to the less fortunate so as to bring about a condition of relative economic equality. However, when it comes to social policy they essentially agree with Libertarians; there should be a clear separation between church and state. Like Marx, many socialists believe institutional religion does more to convince the poor to accept their poverty than it does to eradicate it.

The Green Party. The Green Party is located mid-way between the center of the spectrum where both lines intersect and the Socialists in the upper left hand corner because they—like the Socialist Party—support a more labor friendly and ecologically sound economic system, while also being in favor of a secular social policy. The Green Party is not as extreme in their political views as that of the Socialists, but they are both clearly left-of-center (or liberal) political parties. For explanatory purposes, I have juxtaposed them with what I have labeled "Buchanan's platform" to help illustrate both the similarities as well as differences between Buchanan's conservative movement and the Green Party as personified by Ralph Nader. That is, notice while Buchanan and Nader may share very similar economic views (a distrust of corporations, advocacy on behalf of working Americans, for example) they, nonetheless, are diametrically opposed concerning social issues, with the Green Party being much more "liberal," whereas, Buchanan is much more "conservative."

The Constitution Party. The Constitution Party is placed in the far right bottom corner of our spectrum given their strong support for both a libertarian economic position coupled with their belief in "biblical principles" guiding our social policies.

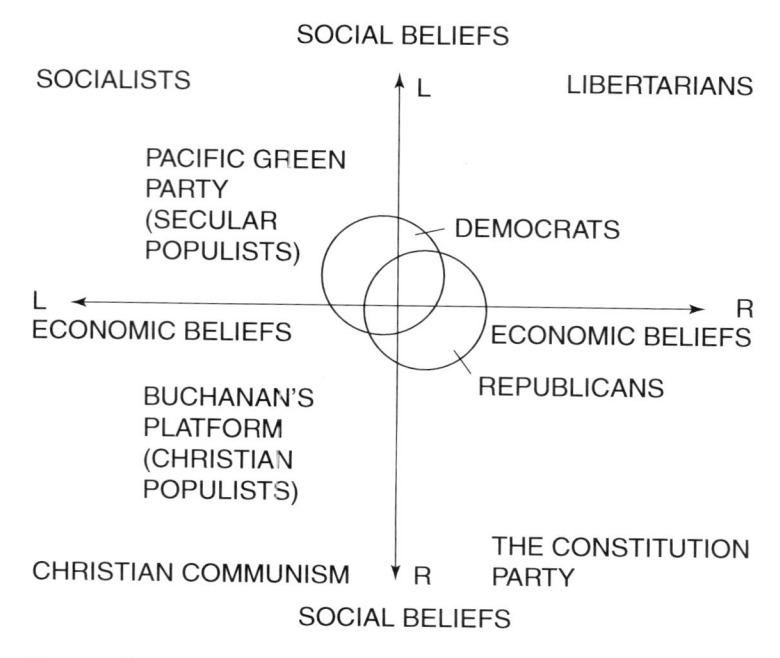

```
                    SOCIAL BELIEFS
  SOCIALISTS            ↑ L         LIBERTARIANS

     PACIFIC GREEN
     PARTY
     (SECULAR              DEMOCRATS
     POPULISTS)
L ←─────────────────────────────────────→ R
ECONOMIC BELIEFS          ECONOMIC BELIEFS
                              REPUBLICANS
     BUCHANAN'S
     PLATFORM
     (CHRISTIAN
     POPULISTS)

                                  THE CONSTITUTION
  CHRISTIAN COMMUNISM  ↓ R        PARTY
                    SOCIAL BELIEFS
```

Figure 4

For symmetry purposes, the philosophy of the early followers of Jesus Christ has been added to fill in the last remaining corner of our spectrum. They are placed in the far left-hand bottom corner to reflect not only their religious devotion but also the historical Jesus' economic vision of a spiritual community in which all share the material benefits of life equally;[44] hence, the term "Christian Communists."

Democratic and Republican Political Parties. In Figure 4, notice we have now placed both the Democrats and the Republicans on our spectrum. They are located in the middle of the spectrum because it represents the status quo, or the way things are presently. Much of each party overlaps with the other as their differences are not as pronounced when compared to other political parties. But take note of the fact that the Democratic Party extends farther left than the Republicans, while the Republican Party extends farther right than the Democrats. Polling data indicates Democrats share the same view as the majority of Americans when it comes to economic issues, whereas, the majority agree with Republicans when it comes to social issues. And, since both parties are very much aware democracy requires persuading a majority of voters, they tailor their message to do just that. Republicans constantly preach social issues because they know most Americans agree with them on these issues, while the Democrats focus on their economic policies for the same reason. This is why during the 2008 presidential election Republican John McCain campaigned on the theme of a "trusted leader," and his foreign policy expertise, whereas, Obama campaigned on the economy. This strategy was necessary because the Democtrats knew that Obama would not be seen

```
                    SOCIAL BELIEFS
   SOCIALISTS              ↑ L        LIBERTARIANS

        PACIFIC GREEN
        PARTY
        (SECULAR              ┌─ DEMOCRATS
        POPULISTS)          ⌒
    L ←─────────────────○─○────────────────→ R
      ECONOMIC BELIEFS    ⌒  ECONOMIC BELIEFS
        REFORM PARTY ┬      REPUBLICANS

        BUCHANAN'S
        PLATFORM
        (CHRISTIAN
        POPULISTS)
                                    THE CONSTITUTION
   CHRISTIAN COMMUNISM    ↓ R        PARTY
                    SOCIAL BELIEFS
```

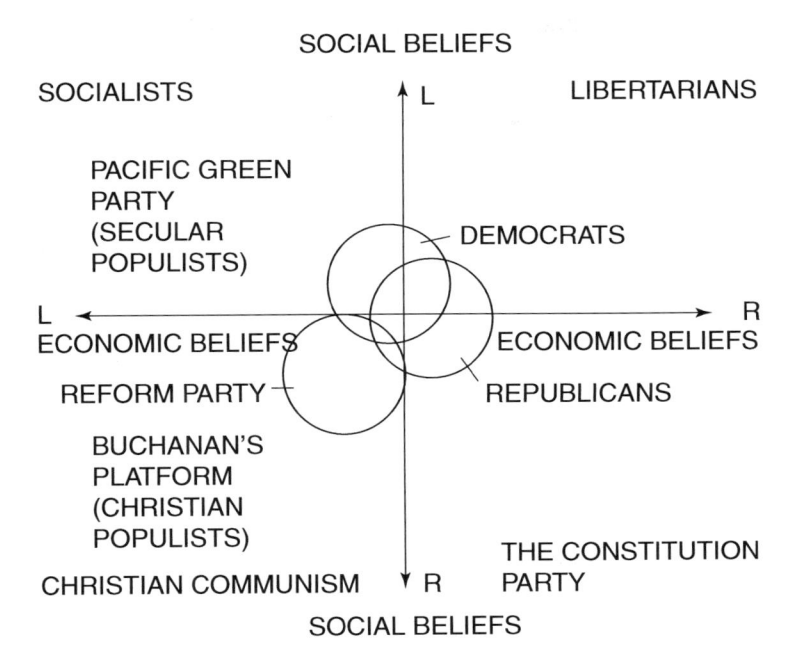

Figure 5

as experienced as his rival; however, Obama's team knew they would win the election as long as they focused their message on the ever-faltering economy.

The Reform Party. In Figure 5 we have now placed the Reform Party on our political spectrum. The Reform Party was created by two leading campaign strategists, one a Democrat, the other a Republican, after each realized if any political party ever promoted the same social *and* economic beliefs as the majority it would come to dominate the American political process for years to come; so, they joined together with Ross Perot for that purpose. This is why the Reform Party tends to favor a slightly right-of-center ("conservative") social policy, while, also, endorsing a slightly left-of-center ("liberal") economic platform.

Given this political strategy, it seems surprising that the Reform Party has not won more elections; however, both major parties regulated the Reform Party to the sidelines of "mainstream" politics by simply co-opting the Reform Party's platform. As mentioned earlier, career politicians are experts at saying whatever they think a particular audience wants to hear. Clinton's campaign team, for example, positioned Clinton politically for both the 1992 and 1996 presidential races so that he would publicly endorse policies that just so happen to coincide with what the Reform Party advocates. In short, since the majority of voters want a government which is slightly left-of-center in the economic sphere, while espousing slightly right-of-center social values, that is exactly what Clinton's people had him propose in his speeches.[45] For example, one political columnist described Clinton's 1997 inaugural address with these words: "The speech was, after all, a clear triumph of [this political] strategy . . . every liberal spending proposal—tax credits for tuition, expanding Head Start—was matched by a conservative values issue—uniforms, charter schools."[46]

It is not a coincidence that Obama has done the exact same thing. He has promised middle-tax relief while publicly refusing to support gay marriage. While promising to put Americans back to work during his inaugural address, he also had pro-life pastor Rick Warren give the invocation. So, like Clinton before him, Obama positioned himself politically to appeal to the voting majority by being right-of-center on social issues but more liberal regarding economic issues. As to how faithful any of these presidents were/are to their professed ideals is for each citizen to decide. Suffice it to say, empirical evidence on these men demonstrates that they were less than true to their political rhetoric.

FINAL THOUGHTS

We have now completed our examination of political parties, political ideologies and the political spectrum in the hope that each of us would gain a better understanding of the American political system. But, there is no reason for any American to accept these parties, ideologies or the spectrum as the limits of our democratic reality. The political possibilities for our American future can be as limitless as our dreams, as grand as our intellects, and as pure as our hearts; or, it will be as limited as our ignorance and as mean-spirited as our arrogance. The choice has been, and always will be, ours. This is why, I believe, democracy has never been a simple governmental procedure, or the mere counting of votes, but rather it has always been about justice—the justice of government treating all members of a community with the equal concern and respect[47] each of us morally deserves as members of our civic community. Yet this democratic justice will never be initiated by the halls of government. It will only come when Americans start thinking with their minds and feeling with their hearts as citizens engaged in a common endeavor, rather than as individuals involved in their own private pursuits. This ideal was nicely summarized by some early Americans who once wrote:

> We the people of the United States, in order to form a more perfect union, establish justice, insure domestic tranquility, provide for the common defense, promote the general welfare, and secure the blessings of liberty to ourselves and our posterity, do ordain and establish this Constitution for the United States of America.[48]

NOTES

1. The following discussion on the history of American political parties paraphrases an essay by Thomas Woodhouse, whose historical expertise was greatly appreciated. For a deeper historical account of the development of America's two dominant political parties the interested reader should consult, Paul Allen Beck and Frank J. Soraut, *Party Politics in America*, 7th ed. (Glenview, Il: Scott, Foresman, 1992).
2. David Broder, "Partisanship is thriving; Congress is flailing," *The Oregonian* (January 29, 2006).
3. Michael Luo, Memo Gives Canada's Account of Obama Campaign's Meeting on NAFTA, The *New York Times*, March 4, 2008.

4. Charlie Savage, "Obama Officials Quietly Endorse Some Bush Anti-Terror Policies," *The Oregonian*, February 22, 2009.
5. Molly Ivins, "Get up and fight, you fools!, *The Oregonian* (January 21, 2006), p. B4.
6. A CNN/USATODAY/Gallup Poll found that 68% of respondents believe that the Democrats have no clear plan for the country, while 67% of respondents thought the same about the Republican Party, CNN.com, "Poll: Most think GOP, Democrats lack vision," (February 15, 2006).
7. A variety of authors share this belief: William Greider (*Who Will Tell the People*), Kevin Phillips (*Boiling Point*), Martin Gross (*A Call for Revolution*), Donald Barlett and James Steele (*America: What Went Wrong?*), and Michael Parenti (*Democracy for the Few*).
8. For a thorough examination of the similarities see, Alexander Cockburn and Jeffrey St. Clair, *Dime's Worth of Difference: Beyond the Lesser of Two Evils* (California: CounterPunch and AK Press, 2004).
9. *The Boston Globe* (February 23, 2004).
10. Robert Landaur, "Labor movement draws new hope from new management—its own," *The Oregonian* (April 5, 1996), p. C8.
11. Greider, *Who Will Tell the People: The Betrayal of American Democracy* (New York: Simon and Schuster, 1992), p. 245.
12. Phillips, *Boiling Point*, p. 79.
13. Betsy Hammond, "U.S. tax system tilts to rich, journalist says," *The Oregonian* (February 7, 2006), p. B5.
14. Lou Dobbs, "Lonely in the Middle," *U.S. News & World Report* (May 2, 2005), U.S.News.com.
15. See Agence France Presse, "*Millionaires Fill U.S. Congress Halls*" (June 30, 2004) at www.commondreams.org/headlines04/0630-05.htm, or Sean Loughlin and Robert Yoon, "*Millionaires populate U.S. Senate*," CNN.com/Inside Politics (June 13, 2003).
16. Michael Moore made this comment on the television show "Hardball with Chris Mathews," June 22, 1999.
17. Quoted at the bottom of page, *The Oregonian* (January 23, 1997) p. C8.
18. See for example, Ed Henry, "Obama Makes Unannounced Stop in Baghdad," CNN.POLITICS.com, April 7, 2009.
19. The so-called father of conservatism, Edmund Burke, wrote in his *Reflections on the Revolution in France*, that "[w]e . . . derive all we possess *as an inheritance from our forefathers*. . . . I hope, nay I am persuaded, that all those which possibly may be made hereafter, will be carefully formed upon analogical precedent, authority, and example. . . . Thus, by preserving the method of nature in the conduct of the state, in what we improve we are never wholly new; in what we retain we are never wholly obsolete. By adhering in this manner and on those principles to our forefathers, we are guided not by the superstition of antiquarians, but by the spirit of philosophic analogy. [italics original]" In short, conservatism seeks to preserve the traditions and mores of the community and places little importance on metaphysical theories of the person that separates individuals from these customs and habits of the community.
20. Terence Ball and Richard Dagger, *Political Ideologies and the Democratic Ideal* (New York: HarperCollins, 1991), p. 91.
21. Michael Oakeshott, "On Being Conservative," *Dogma and Dreams*, ed. Nancy S. Love (New Jersey: Chatham House, 1991), p. 111.
22. J. Salwyn Schapiro, *Liberalism: Its Meaning and History* (Princeton: D. Van Norstrand Company, 1957), pp. 12 and 26.
23. Adam Smith, *An Inquiry Into the Nature and Causes of the Wealth of Nations* (Chicago, Encyclopaedia Britannica, Inc., 1952).
24. Edward S. Greenberg and Benjamin I. Page, *The Struggle for Democracy* (New York: HarperCollins, 1995), p. G2.
25. Karen O'Connor and Larry J. Sabato, *American Government: Roots and Reform* (New York: Macmillan Publishing Company, 1993), glossary, p. 692.
26. Thomas E. Patterson, *The American Democracy*, 3rd ed. (New York: McGraw-Hill, 1996), p. 166.

27. See chapter 7 on foreign policy.
28. Garry Wills, *Reagan's America* (New York: Viking Penguin, 1988), p. 453.
29. O'Connor & Sabato, *American Government*, p. 692.
30. Patterson, *The American Democracy*, 3rd ed., p. 166.
31. Robert L. Lineberry, George C. Edwards III and Martin P. Wattenberg, *Government In America: People, Politics, and Policy*, 6th ed. (New York: HarperCollins, 1994), p. G10.
32. See Jonathan D. Salant, "Obama Won't Accept Public Money in Election Campaign," *Bloomberg*, (June 19, 2008); Shailagh Murray and Perry Bacon Jr., "Obama to Reject Public Funds for Election," *Washington Post*, (June 20, 2008); or 'Obama Recasts the Fund-Raising Landscape." *New York Times*. (October 19, 2008)].
33. Patterson, *The American Democracy*, 2nd ed. (1994), p. 309.
34. David Miller, ed., *The Blackwell Encyclopaedia of Political Thought* (Oxford: Blackwell Publishers, 1991).
35. Nancy Love, ed., *Dogmas and Dreams: Political Ideologies in the Modern World* (Chatham, N.J.: Chatham House Publishers, 1991), p. 179.
36. For those readers who seek further discussion, please refer to *The Blackwell Encyclopaedia of Political Thought*, pp. 485–489.
37. Leon P. Baradat, *Political Ideologies: Their Origins and Impact*, 4th ed. (New Jersey: Simon & Schuster, 1991), pp. 171–2.
38. The distinction between the American socialist and general socialism can be explained simply by noting that the American conception of socialism would allow small businesses and individuals to own property and is sometimes referred to as "market" socialism (see the American socialist party platform). Generally, socialism seeks to command the economy through the control of the means of production. That is, the means of production are owned by the state.
39. Traditional Democrats are sometimes referred to as "New Deal" Democrats. "New Deal" refers to FDR's economic and social policies, sometimes referred to as his "alphabet soup," which included, for example, the WPA (Works Progress Administration) by which the federal government intervened in the Great Depression of the 1930s in an attempt to stabilize the economy by giving unemployed men jobs working on public improvement projects such as building roads and parks. The New Deal also created the Social Security program. New Deal Democrats, then, are those Democrats who defend governmental intervention in the economy and wish to sustain social-welfare programs.
40. Staff Reports, "Corporations and Clinton Consume Nader's Energy," *The Oregonian* (October 19, 1996), p. A12.
41. Molly Ivins, "Choices Aren't Limited to D's and R's," *The Oregonian* (September 9, 1996), p. B7.
52. For a fairly comprehensive list of American political parties visit the web site http://www.politics1.com/parties.htm
43. Further information regarding the American Political Spectrum can be found by the interested reader in Kenneth M. Dolbeare and Linda J. Medcalf, *American Ideologies Today: Shaping the New Politics of the 1990s*, 2nd ed. (New York: McGraw-Hill, Inc., 1993), pp. 205–207.
44. For a superb analysis regarding the economic and religious views of Jesus see, John Dominic Crossan, *The Historical Jesus: The Life a Mediterranean Jewish Peasant* (New York: HarperCollins Publishers, 1991).
45. For example see Dick Morris, *Behind the Oval Office: Winning the Presidency in the 90s* (New York: Random House, 1997).
46. David Sarasohn, "The State of Dick Morris," *The Oregonian* (February 6, 1997), p. C8. 38
47. An excellent discussion on the concept of treating members of society with equal concern and respect can be found in Ronald Dworkin's *Taking Rights Seriously* (Cambridge, MA: Harvard University Press, 1978) and *A Matter of Principle*. (Cambridge, MA: Harvard University Press, 1985).
48. The preamble to the Constitution of the United States.

CHAPTER 5
The Media:
Through the Looking Glass

"A popular government without popular information or the means of acquiring it, is but a prologue to a farce, or a tragedy, or perhaps both."
—James Madison

"Nothing can now be believed which is seen in a newspaper. Truth itself becomes suspicious by being put into that polluted vehicle."
—Thomas Jefferson

"The function of the press is very high. It is almost holy. To misstate . . . the news is a breach of trust."
—Louis D. Brandeis

"If I only had a brain."
—The Scarecrow

INTRODUCTION

This chapter will analyze how the media in both its broadcast forms (television, radio, and Internet) and, to some lesser extent, in its print forms (newspapers and magazines) affect the health of our democratic institutions. We will begin with a brief discussion on the important role the media plays in influencing American political debate. After that, the chapter will focus primarily on the broadcast media, since most Americans name the broadcast media as their main source of news.[1] In doing so, we will scrutinize how the broadcast media makes the news fit its own limitations by covering simple events that appear impressive on TV. In the second part of the chapter we will examine whether the media in general is either liberally or conservatively biased. It will then be argued that it may, in fact, be both. The chapter will conclude with some thoughts on how the Internet has affected the media and American political culture.

But before we proceed any further with our discussion, let us be clear from the outset about one central truth: The mainstream, commercial media, no longer sees its role as constitutionally empowered watchdogs of the political system, even though the

1st Amendment of the Constitution specifically protects the media for that purpose. Instead, the media sees itself as a business operation. In other words, the media no longer sees its role as "informing the public"; it only sees itself as a vehicle to make a profit. The institutions collectively called the "media" are private enterprise corporations out to make money for their shareholders; it is for this purpose they exist and for no other. The reason political scientists study the media is not because these institutions are public (they are not) but because the media so influences those institutions that are. Explaining how the media does so will be the primary purpose of this chapter. To this end, we will analyze how the media fails to perform at a level necessary for a healthy democracy by articulating five basic and closely connected deficiencies: The media's reinvented role as lapdog rather than watchdog of the political system; the media's lack of social scientific sophistication; its obsessive overage of sensational events; its tendency to personalize its coverage; and its inherent class bias.

BROADCAST MEDIA: THE BLIND LEADING . . .
1. Silence of the Lambs: American Journalism Hears No Evil, Sees No Evil, Reports No Evil.[2]

The American media was given constitutional protection in the 1st Amendment of the Constitution so that it would be free from governmental censorship. The constitutional framers did so because they expected the media to be an aggressive, critical watchdog of the political system, instead the modern media has turned this proposition on its head. They now see themselves as lapdogs for political authority whose job it is to defend the political system rather than critique it. In short, the media has rejected its constitutional duty and now acts as a public relations arm of the political system. The best example of this apologetic stance concerns arguably the three most important stories in recent memory—the presidential election of 2000, the terrorist attacks of 9/11, and the Bush administration's propaganda campaign regarding WMD in the run-up to the 2003 invasion of Iraq. In each of these cases the American media has refused to investigate what could be some of the greatest political crimes in American history. If this seems like just so much hyperbole, then this alone proves my point. That is, if the media accepted their constitutional duty the facts regarding these three events would be so well known that there would be no surprise by the above allegation. Let us look at these three events and see how well the American media kept its collective head buried in the sand.

In his book, *The Best Democracy Money Can Buy*,[3] Greg Palast, thoroughly investigated the activities of the election officials in the state of Florida during the 2000 election. Keep in mind that without the state of Florida's electoral votes George Bush Jr. would not have been elected president. So, what we are talking about is the first principle of democratic government—uncorrupted elections. Moreover, in this case, we are talking about the integrity of the process by in which the American people elect the single most powerful person in the American political system, namely the president. So, there can be no argument that this is a story that demands serious investigative journalism, period. But what did we get instead? What we got was a simplified, superficial "analysis" by the American media motivated by the need to *get past* the story rather than by the need to *get out* the story. Palast's reports in his book the following:

> In the days following the presidential election, there were so many stories of African Americans erased from the voter rolls you might think they were targeted by some kind of racial computer program. They were. I have a copy of it: two silvery CD-ROM disks right out of the office computers of [then] Florida Secretary of State Katherine Harris . . . Here's how it worked: Mostly the disks contain data on Florida citizens—57,700 of them. In the months leading up to the November 2000 balloting, Florida Secretary of State Harris, in coordination with Governor Jeb Bush, ordered local elections supervisors to purge these 57,700 from the voter registries. In Harris' computers, they are named as felons who have no right to vote in Florida.
>
> Thomas Cooper is on the list: criminal scum, bad guy, felon, *attempted* voter [emphasis original]. The Harris list says Cooper was convicted of a felony on January 30, 2007. 2007? You may suspect something's wrong with this list. You'd be right. At least 90.2 percent of those on this "scrub" list, targeted to lose their civil rights, are innocent. Notably, over half—about 54 percent are Black and Hispanic voters. Overwhelmingly, it is a list of Democrats. . . . Now, after two years of peeling the Florida election onion, we put the number of voters wrongly barred from voting at over 90,000, mostly Black and Hispanics, and by a wide majority, Democrats. . . . You've seen barely a hair of any of this in the U.S. media. Why? How did 100,000 U.S. journalists sent to cover the election fail to get the vote theft story (and preferably *before* the election) [emphasis original] . . . I freely offered CBS this information: The office of the Governor of Florida, Jeb Bush, brother of the Republican presidential candidate, had illegally ordered the removal of the names of . . . felons who had served time but obtained clemency, with the right to vote under Florida law. As a result, *another 40,000 legal voters* (in addition to the 57,000 on the purge list), almost all of them Democrats, could not vote [emphasis original] . . . The next day I received a call from the producer, who said, "I'm sorry your story didn't hold up." And how do you think the multi-million-dollar CBS network determined this? Answer: "We called Jeb Bush's Office" . . . I wasn't surprised by this type of "investigation." It is, in fact, standard operating procedure for the little lambs of American journalism. One good, slick explanation from a politician or corporate chieftain and it's *case closed,* investigation over [emphasis original].[4]

What Mr. Palast has described is one of the American media's prime tactics to avoid doing real reporting, what I call **"running to authority" reporting**. That is, if the **Pentagon** is charged with using illegal cluster bombs in Afghanistan or Iraq, the American media goes to the Pentagon to check the veracity of said charge. If Dick Cheney is under investigation for his activity as CEO of Halliburton, they go ask Dick if the story has any truth to it. If Clinton has been accused of rape, they check with the Clinton people to see if there is anything to the allegation. If there is evidence that George Bush Jr. was convicted of cocaine possession in his early thirties, the media checks with the Bush entourage to get the "real" story. When there were some serious questions as to President Obama's relationship with the corruption of the Ohio political machine, the media "investigated" the story by seeing if Obama's team thought there was anything to the story. By the way, each of these examples are legitimate charges that have never been investigated, but instead have been dismissed by the person or institution so accused.

Another time-honored tactic the American media employs to avoid real reporting is what is referred to as the "old news" spin-doctor tactic. That is, the person or institution will deny the story until the facts force them to acknowledge the information while immediately dismissing the information as "old news." This, by the way, is the tactic that was employed to ignore what Mr. Palast has uncovered regarding the presidential election of 2000. Mainstream media has taken the collective position that it is time to move on from the 2000 presidential election so it can cover more newsworthy events like Michelle Obamas' well-dressed body and Barack Obama's bowling prowess. After all, a journalist must have his or her priorities straight, right? Why waste time covering a story of electoral criminal activity in a state which determined who would be the next president of the United States? Besides, we all know that Florida declared George Bush the winner by a total 537 votes, case closed.

The Foundation for Critical Thinking, explains the same phenomenon in these words:

> National news media are always sensitive to the power of government. For one, national governments typically license and regulate news media by law. For another, much national news is "given" to news media through high governmental officials and agencies. For these reasons, news media personnel hesitate to criticize the national government in certain fundamental ways. For example, if the national government names some other group or nation as an enemy, the national news media generally present the "enemy" as unfavorably as they can. If the government attacks another nation militarily, the national media line up like cheerleaders at a sporting event. The news media are typically apologists for the policies and acts of the national government.[5]

This leads me to another story that can rightfully be said to be of as great significance to our constitutional system as the above case concerning the presidential election—the attacks of 9/11. Because the media refuses to look into this crime with the effort they reserve for, say, the next blonde that gets abducted in Aruba, it has spawned a cottage industry on the Internet regarding what really happened on that day, and what did the government know about these attacks before they commenced. Moreover, the media's refusal to investigate 9/11 with the seriousness it deserves has led not to support of such government authorized inquiries into these events (see the 9/11 Commission), but to more and more average Americans becoming suspicious of the government's role in this whole affair.

For example, many adults in the United States believe the federal government has not been completely forthcoming on the issue of the 9/11 terrorist attacks, according to a poll by the *New York Times* and CBS News conducted in October 2006. The poll shows that 53% of respondents thought the Bush administration was hiding something, and 28% believe it was lying.

Only 16 percent of respondents say the government headed by U.S. president George W. Bush was telling the truth on what it knew prior to the terrorist attacks, down five points since May 2002.[6]

Given the enormity of the matter of 9/11, I submit that if the Constitution's fundamental guardians, the American people and their representatives in Congress, do not begin to demand a thorough and real investigation into these horrific events, then "Operation Enduring Freedom" becomes more than just an operational name, it becomes a slap in the face to those of us who take seriously representative government and the sacrifices so many Americans have made in freedom's name.[7]

One last example of the media's refusal to cover stories that go the heart of America's political integrity—the propaganda campaign regarding the allegations made by the Bush administration about Iraq's "stockpiles" of WMD. These claims have been thoroughly refuted by experts who knew before the invasion of 2003 that Iraq had no weapons of mass destruction, as nearly 5,000 American dead later has proved beyond a shadow of a doubt. Moreover, these experts knew that almost every claim the Bush administration made was not only non-sense and lies, but that the Bush administration knew it as well. With the enormous consequences the Iraq war has had on America's troops and Iraqi innocent, America's national security, and America's economy, one cannot overstate the level of harm done by the media's refusal to report what these experts were saying. There can be no question that the media, by ignoring all these experts who pleaded with the media to stop repeating what the Bush administration was putting out there, and report on their expert, contrary opinions, helped lead the country into the dire situation it now finds itself in.

Who were these experts? Let me list just some of them and their credentials, which clearly show that these experts were the individuals who would know fact from fiction in Iraq. Before doing so, however, let me remind you that this failure on the part of America's media is yet again the result of the media's "running to authority" reporting—with a twist. That is, the media runs to those who are *in* authority—members of the administration in this case—but ran away from those who are *an* authority on matters pertaining to Iraq's weapon's capability.[8] Now, here are the experts who were ignored by the mainstream press:

- David Albright, Physicist and Former Weapons Inspector with International Atomic Energy Agency Action Team. Mr. Albright has over 20 years of experience monitoring secret nuclear weapons programs.

- Robert Baer, Former **CIA** operative who served covertly in Saddam's Iraq for over 10 years, and nearly getting killed by Saddam numerous times in the process. Mr. Baer also served covertly in Lebanon and was awarded by the CIA "The Career Intelligence Medal."

- Milt Bearden, former head of the CIA's Soviet/ East European Division, and CIA Station Chief in Pakistan. Mr. Bearden served in the CIA for over 30 years.

- John Dean, former White House Counsel to President Richard Nixon.
- Patrick Eddington, Former CIA analyst during the Gulf War. Mr. Eddington was so disgusted with what transpired he commented: "The weapon inspections in Iraq were the most intrusive in history, and they worked, so, in the end, we went to war for nothing."
- Chris Freeman, former Assistant Secretary of Defense, who served as Ambassador to Saudi Arabia during the Gulf War. Mr. Freeman served in the Foreign Service for over 30 years.
- Graham Fuller, former Vice-Chairman of the National Intelligence Council at the CIA. Mr. Fuller has been a professional intelligence officer for 25 years.
- Mel Goodman, Mr. Goodman served for over 20 years as a CIA senior intelligence analyst.
- John Brady Kiesling, served for over 20 years in the US Foreign Service, as well as serving as Political Counselor to the United States Embassy in Greece.
- Karen Kwintkowski, Former United States Air Force Lt. Colonel. Ms. Kwintkowski also served in the Office of the Under Secretary of Defense for Policy, Near East/South Asia and Special Plans.
- Patrick Lang, retired Colonel, US Army, Military Intelligence and Special Forces. Former Chief of Middle East Intelligence at the Defense Intelligence Agency.
- Dr. David C. MacMichael served for 13 years as a CIA analyst.
- Ray McGovern served for 27 years in the CIA. Mr. McGovern served as Chairmen of the National Intelligence Estimate. Mr. McGovern was responsible for preparing the President's Daily Brief (PDB) on intelligence matters.
- Scott Ritter served a Chief Weapons Inspector in Iraq from 1991-1998. Mr. Ritter is a former Captain in the United States Marines.
- Joseph Wilson served for 23 years in America's Foreign Service. Some of his appointments include being the last Ambassador to Iraq before the 2003 invasion. He also worked for then Vice President, Dick Cheney, and was sent to find out if there was any truth to the claim that Saddam tried to buy enriched uranium from Niger. He found that there was no proof of any such attempt, and, in fact, the documents supposing to prove this, were found to be a forgeries—to this day, the media has made no attempts to find out who forged these documents. Nonetheless, even after Mr. Wilson had told the Bush administration that there was no truth to these reports, President Bush still asserted it as proof of Saddam's WMD stockpiles in his 2003 "State of the Union Address."
- Mary Ann Wright, former Colonel in the US Army for over 30 years, she served as Deputy Chief of Mission in the US Embassy in Afghanistan among other places.

- Peter Zimmerman served as former Chief Scientist for the Senate's Foreign Relations Committee, and served as Chief Scientist for the Arms Control Agency.

Again, these are some of the experts who were studiously ignored by the mainstream press because their expertise was not consistent with what the media wanted to hear.[9]

It is time to quote the Constitution's chief author, James Madison, on the difficulty of, if not out-right contradiction in, trying to defend freedom with the instrument of war:

> Of all the enemies of public liberty war is, perhaps, the most to be dreaded, because it comprises and develops the germ of every other. War is the parent of armies; from these proceed debts and taxes; and armies, and debts, and taxes are the known instruments for bringing the many under the domination of the few. In war, too, the discretionary power of the [Presidency] is extended; its influence in dealing out offices, honors, and emoluments is multiplied; and all the means of seducing the minds, are added to those of subduing the force, of the people . . . [There is also an] inequality of fortunes, and opportunities of fraud, growing out of a state of war, and . . . degeneracy of manners and of morals . . . No nation could preserve its freedom in the midst of continual warfare . . . [10]

However, there does seem to be an apparent contradiction in asserting that the media refuses to investigate serious political misdeeds while quoting print media sources; that is until one realizes that this, too, is a time-honored tactic of the American media to avoid digging too deeply into political corruption and crime. It is referred to in political science as "bump and run" reporting. "Bump and run" reporting consists in lightly reporting incriminating facts so the story emerges slowly, piece by piece, until the whole thing is "old news." Let me prove this point simply by listing a few of the stories which were reported by mainstream media either much after the fact or buried in the middle of the dreaded news section of the newspaper. Before doing so, however, I would be remiss if I did not account for the truth that this tactic needs an accomplice to be effective—an apathetic citizenry. Now to some headlines and words, all from what would clearly be categorized as "mainstream media."

- Headline: "Bad Wiring Puts Troops in Danger of Electrocution: Iraq Facilities—Overworked Inspectors Admit That Service Members Face 'Russian Roulette.'" The story reads, "Military inspectors are racing to examine 90,000 US–run facilities in Iraq with the goal of repairing electrical problems before more troops are electrocuted . . . [it ends with these troubling words] "Sen. Byron Dorgan, D-N.D., questioned why KBR [former vice-president, Dick Cheney's company] has been allowed to continue to perform electrical work in Iraq. He said the military should take a more careful look at the electrical work in Afghanistan, too, where KBR also has a large contract." *The Associated Press*, Front Page, *The Oregonian*, March 27, 2009.

- Headline: "Iraq's Agent Orange: An Oregon National Guard Veteran and other Soldier's were Exposed to Hexavalent Chromium While Protecting Contractors After Saddam's Fall." Within the story it reads: "Officials say they didn't learn of the problem themselves until November, when the Army, spurred by lawsuits in Indiana and Texas and a subsequent Senate investigation, alerted the Oregon Guard. The suits claim that KBR ignored a United Nations report and its own employees warnings about the danger." Front Page, *The Oregonian*, March 8, 2009.

- Headline: US Admits 'Precision Strikes' Killed More Civilians than Foes." The story begins: " An operation the US Military first called a 'precision strike' instead killed 13 Afghan civilians . . . " *The Associated Press*, Page A9, *The Oregonian*, February 22, 2009.

- Headline: "Bush and Blair Were Set for War Weeks Before, Memo Shows: Regardless of a second U.N. resolution or proof of weaponry, the president planned to invade." After the first paragraph the story states: "During a private two-hour meeting in the Oval Office on Jan. 31, 2003, Bush made it clear to British Prime Minister Tony Blair that he was determined to invade Iraq without the second resolution, or even if international arms inspectors failed to find unconventional weapons, said a confidential memo about the meeting written by Blair's top foreign policy advisor and reviewed by *The New York Times* . . . The memo also shows that the president and the prime minister acknowledged that no unconventional weapons had been found inside Iraq. Faced with the possibility of not finding any before the planned invasion, Bush talked about several ways to provoke a confrontation, including a proposal to paint a U.S. surveillance plane in the colors of the United Nations in hopes of drawing fire, and assassinating Saddam." *New York Times News Service*; Front Page, *The Oregonian*, March 27, 2006.

- Headline: "Terrorism Suspect Visited White House: Sami Al-Arian, Accused of Being a Terrorist Leader, Attended a Meeting with the President's senior Advisor" The first two sentences of the article contain these lightly reported incriminating facts: " . . . a terrorist leader attended a 2001 group meeting in the White House complex with President Bush's senior advisor . . . Sami Al-Arian . . . had been under investigation by the FBI for at least six years at the time of the June 2001 briefing . . . " *LA Times-Washington Post Service*, February 22, 2003.

- Headline: "U.S. Tests Exposed Sailors to Nerve, Chemical Agents in the 1960s" *New York Times News Service*, May 24, 2002.

- Headline: "Link Found Between Leukemia, Soldiers Exposed to Herbicides." *The Associated Press*, January 24, 2003.

- Headline: "Chemical Weapons Tests by U.S. in 60s" The story begins with these words: "The United States held open-air biological and chemical weapons tests in at least four states—Alaska, Hawaii, Maryland and Florida—during the 1960s." Mat Kelly, *Associated Press* writer, October 8, 2002.

- Headline: "Iraq Cites U.S., French Firms as Suppliers: Two Companies are Identified as the Sources of Foreign Germ Samples Used to Create Biological Weapons." *New York Times News Service*, March 16, 2003.

- Headline: "Spying Allegations May Put U.S. in Fix: A Memo Reportedly Reveals that the United States has been Listening in on U.N. Security Council Members" *LA Times-Washington Post Service*, March 4, 2003

- Headline: "False Figures?" The story begins with these words: "In the year after September 11 attacks, federal prosecutors exaggerated their success in convicting would-be terrorists by wrongly classifying three of every four cases originally labeled as international terrorism, congressional investigators said this week." *Associated Press* wire reports, February 22, 2003.

- Headline: "U.S. Gets Creative with Coalition-Support Figures: The Administration's Claims About the Level of Support are Exaggerations, Analysts Say" The *Associated Press*, March 21, 2003.

- Headline: "State Department Disputes CIA Over Use of Mysterious Trailers" The story begins with these words: "The State Department's Intelligence division is disputing the Central Intelligence Agency's conclusion that mysterious trailers found in Iraq were for making biological weapons, U.S. government officials said Wednesday." *New York Times News Service*, June 26, 2003.

- Headline: "Official Admits Weapons Report Faulty" The story begins with these words: "A British Dossier on Iraqi weapons of mass destruction that included material lifted from a graduate thesis on the Internet was an embarrassment for the government, Foreign Secretary Jack Straw said Tuesday . . . The dossier . . . contained material from a U.S. researcher's 12-year-old thesis that was copied, with a few alterations, from the Internet." The *Associated Press*, June 25, 2003.

- Headline: "U.N. Report on Al-Qiada Sees No Link to Saddam's Regime" *New York Times News Service*, June 27, 2003.

Again, these are just a few randomly chosen stories that constitute **bump and run reporting**. This tactic essentially buries a story by covering it, and usually much after the fact, or by hiding it in plain sight. Notice that these stories were either so old it seems somewhat foolish to now report them as "news," and/or they created no follow-up, no scandal, just a collective yawn by the American media looking for the next big child abduction case. So, by employing "running to authority" reporting, while adopting an authority friendly "old news" mentality, and then "bump and running" a story when necessary, the American media can maintain the façade of an "investigative" journalism without ever actually challenging the status quo. It is only appropriate that I end this section by quoting an American journalist who, so predictably, is ignorant of his own hypocrisy when he condemns the "Arab" press thusly: "[Arab] journalists painted a world in which their leadership was always right. . . . Self-criticism was seen almost as treasonous, implicitly aiding the enemy."[11]

2. General Lack of Social Scientific Sophistication.

The media's lack of specific expertise is a condition that is problematic for both the print and broadcast media, but it especially plagues the broadcast media. Let us be clear on how most members of the broadcast media acquire their jobs: What qualifies one to be a broadcast journalist is simply that you must look good and sound impressive. Period. It seems the networks believe any well-pronounced sentences delivered by an attractive, well-tanned face is thereby news regardless of the substance of the information. In short, it is not what you have to say that is important, but rather, how you look and sound when you say it.

Moreover, the media's lack of academic sophistication contributes to the decaying of both our political institutions and their attendant political debate in two interrelated ways. One, the media hinders the public from thinking of solutions to political problems by limiting them to a menu of rehashed ready-made mainstream positions. Two, the media further promotes the "dumbing down" of political dialogue by limiting the complexity of political debate to a level simple enough for the media to understand and control.[12] Notice, for example, how much of the media's so-called political coverage consists simply of poll watching. Political scientists refer to this phenomenon as the "horse race" syndrome. That is, the media covers politics as if it is a horse race between political candidates. In early 2007 the media was already saturating the airways with a play-by-play account of how Hillary Clinton had an early lead in the polls over her Republican challenger, Mitt Romney. Of course neither of the two actually secured their party's nomination, but do not fret—the media is already covering Sarah Palin's run in 2012. This permits the media to appear to be covering politics while it is actually ignoring the activities of government. This dumbing down also has severe consequences for the media's coverage of international events. The media, given its apparent ignorance, tends to view international events through the lens of a child, seeing the world community as made up of good guys and bad guys. This white hat/black hat orientation skews all its global reporting. Chavez and Hussein wear black hats; American presidents and corporate friendly dictators wear white hats. Needless to say, this very much distorts the complex reality of world events where, more often than not, political actors wear shades of gray.

3. The Media's Focus on Sensational Events.

Given their apparent ignorance, the television media must somehow present as news anything that will require little expert analysis and will seem impressive on television. Hence, the most important factor in deciding what story to cover is whether the story is sensationally dramatic. In other words, for the broadcast media to consider anything newsworthy it must be a limited and exciting event, no matter the importance of the story to the public at large. Or as humorist Dave Barry has written:

> TV news . . . means anything that you can take a picture of, especially if a local TV News Personality can stand in front of it. This is why they are so fond of car accidents, burning buildings, and crowds: these are good for standing in front of. On the other hand, local TV news shows tend to avoid stories about things that a local TV News Personality cannot stand in front of, such as budgets and taxes and the economy. If you want to get a local TV news show to do a story on the budget, your best bet is to involve it in a car crash.[13]

In his own way, Barry has identified a simple truth of the broadcast media: It spends most of its time looking for (and sometimes creating) dramatic events that will attract viewers and, therefore, advertisers.

Needless to say, this type of reporting may help the media, but it is killing our democracy. Since the stakes are so high, we must begin unpacking exactly how this "event centered" approach to the news affects not only how the media presents the "news" to us, but also how it hinders us from improving our political institutions and thereby our communities. To this task we now turn.

First of all, the media's fascination with simpleminded explanations and sensational events affects both what the media considers news and how it presents the news to us. This approach to the news forces the media to prefer style over substance, since style is, by definition, much more user friendly for television and the uninformed reporter. In short, cosmetics are much easier to cover than substantive issues for those who are themselves uninformed. As columnist George Will once suggested, the only way the media would have covered the very important post World War II migration of African-Americans from the South to the North was if someone had stretched a ribbon across the Mason-Dixon line and presented a prize to the one-millionth African-American who crossed it.[14] The media simply cannot cover things that are tedious and complex, like, say, governing, so it must focus on events. In doing so, the media has three primary tactics it uses to ensure it will have the necessary, user-friendly events at its disposal. One, the media tends to exaggerate and distort actual events to make them more exciting; two, the media creates events; or, three, the media itself will become the event. We will now look at each of these three tactics more closely and see how in the process of manufacturing the news the media hinders more than helps the public exercise its democratic responsibilities.

The Media Distorts and Exaggerates Actual Events. One of the broadcast media's favorite tricks is to distort and exaggerate an event either to justify its obsession with it or to hide its ignorance about it. Listen as the media covers any given event that President Obama is involved in, be it a budget discussion, an overseas trip, or a state of the union address, for it will frame the event (no matter how insignificant the event actually is) as the single most important event in Obama's presidency. In doing so, the media will pronounce, "the future of this administration rests on the success of this budget battle (or trip, or speech, or any other presidential photo opportunity)." This, of course, not only distorts and exaggerates whatever presidential event it is spotlighting, it also justifies the media's obsessive coverage. During the early months of the Obama administration, for instance, the media framed every speech and appearance by Obama as the defining event of his presidency. This allowed the media to continue its obsession with America's first African-American president without actually covering his policies.

The media can also exaggerate and distort its coverage by "spinning" an insubstantial event beyond its actual importance. As an example, recall how often the media replayed the video clip showing Hillary Clinton taking shots of whiskey with blue-collar folks in Pennsylvania. What exactly was the significance of this footage? After seeing Ms. Clinton drinking with the boys did the media believe (as Ms. Clinton's campaign team hoped) that this photo-op would somehow convince Americans that ivy-league, former first-lady, Senator from New York, and then presidential candidate, Hillary, was just an average gal? Another example of this tactic was the media's obsessive coverage of whether then Candidate Obama was a "real" American since he didn't wear a flag pin on his lapel!

An example of the media distorting an event is the now infamous "Saving Private Lynch" episode. It seems the media decided to bolster the actual event by adding such an implausible storyline that only the media and an ignorant public would have believed it. The media "enhanced" the story by making the ridiculous claim that a noncombat trained supply troop was captured "fighting for her life" with "multiple gunshot wounds," and then "rescued" by Special Forces under heavy enemy fire. Although none of these exciting details were actually true, they made for a much better story—at least in the media's eye—than the real story of a supply convoy gone astray in a combat zone and, hence, predictably ambushed by enemy combat troops. Another example was the much-repeated scene of "Iraqis" toppling Saddam's statue in Baghdad. What the media presented as the end of the war civilian uprising against the dictator Saddam, was actually American troops and some Iraqi juvenile hoods pulling down a statue that was more about rampant chaos which commenced after the event than about any Hollywood style Paris liberation. A recent example of the media exaggerating a story is the repeating of the spin "that Obama is pulling American troops from Iraq." This distortion conveniently ignores the fact that Obama's planned "removal of troops" still leaves 30,000 to 50,000 so-called contingency troops left to fight for their lives in Iraq. Another recent example of this approach to reporting was the contentious debates the media pundits had over which of the two major-party presidential candidates had Satan as their preacher.

Democracy is predicated on the notion that the people give their allegiance to the law only after they have thoroughly discussed the issue and then approved it through the appropriate majority process. It is a sad commentary on our political system indeed, when those charged with informing the democratic dialogue have become experts, not at their constitutional duty, but at distorting the insignificant and ignoring the important.

The Media Manufactures or Creates Events. If the media cannot find an actual event to distort and exaggerate, then it will simply create one of its own. This not only keeps the media busy so it appears to be doing something important (style over substance, you know), but it also keeps the public distracted and prevents them from legitimately exercising their constitutional responsibility. There is no better example of this than what some political scientists call the "body watch."[15] That is, how often must we endure the media's obsession with watching what the president's body is doing? Notice, for example, how the networks will cover the president playing hoops, reading to children, or walking hand in hand with the first lady. Whatever else one wants to say about these events, one cannot say they qualify as news. Also, why must the media always have a camera crew filming the president getting off a helicopter? What of importance is happening there at the helicopter pad? Is it that the public can rest assured because their beloved president can, in fact, use a step ladder? Along these lines, watch how often one of the White House correspondents will repeat what the anchor person has just stated, but this time the reporter will say it while standing in front of the White House. This, of course, somehow makes what the reporter is saying much more important because, well, the reporter is, after all, on the White House lawn! Moreover, the media distorts events that are not, strictly speaking, political. For example, does anybody remember the fiasco and intellectually demeaning non-sense about "Joe the Plumber" that played out during the 2008 election?

All of this would simply be annoying and of no real importance to political science if it did not have the effect of wasting our public energy on these silly events rather than focusing it on issues of substance. And let us remember, when a democratic society fails to provide the means for serious institutional debate it robs the political system of its only source of moral authority and corrodes the people's faith in their own civic responsibility. Think how much healthier our democracy would be if the media spent as much time covering issues like the economy, or the environment, as it does on creating events with no public importance at all. But, then again, who has time for this when the media is busy showing us things it can stand in front of?

A sad example of the media's body watch was its coverage of then president Bush flying via jet fighter to the aircraft carrier, U.S.S. Abraham Lincoln, to celebrate "Mission Accomplished" in May of 2003. According to the Bush administration and its lapdogs in the media, the fighter jet was necessary because the aircraft carrier was "too far out to sea to be reached by the standard procedure of employing Helicopter One." And, after all, the president wanted to greet his victorious troops as soon as possible so he opted for the more dangerous approach so as to welcome home his exhausted troops out at sea. What the media failed to report, was that this photo-op was so cleverly staged that the carrier was actually within easy reach of the less glamorous Helicopter One, but the media agreed to film from a direction which would only reveal the open sea rather than from the other direction which would have clearly exposed the nearby coastline. Moreover, Bush's concern for his troops was so insincere that he not only ordered the U.S.S. Abraham Lincoln to continue to circle in such a way as to provide the proper backdrop for "his" photo-op flight, he also delayed the sailors' reunion with their families even after their grueling tour of duty all so Bush could play Top Gun.

The Media Will Become the Event. When all else fails, the media will frame everything in relation to its own profession; in short, the media will itself become the event. For example, after NBC's Tim Russet passed away, the news, especially NBC and its sister networks on cable spent days upon days running testimonials about what a wonderful guy Mr. Russet was. Now, he may have indeed been a good man—as were the millions other individuals who died that same week. The media has also decided the main reason people are tuning out the major political parties is because, "of the constant negative commercials run in the media!" A much better explanation for why the public is turning away from the two major political parties could be the general public no longer feels either party represents their interests in the political arena.

Again, this fascination the media has with itself taints all of its coverage. For example, during the 2008 elections Tina Fey became more Sarah Palin than Sarah Palin. This very talented comedian, played Ms. Palin better than real Ms. Palin played herself. As a matter of fact, how many times did you hear people ridicule the real Ms. Palin about her statement that she knew foreign policy "because she could see Russia from her home"? I wonder how many people who repeated this line realized that Sarah Palin never said it—Tina Fey did, or was that Sarah Palin? Another tragic example of this media self-absorption was its coverage of the war in Iraq. Most of its coverage was concerned with the idea of "embedded reporters." It seems the political system has learned of the media's constant fascination with itself, hence the Bush Administration used this as a way to give the media something it loves to discuss—itself. Of course this prevented them from covering the story as independent journalists and, thereby, created a distorted image for the American public of what was actually happening in Iraq.

So, the media succeeds yet again in hiding its ignorance and in harming our democracy—now there is a story. Too bad there is no one willing to report it. Again, the reason this is so detrimental to democracy is because the time it wastes on itself is time it could spend focusing on the business of the community—namely, the business of fostering the substantive political conversations which are the only remedy to the political problems around us. Imagine what a different world we would live in if the media would only spend as much time on the public's business as it does on its own. Alas, how does one involve such a noble purpose in a car crash anyway?

4. The Media's Tendency to "Personalize" Their Coverage.

The media also tends to favor personal interpretations of events. Hence, the media reduces almost all of its so-called political coverage to simply gossiping about individuals. For example, notice how many "political" stories merely revolve around an individual by the name of Barack Obama. It is as if the media believes Obama *is* the government, rather than just one of millions of federal and state governing officials. This "Obama-as-government" bias so permeates the media's coverage of American politics, most Americans have no idea how institutionally weak the presidency actually is (I will have much more to say on this matter later in the chapter on the presidency). Furthermore, most Americans not only have unreal expectations of what any president can or cannot accomplish in office (which may explain why so many Americans feel frustrated by each president's inability to get things done), they also much underestimate the importance of the other branches of the federal government and their own state governments (which may explain why voter turnout is always substantially lower in non-presidential election years). This personalization extends to the media's international coverage as well. For example, the media reports as if the invasion of Iraq was directed at Saddam rather than the millions of innocent Iraqis who are bearing the brunt of the occupation. Moreover the media has reduced the fight against terrorism and the complexities of the Muslim world into a single individual—Osama bin Laden.

The media's instinct to personalize their coverage also distorts most people's understanding of the economy. Notice how often the media covers economic issues in a personalized manner, as if wealth and poverty were the product not of systemic causes but of personal merit. That is, the media's take on why so few do so well and so many, many more work hard all their lives just to get by is characteristically simplistic individualistic analysis. For example, according to the media, the primary reason the wealthy stay rich is because of their unique ingenuity and entrepreneurial skills and not because the system is skewed in their favor (a **regressive tax** code, insider trading, or, simply through inheritance, for example). And, of course, the corollary is true as well—individuals are struggling to get by not because of any sociological reasons (inadequate educational systems, exploited labor, unfair banking practices, etc.), but because they are either lazy, stupid, or "lack the necessary job skills." Needless to say, the media's inability to confront the complexity of the American political system hardly helps citizens perform their civic duty in any meaningful way. Of course this personalized coverage is necessary given the general lack of social scientific sophistication among the press; it is always easier for the ignorant to gossip about the activities of an individual than to understand and explain the institutional and theoretical interplay of political affairs.

5. The Class Bias of the Media.

The media also tends to bias their reporting in favor of the economic elite.[16] This should come as no surprise since the media, particularly in recent times and at the national level, is dominated by reporters who happen to earn relatively high incomes creating within them "the desire to maintain the economic fruits of their own accomplishments."[17] The media's generally high income status may explain why one political scientist, after extensive research on the question of bias in the press, wrote, "there is reason to doubt [the media] is very liberal on economic issues of importance to lower-status people . . . [for example] they were less liberal than the general public on the question of using government to reduce income inequalities."[18] Moreover, one study has found that 48% of media respondents claimed expanding free trade was either "one of the top few priorities" or "near the top of the list" regarding issues facing the country. In contrast, 44% of the general public regarded expanding free trade as "toward the bottom of the list." On the issue of corporate power, only 24% of media respondents, compared with 62% of the public, "strongly agree" that "too much power is concentrated in the hands of a few large companies." Lastly, the study revealed that, in comparison to 18% of the public, 43% of the media "strongly agree" that "the largest companies do not have too much power."[19]

This economic bias in favor of the fortunate few may help explain why the media not only favors individual economic interpretations (they must, after all, be well-off because of their own individual merit) but also why liberals and conservatives alike view the media as biased against them. As we will see in more detail below, conservatives claim the media is biased against religion and rural America, which is not surprising since the professional elite tend to find such things quaint at best. At the same time, liberals believe the media is too much the apologist for corporate interests, which also is predictable since so many of them are wealthy corporate shareholders. Hence, the only consistent bias to be found in the media is economical not ideological; in other words, it seems very few well-off journalists are critical of their own wealth or favorable to such blue-collar images as rural, religious America. This bias helps explain the media's economic preconceptions: According to the media orthodoxy, it is always good news when stocks climb (though this typically means workers have either taken a pay cut or been downsized altogether;[20] **inflation** is low (not always good news for working families);[21] and, free trade triumphs over protectionist policies. This also helps explain why the media kept repeating throughout much of this decade that, "the economy is booming," despite mountains of evidence demonstrating that working families actually fell behind in real economic terms.[22] It also helps explain how the media could have been taken by surprise by the "sudden collapse" of the economy in late 2008. Every expert who cared (including this one) and most working Americans who have been dealing with decades of diminishing economic opportunities were hardly surprised at all.

BIAS IN THE MEDIA: LIBERAL OR CONSERVATIVE?

There is no more enduring debate regarding the media than the question of whether the media has a liberal or conservative bias. Ask so-called conservatives if the media has a bias, and they will invariably exclaim, "the media is most assuredly biased in favor of the liberal." On the other hand, ask so-called liberals and they will claim the opposite, "the media favors the conservative perspective." Who is right, the liberal or the conservative? I will argue they are, in fact, both right.[23] Conservatives are correct when they complain about the media's liberal bias when reporting social policy; whereas, liberals are correct to criticize the media's conservative bias when covering economic policy. Below we will look closely at both the conservative and liberal critiques of the media.

The Conservative Critique: "The Media Is too Liberal!"

The conservative claims the media reveals a liberal bias when covering social policy. That is, it seems to the conservative the media slants its social commentary to reflect the values of the liberal "elite." The conservative critique of the media can be reduced to the three following arguments:

1. *The Media Mindlessly Accepts Liberal Beliefs and Explanations Regarding Social Policy.* Examples of the media acting more as advocates for certain "politically correct" positions rather than as objective journalists in search of the facts are so numerous it is difficult to know where to begin. Nonetheless, the media's coverage of the partial birth abortion debate in Congress clearly illustrates the media's mindless acceptance of so-called politically correct views. While the debate was taking place, the media widely reported as fact a comment made by Ron Fitsimmons, of the National Coalition of Abortion Providers, that the majority of partial birth abortions are performed only to protect the life of the mother or in cases of severe fetal deformity. His connection with an obviously interested and liberal organization apparently did not seem to trouble most media sorts since they never thought to double check his claim for accuracy. Not surprisingly, it was later revealed that most partial birth abortions are in fact performed on healthy mothers and fetuses. This, along with a long line of instances of the media contaminating the political process with its liberal bias, led one disgusted veteran journalist to write:

> If it hadn't been for those [partial birth abortion] lies, eagerly accepted and passed along as gospel by the printed press and broadcast news, President Clinton would not have dared veto a bill that outlawed the procedure. And Congress wouldn't have buckled and failed to override his veto . . . what is so infuriating [is] . . . the willingness of the press to accept the lie and pass it along as fact. If more sheep are cloned, don't be surprised if some come out looking like modern journalists. It isn't the first big lie that the media have bought and resold. Some years ago, gay organizations and public health people launched an intense "We're All at Risk" campaign. This meant that we were all equally vulnerable to the threat of AIDs. Common sense and existing evidence said otherwise . . . But those who launched the propaganda campaign later admitted that they believed the fear would create sympathy for gays and spur increase spending on AIDs research. Eventually, a few skeptical reporters shot holes in the campaign. But not until others who questioned it had been labeled bigots and homophobes. . . . More recently, there was the media hysteria over the burning of black churches. Remember? Night riders were thought to be galloping all over the country, burning black churches. A massive racists conspiracy, possibly inspired by the oratory of political conservatives like Pat Buchanan. Clinton, concerned frown and all, visited churches and recalled similar evil arsons in Arkansas when he was a youth—memories that turned out to be pure fiction. Turned out it was more smoke than fire. After the nation's press spread the arson story calmer heads took a closer look. Most of the fires weren't arson. No conspiracy. Black arsonists as well as white arsonists were arrested, proving a nut is a nut, regardless of color.[24]

During Super Bowl XXVII, the media proved once again their liberal bias. They reported relentlessly that, "there are more instances of domestic abuse on Super Bowl Sunday than on any other day of the year." The only problem with this claim was that it simply was not true.[25] Nonetheless, the media repeated this accusation as truth without ever thinking to check its validity. In another example, the American Association of University Women released a series of studies in which they charged America's schools were irreparably harming girls' self-esteem.[26] As evidence of this, they cited two findings from the studies: One, the study demonstrated boys were called on eight to ten times as often as girls in America's public schools. Two, due to this lack of attention, girls suffered from what the authors of the studies called the "glamor-gap."[27] When girls were asked, what they wanted to be when they grow up, the three most popular responses were, "lawyer, doctor, or scientist." This apparently disturbed the AAUW, because, when asked the same question, boys had declared they wanted to be, "sports stars and rock stars." As some scholars suggested, these responses reveal not a "glamor gap" but rather "a reality gap" between girls (who mature faster) and boys. In other words, boys tend to believe they will be rock-n-roll stars or celebrity athletes longer than girls who, given their maturity, no longer have such unrealistic aspirations. In response to the first issue, concerning the extra attention boys were receiving in America's public schools, objective reviewers pointed out what accounted for this disparity of attention was the fact boys were scolded or punished much more often than girls.[28] Ignoring for the moment the troubling fact the media did not think it worth reporting boys are being punished at a much greater rate than girls, why did the media not think to background check this story? Is it because the media is the liberal apologist the conservative critic makes it out to be? This story became such media orthodoxy a Senator actually presented the study as proof of why the federal government should enact legislation to address this calamity.[29]

Such examples seem endless (including reports that the phrase "rule of thumb" originated in the South where a man could legally beat his wife if the stick was no bigger than the circumference of the husband's thumb [untrue][30] to the media's chant, "women earn 60 cents on the dollar compared to men" [essentially incorrect])[31] making a compelling case the media does in fact favor the liberal perspective when covering social issues. For example, since the media seems so obsessed with how gender affects public policy in America, then why does the media refuse to tell the other side of the story? For example, what of the fact the vast majority of prison inmates in America are male;[32] more boys drop out of school than girls;[33] fewer men graduate college than women;[34] more young men kill themselves or are killed by others than any other demographic group in America;[35] as many men die of prostate cancer as women do from breast cancer;[36] or men, as a group, die sooner than women?[37] Are these facts not important enough to report? Could it be that the conservative is correct after all? Is a fact only as good as the liberal policy it supports?

2. *The Media Is Biased Against Religion.* The conservative argues the media presents institutional religion and its participants as, at best, quaint and naive, or, at worst, ignorant and backwards. As proof, they point to the proliferation of stories in the media which either focus on the most eccentric and bizarre behavior of religious leaders or have as a theme a story of a religious figure gone astray. In other words, the conservative believes if one's only acquaintance with religion came from the media, then one would think the only thing church members do is either kiss snakes, molest children, or frequent prostitutes. Not only does this do a grave injustice to the sincerity and commitment persons of faith bring to their communities, it also badly distorts the actual record of most religious institutions; after all, these are the institutions which feed the poor, shelter the homeless, advocate for peace, comfort the sick and downtrodden, and do other socially constructive activities. Conservatives argue, this side of the religious experience is very rarely reported by the media because the liberal media is so predisposed to disbelieve it. It is as if the media's own liberal faith would be tested and found wanting if it reported such heresy by exposing the rich contributions that institutional religion promotes and fosters in America and around the world.

To further document the liberal bias of the media when it comes to religion, the conservative points out the print media's idea of "balance" is having a weekly "Religion Page" (usually Saturday) which articulates the "religious perspective." This just reinforces the conservative's point that newspapers are, simply stated, the "Secular Pages." This hardly seems like balance. According to the conservative, if the press really wanted balance, then it would not delegate only one page of the paper, once a week, to the religious perspective; but, the conservative knows, the press is not concerned with presenting a fair picture of the world at all, it is only interested in presenting a liberally biased one. The liberal picture is one where liberal superiors in the media wink and nod knowingly to each other as they humor their religious inferiors by allowing them one page a week to explain their silly beliefs to those equally silly enough to want to listen.

3. *The Media Is Biased Against Rural America.* Conservatives argue the media has a subtle, yet explicit, contempt for all things rural. They believe the media tends to present farming America as less sophisticated and intelligent than urban and suburban America. For example, when was the last time anchorpersons were asked to lose their urban or suburban accents because they made them sound stupid? Also, what compelled a reporter to sum up a story on the militia movement by commenting that these militia members were, after all, "only farmers, ranchers, and small town people?" As if this fact, in and of itself, diminished these people's concerns about the federal government being out of control and abusive to Americans. Moreover, it does not help the media's image of rural Americans that they are also (wink and nod) religious as well as small town. As the conservative points out, it seems to the media if your religious faith does not actually prove you are ignorant then coupling it with a rural accent certainly does.

The conservative also argues this contempt of rural America is much deeper than a mere discussion of the strictly political news can unveil. They believe one must view the media in its entirety to understand the media's contempt for rural America. For example, why is it whenever sitcoms want to present a character as a buffoon they so often give the character a rural flavor? Some of you may recall a series called, "Green Acres," which makes the point nicely. Or, recall the program "Married With Children" where the only "clan" dumber than the Bundys were Peg's "backwoods" relatives. How many of you remember the "National Lampoon Vacation" movies where Chevy Chase's character, Clark, is constantly plagued by his unemployed, good-for-nothing rural in-laws? If you do not think this type of stereotyping is all that hurtful, just imagine how Americans would react if such type casting was done on account of race, sex, or sexual preference, instead of by geography. It seems even if you do not agree with the conservative, you must, at least, recognize the conservative has plenty of valid reasons for believing the media is in fact liberally biased when covering social issues.

The Liberal Critique: "The Media Is too Conservative!"

The liberal critics of the media challenge one of the central tenets of the American civic faith—the belief in the freedom of the press. Liberals argue, rather than being free and independent, the media is bought and paid for by corporate interests. In support of this contention, liberals call attention to the fact the vast majority of media outlets (television stations, radio stations, newspapers and magazines) are controlled by large corporations whose primary purpose is not to inform the public but rather to indoctrinate it with the corporate party-line.[38] As reported by the Media Reform Information Center, in November 2008:

> In 1983, 50 corporations controlled the vast majority of all news media in the U.S. At the time, Ben Bagdikian was called "alarmist" for pointing this out in his book, *The Media Monopoly*. In his 4th edition, published in 1992, he wrote "in the U.S., fewer than two dozen of these extraordinary creatures own and operate 90% of the mass media"—controlling almost all of America's newspapers, magazines, TV and radio stations, books, records, movies, videos, wire services and photo agencies. He predicted then that eventually this number would fall to about half a dozen companies. This was greeted with skepticism at the time. When the 6th edition of *The Media Monopoly* was published in 2000, the number had fallen to six. Since then, there have been more mergers and the scope has expanded to include new media like the Internet market. More than 1 in 4 Internet users in the U.S. now log in with AOL Time-Warner, the world's largest media corporation.
>
> In 2004, Bagdikian's revised and expanded book, *The New Media Monopoly*, shows that only 5 huge corporations—Time Warner, Disney, Murdoch's News Corporation, Bertelsmann of Germany, and Viacom (formerly CBS)—now control most of the media industry in the U.S. General Electric's NBC is a close sixth.[39]

This intimate relationship with the corporate system leaves little room for the media to investigate or report on anything which might reflect poorly on its owners or customers; in other words, liberals charge the media is neither free nor independent. As a market driven enterprise, the media is dependent on advertising for its economic existence, making it very reluctant to either challenge the system in general, or its advertisers in particular. Hence, the media cannot have anything more than cosmetic debates regarding economic questions. There is no better example of this than the façade that takes place on most major newspapers' editorial page between the so-called liberal and conservative columnists. The columnists will play the role of adversaries as they passionately argue with each other over trivial differences of economic policy. For example, the liberal will advocate strongly for a "raise in the minimum wage," while the conservative will explain contemptuously such a policy is "fiscally irresponsible." By the tone of the debate one would think there is actually some real disagreement between the two, until one realizes they are arguing over whether the minimum wage should be $7 or $8 an hour—for a net difference of $1! Another example of this fakery is the "debate" over the time line for a balanced federal budget. Again, the two politically opposed columnists will make nice theater of the fact the liberal thinks it should be done in nine years, whereas, the conservative believes it is best to balance the budget in seven years. Of course, neither columnist will ever question the legitimacy of the debt to begin with or why the middle class alone is left holding the bill. In addition, you will notice that on the big economic issues they will always agree. For example, both are always for "free trade" (whatever that is) and against "**protectionism**" (whatever that is). They will also agree the reason most working Americans are falling behind economically is because "they lack the necessary job skills" and not because of any system-wide flaw.

It is no coincidence unions have always claimed they get very little fair and accurate treatment by a media which just so happens to be owned by the very corporate interests who so despise organized labor. Examples of biased coverage of management-labor disputes by the media could fill an entire book by themselves, and is much beyond the scope of this chapter. Suffice it to say, American's support of unions has tracked consistently downward as the media became more and more centralized by corporate power.

Other examples of the media's conservative bias is its constant refrain—"tax cuts for the wealthy will stimulate the economy." No matter how often the facts say otherwise, the media keeps preaching this corporate line. No matter the fact working Americans have been confronted with the reality of stagnant wages since 1973; home ownership becoming more the American myth and less the American dream; vacations and pensions becoming nothing more than anachronisms; employment becoming part time and of limited duration; and, social security becoming an economic burden rather than an economic insurance policy.[40] Still, the media ignores this side of the economic story, proving, it seems, the truth in the liberal's belief that the media is conservatively biased when it comes to economic issues.

The recent taxpayer funded bailouts of the financial system was treated by the media as a non-partisan issue since everyone agreed it was the first step back to economic recovery. The fact economists and political scientists who thought this opinion was misleading and politically motivated were left out of the "discussion" comes as no surprise given the bias of the press. The corporate media presented the bailouts to average Americans as good for them, because these banks are simply "too big to fail." Yet not one mainstream news source found it odd that the tax payer was being compelled to give what little cash they had to these banks so these banks would have some cash to lend back to these very same tax-payers.

THE EMERGENCE OF THE INTERNET

No chapter on the media can ignore the profound effect the Internet has played in reshaping, not only our news habits, but also our political culture. Gone are the days when the news is controlled by the establishment press. No more monopolies on information and opinion; every opinion has its on web site, and every subject can be researched with a computer. This is the reality of the contemporary promulgation of information.

The Internet found its beginnings when the United States national security establishment needed to respond to the Soviet Union's launching of the space probe "Sputnik" in the 1950s. Due to the need to maintain its technological superiority during the **Cold War**, the United States began dedicating its defense dollars to rapidly expanding its technological know-how; from these efforts emerged the Internet. So, what began as a way to centralize real time sharing of information for the defense establishment evolved into a mechanism that has democratized information.

The amount of literature explaining the deficiencies of the Internet as a reliable source of information has become its own flourishing industry, and need not be retold here. Suffice it to say, that critics of the Internet are correct in claiming that much of what one finds on the Internet—particularly as it applies to political information—is not worth the screen it appears upon. However, the same could be said of all sources of news, be they such established purveyors of news as *The New York Times* or NBC. The majority of what appears in these establishment news institutions is no more reliable than what one finds on the Internet. In fact, I would assert that the explosion of politically minded web sites on the Internet is itself a result of establishment news sources' inability and resistance to doing the job the Constitution protected them to do—report government crimes and corruption, and be suspicious of government and not its enabler. But as this chapter has demonstrated, the establishment media long ago let go of that constitutional mission. So, consumers of news who have longed for a more aggressive and investigation-minded press have migrated to the one place that provides it in droves—the Internet.

So, what can students of politics take from this reaction? The same lesson that has always applied to political information since time immemorial: be skeptical of any political news regardless of its source, and be sure to filter it with your knowledge and with the consultation of political scientists and other experts in the field. The differing views and theories that exist in cyber-space is a healthy thing for a democracy that relies on a robust market-place of ideas for its continued health; the more differing opinions the better, *unless one avoids any information that does not already square with one's political viewpoint.* One scholar has written: "One 12-nation study found Americans the least likely to discuss politics with people of different views, and this particularly true of the well-educated. High school dropouts had the most diverse group of discussion-mates, while college graduates managed to shelter themselves from uncomfortable perspectives . . . The danger is that this self-selected 'news' acts as a narcotic, lulling us into a stupor through which we will perceive in blacks and whites a world that unfolds in greys . . . So perhaps the only way forward is for each of us to struggle on our own to work out intellectually with sparring partners whose views we deplore. Think of it as a daily mental workout analogous to a trip to a gym; if you don't work up a sweat, it doesn't count."[41] Good advice, indeed, now off to the gym.

FINAL THOUGHTS

It is time to end this chapter where it began, with a reminder of why political scientists and, for that matter, all Americans should concern themselves with the media in the first place. We should be concerned with the media because the integrity of our constitutional political system depends on it. A democracy without a competent and professional media will never foster the necessary political debate which is the backbone of our political freedom. For if it is true that knowledge is power (and it is) then the opposite must also be true—ignorance is powerlessness. And, in a democracy, an ill-informed public is a reality we simply cannot tolerate, for it robs our public institutions of their only source of legitimacy—the people's informed consent to their authority. Without this informed consent we make a mockery of both our freedom and our political system.

NOTES

1. General Social Surveys, 1972-1989: Machine Readable Data File (Chicago: The National Opinion Research Center, University of Chicago, 1989).
2. This title is taken directly from Greg Palast's superb book, *The Best Democracy Can Buy: The Truth about Corporate Cons, Globalization, and High-Finance Fraudsters*, revised American edition, (London: Penguin Books, 2003) p.14.
3. Ibid
4. Ibid., p.11–15
5. Richard Paul and Linda Elder, *How to Detect Media Bias and Propaganda in National and World News, The Miniature Guide,* 2002 Foundation for Critical Thinking, www.criticalthinking.org.
6. Source: The New York Times/CBS News Methodology: Telephone interviews with 983 American adults, conducted from Oct. 5 to Oct. 8, 2006. Margin of error is 4 percent.
7. For an excellent scholarly look into the 9/11 attacks see, Nafeez Mosaddeq Ahmed, *The War on Freedom: How and Why America was Attacked September 11, 2001,* (Joshua Tree, California: Tree of Life Publications, 2002). Nafeez Mosaddeq Ahmed details nearly 600 reported facts alleging that the U.S. Government had prior knowledge of the attacks and were either criminally negligent or accessories in the execution of the attacks. Here are just a few of the confirmed facts regarding the horrific events of 9/11 as reported by Ahmed:
    - The activities of a former U.S. Army Sergeant who trained Al-Qaeda and participated in the Embassy bombings suggest that the U.S. continues to protect bin Laden as a strategic asset. This may explain why Ted Bridis and John Solomon of the *Associated Press* reported that, "Although Predator Drones spotted Osama bin Laden as many as three times in late 2000, the Bush administration didn't fly the unmanned planes over Afghanistan during its first eight months, current and former officials say (from *The Oregonian,* June 25, 2003, p. A2)."
    - The Sudanese government had captured bin Laden in March of 1996 and offered to extradite him to the U.S. for criminal prosecution, instead of accepting the offer, the U.S. Government, according to Sudanese Minister of State, as reported in the *Washington Post* on October 3, 2001, "said 'just ask him to leave the country. Just don't let him go to Somalia,'" and the Sudanese Government responded, "'he will go to Afghanistan' and the U.S. said 'let him.'"
    - Two years later the U.S. Government launched an attack on a Sudanese pharmaceutical plant after falsely charging that it was a chemical weapons plant.
    - The CIA in the U.S.A. trained members of Al-Qaeda in terrorism, and the hijackers themselves were trained by the U.S. military at U.S. military institutions.
    - High-level elements of the U.S. government, military, intelligence and law enforcement agencies received numerous credible and urgent warnings of the 11th September attacks, which were of such a nature as to successively reinforce one another. Only a full-fledged inquiry would suffice to clarify in a definite manner why the American intelligence community failed to act on the warnings received. However, the nature of the multiple warnings received, along with the false claims by U.S. intelligence agencies that they had no specific warnings of what was about

to occur, suggests that they indeed had extensive foreknowledge of the attacks, but are now attempting to prevent public recognition of this.

- Independent journalists revealed that Mahmoud Ahmed, as ISI Director-General [of the Pakistani Secret Police], had channeled U.S. government funding to Mohamed Atta, described as the "lead hijacker" by the FBI. The U.S. government protected him, and itself, by asking him to resign quietly after the discovery, thus blocking a further inquiry and a potential scandal.
- Three FBI officers testified that they had known the names of the hijackers and the date of the planned attack weeks before it happened, but were muzzled by superiors under threat of prosecution. Moreover, on May 9, 2002, the New York Post reported that: "FBI headquarters ignored its own agents' red-flag warning a month before 9/11 that Zacarias Moussaoui [the so-called, "twentieth hijacker"] was the kind of person who might 'fly something into the World Trade Center,' FBI Director Robert Mueller admitted yesterday."
- Two days after the attacks, Mr. David Schippers publicly declared, on WRRK in Pittsburgh PA., that he had attempted to warn U.S. Attorney General John Ashcroft, along with other federal officials, about the terrorist attacks weeks before they occurred. Citing U.S. intelligence officials, including FBI agents, Schippers stated that these agents knew, months before 9/11 attacks, the names of the hijackers, the targets of their attacks, the proposed dates . . . along with other information. Here are a few of Mr. Schipper's credentials: Chief Counsel to the U.S. House of Representatives managers for the impeachment trial of Bill Clinton; Chief Investigative Counsel for the U.S. House of Representatives' Judiciary Committee in 1998, handling the committee's oversight of the U.S. Department of Justice; Senior partner of the Chicago law firm of Schippers & Bailey; former member and Chief of the Organized Crime and Racketeering Section of the U.S. Department of Justice; former assistant U.S. Attorney; and, he is the recipient of the Loyola University Law Alumni Medal of Excellence, The Loyola University Alumni Association citation for distinguished service to the legal community and the Award of Appreciation from the Federal Criminal Investigators Association.
- In spite of extensive forewarnings, the U.S. Air Force emergency response systems collapsed systematically on 11th September, in violation of the clear rules that are normally and routinely followed on a strict basis. This is an event that could only conceivably occur as a result of deliberate obstructions to the following of Standard Operating Procedures for emergency response.
- In addition to the numerous warnings, Paul Monk, Senior Fellow at the Australian Thinking Skills Institute and Professor at the Australian Defense University, points out the date September 11 should already have been a high alert date because on that date in 1996 Ramzi Yousef was convicted for the first WTC attacks in 1993. "From that point, given the fascination terrorists have with anniversaries, 11 September should surely have become a watch date." Keep this in mind as the next September 11 rolls around and the federal government heightens the nation's terrorist alert status for just this reason.
- The Bush administration, to this day, has failed to account for the inconsistencies concerning the official explanations of what President Bush knew about the attacks and when exactly he became aware of said attacks on the morning of 9/11.
- Increases of so-called "put-options" (a bet that a stock will fall in price dramatically on a certain date) on United Airlines, American Airlines, Morgan Stanley Dean Witter, and Merrill Lynch Company (two of the largest occupants of the World Trade Centers) increased up to 1200 percent above normal from September 6 through September 10 at both the New York Stock Exchange and the Chicago Board Options. This activity led to the closure of NYSE. To this day, no one has collected the money on these put options. The *London Times* reported about this pre 9/11 stock trading on September 18, 2001: "American authorities are investigating unusually large numbers of shares in airlines, insurance companies and arms manufacturers that were sold off in the days and weeks before the attacks. They believe that the sales were by people who knew about the impending disaster."

- *Newsweek* reported, on September 13, 2001, that on the day before the attacks, "Top Pentagon officials suddenly cancelled travel plans for the next morning, apparently because of security concerns." Moreover, the *San Francisco Chronicle* reported San Francisco Mayor Willie Brown was booked to fly from the Bay Area to New York on September 11, 2001, but cancelled his plans "when he got a call that he described as his airport security—a full eight hours before yesterday's string of terrorist attacks—advising him that Americans should be cautious about their air travel . . . Exactly where the call came from is a bit of a mystery. The mayor would only say that it came from 'my security people at the airport.'"
- It is a fact that no top World Trade Center executives were killed in the attacks. It is a fact that the thousands of victims who were killed in the attacks constitute a fraction of the total number of employees who work at the World Trade Centers. It is a fact that none of the Pentagon employees who died were members of the top military establishment.

8. See for a thorough analysis of the media's failure is Greg Mitchell, *So Wrong for so long: How the Press, the Pundits, and The President, Failed In Iraq,* Union Square Press, New York, 2008.
9. To hear these experts explain how deep the lies and distortions about Iraq's WMD programs were, watch "Uncovered: The War on Iraq," by Robert Greenwald, Cinema Libre Distribution, 2004.
10. Ibid., p. 329. Or, for some empirical evidence to prove the wisdom of Mr. Madison's fears, see chapter 7 on foreign policy.
11. David Ignatius, "A Bit of Advise to Intellectuals of Arab World," *The Oregonian,* (June 25, 2003) p. C9.
12. In class I often refer to this as a "conspiracy of ignorance." By this I mean the media is unaware (due to its apparent ignorance) of its transgressions against representative government.
13. Dave Barry, 1996 Day Calendar, Thursday, November 30th.
14. Will made this comment at the annual meeting of the American Association of Political Consultants, Washington, D.C., 1977.
15. The phrase "body watch" refers to the media's habit of fixating on the "movements" of the president, such as his jogging, eating, traveling, golfing, or simply walking. See for example, Robert L. Lineberry, George C. Edwards III, and Martin P. Wattenberg, *Government in America: Politics and Policy,* 6th ed. (New York: HarperCollins, 1994), p.491, where they write: "Most of the news coverage of the White House comes under the heading 'body watch.' In other words, reporters focus on the most visible layer of presidents' personal and official activities and provide the public with step-by-step accounts."
16. For an excellent analysis of the class bias inherent in the modern media see, James Fallows, *Breaking the News: How the Media Undermines American Democracy* (New York: First Vintage Books, 1997).
17. Stephen E. Frantzich and Stephen L. Percy, *American Government: The Political Game* (Madison: Brown & Benchmark, 1994), p. 171; see also, Robert Lichter and Stanley Rothman, "Media and Business Elites," *Public Opinion,* October/November 1981.
18. John J. Harrigan, Empty Dreams, *Empty Pockets: Class and Bias in American Politics* (New York: Macmillian Publishing Company, 1993), p.112; see also, Daniel Hellinger and Dennis R. Judd, *The Democratic Facade,* 2nd ed. (Belmont, CA: Wadsworth Publishing Co., 1994), particularly pages 60–69.
19. David Croteau, "Challenging the 'Liberal Myth' Claim," *Extra, the Magazine of FAIR,* vol.11, no.4 (July/August 1998).
20. Molly Ivins, "Analyzing the Ups and Downs of the Stock Market," *The Oregonian* (November 24, 1996) p. C6.
21. See chapter 6 on how low inflation is not necessarily a good indicator of the health of the economy for working Americans.
22. Staff Reports, "Families Work Harder for Less Money, Studies Show," *The Oregonian* (September 9, 1996), p. B12.
23. Steven Kelman makes a similar point in his book, *American Democracy and the Public Good* (Fort Worth: Harcourt Brace, 1996), p. 383.

24. Mike Royko, "Another Lie Exposed," *The Oregonian* (February 1, 1997), p. D8.
25. Ken Ringle, "Wife-Beating Claims Called Out of Bounds," *Washington Post* (January 31, 1993), p. A1.
26. "How Schools Shortchange Girls" (Washington, D.C.: AAUW Educational Foundation, 1992).
27. "Summary: Shortchanging Girls, Shortchanging America" Washington, D.C.: American Association of University Women, 1991.
28. David Sadker, Myra Sadker, and Dawn Thomas, "Sex Equity and Special Education," *The Pointer* 26, no. 1 (1981): 36.
29. Senator Edward Kennedy used the AAUW study to support the Gender Equity in Education Act (HR 1793) in 1993: "[It] refutes the common assumption that boys and girls are treated equally in our educational system. Clearly they are not." *Boston Globe* (September 16, 1993), p. 5.
30. Women's Studies Network (Internet: listserv@umdd.umd.edu), May 11, 1993.
31. June O'Neill and Solomon Polachek, "Why the Gender Gap in Wages Narrowed in the 1980s," *Journal of Labor Economics* 11, no. 1 (January 1993), part 1: 205–28. Additionally, a Stanford economist, Lawrence Baker, published evidence in the *New England Journal of Medicine* (1996) stating, among other reasons, that any difference in the pay between men and women doctors is due to the amount of hours men work compared to their female counterparts. Male doctors tend to work, according to Baker, an average of 62 hours per week while women work 51 hours per week. See Julianne Malveaux, "Medical Fields Still Short of Gender Equity," *The Oregonian* (April 15, 1996), p. B5.
32. Bureau of Justice Statistics, "Correctional Populations in the United States, 1993" (Washington, D.C.: Office of Justice Programs, U.S. Department of Justice, October 1995). This report states that in 1993 there were 1.3 million adult males incarcerated in local jails or prisons within the United States. Contrast this with the comparatively low figure of 95,000 incarcerated adult females.
33. Bruce Bower, "Tracking Teen Self-Esteem," *Science News* (March 23, 1991), p. 184.
34. Digest of Education Statistics (Washington, D.C.: National Center for Education Statistics, U.S. Department of Education, 1992), p. 273.
35. Monthly Vital Statistics Report, "Advance Report of Final Mortality Statistics, 1990" (Washington, D.C.: U.S. Department of Health and Human Services, January 1993).
36. National Cancer Institute, *Cancer Statistics Review*, 1973–1991, 1994. The lifetime risk of a male dying of prostate cancer in the United States is roughly 3.5 percent; the lifetime chance of a female dying of breast cancer is roughly the same.
37. According to the National Center for Health Statistics, males can expect to live to be 72 years of age while females can expect to live to be 79 years of age. National Center for Health Statistics. "Annual Summary of Births, Marriages, Divorces, and Deaths: United States, 1993." Monthly Vital Statistics Report. 42(13). Hyattsville, MD: National Center for Health Statistics, 1994.
38. The good news, so to speak, is it appears a healthy number of Americans are aware and concerned about the growing influence and power of big money over the media. As reported in *Parade* magazine ("Do you believe what news people tell you?" March, 2, 1997 edition), a survey conducted by the Roper Center and commissioned by Newseum, revealed that "88% of respondents believed corporate owners improperly influenced news reporting—and that big corporations seem to be getting bigger."
39. Source http://www.corporations.org/media/
40. The interested reader will find these and other topics explored in more detail in the following books: William Greider (*Who Will Tell the People*), Kevin Phillips (*Boiling Point*), Martin Gross (*A Call for Revolution*), Donald Barlett and James Steele (*America: What Went Wrong?*), Michael Parenti (*Democracy for the Few*), and John Kenneth Galbraith (*The Culture of Contentment*).
41. Nicholas Kristof, "The Slippery Slope to the Daily Me," *The Oregonian*, March 20, 2009, p. C5.

CHAPTER 6
Economic Policy:
The Divine Command

"Banking establishments are more dangerous than standing armies."
—*Thomas Jefferson*

"All the measures of government are directed to the purpose of making the rich richer and the poor poorer"
—*William Henry Harrison*

"You mean to tell me that the success of the [economic] program and my reelection hinges on the Federal Reserve and a bunch of f***ing bond traders?"
—*Bill Clinton*

"And I have sufficient witness to the truth of what I say—my poverty."
—*Socrates*

INTRODUCTION

This chapter will focus on that most ordinary, yet mysterious, concept known as money. Americans like to think of themselves as members of the ultimate money society, while at the same time, they know very little about the subject themselves. In other words, we may love our money, but we know very little about the thing we love. Given the realities of economic policy which this chapter will expose, it may be good so few Americans comprehend money and its attendant private and public institutions. Or as Henry Ford once said:

> It is well enough that the people of the nation do not understand our banking and monetary system for, if they did, I believe there would be a revolution before tomorrow morning.[1]

But as students of politics, we cannot afford the luxury of economic ignorance if we are to help our families and improve our communities.

Our analysis of economic policy will dispel many of the myths and resolve many of the mysteries that support the American economy. However, as we proceed, we must be aware much about money remains a mystery to even the most astute political and economic scholars. It seems the study of political economics has as much to do with religion as it does with science. As William Greider has written:

> Above all, money [is] a function of faith. It requires an implicit and universal social consent that is indeed mysterious. To create money and use it, each one must believe and everyone must believe. Only then [do] worthless pieces of paper take on value. . . . The money process . . . [is] so mysterious that it could easily be confused with divine powers.[2]

It is this "money process" we will be examining in this chapter. In doing so, we will break down economic policy into its three main components: monetary policy, fiscal policy and **trade policy**. We will then examine each of these components in detail by asking three basic questions about them: What is it?, Who does it?, and How do they do it?

MONETARY POLICY: THE SECRETS OF THE TEMPLE[3]

1. What is Monetary Policy? Monetary policy is simply a pretentious phrase referring to the idea that someone must regulate the amount of money that physically exists in the economy. In other words, monetary policy controls the supply of actual dollars circulating in the economy.

2. Who Controls Monetary Policy? The Federal Reserve System controls monetary policy in the American political system. It was created with the enactment of the 1913 Federal Reserve Act, promoted by then President Woodrow Wilson and Senator Carter Glass of Virginia, who was the chief congressional sponsor of the law. It has been revised by two subsequent acts: In 1935, Congress centralized policy control in Washington, and in 1980, Congress granted the Federal Reserve System universal authority over the reserves of private banks. The Federal Reserve System has four main institutional components. They are: The **Federal Reserve Board**, the **Federal Open Market Committee**, the Federal Reserve Banks, and commercial banks and credit unions.

The Federal Reserve Board (AKA: "The Fed"): The Federal Reserve Board—most commonly referred to as the "Fed"—is made up of seven "Governors" who serve fourteen-year terms, except for the chair and vice-chair, who serve for four years. All members of the board are appointed by the President and confirmed by the **Senate**.

The Federal Open Market Committee (AKA: "The FOMC"): The Federal Open Market Committee is the main policy making body of the Federal Reserve System. It consists of the seven Governors of the Federal Reserve Board and five of the presidents of the twelve Federal Reserve Banks, for a total of twelve members. When choosing the five Reserve Bank presidents for the FOMC, the committee rotates the membership amongst the twelve presidents. The president of the Federal Reserve Bank of New York serves on a continuous basis; the presidents of the other Reserve Banks serve one-year terms on a rotating basis beginning January 1 of each year.

The Federal Reserve Banks: The twelve Federal Reserve Banks are lenders of cash to commercial banks. They are distributed throughout the United States to provide an even supply of cash to various geographical regions of the country. The Federal

Reserve Banks are located in the following cities: Atlanta; Boston; Chicago; Cleveland; Dallas; Kansas City; Minneapolis; Philadelphia; Richmond; San Francisco; St. Louis; and, New York (the most influential of the Federal Reserve banks).

Commercial Banks and Credit Unions: These are the depository and lending institutions (banks) that serve the public.

Originally, the Federal Reserve System was designed to be part of the policy-making authority of the president. That is, under the original law, it was never intended for the Federal Reserve System to be independent of the political process and, thereby, the concerns of working Americans. Yet, through the manipulations of the wealthy and their media cohorts, Americans were convinced monetary policy was best left to the "experts" and citizens should simply accept the Federal Reserve System's policies as economic necessities. Today, for instance, Americans will complain about how the "Fed just increased **interest rates**," without ever thinking they, or their elected representatives, can do anything about it. That is the first myth we need to dispel. The only thing working Americans need to do, to gain control of monetary policy, is to elect politicians who will do so. There is no reason, legal, political, or otherwise, why it could not happen; Americans simply need to want to accomplish monetary reform and it is done.

3. How Does the Federal Reserve System Control Monetary Policy? That is, how does the Federal Reserve System regulate the supply of money? To answer this question, we must first examine two concepts, which dominate monetary policy (namely, inflation and **recession**) before we can fully appreciate the activities of the Federal Reserve System. "Inflation" and "recession" are two of the most overused and least understood concepts in America's political vocabulary. At this point, each of you ask yourself this question: Can I, an American citizen, explain what either of these two terms mean? If you cannot, do not feel bad, most Americans cannot either. But as emerging political scientists we must learn to do just that, because our families are depending on it. But, be forewarned: As you read on, you are about to understand Mr. Jefferson's and Mr. Ford's comments which introduced this chapter.

Inflation is best defined as too much money chasing too few goods. This simply means the supply of actual dollars has increased, although the production behind those dollars has not, so each dollar is now worth less than before, hence, prices go up during times of inflation. Recession is the opposite of inflation, too little money chasing too many goods. And, since there is now less money in comparison to production, each dollar is worth more than before; hence, prices go down in times of recession. This fluctuation of the money supply (between inflation and recession) is what the Federal Reserve System is primarily concerned with regulating, but it does not do so without a political bias. In other words, the Federal Reserve System is by no means neutral in its policies; its policies tend to favor the wealthy, while working against the interests of middle class Americans. Below, we will find out exactly how and why.

Before we precede any further with our particular discussion, I need to make some preliminary remarks concerning the concept inflation in general. I will be arguing below inflation is not as harmful to working Americans as they have been led to believe; indeed,

I will argue it has mostly beneficial aspects for the vast majority of Americans. Nonetheless, this must not be taken to mean I am advocating an economy awash in worthless dollars, anymore than those fiscal conservatives who disagree with me are, therefore, advocating the removal of all available dollars. And, in fact, the debate between those who favor the interests of banks and the wealthy (monetary conservatives) and those of us who favor the interests of working Americans and their families (monetary liberals) is not really a debate about inflation at all. What the debate actually centers on is the question: How much money should be in circulation for the economy to be considered healthy? Therefore, a monetary supply acceptable to say, economists for either the Fed or Citibank, fiscal liberals (like myself) would find unduly scarce (or recessionary), whereas, a monetary supply acceptable to fiscal liberals would seem much too plentiful (inflationary) to them. The reasons for this dichotomy will be explained in much more detail below, at this point just think of it as an economic glass of water—neither party disagrees on how much water is in the glass, but they do disagree on if the amount means the glass is half empty or half full. Nonetheless, I will continue to use both terms (inflation and recession) in their more traditional sense for readability purposes.

There is a story of a robber, who, when asked why he robbed a bank, replied, "because that's where the money is." Well, the robber is right, banks are in fact where the money is. They have the money because the wealthy use the institutional apparatus of the banking industry to sell their excessive money for a profit to those Americans who do not have enough money to begin with. That is, the banks (the institutional side) and the wealthy (the individual side) are two sides of the same coin, and the Federal Reserve System is dominated by those concerned with keeping it this way. To do so, the Federal Reserve System will do all it can to prevent inflation, which is the main monetary threat to the rich's privileged economic status.

The wealthy depend on a scarce money supply (recession) for two primary reasons. First, their incomes are the result of money working for them rather than (as with most of us) them working for money. The primary way they accomplish this is not by laboring for wages, but by selling their excess money at banking institutions; what most Americans call a "loan." Hence, the term loan is a misnomer, for what one is really doing at the bank is not "borrowing" money but buying it; interest on a loan is simply the price one paid for that money. In other words, if one wants to buy, say, $100 (borrow), the bank will demand one pay them back the original $100, plus, say, $10 more as a profit on the sale (a 10% interest rate). Now imagine you are a wealthy lender and you make the above loan expecting a profit of $10 when the loan is paid back. But, unfortunately for you the banker, by the time the loan is paid back, inflation (the money supply) has increased by 10% and eroded your profit margin. That is, though you received $110 from your original "loan" of $100, there's no real profit, since your $110 won't buy any more than your original $100. In short, you failed to make a profit, which was the reason you entered the banking business to begin with.

The second reason why the wealthy depend on a limited money supply (recession) is because this keeps the value of their money high, since dollars in general are scarce during a recession. In short, dollars are like diamonds, and what makes a rock or a piece of paper valuable to people is the fact that there are very few of them. So, if inflation decreases the value of money by increasing its supply, then conversely, recessions increase the value of money by decreasing its supply. This is why the Federal Reserve System, which represents primarily the interests of the wealthy, spends its time promoting recessions and fighting inflation. It is also why the wealthy spend so much energy successfully lobbying the Federal Reserve System, while, at the same time, convincing working Americans, through the media, it is in everybody's interest to fight inflation—and most believe them.

Because the wealthy have been so successful at influencing beliefs, the idea marginal inflation is "bad for the economy" has become one of America's most sacred economic myths. Though this is utter nonsense, the vast majority of Americans will not believe the truth, even if it is proven to them; nonetheless, here goes. Inflation only hurts the creditor but it is an economic windfall for the majority of Americans. As Greider has written about the inflationary 1970s:

> While the [wealthy] suffered loss, the [middle class] enjoyed real gains. Rising prices aggravated everyone, but inflation actually improved the financial status of large classes of ordinary Americans. . . . Inflation particularly benefited the broad middle class of families that owned their own homes, that depended on wages for their income, not on interest and dividends from financial assets. This consequence was familiar to many economists, but not to most ordinary citizens, including many of those whose personal balance sheets were enhanced by inflation. [4]

Or, as Joseph J. Minarik, an economist for the Brookings Institution who authored an exhaustive study of how inflation affects Americans, concluded, "the average-income homeowner is the big winner in inflation. His labor income keeps up with prices, his home appreciates in real terms, and his home mortgage payment does not increase at all."[5] In other words, because of inflation many Americans were able to sell their homes for large **capital gains**; the value of their houses soared but their mortgages remained the same as when they purchased their homes. For example, if someone bought a home for, say, $10,000 in 1970, by 1990, it became worth over $100,000 due to inflation, without any corresponding increase in the owner's $10,000 mortgage. So, even though the value of the home in 1990 is now worth ten times as much as in 1970, the owner only had to pay on a $10,000 loan (mortgage). In short, the owner bought a $100,000 home for $10,000.

Another positive aspect of inflation for most Americans is while everything from wages to prices increase, *debts actually decrease in proportion to the inflation rate.* For an extreme example, imagine charging $100 on a credit card on Monday, but on Tuesday inflation suddenly increases by 50%. Guess what? Your debt has just been cut in half! How did this miraculous event occur? Because inflation, by decreasing the value of each dollar, just reduced the value of your debt by 50%, since each dollar is now worth half of what it was worth when you spent it. In short, you just borrowed twice as much as you will have to pay back.

Inflation also serves the economic interests of the working majority by reducing their dependence on the expensive money of the wealthy since a larger supply of money means the middle class no longer needs to buy (borrow) so much of it. Lastly, and very importantly, inflation also helps level the political playing field by reducing the economic, and thereby the political, gap between the elite few and the working majority. That is, imagine a community of 100 persons in which there are a total of 100 one dollar bills and 10 individuals control close to 70 of these dollars (this is very close to the American economy, by the way). Given this economic situation, ask yourself the following political question: Do you think the rest of this community will be granted the same political respect as these 10 individuals? Now, imagine an "inflationary" monetary policy has just increased the money supply of the other 90 members of this hypothetical community by, say, 100%. Such a change in the money supply would mean the majority would now control close to the same amount of money as those 10 individuals. Hence, inflation has leveled the political playing field by reducing the political influence of this elite group by offsetting their wealth against the collective economic power of the majority. In short, it is a truism of political science that with economic power comes political respect.

The only apparent drawback to inflation for working Americans (and the one thing the wealthy and their cohorts in the media constantly focus the majority's attention on) is the fact prices increase during times of inflation. This occurs because the dollar becomes less valuable during inflation, hence, it takes more of it (higher prices) to buy any given product. Under closer inspection, we will discover rising prices have no real effect on the spending power of working Americans. Why? Well, because inflation, by definition, demands wages keep up with prices for the very same reason prices increased to begin with. In other words, if inflation causes prices to increase due to the lessening value of the dollar, then it stands to reason the *price of labor* (your wages) must also increase at the same rate.[6] If wages do not increase during inflation as they should, then working Americans have not been denied a raise (as so many of them apparently believe) but have in fact taken a pay cut. That is, you are now receiving less in spendable income for each hour worked than you did prior to an increase in the money supply (inflation). So, rising prices due to inflation should be no real concern to working Americans since their wages must increase at the same rate, making it at worst a wash economically speaking.

This is why no professional organization that has experts negotiating their wage contract would ever accept a wage offer without a cost of living adjustment. In the language of finance, a "cost of living adjustment" is referred to as a "COLA." In short, those that know money always make sure that their wages are tied to a COLA, so that their wages keep up with inflation. If a COLA is good for professionals, then one should surmise that COLA's are good for working Americans as well. And, in fact, it is no coincidence that as union membership has decreased among American workers over the last twenty plus years, so have American workers' COLA's, along with their awareness of a COLA's existence and necessity, too.

Let us review: There are at least four primary ways in which inflation actually improves the economic and political position of the vast majority of American citizens.

1. **As price increases are offset by wage increases, all real and estate property appreciates;**

2. **All debts decrease in direct relation to increases in inflation;**

3. **Working Americans become less dependent on "borrowing" money from the wealthy; and,**

4. **Working Americans become much more politically equal since inflation levels the economic playing field by decreasing the income disparity between them and the wealthy few.**

For these reasons Greider has written:

> A social philosopher, searching for a progressive theory of justice, might contemplate the underlying consequences of inflation and conclude that this system was a promising model for social equity. Inflation, after all, discreetly redistributed wealth from creditors to debtors, from those who had an excess to those who had none. It took the most from those who had the largest accumulations of wealth but without subjecting them to real suffering. They were not impoverished, after all, merely made less wealthy.[7]

On the other hand, as we have seen, inflation has dire consequences for the wealthy. In summary, here are the four reasons the wealthy regard inflation as such an economic (and political) evil:

1. **Inflation diminishes their ability to generate income simply by selling their money for a profit since inflation makes it less likely the working majority will need it;**

2. **Inflation reduces the wealthy's profit margin on the loans it does extend;**

3. **Inflation reduces the value of their money by increasing its supply; and,**

4. **Inflation levels the political playing field by dispersing economic strength, and, therefore, political power to the majority.**

For these reasons the wealthy and their faithful servants in the Federal Reserve System fear inflation; and, again, this is why they spend so much money convincing Americans they should fear inflation, too. Because the wealthy have been so successful at this, Americans will accept thousands of themselves losing their jobs and their small businesses in the name of fighting the one thing, which works to their advantage, inflation. It seems Mr. Jefferson's and Mr. Ford's comments are making more and more sense as we go.

We may now begin answering the question that began this section, how does the Federal Reserve System go about regulating monetary policy? The Federal Reserve System manages the money supply by adjusting interest rates (that is, it changes the price of money) and it adjusts deposit requirements of commercial banks and credit unions. Let us look at each these activities separately so as to gain a better understanding of monetary policy.

If the Federal Reserve System believes there is too much money in the economy (inflation) it will simply increase the cost of borrowing it by raising interest rates. Here, the Federal Reserve System applies a basic law of economics (the more expensive something is the less people will be able to afford it) to restrict the amount of money entering the economy. That is, because less people will be able to afford money (interest on a loan, remember, is the price of money), less money will enter into the economy, which will slow the inflation rate. So, by raising interest rates (making money more expensive) the Federal Reserve System has lessened the amount of money entering the economy by suppressing the demand for so-called loans. On those rare occasions when the Federal Reserve System attempts to "loosen" the money supply, to alleviate some of the suffering caused by their recessionary policies, it simply does the opposite: It lowers the cost of money (lower interest rates) so people are able to afford to buy (borrow) more of it, thus increasing the amount of dollars in the economy.

There are two primary interest rates that affect the monetary policy of the United States. They are the Discount Rate and the Federal Funds Rate. Of these two the most influential and important rate is the Federal Funds Rate.

Discount Rate: The Discount Rate (also referred to as "prime credit") is set by the Federal Reserve Board alone. The Discount Rate is charged to commercial banks and other depository institutions on loans they receive from their regional Federal Reserve Bank's lending facility. Most banks are much more likely to borrow from each other so this interest rate has less of an impact on monetary policy than the Federal Funds Rate.

The Federal Funds Rate: The Federal Funds Rate is the interest rate at which commercial banks lend balances to other commercial banks through the Federal Reserve Banks. This is the most important policy tool of the Federal Reserve System and is set by the Federal Open Market Committee. In fact, when the media reports that the Fed has increased or decreased interest rates, the media is almost always referring to the Federal Funds rate and not the Discount Rate.

Moreover, the Federal Funds Rate is not actually "set" by the FOMC, unlike the Discount Rate that is set directly by the Federal Reserve Board. It is more accurate to say that the FOMC influences the Federal Funds Rate, than to say it sets the Federal Funds Rate (that is, decides the exact Federal Funds Rate). The FOMC influences the Federal Funds Rate by its "open market transactions." That is, the FOMC influences the Federal Funds Rate by buying and selling government **securities**. For present purposes, do not worry about what a security actually is; just think of it as any given commodity, like, say, a toaster.[8] Now, if the FOMC thinks there is too much money in the economy (inflation), it will simply sell its toasters (securities) in exchange for the bank's cash, thus removing dollars from the banks. Think about it; when you sell something, you increase your money supply, and when you buy something, you decrease your money supply. The FOMC to control inflation, is simply applying this basic economic principle to the buying and selling of securities. If there is inflation, then it will sell the banks a security to lessen the bank's cash on hand. Of course, if it wants to lessen the severity of a recession, it just reverses the process and buys securities from the banks.

In other words, when the FOMC wants banks to increase the Federal Funds Rate they will sell securities to a bank in exchange for that bank's cash, thereby leaving that bank with less cash to lend than it had before the bank bought those securities. So, that bank will increase its Federal Funds Rate (that is, increase the cost of borrowing from it) so as to weaken the demand on its diminished cash supply. When the FOMC wants to "push" the Federal Funds Rate downward (that is, decrease the Federal Funds Rate) it will buy securities from banks in exchange for cash. In doing so, the FOMC has increased the cash a bank has, which will cause the bank to lower the Federal Funds Rate to encourage other banks to borrow its excessive cash reserves.

Adjusting Deposit Requirements of Banks. Another way the Fed lessens the amount of money entering the economy is to reduce the amount of money banks can sell (lend) to customers. This occurs when the Fed increases the deposit requirement of banks. Imagine a bank that has a total of $100 in deposits, but is required to keep 10% of its total deposits in the vault. This leaves the bank with a net total of $90 to sell (lend) to its customers. If the Fed increases its deposit requirement to 20%, then it has reduced the available pool of money for sale by 10%; or, in other words, the bank went from having $90 to lend to having $80 to lend, reducing the available money from the bank by $10. Again, to mollify recessionary conditions, the Fed will do the opposite and decrease the deposit requirement of banks to stimulate the economy.

Given the political ramifications of monetary policy, why does the Fed primarily concern itself with the economic interests of the wealthy? Why do our elected representatives only appoint people to the Fed who share this bias? And, why is it that they claim to be outside the reach of elected officials? Well, it is because we, the people, let them.

FISCAL POLICY: SMOKE AND MIRRORS

1. What is Fiscal Policy? **Fiscal policy** is, simply stated, to tax and to spend. That is, fiscal policy is the determination of which Americans the government will take money from (tax) and which Americans the government will give money to (spend). This taking of money from some and giving it to others, is the main function of the federal government; the final document which spells out who wins (gets) and who loses (gives) is referred to as the budget.

2. Who Determines Fiscal Policy? Congress and the President share authority over fiscal policy in the American political system. A simplified explanation of the fiscal process (and a strictly constitutional one) states Congress determines tax and spend policy and then submits its plan to the President for approval. However, a much more accurate explanation of the political process of fiscal policy is one which explains it is the President, through the Office of Management and Budget, who actually initiates and formulates the budget and then submits it to Congress for approval. To be sure, Congress can and does modify the budget as it sees fit, nonetheless, once the President became the initiator of fiscal policy he became the main player in the budget process—no matter what the Constitution had intended.

3. How Do Congress and the President Control Fiscal Policy? They accomplish this by exercising their constitutional authority as chief lawmakers and executive respectively. That is, Congress and the President are granted the political authority to make and enforce the laws Americans must obey; and there are no more important laws to write or enforce than the laws which stipulate who in America pays taxes and who in America receives Federal monies. At this point, it would behoove us to divide our discussion of fiscal policy into its two main elements (tax and spend) to best grasp the political realities of the federal budget.

Government can receive money in a variety of ways (from excise taxes to social security taxes) but its main source of revenue, since the ratification of the 16th Amendment in 1913, is the dreaded income tax.[9] There are in essence three possible income tax systems: regressive, progressive, and flat. A regressive tax system is one in which the smaller a person's income the higher percentage of income taxes he or she will pay; a **progressive tax** system is one in which the higher a person's income the higher percentage of income tax is paid; and, a **flat tax** system is one in which all citizens pay the same percentage of tax regardless of income level.

The American income tax system is regressive in nature. This strikes many Americans as incorrect given the large tax bills the wealthy are constantly complaining about; but this is misleading in two ways. First, people very rarely check to see if the wealthy actually pay the amount of taxes they complain they do (most scholars who have looked find their claims grossly distorted).[10] Second, even if they do indeed pay more in income taxes, substantially more, this would in no way prove the American tax system is indeed progressive or even flat. Such a finding is irrelevant as far as identifying the type of tax system the American political system employs because *it focuses on how much tax is paid rather than on what percentage of income was taken*. Let me provide an example: Imagine two citizens, one with an income $100 and the other with an income of $100,000. Now, say we enact a regressive tax system in which the poorer citizen is taxed at a rate of 10% of her income, whereas, the richer of the two is taxed at a rate of 1% of her income. Notice that even though the poorer citizen was taxed at a rate ten times greater than her more fortunate neighbor (a truly regressive system) she, nonetheless, paid "only" $10 in taxes compared to the much richer citizen who paid $1,000 in taxes. Hence, even though the less fortunate citizen was taxed at a rate ten times as great as the wealthy citizen, the better off citizen *by focusing on taxes paid* can argue convincingly she is over taxed in relation to her less fortunate neighbor.

Mark Twain, when quoting Disraeli, once remarked, "There are three kinds of lies: lies, damned lies and statistics."[11] Allow me to demonstrate why he might have been motivated to articulate such an important truth. Say we know the following statistical information to be true—drunken drivers cause 40% of all accidents. Statistically, what is the surest way to make the roads safer? To make the roads safer statistically, all we need to do is get rid of all sober drivers and we will have eliminated 60% of all traffic accidents.[12] The moral of the story? Be careful of statistical arguments, particularly when they try to convince you of something your common sense refutes. (For example, statistics reportedly demonstrating the wealthy are being impoverished by the tax code. If this is true, then why are they still so wealthy while the rest of us cannot seem to get ahead, or even catch up?)

Given the complexity and confusing nature of statistics in general and economic ones in particular, it should come as no surprise to the student of politics that much of the substance of fiscal policy is concerned with protecting the interests of the economic elite while shifting the tab to hard working middle class Americans. As the authors of *America: Who Really Pays the Taxes?* explain:

> For over thirty years, members of Congress and Presidents—Democrats and Republicans alike—have enacted one law after another to create two separate and distinct tax systems: One for the rich and powerful—call it the Privileged Person's Tax Law; another for you and everyone else—call it the Common Person's Tax Law . . . In short, they have taken tax and economic policies that once nurtured the growth of history's largest middle class, and replaced them with policies that are driving the nation toward a two-class society, eroding living standards for most Americans, and causing—for the first time since the Great Depression—a decline in the population [of the middle class].[13]

The authors go on to prove this claim for over 300 nauseating pages, describing in exact detail how the middle class gets poorer and the rich get richer—all thanks to our beloved leaders in Washington and their fiscal policy. To reverse this trend and promote real tax equity, the authors suggest the following reforms:

INCOME: Define income to be taxed in the concise terms of the sixteenth Amendment—"lay and collect taxes on incomes, from whatever source derived." A dollar is a dollar, whether earned in a factory, by speculating in stock options, or by selling real estate. No exceptions. No special treatment for anyone [as the fourteenth Amendment's equal protection clause requires.]

ITEMIZED DEDUCTIONS: Eliminate all itemized deductions from mortgage interests to state and local taxes, from gambling losses to medical expenses. Every exception to tax law, no matter how well intended . . . leads to inequities.

TAX RATES: If all itemized deductions were gone, it would be possible to restore a truly progressive tax structure. The bottom rate, now fixed at 15 percent, could be lowered to 5 percent. The top rate, on the other hand, would be boosted back up to 70 percent—but instead of beginning on taxable income above $250,000, as it does now, it would not kick in until taxable income reached several million dollars. There should be at least a dozen different rates in between, so that people in dissimilar economic situations no longer occupied the same tax bracket. The brackets would be indexed for inflation.

CAPITAL GAINS: Eliminate the preferential rate for capital gains. All capital gains would be taxed as normal income.

EXCEPTIONS: The only exception would be a return to income averaging, so that windfall income in a single year—such as that from the sale of investments held for many years—would not be subject to tax at the highest rate. (This was the original purpose of the capital gains preference.)

CAPITAL GAINS TAX AT DEATH: Impose the income tax on increase in value of all holdings at death.

TAX-EXEMPT SECURITIES: End the tax exemption for local and state government securities. While the community that issues the tax-exempt bonds may benefit because it pays less interest, the cost to the country at large exceeds the savings. And the damage in terms of fairness is incalculable. To ease the anxieties of state and local governments over the loss of tax exemptions, Congress could grant those governments the authority to tax U.S. Treasury securities.

WITHHOLDING: To help curtail tax avoidance, begin withholding on all income—from Wall Street brokerage accounts to interest on savings accounts to stock dividends. And require withholding on everyone—including foreign investors.

PERSONAL EXEMPTION: The only holdover from the current system would be the personal exemption, which would assure people living below the poverty level are not taxed.

SOCIAL SECURITY: Remove Social Security from the unified budget, return it to a pay-as-you-go system, and lower the tax rate from the current 6.2 percent level. At the same time, impose the tax on all wage and salary income, rather than limiting it to $60,600 . . . In addition, raise the retirement age and end payments to people whose other income exceeds, say, two to three times the median family income, but only after they have gotten back what they have paid in.

MEANS TESTING: To reduce conflicts and injustices between generations, begin **means testing** for all government benefits. A Philadelphia physician summed up the issue this way: "I have patients who come to my office in chauffeur-driven limousines. They own three or four homes. And Medicare pays their bills. Does this make sense?"

NEW TAXES: Throughout this century, a wide range of products and services used by low-income and middle-income people have been subject to excise taxes—from the telephone to gasoline. With the exception of a brief period during the Depression, one item has escaped untaxed—Wall Street securities transactions. An excise tax of up to 1 percent should be imposed on the value of all securities and options trading. At the same time, the investment income retirement plans should be taxed. With $3 trillion—that's trillion—in assets, these plans represent the largest pool of untaxed wealth in the country.

CORPORATE TAXES: It might be worth scrapping the entire net-income approach and replacing it with a graduated gross-receipts tax. The tax rates should be set to generate revenue equivalent to 25 percent of total income tax collections from individuals and businesses. In the case of multinational corporations, the tax could be calculated on the formula basis once used by California . . . Such an approach would also render meaningless the tax-avoidance devices used by corporations, such as transfer pricing.[14]

These are the tax remedies the authors suggest. I encourage, no make that beg, each and every American to read their book—but make sure you have antidepressants handy, for it is not a pleasant read.[15] On the other hand, if we fail to educate ourselves about the reality of American tax policy, then, in the words of Congressman Peter DeFazio, we will continue "the days when 130 companies ranging from Aetna to Xerox earned a combined $72.9 billion in pretax domestic profits and, instead of paying taxes, received a total of $6.1 billion in tax rebates."[16] What accounts for this betrayal of the American middle class? Why does Congress refuse to enact real tax reform like that suggested above? Sadly, the authors of *America: Who Really Pays the Taxes?* identify the reason why:

> You will hear a litany of reasons why such a simplified system will never work. Members of the tax industry will tell you so. Members of Congress will tell you so. Special-interest groups will tell you so. [Most] Academicians will tell you so. Economists will tell you so. They have one thing in common: a vested interest in preserving two tax laws—one for the privileged person, whom they represent, and, another for the common person, who has no representation.[17]

Given that the numbers involved in fiscal policy are so enormous, where billions of dollars seem like pennies, most Americans have given up attempting to make sense of their ever increasing tax burden. Let me try to help us all comprehend the reality of these numbers by listing the most pertinent facts regarding American fiscal policy. Let me start by clarifying a distinction that too few Americans are aware of—the difference between the federal deficit and the federal debt; that is, they are not synonyms for the same fiscal reality, even though too many politicians employ them as if they were. The deficit is the total amount the U.S. government spent above and beyond its total tax revenues *for that fiscal year alone,* whereas the federal debt is the total of all previous deficits. Hence, the deficits the U.S. government has run continually—with the exception of just four years—from 1974 to the present has led to a total debt of somewhere in the neighborhood of $11 plus trillion dollars—and the debt just increased by literally millions of dollars by the time you finished reading this paragraph.

Moreover, the U.S. Government makes up the difference between what it receives in taxes and the amount it over spent (that is, creating a deficit between tax revenues and governmental expenditures) by borrowing on the backs of working Americans. They do this by selling so-called **Treasury Bonds** (see Clinton's quote which begins this chapter). So, Americans are not only paying taxes that they will never see any real return on, but are also paying interest to those who have the capital to invest heavily in federal Treasury Bonds, or, in other words, the federal debt. That is, the federal debt has become a well-financed investor's best long-term bet. In short, the super-wealthy are making a fortune on the debt—and not all are even American citizens. In fact, non-American citizens own 40 percent of the U.S. treasury debt.[18] This means that all that interest (or debt service in the language of finance) and principal, all that American capital which could be available to help Americans here at home, is being transferred out of the very hands of those who produced the wealth to foreign investors to do with as they like.

Furthermore, in the fiscal year 2008, interest on the debt (recall this does not include the principal) was a staggering $412 billion dollars. To help us find some fiscal terra firma regarding these colossal numbers, allow me to explain it this way: If interest on the national debt were a government department, it would be second only to the Department of Defense in total expenditures.[19] That is, the only activity of the American federal government that requires more tax money from working Americans than interest on the national debt is the Pentagon.

The Bush Administrations' fiscal policy hardly improved the fiscal situation for those Americans who work for their incomes. In fact since the election of Bush in 2000, "the $5.6 trillion projected budget surplus has turned into a $4 trillion deficit—a $10 trillion dollar turnaround, the worst reversal in U.S. history," according to Congressman, Peter DeFazio.[20] Additionally, the Congressman points out:

> Congressional spending is not the primary cause of the rising federal debt: Sixty percent of the increase is caused by tax cuts, 19 percent is spending on homeland security and the recent wars and 21 percent is related to other . . . nonwar-related defense increases requested by the president. Even if we eliminated all spending on education and social services, we wouldn't come close to balancing the budget. . . . Tax cuts targeted at those most in need can indeed boost the economy. But President Bush's latest tax cut targets only around 20 percent of those making less than $100,000."[21]

In support of these fiscal facts, the *New York Times News Service* recently ran a story with this telling headline: "Incomes of the Wealthiest Rise While Their Income Tax Burden Falls."[22] Moreover, with this type of fiscal policy, coupled with the super-rich friendly monetary policy discussed previously and the American worker adverse trade policy to be discussed shortly, is it any wonder that the same article pointed out that 50 percent of Americans earned "less than $27,682 a year."

As should be evident by this point in the chapter: all aspects of governmental economic policy have an underlying political purpose. For example, monetary policy is designed so as to protect the wealthy from the dreaded peril of the creditor class, inflation. By the way, the Fed has been so successful at this, we now find ourselves in a deep recession with over 3 million net jobs eliminated from the American economy in a little over two years. And we must keep in mind that all three elements of economic policy work in concert to fulfill whatever the political class sets out as its long-term political strategy. And let me be perfectly clear: The long term goal of economic policy in the American governmental scheme is to shift, continually, wealth from those who earn it through work to those who acquire it through shrewd financial maneuvering of choosing the right parents. Hence, one economist, explaining the connection between monetary and fiscal policy, wrote:

> Fiscal policy is effectively off the table, in part because of long-term deficits worsened by [Fed Chairman] Greenspan's own bad advice. Funny how he wasn't sure that Nasdaq 5,000 was a bubble, but believed that 10-year surplus projections were reliable enough to justify a huge tax cut. In any case, serious fiscal action is ruled out by the Bush administration's relentless opportunism; every proposal for short-term stimulus turns into an attempt to lock in permanent tax cuts for corporations and the wealthy.[23]

In other words, recent fiscal policy was not just about tax cuts for the wealthy; it also entailed dismantling what little government programs were left which benefited working Americans. Hence, David S. Broder, of *The Washington Post,* wrote the following stunning column regarding the political agenda of the Bush administration in particular and the Republican Party in general when it comes to fiscal policy:

> Grover Norquist . . . [t]he president of Americans for Tax Reform and influential presiding officer at a famous weekly strategy session of conservative organizations honored *The Washington Post* last week with an op-ed article modestly headlined "Step-by Step Tax Reform." In it, Norquist . . . hailed the Bush administration for pushing through a fresh tax cut in each of his three years in office. It will continue to do so, he said, because this president . . . can operate with confidence that Republican control of Washington will provide him eight years to pursue his economic agenda . . . [this agenda] foresees Bush signing into law measures to abolish the estate tax . . . and the capital gains tax . . . This is hardly speculative. Bush already has seen Congress pass a phaseout of estate taxes and a reduction in capital gains levies . . . With an increase in corporate deductions for capital investment and an end to the alternative minimum tax—designed to catch those individuals who would otherwise shelter all their income—Norquist says the Bush era will eventually produce the conservatives' dream of a flat-rate income tax. When janitors and CEOs have to give up the same share of their paychecks to Uncle Sam, Norquist foresees virtually all voters uniting in a continuing demand for ever-lower rates—and no longer will Democrats be able to advocate tax hikes that target only the top brackets. The consequence of this . . . is a massive rollback in federal revenues and what he regards as the desirable shrinkage of federal services and benefits. In short, the goal is a system of government wiped clean, on both the revenue and spending side, of almost a full century's accumulation of social programs designed to provide a safety net beneath the private economy. When I asked Norquist what had prompted his exercise in candor, he said . . . he saw it as an opportunity to show his fellow conservatives that "We don't have to operate under the radar screen. We can be very open about our agenda." And the White House reaction? "They didn't ask me to do it, but they certainly didn't complain about what I did. I have exchanged several e-mails with [senior political advisor to Bush] Karl Rove since then, and it's never come up."[24]

Moreover, with the results of the 2008 elections, America's fiscal situation is hardly looking to improve with a Democratic administration. As the *Washington Post* reported:

> "President Obama's ambitious plans to cut middle-class taxes, overhaul health care and expand access to college would require massive borrowing over the next decade, leaving the nation mired far deeper in debt than the White House previously estimated, congressional budget analysts said yesterday. In the first independent analysis of Obama's budget proposal, the nonpartisan Congressional Budget Office

concluded that Obama's policies would cause government spending to swell above historic levels even after costly programs to ease the recession and stabilize the nation's financial system have ended. Tax collections, meanwhile, would lag well behind spending, producing huge annual budget deficits that would force the nation to borrow nearly $9.3 trillion over the next decade—$2.3 trillion more than the president predicted when he unveiled his budget request just one month ago . . . the CBO predicts that deficits under his policies would exceed 4 percent of the overall economy over the next 10 years, a level White House budget director Peter R. Orszag yesterday acknowledged would "not be sustainable." The result, according to the CBO, would be an ever-expanding national debt that would exceed 82 percent of the overall economy by 2019—double last year's level—and threaten the nation's financial stability. "This clearly creates a scenario where the country's going to go bankrupt. It's almost that simple," said Sen. Judd Gregg (N.H.), the senior Republican on the Senate Budget Committee, who briefly considered joining the Obama administration as commerce secretary. "One would hope these numbers would wake somebody up," Gregg said . . . The White House's economic assumptions have come under fire for being too optimistic: Over the next decade, the administration projects that the economy will grow at an average annual rate of 2.8 percent, rosier than forecasts by the CBO (2.5 percent) and the Blue Chip economic consensus (2.3 percent) . . . In a speech to state legislators at the White House yesterday, Obama said his budget "makes hard choices about where to save and where to spend" . . . The CBO is the official scorekeeper for budgeting on Capitol Hill, and the new report could complicate efforts to win congressional approval for Obama's $3.6 trillion request for the fiscal year that begins Oct. 1. While Obama had predicted a deficit of nearly $1.2 trillion for 2010, the CBO puts next year's budget gap at nearly $1.4 trillion. And this year's deficit is now projected to soar past $1.8 trillion, or 13 percent of the economy—the deepest well of red ink since the end of World War II."

The *Washington Post* article concludes with a comment about why Obama's fiscal plan is so deep in red ink. In doing so, the article also serves as a sad, but accurate, indicator of what both major political parties' inability to practice sound fiscal policy has done to America's present financial reality:

"Deteriorating economic conditions are a major cause of the darkening fiscal picture, according to the CBO. But other factors also are weighing heavily on the budget this year and next. For example, the $700 billion financial-system bailout is now expected to cost taxpayers at least $350 billion, by CBO estimates, because the investments the Treasury Department has made in banks and other financial institutions are worth considerably less than when the bailout was approved. In addition, Obama proposes to use a portion of the money to buy down troubled mortgages, a program that will provide no return to the taxpayer." [25]

TRADE POLICY: THE EXPORTING OF AMERICAN PROSPERITY

1. What Is Trade Policy? Trade policy is the federal government's regulation of the flow of goods and capital across America's borders. Consumer goods which exit the

United States are called exports; consumer goods which enter the nation are referred to as imports. The United States has been regulating imports and exports since the nation's inception.

2. Who Regulates Imports and Exports in the American Political System? Strictly speaking, the constitutional authority over trade policy resides with Congress. Nevertheless, like with so much of present politics, actual governing authority has migrated elsewhere. Today, control over trade policy is exercised by federal bureaucracies under the direction of the President if it is exercised by the United States government at all. Although federal bureaucracies have always played a significant role in the formulation of trade policy, their role was greatly amplified under the New Deal Democrats of the 1930s and has continued to grow ever since.[26] With the approval of the North American Free Trade Agreement (NAFTA) in 1993, and the **General Agreement on Tariffs and Trade (GATT)** in 1994, the Office of U.S. Trade Representative became the dominant **bureaucracy regulating trade**. The Office of U.S. Trade Representative is treated as a cabinet-level bureaucracy and works directly under the authority of the White House. However, trade policy is not the sole purview of the federal government, as much of its regulatory authority has been ceded to various international trade organizations. For example, with the establishment of GATT, trade matters affecting the member nations now reside with the newly created **World Trade Organization (WTO)**, which has the authority to decide when violations occur and what punishments they entail. In effect, the United States is no longer sovereign when it comes to matters of international trade.

This forfeiture of national sovereignty has led many critics to question the democratic ramifications of this new world order. As Ralph Nader has written:

> It is hard enough when people in local communities have to defer to the state government, or when the state government has to defer to the federal government. But it is quite another order of democratic surrender to defer to trade agreement bureaucracies, where the decisions are made by unaccountable members of tribunals in Geneva, Rome, or elsewhere.[27]

William Greider has also commented on this new political reality:

> For Americans, this is a new experience, profoundly at odds with national history and democratic legacy. We are now, suddenly, a nation whose citizens can no longer decide their own destiny . . . American politics, in other words, is moving offshore. The nature of global economy pushes every political debate in that direction—further and further away from the citizens . . . Arguments that were once decided, up or down, in the public forums of democratic debate are now floating off into the murk of international diplomacy and deal making. They are to be decided in settings where neither American citizens nor their elected representatives can be heard, where no institutional rules exist to guarantee democratic access and accountability.[28]

And, if this seems like so much hyperbole, let me conclude this section with a reminder by Greider on the political magnitude of this issue. He writes:

> If democracy is to retain any meaning, Americans will need to draw a hard line in defense of their own national sovereignty. This is not just about protecting American

jobs, but also about protecting the very core of self-government—laws that are fashioned in open debate by representatives who are directly accountable to the people.[29]

3. How Is Trade Regulated? The United States, like most governments, can influence the flow of goods in two ways. The first way to regulate trade is by the use of governmental tariffs; tariffs are essentially taxes on imported goods. Tariffs are an extremely effective way of protecting the wages of working Americans as they level the economic playing field with imported goods from low wage nations. By bringing the price of low wage, imported goods in line with the high wage, domestic goods, products compete on quality grounds rather than by price advantage brought about through labor exploitation. In 1907, Theodore Roosevelt, in his seventh address to Congress, expressed this basic maxim of wage economics: "There must always be as a minimum a tariff . . . which will at least make good the difference in the cost of production here and abroad; that is, the difference in labor cost here and abroad, for the well-being of the wage-worker must ever be a cardinal point of American policy."[30] Abraham Lincoln, with his usual brilliant brevity, echoed the point: "Give us a protective tariff, and we will have the greatest country on earth."[31] Moreover, experience has shown that the price of consumer goods does not increase in times of high tariffs, as is so often argued by proponents of free trade. A quick review of the history of the **Consumer Price Index** (CPI) clearly shows that the largest increase in prices has occurred with the expansion of non-tariff, free trade agreements. According to the U.S. Bureau of Labor, consumer prices, as measured against the 1967 dollar, increased an astonishing 225% since the early 1980s when the government began removing tariffs on imported goods.[32] Nonetheless, defenders of free trade continue to claim tariffs have negative consequences for consumer prices.

The second way to regulate trade is by placing **non-tariff trade barriers** on imported goods. Non-tariff trade barriers are just what they sound like, they place certain non-monetary restrictions on imports. Examples of non-tariff trade barriers would be prohibiting the importation of agricultural goods with too much pesticides or consumer products which fail to meet certain child safety measures. As mentioned above, today such non-tariff trade barriers could be found unlawful by any number of international trade organizations. For instance, in 1991 the Mexican government filed a challenge with the WTO over a U.S. trade barrier preventing the importation of tuna caught in mile-long nets which were killing over 100,000 dolphins a year.[33] The dolphins were being drowned and crushed mostly by commercial tuna fleets from Mexico, Venezuela, Vanuatu, Ecuador, and Panama. Mexico claimed any import restriction on this tuna constituted an illegal trade barrier in violation of GATT. Meeting in Geneva, the WTO agreed and ordered the lifting of the ban in August 1991. Moreover, since that time the United States has lost 80% of the cases in which it has been the defendant before the WTO tribunals, and the WTO has ruled against the United States in more than 90% of the cases tried against Asian countries.[34]

Today, any trade policy that calls for tariffs and non-tariff barriers is dismissed by most members of the national parties, the media, and establishment economists, as protectionist and economically faulty. No matter that just such a protectionist policy was endorsed by such American luminaries as Washington, Hamilton, Madison, Jackson, Lincoln and T. Roosevelt. No matter that even Jefferson came to see the error of his own free trade views and refuted them in favor of protectionist policy. To the modern economic sophisticate, the age of protectionism is over; modern economic conditions call for an unqualified support for free trade policies. But before we examine if the facts support this unbridled enthusiasm for free trade, let us first look more closely at the concept.

The core principle of free trade policy is to remove impediments to the free flow of goods and services between nations.[35] That is to say, free trade proponents hope to create a unified, or, in the words of the corporate establishment, harmonized, world economic community by removing all tariffs and non-tariff barriers. In this way, political borders bow to the needs of global capital. If, for example, a corporation wants to relocate its production facilities offshore, then it should be free to do so. Moreover, there should be no trade barriers obstructing its ability to import goods back into the nation it just abandoned. To the proponents of free trade, the idea of patriotism is as silly and obsolete as the notion of protectionism. Gulf and Western CEO, Martin S. Davis, declares. "all such allegiances are viewed as expendable under the new rules."[36] When asked about the problem of American working people, the president of NCR, Gilbert Williamson, arrogantly exclaimed: "I was asked the other day about U.S. competitiveness, and I replied that I don't think about it at all. We at NCR think of ourselves as a globally competitive company that happens to be headquartered in the United States."[37] Carl A. Gerstacker of the Dow Chemical Company said: "I have dreamed of buying an island owned by no nation and of establishing the World Head Quarters of the Dow Company on the truly neutral ground of such an island, beholden to no nation or society." As Patrick Buchanan has pointed out, it is America he is dreaming of being rid of.[38] A spokesman for Union Carbide proclaimed: "It is not proper for an international corporation to put the welfare of any country in which it does business above that of any other."[39] Microsoft alone has invested hundreds of millions dollars into India's training and workforce development since just 2003. *The Times of India* estimates that work on Microsoft products constitutes nearly a quarter of the $8 billion dollars worth of outsourced work done in India.[40] An obviously sophisticated reporter from the *Washington Post* approvingly summarized these thoughts: "The modern corporation looks first to satisfying customers and to rolling up profits—forget the salute to the flag."[41] One cannot help but wonder why these corporations never forget to wave the flag whenever they need the assistance of the U.S. armed forces or a tax break at the expense of the American worker. Former Secretary of Labor, Robert Reich, captures the sad truth when he writes: "Gone is the connection between the company, its community, even its country."[42]

Free trade advocates argue this is all beside the point, it is in the realm of economics, after all, not politics, in which free trade carries the day. Free trade, they argue, brings such overwhelming economic benefits only the thick-headed would allow for its obstruction on political grounds. According to free trade orthodoxy, free trade has the following economic benefits:

- Competition spurs innovation, raises productivity, and lowers prices.
- The division of labor allows specialization, which raises productivity and lowers prices.
- The bigger the production unit, the greater the division of labor and specialization, thus the greater the benefits.

Or, as one economist states:

> Proponents of free trade argue that it fosters growth by removing artificial barriers, thus rewarding efficient firms. All nations benefit. Without tariffs and subsidies, countries specialize in goods they make cheaply. Higher efficiency means lower prices, so workers see their purchasing power grow. While some people lose their jobs in the shakeup that follows newly liberalized trade, other jobs open in expanding industries. In the case of North America, by further opening Mexico's consumer market to imports, NAFTA will supposedly create hundreds of thousands of export-related jobs in the United States and Canada. So the theory goes. In the real world; however, the touted benefits won't necessarily come to pass.[43]

We have already seen how one touted benefit has not come to pass—the promise of lower consumer prices. In fact, free trade policies do nothing to lower consumer prices and have tended to raise them substantially (compare, for example, the price of a Nike shoe with a domestic brand for a real world example of this phenomenon). To be sure, with the expansion of free trade policies in the 1990s, corporate profits, not to mention the stock market, had never been healthier. But this economic "boom" did not trickle down to the majority of Americans who depended on wages to feed their families. It seems free trade consistently delivered only one price reduction—the price of labor.

If we look beyond the promises of free trade theory, we will discover the reality of what it has wrought. By examining the economic facts, the stark and often ugly economic truths, we will be compelled to confront the dark underbelly of the so-called "benefits" of free trade. CNN commentator, Lou Dobbs, in his superb book, *Exporting America: Why Corporate Greed is Shipping American Jobs Overseas*, details the havoc so-called "free trade" has wrought on working Americans.[44] Here are just a few of the facts that Mr. Dobbs provides:

- From 2000–2004, employment in the US auto industry dropped by 200,000 jobs. During that same time, imports of Chinese auto parts doubled.
- Today, 96% of all clothing purchased in the United States is now imported.
- $750,000,000 billion dollars' worth of goods comes into the United States on ships each year, but not one of the top ten international shipping companies is American-owned.

- According to the Economic Policy Institute, the average American worker has added 199 hours to a year's work since 1973, while wages for that same time period have remained stagnant or have fallen.
- Forrester Research estimates that $151.2 billion in wages will be shifted from the United States to lower-wage countries by 2015.
- 40 state governments are now outsourcing government jobs to foreign nationals.
- While wages in the United States have remained stagnant for the past three decades, CEO compensation has risen astronomically, now amounting to about 400 times what the average employee earns.
- The world's former greatest creditor nation has now become history's greatest debtor nation.
- Net imports of petroleum are expected to rise to 68% of demand by 2025.
- In 2004, Wal-Mart alone imported nearly $15 billion in goods from China. In fact, Wal-Mart as a single company is China's fifth largest export market in the world.
- The Economic Policy Institute estimates that 99% of our **trade deficit** comes from goods we now buy overseas because we no longer make them in the United States.
- Around 80% of the toys Americans buy are now foreign-made (I'll have more to say about this below).
- Service sector jobs now account for over 60% of the employment in the United States, compared to 14% for manufacturing.
- A.T. Kearney predicts that 500,000–700,000 financial services jobs will go offshore by 2008.

Moreover, its not just America's economic future that US trade policy has endangered. With the political systems' rush to outsource America's high-wage jobs has come the importation of seriously dangerous low-quality goods into America. For example, as *The New York Times* reported in 2007:

> The head of a Chinese company that was behind the recall earlier this month of more than a million Mattel toys committed suicide over the weekend, China's state-controlled media reported today . . . The death is the latest development in a year filled with prominent recalls and product safety scandals involving goods that were made in China.
>
> Mattel, which makes Barbie dolls and Hot Wheels cars, recalled more than a million toys worldwide after discovering that they were coated with lead paint. The recall was one of the largest this year and included 83 types of toys, including Sesame Street and Dora the Explorer characters made under the Fisher-Price brand and sold worldwide.
>
> A string of troubling recalls of Chinese-made products this year has heightened trade tensions between the United States and China and created a public relations

disaster for China, whose economy and trade surpluses are growing at a blistering pace.

Experts here say many Chinese factory owners—often under intense pressure to lower production costs—cut corners in making products and regularly use cheap and illegal substitutes. And indeed, in several of the recalls involving China this year, the government says companies intentionally used cheap or illegal substitutes.

For instance, after the United States announced one of the largest pet food recalls in history, Chinese regulators said they found that two makers of food ingredients here intentionally added an industrial chemical called melamine into the feed to save money and artificially increase the protein count. Instead, they created a toxic potion that sickened or killed thousands of animals . . .

China now makes about 80 percent of the world's toys and many of the world's biggest brand name companies, including Mattel, Hasbro and McDonald's, use contract toy manufacturers in China.[45]

Finally, here is a list of America's fifteen highest trade deficits by country. Before looking at the list, let me explain what a trade deficit means. When the US sells a product to another country that product is an export, when the US buys a product from a foreign country that is an import. When any country sells more than it buys from foreign countries, that country is running a trade surplus, meaning they made more money on exports than they lost buying imports. However, when a country buys more imports than it sells exports that country is running a trade deficit. So, the numbers below show that the United States is buying a lot more goods from foreign countries than we are selling to them. Another way to look at this is to understand that by the time the US has imported and exported to the countries listed below the US economy has lost a total of $718 billion dollars to its so-called "trading partners" during the 2007 year alone.

The list below shows America's deficit amounts for its top 15 trading partners in 2007.

1. China . . . US$259.1 billion (up 11.4% from 2006, up 59.9% from 2004)
2. Japan . . . $83.1 billion (down 6.1%, up 10.5%)
3. Mexico . . . $74 billion (up 15.4%, up 64.4%)
4. Canada . . . $65 billion (down 10.7%, down 1%)
5. Germany . . . $44.5 billion (down 6.9%, down 2.8%)
6. Nigeria . . . $28.9 billion (up 12.5%, up 97.3%)
7. Venezuela . . . $28.4 billion (up 0.6%, up 40.4%)
8. Saudi Arabia . . . $24.5 billion (up 1.8%, up 57.3%)
9. Ireland . . . $21.6 billion (up 7.5%, up 12.5%)
10. Italy . . . $20.9 billion (up 3.7%, up 20.4%)
11. Malaysia . . . $20.8 billion (down 13.2%, up 20.4%)

12. France . . . $14.5 billion (up 12.5%, down 36.9%)

13. South Korea . . . $13.6 billion (up 2.5%, down 31.5%)

14. Taiwan . . . $12.7 billion (down 16.7%, down 1.9%)

15. United Kingdom . . . $6.7 billion (down 16.8%, down 36%).[46]

It seems free trade is not free after all. Or, to put it another way, it seems only the select few have enjoyed a free ride while the rest of us have paid dearly for their privilege. Upon closer inspection, it turns out the issue was never an academic issue over free trade versus protectionist economic theory. It seems the real issue—as it always is in politics—concerned who got protected. According to Congressman DeFazio, it certainly wasn't the American public who were the beneficiaries of these economic policies. Hence, he writes, "I fear for the financial stability of the United States. The threat posed by the rapidly accelerating twin federal deficits—the budget and the trade deficit—has grown so grave that our nation teeters on the brink of financial catastrophe."[47]

FINAL THOUGHTS

The word economics comes from the Greek word "oikonomia," meaning the management of the household and husbandry of its valuable assets.[48] How far we have come from this more morally defensible, not to mention common sense, definition of economics. To think economic health used to be measured by the health of one's family, one's household, rather than by the theorems of some well-financed economist. Economic orthodoxy has become so disconnected from daily life, so esoteric, it can declare the economy booming even when most of our individual households are hurting. How did our political system become a party to this irrationality? More importantly, what can be done about it? After reading this chapter, it will be understandable if you believe Ford was right all along—what the country requires is indeed a good old fashioned revolution. However, this revolution need not be a bloody and violent act, only a peaceful and political one. That is, the only revolutionary act required of Americans to regain control over their economic lives is to elect representatives who will make it happen.

NOTES

1. Quoted in Wickliffe B. Vennard, Sr., *The Federal Reserve Hoax,* privately published, circa 1962. Just one of many works of interest highly critical of the Federal Reserve Board that can be found in the Federal Reserve Board library.
2. William Greider, *Secrets of the Temple: How the Federal Reserve Runs the Country* (New York: Simon & Schuster, 1987), p. 53.
3. The title for this section is borrowed from Greider's book, *Secrets of the Temple.*
4. Grieder, *Secrets of the Temple,* p. 41.
5. Joseph J. Minarik, "The Distributional Effects of Inflation and Their Implications," in *Stagflation: The Causes, Effects and Solutions,* Joint Economic Committee, U.S. Congress, 1980.
6. This is known in the lexicon of economics as the "wage-price spiral."

7. Grieder, *Secrets of the Temple*, p. 44.
8. There are three types of governmental securities: Treasury bills (which mature in one year); Treasury notes (which mature in five years); and Treasury bonds (which mature in 30 years).
9. Office of Management and Budget, Press Office, 1992.
10. See for example, Donald L. Barlett and James B. Steele, *America: Who Really Pays the Taxes?* (New York: Simon & Schuster, 1994).
11. From Mark Twain's *Autobiography* (New York: Oxford University Press, 1996): "Figures often beguile me, particularly when I have the pleasure of arranging them myself; in which case the remark attributed to Disraeli would often apply with justice and force: 'There are three kinds of lies: lies, damned lies and statistics.'"
12. I am indebted to Craig Carr, professor of political science, Portland State University, for this statistical analogy.
13. Barlett and Steele, *America: Who Really Pays the Taxes?*, p.14.
14. Ibid., pp. 338-340.
15. In addition, read Martin Gross, *The Tax Racket*.
16. Peter DeFazio, "Lonely Opposition," *The Oregonian* (October 12, 1998) p. C8.
17. Barlett and Steele, *America: Who Really Pays the Taxes?*, p. 342.
18. Peter DeFazio, "Twin Deficits Put America on the Brink," *The Oregonian*, (June 26, 2003) p. C11.
19. Source Congressional Quarterly and Congressional Budget Office, *The Oregonian*, (March 8, 2003) p. A7.
20. Peter DeFazio, "Twin Deficits Put America on the Brink" *The Oregonian*, (June 26, 2003) p. C11.
21. Ibid
22. David Cay Johnston, (June 26, 2003) p.A6.
23. Paul Krugman, "Greenspan Evades Wall Street Responsibility," *The Oregonian*, (September 4, 2002), p. C9
24. "Grover Norquist's Vision for America," *The Oregonian*, (June 18, 2003) p. D7.
25. Lori Montgomery, "Deficit Projected To Swell Beyond Earlier Estimates: CBO Expects Trillions More in Borrowing," *Washington Post*, (March 21, 2009), p. A01.
26. Patrick Buchanan, *The Great Betrayal: How American Sovereignty and Social Justice are Being Sacrificed to the Gods of the Global Economy* (Boston: Little, Brown and Company, 1998), p.33.
27. Ralph Nader, "Introduction: Free Trade & The Decline of Democracy," in *The Case Against Free Trade: GATT, NAFTA, and the Globalization of Corporate Power* (San Francisco: Earth Island Press and North Atlantic Books, 1993) p.11.
28. William Greider, "The Global Marketplace: A Closet Dictator," in *The Case Against Free Trade: GATT, NAFTA, and the Globalization of Corporate Power*, pp. 204–205.
29. Ibid., p. 208.
30. Patrick Buchanan, *The Great Betrayal: How American Sovereignty and Social Justice are Being Sacrificed to the Gods of the Global Economy*, p. 302.
31. Ibid., p. 157.
32. Ibid., p. 64.
33. See for a thorough discussion of this event David Phillips, "Dolphins and GATT," in *The Case Against Free Trade: GATT, NAFTA, and the Globalization of Corporate Power*, pp. 133–138.
34. Lou Dobbs, *Exporting America: Why Corporate Greed is Shipping American Jobs Overseas*, (New York: Time Warner Book Group, 2004), p.142.
35. For an excellent discussion on the essence of free trade theory see Lori Wallach, "Hidden Dangers of GATT and NAFTA," in *The Case Against GATT, NAFTA, and the Globalization of Corporate Power*, pp. 23–64.
36. Patrick Buchanan, *The Great Betrayal: How American Sovereignty and Social Justice are Being Sacrificed to the Gods of the Global Economy*, p. 98.
37. Ibid., p. 99.
38. Ibid., p. 105.

39. Ibid., p. 105.
40. Lou Dobbs, *Exporting America: Why Corporate Greed is Shipping American Jobs Overseas*, pp. 88–89
41. Patrick Buchanan, *The Great Betrayal: How American Sovereignty and Social Justice are Being Sacrificed to the Gods of the Global Economy*, p. 99.
42. Ibid. p. 93.
43. Thea Lee, "Happily Never NAFTA: There's No Such Thing as a Free Trade," in *The Case Against GATT, NAFTA, and the Globalization of Corporate Power*, p. 71.
44. Lou Dobbs, *Exporting America: Why Corporate Greed is Shipping American Jobs Overseas*.
45. David Barboza, "Head of Chinese Toy Company Said to Kill Himself," *The New York Times*, (August 13, 2007)
46. This list presents independent calculations and insights based on data drawn from the CIA World Factbook and the U.S. Census Bureau—Foreign Trade Statistics (annualized for 2007 based on statistics on year-to-date data to November 2007).
47. Peter DeFazio, "Twin Deficits Put America on the Brink" *The Oregonian,* (June 26, 2003) p. C11.
48. This definition comes from William Greider, *One World, Ready or Not: The Manic Logic of Global Capitalism* (New York: Simon & Schuster, 1997), p. 444.

CHAPTER 7
Foreign Policy: Minding the Empire

"I have always given it as my decided opinion that no nation has a right to intermeddle in the internal concerns of another."
—George Washington

"I have deemed it fundamental for the United States never to take an active part in the quarrels of Europe. . . . They are nations of eternal war."
—Thomas Jefferson

"Military glory—that attractive rainbow that rises in showers of blood."
—Abraham Lincoln

"You will kill ten of our men, and we will kill one of yours, and in the end it will be you who tire of it."
—Ho Chi Minh

INTRODUCTION

Needless to say, America has not heeded the advice of its first president regarding the proper role for the United States in world affairs. Some political scientists claim it was necessary for the government of the United States to pursue a more active role in world events, given America's historic role as torch bearer for freedom and democracy. Still, other scholars claim, that in diverging from Washington's advised path, the U.S. government has become another in a long line of morally corrupt, aging empires exploiting its weaker neighbors in the international community. Other scholars, however, would argue the truth lies somewhere between these two extremes, with an accent, nonetheless, on the U.S. government's tendency to favor exploitation over democracy in its foreign policy.

This chapter will follow the lead of the critics of American foreign policy by flavoring its analysis with this last interpretation of American foreign policy. In doing so, this chapter will introduce the reader to some of the political complexity that entangles American foreign policy and helps explain its exploitative nature. To this end, we will use the same approach as the proceeding chapter and simplify our analysis by asking three basic questions about foreign policy: What is the purpose of foreign policy? Who controls foreign policy? And, how do they go about executing foreign policy?

WHAT IS THE PURPOSE OF FOREIGN POLICY?

Foreign policy can be differentiated from domestic policy by the common sense observation that foreign policy is focused on activity outside the borders of the United States. However, before we begin evaluating American foreign policy, we must first state explicitly the two purposes that, at a minimum, legitimize the exercise of the United States government's foreign policy capabilities. The most minimal moral standard that justifies the necessary loss of American life, liberty, and property, which supporting foreign policy may entail, is either:

1. to protect the territorial integrity of the United States; and/or,

2. to promote the American standard of living.

Again, these are the most minimal ends that justify the expenditure of American lives and resources. And, it is with this in mind, that we will gauge the appropriateness of American foreign policy. Therefore, by identifying the main actors who influence American foreign policy, and by tracing a relatively recent history of American foreign policy, this chapter will expose some of the less savory aspects of America's international activities. This will entail examining foreign policy from a critical perspective while keeping in mind some obvious and basic questions of American foreign policy. For example, how did supporting such regimes as the **Taliban** in the 1990s or Saddam's Iraq in the 1980s protect America? And how are we promoting the American standard of living by mortgaging our financial futures fighting wars in Afghanistan and Iraq? What possible benefit is there for America to be destabilizing North Korea? And how can we afford to continue to be militarily deployed in dozens of countries while the nation keeps deficit spending with many of America's lenders being foreign interests or governments? Furthermore, contrary to popular opinion, those who raise these issues are not enemies of the United States; they are rather the true heirs of its founding principles. As George Washington warned, "a free people ought to . . . avoid the necessity of those overgrown military establishments which, under any form of government, are inauspicious to liberty."[1] Or as Thomas Jefferson wrote to James Madison when discussing the proper role for a military in a democracy, "it is better . . . to abolish standing armies in times of peace" and "if no check can be found to keep the number of standing troops within safe bounds, while they are tolerated as far as necessary, abandon them all together . . . "[2]

These early American leaders were very much aware of the sad history of democratic governments. A history that clearly reveals a simple yet profound truth concerning standing armies and democratic regimes: A large military establishment, no matter how benign in its formulation, will eventually demand the country serve it and not the other way around. And, for much of the country's history, the government seemed to respect this political wisdom. Hence, before the advent of the so-called "Cold War" with the Soviet Union, America maintained, particularly in relation to today's military levels, what could only be described as a minimal defense capability. To be sure, the military grew during times of war but would always quickly shrink back to the necessary minimum immediately afterwards. For example, as soon as General Lee surrendered to General Grant at Appomattox Court House to end the Civil War, the army went from more than two million soldiers to an army of less than 25,000 men, and this is while it was busy fighting the so-called "Indian Wars" of the late 19th century.[3] The phenomenon of the American military growing only when the country was at war and quickly demobilizing afterwards continued up until the end of the Second World War. This changed, however, when the foreign policy establishment used the Cold War as justification for taking a permanent and prominent position in the post-WWII American political system.

A complete explanation for this dramatic shift in American foreign policy is much beyond the scope of this chapter. Suffice it to say, this increase in the American military presence was not solely motivated by concerns for protecting America from the threat of the "evil empire." Some of it was motivated by the fact that a well placed investment in the arms industry could turn a handsome profit given the public's fear of the communist threat and their corresponding enthusiasm for increasing the defense budget accordingly. This combination of fear and profit created the necessary political recipe to help create what was soon coined the "military-industrial complex" (which will be discussed in much greater detail later in this chapter). This term refers to both the growth and entanglement of weapons manufacturers and related industries with America's foreign policy establishment. In one of the amazing stories of empire building, America grew from a small rural nation in 1789, with an original foreign policy establishment consisting of twelve bureaucrats in the State and War departments[4] and an army of 3,000 men,[5] into an industrial super power equipped with a military empire so vast its "fleets roamed all the seas, her military bases extended around the earth's periphery, her soldiers stood guard from Berlin to Okinawa, and her alliances spanned the earth."[6] And, of course, this empire was built with the blood of the American soldier and the money of the American taxpayer. We will now turn our attention to those actors who have the authority in the American political system to determine where the bodies are sent and where the tax dollars are spent.

WHO CONTROLS FOREIGN POLICY IN THE AMERICAN POLITICAL SYSTEM?

The President

Any discussion of American foreign policy must begin and end with the president of the United States. As one student of American politics states:

> [I]t is quite true that of a President's substantive powers, only one—more through tradition and the accidental attrition of congressional power than through law—approaches the absolutism of one-man rule. This is his power that comes through the creation of foreign policy.[7]

As this quote mentions, pure constitutional theory declares the president shall share foreign power authority with Congress, but actual political practice has dictated that the president shares this power with no one. This is why the designers of the Constitution, when attempting to convince Americans to accept it, wrote that the president's foreign policy authority:

> [W]ould amount to nothing more than the supreme command and direction of the military and naval forces . . . while that of the British king extends to the *declaring* of war and to the *raising* and *regulating* of fleets and armies—all which, by the Constitution under consideration, would appertain to the [Congress]. [italics original][8]

While a more contemporary scholar claims, "the President can deploy the Armed Forces and order them into active operation. In an age of missiles and hydrogen warheads, his powers are as large as the situation requires."[9] Or as another political scientist stated, though the president does not exercise his foreign policy authority in a political vacuum:

> [T]he operational realities—the advanced state of weaponry and the unrelenting persistence and impatience of international adversaries who are not bound by the constraints of constitutional democracy—require that he be accorded ample latitude to act independently and often secretly.[10]

That is, though the Constitution stipulates that Congress shall declare war and appropriate funds for its execution as a check on the president's war-making authority, political reality has determined that this constitutional check is no check at all.

History has shown a president can easily manipulate Congress into financially supporting his foreign policy initiatives with clever political maneuvering. For example, when President Theodore Roosevelt wished to show off the new American Navy to impress the world, Congress refused to fund his excursion so he notified them that he had enough money previously appropriated to send the boys halfway around the world; if the lawmakers wanted the fleet back home, they would have to provide the money for the return trip—and they did.[11] Imagine, for instance, a congressperson explaining to the people that the constitutional principle of separation-of-powers demands that she force the soldiers in, say, Iraq, to fight without the necessary financial support to buy ammunition, food, and air support. Her argument may be constitutionally correct, but it would also be political suicide—and presidents know it. As the authors of a book on the presidency wrote:

> Historical practice . . . has resulted in a vast expansion of presidential authority to use force at the expense of the powers of Congress. The dominance of the President in this regard has been almost total in wartime . . . [and] the result has been the continual aggrandizement of presidential power.[12]

The best historical evidence of this aggrandizement of presidential power is the fact that only five of the over two hundred foreign military adventures the United States has been involved in have been constitutionally declared by Congress.[13] In short, Congress' check on the president's foreign policy authority becomes (like so much in American politics) nothing more than another constitutional sacrifice at the altar of political necessity.

In closing, let me emphasize again that any discussion on American foreign policy must begin and end with the president of the United States. He is, so to speak, the top taco, el mucky muck, and grand pooh-bah, all rolled into one. On a more serious note, when it comes to the president and foreign policy, it is no exaggeration to say he has the world at his fingertips.

The National Security Council

With the onset of the Cold War in 1947, Congress created a bureaucratic institution to help further streamline the president's domination of foreign policy in the American political system. This bureaucracy is the **National Security Council, or NSC** for short. The president, with the help of the vice-president, chairs it. These two theoretically represent the concerns of the public who elected them. Other members include: The Secretary of State, who represents the American diplomatic community; the Secretary of Defense, who represents the military community; the Secretary of the Treasury, who represents American economic interests; the Director of National Intelligence, who represents the intelligence community; the Chairman of the Joint Chiefs of Staff, who represents the tactical advice of the individual armed services; and a National Security Advisor and his staff to help implement the plans of the council. The NSC is the main institutional authority on forming and implementing foreign policy for the U.S. Government. The NSC, while allowing the president to respond much more quickly to immediate danger from foreign enemies by bypassing the rigors of congressional approval or the bureaucratic morass of the State and Defense departments, may also lead the president into trouble due to its expediency. For instance, it was while a member of the NSC staff that Col. Oliver North committed an allegedly criminal act by setting up an independent source of funding for the Executive Branch by selling arms to Iran to generate cash to help buy weapons for the so-called "contras" of Nicaragua. These activities violated the expressed wishes of Congress, and have come down to us in history as the "Iran-Contra Affair." Nonetheless, for better or for worse, the NSC is now the headquarters of the American foreign policy establishment.

The Military-Industrial Complex

As mentioned earlier, the term "military-industrial complex" refers to the incestuous relationship between the government and weapons related industries. This relationship is one in which various weapons manufactures make the majority of their profits selling weapons to the federal government while the politicians who keep the government contracts coming are guaranteed nice campaign contributions and post-political career opportunities from the weapons industry in return. Since the beginning of the Cold War in the late 1940s, the military-industrial complex has been one of the main actors influencing American foreign policy—and not everyone sees this involvement as healthy for America. As President Eisenhower, who, by the way, was also the Supreme Allied Commander during WWII, cautioned Americans when leaving the White House after two terms at the height of the Cold War:

> The conjunction of an immense military establishment and a large arms industry is new in the American experience. . . . In the councils of government, we must guard against the acquisition of unwarranted influence, whether sought or unsought, by the military-industrial complex. The potential for the disastrous rise of misplaced power exists and will persist.[14]

Please note the word "new" in President Eisenhower's speech. As mentioned earlier, contrary to what many contemporary so-called conservatives claim, a huge military establishment is not what made America great, but rather, it was the lack of any such public and private military entanglements that kept America democratic. This is why the Founders cautioned against standing armies in America. They were well aware of the basic maxim of political science that the freedom of a democratic people is in inverse relation to the size of its military—the smaller the military establishment the freer the people. In short, the Founders, Eisenhower, and many other concerned Americans, feared that by wedding a corporation's profit motive with the nation's security needs, America would be creating a recipe for both financial and constitutional disaster. And, as even a cursory review of America's recent foreign policy history and financial situation would indicate, these fears seem to be more than justified as they border on the prophetic.

Nonetheless, with the rise of the Cold War and its nuclear realities, the arms industry and their political lackeys had the perfect excuse to reject the wisdom of our Founders and begin building up America's war-making capabilities. Hence, they kept up a constant public relations campaign designed to create a political climate dominated by the premise that the country was now confronted with such a severe security risk it could no longer afford to worry about things like constitutional restrictions or rising taxes. Most Americans believed this government sponsored campaign declaring that the Cold War had created a world rife with danger, where nuclear devastation was always just a missile launch away, and, therefore, accepted their ever-increasing tax bills as a necessary price of security. Many Americans, however, did not. They questioned the constant clamoring of military peril emanating from the very politicians and industries whose pocketbooks were being lined with the tax dollars appropriated to prevent them. One such American, General Douglas MacArthur, best summarized the thoughts of all these concerned Americans, when in 1952, he said:

> Indeed, it is part of the general pattern of misguided policy that our country is now geared to an arms economy which was bred in an artificially induced psychosis of war hysteria and nurtured upon an incessant propaganda of fear. While such an

economy may produce a sense of seeming prosperity for the moment, it rests on an illusionary foundation of complete unreliability and renders among our leaders almost a greater fear of peace than is their fear of war.[15]

And, when he said in 1957:

> Our government has kept us in a perpetual state of fear—kept us in a continuous stampede of patriotic fervor—with the cry of a grave national emergency. . . . Yet, in retrospect, these disasters seem never to have happened, seem never to have been real.[16]

Needless to say, very few politicians (or voting Americans, for that matter) have taken the concerns of Eisenhower or MacArthur seriously enough to stop the constant buildup of the American military-industrial complex to the point that many political pundits claim it is now too late to even try. As proof of this, they point to the economic fact that one out of every ten jobs in America depends, either directly or indirectly, on the arms industry. This may account for why America now finds itself in a global **war on terrorism**. In fact, I would submit that much of the so-called "War on Terrorism" has as much to do with political economics as it does with national security. That is, the War on Terrorism provides ample proof that the concerns voiced by Eisenhower and MacArthur are more relevant today than at anytime in American history. In fact, contrary to American tradition, the War on Terrorism has been a war profiteer's dream investment portfolio (I will have much more to say about this later under the section concerning multinational corporations). Unlike WWII, when President Roosevelt declared that there shall not be "a single war millionaire created in the United States as a result of this world disaster,"[17] the military actions in Afghanistan and Iraq were launched by a president whose father, a former president, happened to be a Senior Advisor to one of the world's largest private military-industrial firms, The Carlyle Group, up until October 2003. According to its own web page, The Carlyle Group, established in 1987, manages $34.9 billion in assets as of 2005.[18] Other politically notable and powerful members of The Carlyle Group, both past and present, include: Carlyle Chairman Emeritus, Frank Carlucci, former Secretary of Defense, Reagan/Bush Administration; Carlyle Senior Counselor, James Baker, III, former Secretary of State for Bush Sr. and Secretary of Treasury under Reagan; Carlyle Managing Director, Richard Darman, former White House Budget Advisor for both Bush Sr. and Clinton; Chairman of Carlyle Europe, John Major, former Prime Minister of Britain; to name just a few.[19] As a private equity firm, The Carlyle Group's activities are hard to trace in precise detail, but one would be hard pressed to believe its earnings from these engagements will be anything but robust. Moreover, to think such politically influential individuals do not affect American foreign policy just as Eisenhower and MacArthur warned is an exercise of such extreme gullibility and wishful thinking that it renders any rational response fruitless. It seems many people, for either purely selfish reasons or because they believe it is an economic necessity, think America simply cannot afford to deescalate its arms dependent economy.

Still others (this author included) would argue the opposite: We, the American people, simply cannot afford to continue to spend ourselves into moral and economic bankruptcy by building and selling war machines to the United States government and other regimes throughout the world. Such a foreign policy may be good for some people's financial situations but it is killing America's democratic possibilities. That is, how is it we cannot afford health care for the young, but we can afford global military supremacy? Or, though we can no longer afford to police America's cities, we can somehow afford to police Baghdad? And, why is it that even though we cannot afford to help feed the American working poor, we can somehow afford to rebuild Iraq? Given that America is already somewhere in the neighborhood of $11 trillion in debt, why do we continue building machines which produce nothing economically productive, but produce only death and destruction? What type of life is this and why do we allow the very people who feed off of this misery to determine American foreign policy for the rest of us? It seems only appropriate to end this section with a quote from the same American who first warned us of the danger the military-industrial complex presented to the country's moral and economic future. Again, President Dwight D. Eisenhower:

> Every gun that is made, every warship launched, every rocket fired signifies, in the final sense, a theft from those that hunger and are not fed, those who are cold and not clothed. This world in arms is not spending money alone. It is spending the sweat of its laborers, the genius of its scientists, the hopes of its children. . . . This is not a way of life at all in any true sense. Under the cloud of threatening war, it is humanity hanging from a cross of iron.[20]

Congress

As mentioned in the section on the president, Congress was constitutionally intended to be the main player in the foreign policy community, but political reality has relegated it to subservient status vis-à-vis the Executive Branch.[21] To be sure, much of this has been due to their own reluctance to take on the president or their wealthy friends in the arms industry when it comes to issues involving foreign policy. Nonetheless, Congress still wields substantial institutional authority over American foreign policy through its lawmaking power. Congress, mainly through the committee and subcommittees which deal with foreign policy, determines (at least constitutionally) the size of the military, its training, how much money is spent to support the same, and if, when and for what purposes the troops will be used. Still, all in all, Congress has become much more the deputy to the president's sheriff with respect to making foreign policy in the American political system. Sadly to say, this abdication of Congress' constitutional prerogatives has been no more exposed than during this decade's war-torn foreign policy. While numerous congresspersons have made their objections to this policy apparent in front of the news cameras, they have done nothing but facilitate its war-first mentality when it counts—that is, through authorizing legislation.

The Public

The public influences foreign policy in many ways, the most obvious one is via elections. The primary public check on the government's foreign policy activities is the public's acceptance or rejection of them at the voting booth. In addition, the public also affects foreign policy by protesting (peaceful or otherwise) the government's foreign policies, by their purchases at the local mall, or (arguably the most common) by their silence concerning their government's overseas activity.

The Media

The media affects foreign policy, first and foremost, by simply deciding if, and to what degree, it will or will not cover any given foreign policy event. By covering a foreign policy activity, the media focuses the public's attention on that particular issue and, consequently, keeps the public's attention off any other events that might be occurring simultaneously. For example, American troops were sent to Kosovo and not Sudan, in the summer of 1999, because the media's attention focused on the conflict in Europe and not on the conflict in Africa, which served to draw the American public's attention there as well. One of the most striking examples of the media influencing foreign policy is the much repeated story of William Randolph Hearst's role in involving America in the Spanish-American War at the turn of the 19th century. Realizing a war would increase his paper's advertising revenues, Hearst's papers harped on the "Spanish atrocities" in then Spanish-held Cuba, stirring up the American public until they demanded a military response.[22] Upon learning of his success in entangling America in Cuba (and increasing the sales of his papers accordingly) so the story goes, Hearst strode into his board room and announced, "gentlemen, how do you like my splendid little war?" A more recent example is when, in 1991, the wealthy monarchs of Kuwait involved America in their dispute with Iraq by paying for, what was at the time, the largest public relations campaign in the history of American media. By buying huge blocks of American media time, they convinced Americans they would protect democracy by fighting and dying for a morally suspect monarchy.[23]

Of course, the television networks are also well aware of the huge ratings any foreign crisis generates. Why else would CNN spend much of the winter of 1996 rerunning its coverage of Desert Storm? Of course, we now are engaged in the War on Terrorism that has led, as of this writing, to full-on military invasions of two countries, all with the requisite media heavy breathing. The media, so enamored with the ratings windfall that is war, resorted to what amounted to selling these wars as if they were made-for-TV movies, or better yet, reality shows for all those armchair generals who love watching sanitized war from the comfort of their living rooms; how ironic that these living room ratings came at the expense of those less fortunate souls who found themselves enmeshed in the killing fields of war. For example, before the political system had actually formally announced war with Iraq on March 20, 2003, many television networks were framing the issue with such catchy slogans as "Countdown to Iraq," "Showdown with Saddam," and other despicable war mongering antics such as the "Saddam-a-meter." Notice how all the pre-war coverage assumed the war was inevitable and would go on as scheduled—like any well-managed television event. They do so, not only because it improves their corporate revenues, but because it also enhances an individual correspondent's professional reputation to be seen covering a dangerous, yet "sexy," foreign policy event. In this way, reporters can be seen in combat fatigues, heroically ignoring the danger swirling around them, as they dig to get the real story while asking the tough questions—call it the Dan Rather syndrome.

The political system is very aware of how the media impacts American's foreign policy opinions. In one of the most egregious examples of an administration trying to use the media to push war on Americans, is the story reported by *The New York Times* regarding how at least 75 retired military officers were drafted to promote the war in Iraq. These so-called "objective" retired military officers were hardly the objective experts they were depicted to be on T.V. It was reported that many of these same analysts just so happen to have been lobbyists for many of the corporations that would profit from the war they were "objectively" commenting about while they were also being given special treatment and "facts" by the Pentagon.[24]

Moreover, as the *Washington Post* reported:

> That the news divisions of NBC, ABC, CBS, CNN and Fox sanctioned this domination by military types was a further assault on what the public deserves: independent, balanced and impartial journalism. The tube turned into a parade ground for military men—all well-groomed white males—saluting the ethic that war is rational, that bombing and shooting are the way to win peace, and that their uniformed pals in Iraq were there to free people, not slaughter them. Perspective vanished, as if caught in a sandstorm of hype and war-whooping. If the U.S. military embedded journalists to report the war from Iraq, journalists back in network studios embedded militarists to explain it. Either way, it was one-version news.
>
> If the stateside studios are dominated by militarists, coverage from Iraq also offered mostly the military perspective. Whether it was celebrity news people such as Ted Koppel or Brian Williams roughing it by donning helmets, gas masks and goggles, or Geraldo Rivera gushing from Afghanistan that "we have liberated this country"—"Hallelujah," shouted his anchorman back at Fox—the media are tethered to the military. They become beholden, which leads not to Pentagon censorship, as in 1991, but a worse kind: self-censorship.[25]

So, Americans will pay with their treasure and blood for the privilege of increasing media profits and enhancing journalistic reputations. Nonetheless, for better or for worse, the media will continue to be an important factor in setting American foreign policy.[26]

Academics

Of all the actors who influence American foreign policy probably the least recognized by the public at large are the academics in the international relations field. These academics are found in universities, government organizations, and private "think tanks" (which is a group of scholars who are paid for their expert opinion). Their impact on American foreign policy cannot be overstated because the ideas that the intellectual elite generate will come to dominate both the direction of American foreign policy and the lives of average Americans for years to come. There is no better example of this phenomenon than, foreign policy scholar, George F. Kennan's **"containment" doctrine (a.k.a. "the domino theory")**.[27] His theory so enthralled the American foreign policy establishment, it cost upwards of 100,000 American lives, in places like Korea and Vietnam, not to mention the billions of dollars it cost the American taxpayer to implement. The domino theory is a painfully simple understanding of international relations and **geopolitics**—first one country falls to **communism**, then another, then another, until, like a row of dominos, the world is enslaved by the "red menace."[28] For example, Secretary of State Dean Acheson, defended President Truman's attempt to stop communism in Greece by arguing if Americans do not contain communism there they might have to ward off the commies on the shores of Maryland.[29] President Johnson defended his escalation of American troop involvement in Vietnam by arguing if Americans did not stop communism in Vietnam, then they most assuredly would have to repel it in the streets of San Francisco.[30]

President Reagan also used the same metaphor in defense of his aggressive military actions in Central America, arguing military involvement was necessary in places like El Salvador because without it, "the killing will increase, and so will the threat to Panama, the Canal and ultimately Mexico." Furthermore, Reagan continued, what is "at stake in the Caribbean and Central America . . . is the United States' national security."[31] Forgiving for the moment the absolute silliness of all of this, there does seem to be a simple contradiction within the domino theory itself. If communism is so popular it spreads like wild fire, then why would we want to stop it since it is what the people apparently want? Or, if it is such a terrible thing, then why is it so popular and, hence, expands so easily? In the second edition of this book, published in 2001, I ended this section with the following words:

> In any event, the academic community is now busy trying to lend some substance to what [first] President Bush called "the new world order," as the new paradigm of American foreign policy. And when they do Americans be forewarned: It will most assuredly end up being as deadly and expensive to working class Americans as Kennan's 'containment' doctrine ever was.

It seems the academic community was very successful in their quest to find some nebulous global threat to replace the expansionist communist threat—the so-called War on Terrorism. We now have unconstitutionally announced war on what amounts to a military tactic that, in the words of previous vice-president, "won't end in our lifetime." Terrorism, like communism, is so nebulous, so fuzzy, that it easily lends itself to political maneuvering and sophistry so as to fit the needs of those in political authority. Moreover, as the military and political situations in Afghanistan and Iraq are demonstrating, I was hardly overstating the impact such academic theories would have on average Americans.

For example, in 1997, political scientist and former United States National Security Advisor, Zbigniew Brzezinski, published his book, *The Grand Chessboard: American Primacy and Its Geostrategic Imperatives*.[32] In the book, Dr. Brzezinski not only outlines why no price is too large to pay to control the untapped energy reserves of the Caspian Sea region, he actually provides a map on page 124 with the area circled where the United States government commenced its war on terrorism five years later. Moreover, on page 146 of the same book he provides a map which literally includes a "UNOCAL pipeline" from Uzbekistan through Turkmenistan and, lo and behold, through Afghanistan and eventually concluding at the Arabian Sea. Here we see a perfect example of how academics are more than the "ivory tower" do nothings they are stereotyped to be by those who know little of political power and its realities. One last chilling note regarding Brzezinski's book: In the conclusion he begins discussing how difficult it could be to persuade Americans to recognize the need to sacrifice their lives, liberty, and property to the cause of controlling the vast energy resources of near Asia. Here is what he wrote:

> Indeed, the critical uncertainty regarding the future may well be whether America might become the first superpower unable or unwilling to wield its power. Might it become an impotent global power? Public opinion polls suggest that only a small minority (13 percent) of Americans favor the proposition that "as the sole remaining superpower, the U.S. should continue to be the preeminent world leader in solving international problems." An overwhelming majority (74 percent) prefers that America "do its fair share in efforts to solve international problems together with other countries."
>
> Moreover, as America becomes an increasingly multicultural society, it may find it more difficult to fashion a consensus on foreign policy issues, *except in the circumstances of a truly massive and widely perceived direct external threat* [emphasis added].... In the absence of a comparable external challenge, American society may find it much more difficult to reach agreement regarding foreign policies that cannot be directly related to central beliefs and widely shared cultural ethnic sympathies and that still require an enduring and sometimes costly imperial engagement.[33]

In other words, Brzezinski is saying that without what political scientists refer to as a "black Sunday" event, Americans will be more than reluctant to engage in theater wars on a global scale all in the name of securing not their own lives, liberties and property, but for some theoretical concept—namely, corporate globalization and American primacy under the guise of protecting national security. Therefore, it is more than fair to ask: Could the 9/11/01 attacks have been the "truly massive and widely perceived direct external threat" Dr. Brzezinski had eluded to?[34] How tragic that just when the proponents of American geopolitical preeminence needed it, New York and Washington, D.C. were struck—again and again, as seen on television and repeated in most major speeches by every major player in the former Bush Administration. Moreover, how tragic that there was a total breakdown in all aspects of America's intelligence and national defense apparatus which should have prevented the attacks.[35] In any event, this again demonstrates that what a political scientist first asserts in a political theory will later be what working Americans will react to as their political reality.

Further proof of the importance and power of academics in forming American foreign policy can be found in the document, *Rebuilding America's Defenses: Strategy,*

Forces and Resources, for a New Century published in September 2000.[36] The document, better known by its authorizing body, *The **Project for the New American Century***, outlines in detail the what, why and how of American foreign policy. Those who constitute this *Project for the New American Century* are some of the most influential academic and political people in America. The academic component includes professors from both the army and naval academies, the National Defense University, Harvard, Yale, and Johns Hopkins Universities, just to name a few. The political component is equally impressive. Consisting of such political heavyweights as former Vice-President, Dick Cheney; the former Secretary of Defense, Donald Rumsfeld; the former Under-Secretary of Defense, Paul Wolfowitz; the former Governor of Florida, Jeb Bush; and former Bush Sr. Vice-President, Dan Quayle; again, just to name a few. In short, although the *Project* came out before the 2000 presidential election, with the results of said election, this became the game plan of Bush's foreign policy. And as I'll discuss later in this chapter, it is becoming apparent that it reflects much of Obama's foreign policy as well.

The *Project* calls for a massive increase in defense spending of anywhere from $26 billion to $100 billion annually (while clearly endorsing the higher figure);[37] it argues for a missile defense system and creation of a new branch of the military to be called U.S. Space Forces;[38] it declares that America's new strategic goal is to "preserve Pax Americana" (that is global supremacy); it stipulates that the United States' "main military threat" is "potential theater wars spread across the globe" while its "focus of strategic competition" is "East Asia" (read China);[39] it identifies three nation-states as particularly problematic, North Korea, Iran, and Iraq;[40] it argues for a new geopolitical permanent presence in the Persian Gulf region (read move troops from Saudi Arabia to a newly established Iraq);[41] it argues for instability in North Korea as a tactical move to contain China;[42] and, so forth. By comparing the academic report with political reality of the Bush administration, one can see how easily theory becomes reality in politics. Defense spending has created deficits as far as the fiscal eye can see; we are currently involved in theater wars on a global scale, in places such as Iraq, Afghanistan, Columbia, the Balkans, etc.; President Bush in one of his State of the Union Addresses labeled Iraq, Iran and North Korea as constituting an "axis of evil" nearly two years after the *Project;* the Bush Administration did, indeed, help destabilize the Korean peninsula as the *Project* directed.

Let me take this opportunity to address the North Korea situation circa 2008 and its fidelity to the strategic reasoning found in the *Project*. Most Americans and the media have struggled with what seemed to be an apparent contradiction regarding America's reaction to Iraq as compared to North Korea. America invaded Iraq even though it posed no real threat to security of the United States, while seemingly ignoring North Korea's nuclear program. As with most things political, there is much more to the story than the simple narrative repeated on almost all broadcast media. Let us begin addressing what appears to be an incoherent foreign policy regarding both Iraq and North Korea. I will be discussing the Iraq situation in much more detail later in this chapter, so I will concentrate at this stage on explaining the motivation behind the Bush administration's Korean strategy.

Once one reads the *Project*, the North Korean situation makes perfect sense under the assumptions of the document. Recall that the *Project* argues the greatest threat to American global supremacy is the People's Republic of China and that is where North Korea fits, literally. Political scientists use the concept 'geopolitics' to explain how a country's geography affects its politics. In other words, North Korea is geopolitically important because it sits on the doorstep of China. Hence, the *Project* warns of the danger of removing troops from the Korean peninsula because they "still have a vital role to play in U.S. security strategy in the event of Korean unification and with the rise of Chinese military power."[43] So, what American media presented as simply an evil/crazy North Korea which, without provocation, suddenly decided to test U.S. resolve by announcing it had continued its nuclear program in noncompliance with its previous agreements was not quite the neat little "white hat/black hat" scenario that fit the mainstream media's inability to deal with complexity. The rest of the story is that just as the *Project* directs, the Bush administration took a very bellicose stance toward North Korea so as to foment instability on the Korean peninsula by refusing to sign a non-aggression pact promising not to invade North Korea. Why? Well, the U.S. intelligence community has known for years that many Koreans are opposed to the American military presence on the peninsula while desiring reunification. This is unacceptable to the present U.S. administration given its position regarding China, so they pushed North Korea into a position where it would threaten South Korea and Japan thereby creating the political climate necessary either for a continual American military presence to "protect" South Korea and Japan, or sow the seeds of war which would require an American invasion of North Korea. What if the Koreas go ahead with reunification? Well as the *Project* reminds, "in any realistic post-unification scenario, U.S. forces are likely to have some role in stability operations in North Korea."[44] So, the U.S., under the *Project*'s theory, helps create tensions on the peninsula to justify its presence in a region where it finds itself less and less welcome so as to maintain a forward base of operations in a future war with China. If the Koreas stay separate, fine, U.S. troops will ostensibly be there to protect South Korea; if war breaks out, then the U.S. will play a dominate role in the reunification of the Koreas, which provides the opportunity for an even greater presence on China's doorstep. Lastly, tensions on the Korean peninsula have a further benefit of allowing the U.S. to maintain a forward military operations presence in Japan as well. Or as the *Project* puts it: "A similar rationale argues in favor of retaining substantial forces in Japan. In recent years, the stationing of large forces in Okinawa has become increasingly controversial in Japanese domestic politics, and while efforts to accommodate local sensibilities are warranted, it is essential to retain the capabilities U.S. forces in Okinawa represent."[45] In other words, if the Japanese don't feel threatened by North Korea, then they might demand American troops be withdrawn from Okinawa, and the U.S. would lose an essential forward operations base in a war with China. On a more hopeful note: With the war in Iraq and Afghanistan, not going anywhere near as well as the Bush or Obama Administration officials had planned, it seems the United States is apparently allowing its North Korean policy to mature beyond the *Project*'s parameters. In fact the United States recently resurrected much of the Clinton administration's North Korea policy while engaging in multi-party talks with North Korea that many believe will lead to a lessening of tensions on the Korean peninsula.

So, it seems the biggest myth we must address is the belief that academics don't impact the "real" world; the truth is that political theorists create not only the world we call real, but contemplate ending it as well. So, if you're wondering what your future holds tomorrow, you might want to visit the political science section of your library today.

Multinational Corporations (MNCs)

Some of the most powerful actors influencing American foreign policy (and indeed all international relations) are so-called **multinational corporations**. A multinational (or transnational) corporation is any private enterprise business collective which has subsidiaries operating in more than one country and whose sole purpose is to make money for its shareholders. With the very recent development of the so-called "global economy,"[46] MNCs have become some of the most powerful actors on the world stage. To be sure, MNCs are nothing new in the international arena, their lineage traces back to Europe's large trading companies of the late 17th century, for instance, the Dutch East India Trading Co. Nonetheless, the growth of MNCs in both numbers and economic power has radically accelerated since World War II.[47] And, given their economic strength, it is no stretch to imagine they can and do affect American foreign policy. As one international relations expert wrote:

> [An] example of the political influence of MNCs took place between 1970 and 1973 in Chile when ITT [International Telegraph and Telephone] in conjunction with the U.S. Central Intelligence Agency helped overthrow the government of Salvador Allende, all in the pursuit, from ITT's perspective, of establishing a more favorable environment in which it could do business.[48]

The prominence of MNCs in foreign policy was again evident in the U.S. government's exemption of U.S. centered oil companies from an economic boycott the government had imposed on Libya to punish it for its anti-Western terrorism.[49] In other words, the U.S. government believed it had a higher duty to protect the interests of the oil companies than it did to protect innocent Americans from terrorism. The war in Iraq is the epitome of what happens when foreign policy is dictated by the needs of corporate finance. No reasonable person can doubt that the Carlyle Group (discussed earlier) will not benefit tremendously from America's aggressive foreign policy. But the story of corporate political insider trading does not end with the current president and his father's former equity firm. Vice-President Dick Cheney's former company, Halliburton, just so happened to garner a non-competitive bid worth hundreds of millions of dollars to help rebuild Iraq's degenerating oil facility industry. At least we know they are well prepared for the job, because according to *The Washington Post*,[50] when Mr. Cheney was still CEO of Halliburton, it signed contracts worth $73 million with Saddam Hussein during the 1990s through foreign subsidiaries. Also, while Cheney was CEO of Halliburton, the corporation consistently did business with some of the most notorious regimes in the world. For example, Halliburton dealt with Burma (aka Myanmar), Algeria, Angola, and Iran, among others. And, as reported by one journalist, "Halliburton's subsidiary Brown & Root . . . was fined $3.8 million for re-exporting goods to Libya in violation of U.S. Sanctions."[51] The defenders of such behavior respond that Cheney no longer runs Halliburton so all of this is mere old news of a profitable businessman doing what he, as CEO, should be doing—making money for his shareholders. However, what does one make of the fact that Cheney received a $20 million severance package when he left Halliburton in 2000 to become vice-president, after which, his previous corporation (Halliburton) hits it rich when the country that Cheney was then co-directing invades a country to remove the very same person his former corporation used to do business with? Is it any wonder that Mr. Cheney refused to inform Congress of what took place during his so-called energy summit held in the first months of his first term as vice-president? Moreover, as to his responsibility to his shareholders, what does one think of the fact that Halliburton had to pay $6 million to settle shareholders' lawsuits because of "deceptive accounting practices while Vice-President Dick Cheney led the Company?"[52]

The real victor in Iraq is what I refer to as the "energy-industrial complex" of which Halliburton is but one of numerous huge transnational corporations involved in the Iraq War sweepstakes. Or, as the *LA Times-Washington Post* service wrote:

> Maybe it's a coincidence, but U.S. and British oil companies would be long-term beneficiaries of a successful military offensive led by the United States and Britain to remove Iraqi President Saddam . . . A post-Saddam Iraq also would be a bonanza for U.S.-dominated oil-services industry . . . The confluence of foreign policy and commercial interests is fueling suspicions that U.S. and British war plans are motivated in part by a thirst for Iraqi oil.[53]

Indeed they are. But the story of this despicable war profiteering is so deep only an oil rig could pump it all out. For example, according to *The Associated Press,* Bechtel Corporation:

> Not only has close ties with elder Republican statesmen, but also its executives enjoy direct links to the Bush administration, which has critics crying cronyism . . . The initial $34.6 million contract . . . could spiral far beyond its projected $680 million price tag. And Bechtel is widely perceived as the front-runner for future business as the United States spends as much as $100 billion in what's seen as the biggest reconstruction project since World War II's aftermath . . . At least two Bechtel executives have ties to the Bush administration. Jack Sheehan, a senior vice-president, sits on the Defense Policy Board formed to advise Defense Secretary Donald Rumsfeld who once lobbied for a Bechtel project . . . And President Bush appointed Bechtel's chairman, Riley Bechtel . . . to the export council which advises the president on international trade matters . . . the company has backed its personal contacts within Washington with sizable campaign contributions.[54]

Speaking of the Defense Policy Board, its former chairman, Richard Perle had to resign in late March 2003 after he was found profiteering from his position with Global Crossing Ltd. and Trireme Corporation. Of course the story gets worse. Recall that the Board advises then Secretary of Defense, Donald Rumsfeld. Well, Rumsfeld didn't actually force Perle to leave the board, he just asked him to resign as its chairman even though the *Los Angeles Times* reported the following: "Last February Perle and the Board received a classified briefing on the potential for conflict in Iraq and North Korea, including information on new communications. Three weeks later, the then chairman of the board, Richard Perle, offered a briefing of his own at an investment seminar on ways to profit on possible conflicts with both countries."[55]

If this information doesn't curdle one's democratic skin, then the American experiment in self-government has become just another failed democracy due to the political indifference of its citizenry. Or as veteran journalist Georgie Anne Geyer, of the *Universal Press Syndicate*, wrote, "Eventually, this whole story will be told. It will be a story of distrust and deception, of new forms of conspiracy, coups and hijackings, all of them far removed from our American historical experience."[56] Unfortunately there is more to this sordid tale. Some of you may remember General Garner who was imposed upon the Iraqis as the first "post-combat phase" American administrator of Iraq. He proved to be a failure at his reported job, which was to bring order to "post war" Iraq. He failed for two fundamental reasons. One, there is no "post-war Iraq," as most of us should be aware, the killing hasn't stopped in Iraq no matter how the political class phrases it. Nor has there been any real pre-war Iraq since at least 1980. So, this leads us to the second reason he failed—he was never qualified to do the job assigned as his expertise is war making and selling homeland security technology and consultation. In short, he is an expert in creating and profiting from disorder caused by continual war, hardly the requisite qualifications for a post-war anything. Yet, as what seems to be a constant in modern American politics, the story turns more tragic as one digs deeper into the political story. Which brings me to Garner's replacement, Paul Bremer. Mr. Bremer was presented by the Bush administration as a career diplomat whose expertise was civil reconstruction of just the sort required in "continual war" Iraq, and this information was obediently repeated by the broadcast media to a never skeptical public. However, the truth is much less palatable. It seems Mr. Bremer's company, Crisis Consulting Practice, is established after the 9/11 attacks to advise corporate clients on how to deal with terrorists. *The Nation's* Naomi Klein wrote:

> "Many have pointed out that Bremer is no expert on Iraqi politics. But that was never the point. He is an expert at profiting from the war on terror and at helping U.S. multinationals make money in far-off places where they are unpopular and unwelcome."[57]

So, it seems he was not there to stop the looting in Iraq after all, but rather he was there to ensure that the connected corporations kept their ill-gotten gain. In short, the

United States spent its moral and financial capital—not to mention the blood of its finest and the innocent of Iraq—so as to allow corporations to raid Iraq.

HOW DOES THE UNITED STATES EXECUTE ITS FOREIGN POLICY ?

Foreign policy may be implemented, simply stated, in one of two ways, either peacefully (through diplomacy) or violently (by armed force). Examples of the former are diplomatic agreements such as the North American Free Trade Agreement (NAFTA), or the General Agreement on Tariffs and Trade (GATT). These are international contracts between the United States and other designated nation-states that do not depend on coercion (the threat or use of force) for their compliance. Examples of the latter would be any time the United States resorts to the use of force to exercise its will in the international community, for example, as we did in WWII, Vietnam, and Iraq. The use of force can be exercised in one of two ways, either overtly (openly) or covertly (secretly). To help illustrate the difference between the two, we will now briefly review the United States' recent use of these two tools of force.[58]

The 1950s

Between the years 1950 and 1953, the United States was involved in an overt United Nations sponsored "police action" to stop the communist advance in Korea. Though the war was never officially declared, this attempt to implement Kennan's "containment" doctrine (discussed earlier), nonetheless, cost around 48,000 American lives and billions more in tax revenues. In addition to this overt activity, the United States government was also involved in many covert foreign policy activities during the 1950s. For example, in 1954, the Central Intelligence Agency masterminded the overthrow of the legitimate Guatemalan government by capturing the communications system of the country and staging a fake invasion of the Guatemalan mainland. This CIA orchestrated coup was celebrated as a great success as it maintained the United Fruit Company's stranglehold on the Guatemalan economy, even though it threw the country into a blood-bath that continues today. It has been estimated that as many as 100,000 Guatemalan people have been killed because of the CIA's "success" at destabilizing the country.[59]

The 1960s

The decade of the 1960s, as well as much of the 1970s, was dominated by the United States' overt military activity in a place called Vietnam. Again, like Korea, this war was never officially declared and was part of the attempt to "contain" communism. It cost upwards of 58,000 American lives, while also calling into question the very moral fiber of the country. President Kennedy's failed attempt at "liberating" Cuba from communism in the early sixties (which came to be known as the Bay of Pigs fiasco) is a prime example of covert activity. Invigorated by its "success" in Guatemala, the CIA decided to arm wealthy Cubans (who had fled the country during the uprising of the Cuban majority under Fidel Castro) and retake the country for the resort owners and their corporate friends. Needless to say, it did not work out as planned and the Cuban wealthy were captured and imprisoned by the very same Cuban majority who had kicked them out to begin with. It seems Castro was well aware of the tactics used in the Guatemalan coup of 1954, and had trained his men accordingly.

The 1970s

As mentioned earlier, the overt operation in Vietnam still raged early in the decade of the 1970s and before we go any further, we need to take some time reviewing the history of America's longest war. Vietnam deserves special attention since it haunts all contemporary American foreign policy and our nation's collective conscience as well. Americans still have not come to grips with our only military defeat as a nation. So many questions remain: Why and how did we get involved? Once involved, what happened there? How did a small underdeveloped country defeat the world's most dominant superpower? And, what can we learn from this painful experience?

The Vietnam War, like so many of our Cold War policies, was an attempt to fight the spread of communism. And, again, like so many of our Cold War activities, American policy toward Vietnam was dominated by men so blinded by their hatred of communism, they failed to take into account the culture or history of the very same people Americans were sent to either liberate or kill.[60] If they had done some research, they would have discovered that the Vietnamese people were hardly the meek little Asians the Kennedy and Johnson administrations took them to be (first lesson, racism kills). Instead, the Vietnamese are a warrior people who have been engaged in constant struggles to fight off the oppressive rule of foreign empires, be it the Chinese, the French, the Japanese, or, lastly, the Americans. As a matter of fact, the Vietnamese were allies of ours during World War II as they helped us defeat the Japanese who had occupied the region during the war. (Immediately after the war, Ho Chi Minh, the Vietnamese leader, read directly from the American *Declaration of Independence* as hundreds of thousands of Vietnamese cheered their hard won independence, which America saluted with a military flyover.) Nonetheless, from about the 1860s to the start of World War II, the Vietnamese had been resisting the colonial rule of the French, who desired Vietnam's rice, rubber, and coal.[61] French occupation was so cruel that in addition to the French sending postcards to their sweethearts with pictures of decapitated Vietnamese heads, they also referred to the Vietnamese dead as "fertilizer," since they would often bury them under the very same rubber trees they had spent their lives tending for the French company, Michelin.

The story of how the British helped the French reestablish their colonial rule after the end of the Second World War is much beyond the scope of this chapter, nevertheless, suffice it to say, it was one of the most disdainful acts ever committed against a war time ally. In any event, the Vietnamese finally dislodged the French in 1954, after the French defeat at Dienbienphu, and from that moment on Vietnam became an American nightmare (we withdrew in 1973 and the American puppet state, South Vietnam fell in 1975). And, just like the French before us, the American military dominated the action on the ground and in the air, but could never win the hearts and minds of the Vietnamese (it seems killing people by the hundreds of thousands makes very few friends). Contrary to popular belief, the American military fought this war with both hands, both legs, the neighbor's legs and the kitchen sink (second lesson, no more nonsense about us fighting Vietnam with one hand tied behind our back). A few facts should put this myth to rest once and for all: By the end of the war, the United States had dropped 7 million tons of bombs on Vietnam, Cambodia, and Laos; this was more than twice the tonnage dropped on Europe and Asia during all of WWII.[62] Moreover, we dropped the equivalent of three atomic bombs on Hanoi while spraying 12 million gallons of the chemical defoliant, Agent Orange, on Vietnam from 1962 to 1971, covering over more than 10% of its entire land mass. This chemical agent is now believed to be causing the severe birth defects of tens of thousands of Vietnamese children.[63]

Nevertheless, none of this American military power did anything but devastate and kill; it did very little to help the Vietnamese, or the Americans sent to use it (by the way, during the Vietnam War the military stocked its ranks with some of the poorest and youngest foot soldiers in American history). The Cold War mentality was one where the only acceptable policy seemed to be, "shoot first, ask questions later." Which is exactly what we got: We shot first and now we are left with the questions that began this discussion (third lesson, ignorance kills). We lost the war because there never was a war to win (and let no one question the bravery of the American or Vietnamese foot soldier, as each fought with a valor known only to the combat veteran); the Vietnamese people sought peace and independence, hence, what they needed was political and humanitarian help not military slaughter. Yet this is the danger of building and maintaining a huge military establishment, our political leaders cannot help but conceive of every international issue as a military problem, be it Vietnam, Afghanistan, or Iraq (last lesson, when all you carry is a hammer, everything begins to look like a nail).

We have already encountered an example of American covert activity in the 1970s during our discussion of MNCs. In 1973, the CIA, at the prodding of ITT, covertly orchestrated the murder of Salvador Allende, the freely elected president of Chile, for being a communist.[64]

The 1980s

The 1980s provided very fertile political soil for American overt and covert military action. The American government, in a pathetic attempt to exorcize the ghosts of Vietnam, involved itself in a number of fruitless and morally questionable overt engagements, which ranged from bombing Libya to invading that well-known Caribbean power, Grenada, to sacrificing over 200 hundred Marines in Beruit. In addition to these overt activities, the United States government was also involved in many questionable covert activities. None more suspect than Col. North's attempt to circumvent the Constitution by selling arms to Iran (a well known anti-American state) to generate funds (Congress had refused to do so) necessary to supply arms for a group of Central American thugs, known as the "contras," in their attempt to overthrow the popular leaders of Nicaragua.

The 1980s closed with an American overt military exercise in Panama, ironically titled, "Operation Just Cause." This so-called just cause wound up costing anywhere from several hundred to several thousand civilian lives all to illegally capture a South American punk, General Manuel Noriega, who allegedly had worked with the CIA under George H.W. Bush but had since been deemed expendable.[65]

The 1990s

The last decade of the 20th century was a busy one for the American foreign policy establishment. The 1990s found America engaged in major overt operations in Iraq, Bosnia, and the Serbian-Montenegro province of Kosovo. The first overt action began as a full-tilt war, labeled Desert Storm, and then degenerated into a series of daily air campaigns against an essentially defenseless people. The last two overt operations consist of peacekeeping exercises in the war-torn Balkans.

The war against Iraq has gone on so long now most Americans have forgotten the Iraq war began over a decade before the 2003 invasion. To help us remember, let me enumerate the basic facts of the conflict. During 1990 the United States, under President Bush Sr., spent almost six months preparing for an attack determined to drive Iraqi forces out of Kuwait. The military operation was so successful that the Iraqi military was not only driven from Kuwait, those Iraqi forces engaged were essentially destroyed after 38 days of air attacks followed by 100 hours of ground fighting. At the close of this initial stage of the conflict, the deaths equaled about 300 Americans and somewhere in the neighborhood of 20,000 to 100,000 plus Iraqis. After the war, the United States, Britain, and France, without United Nations authorization, created so-called "no-fly" zones over much of northern and southern Iraq to protect Kurds in the north and Shiite Arabs in the south from reprisal by Saddam Hussein's regime.[66] The United States and Britain enforced these no-fly zones with vigor, creating a climate of almost daily aerial bombardment of Iraq throughout the 1990s. Attacks were particularly intense in 1998 when the Clinton administration initiated operation "Desert Fox." Moreover, the United Nations Security Council imposed economic sanctions against Iraq that, according to the most respected academic source, Columbia University public health expert, Richard Garfield, claimed the lives of hundreds of thousands of Iraqi children under the age of five.[67]

Harvard University put together a team of lawyers and public health specialists to investigate the tragedy that was 1990s Iraq; the 87 member team of international experts visited 46 hospitals, 28 water and sewage treatment facilities and made around 9,000 random household surveys. Team member Dr. Eric Hoskyns reported that this was "the most comprehensive study ever done of the impact of the conflict," and the team's findings represented "a definitive assessment of the Gulf crisis on children." The report details a humanitarian crisis of such enormity, the best way to relay its anguish in such a short space is to repeat just a couple of statements expressed by a group of child psychologists with experience of the wars in Uganda, Sudan and Mozambique. According to these experts on the affect of war on children, the children of Iraq were "the most traumatized children of war ever described." One of the team members, Dr. Magne Raudalen, director of the Research for Children Program at the Center for Crisis Psychology at Bergen University, Norway, pleaded: "We must not keep this a secret, what has happened to these children."[68]

To address the growing crisis in Iraq, Saddam Hussein, after years of refusing to allow for a more humanitarian sensitive sanctions program, finally agreed to a United Nations Oil-for-Food program that was designed to lessen the hardship on the Iraqi people. The deal would allow Hussein's regime to export oil in exchange for food and medical supplies. The program did help alleviate some of the difficulties caused by the sanctions. Since the fall of Hussein's regime, much evidence has surfaced exposing corruption within the Oil-for-Food program. Contrary to original reports, the corruption was not a simple case of Saddam enriching himself at the expense of his people. It seems that members of the United Nations Security Council, including the United States, were aware of the shenanigans and even approved them for various political reasons.[69] Without excusing Saddam Hussein's culpability in this humanitarian catastrophe and its resulting scandal, the fact remains that the United States government shares responsibility for this humanitarian crime because it insisted on maintaining the sanctions with full knowledge of the devastation they wrought upon the Iraqi people, not to mention the outrage the sanctions caused among the international community. This compelled Denis Halliday, United Nations Director of the Oil-for-Food program, to resign from his position in 1998 to protest what he considered an unjustified, "genocidal" policy against the people of Iraq. On December 16, 1998, he issued the following press release:

> It is time after years of humanitarian tragedy, we acknowledge that this conflict has brutalized the resolutions of the U.N. Security Council. It has sustained economic sanctions, in full knowledge of their catastrophic impact on the people of Iraq, and represents the effective abandonment of civilized values.

He was not alone in his moral outrage. Mr. Halliday's successor at the United Nations, Hans von Sponeck, also resigned in protest "against the sanctions policy of the Security Council and in particular the USA, responsible for the death of several hundred thousand Iraqi children."

This whole scenario was, of course, instigated by Saddam Hussein's illegal invasion and occupation of a neighboring country. Although Kuwait has a terrible human rights record and was governed in a dictatorial style by the ruling al-Sabah family, nonetheless, it has internationally recognized borders whose integrity was violated by Iraq. However, as is so often the case in politics, there is much more to the story. Saddam Hussein, a thug of monumental proportions, assumed power in 1979 after years as an official with the ruling Ba'ath party of Iraq. As fate would have it, during this period the U.S. was looking for a way to address the recent events in the Persian Gulf where the anti-American Iranian revolution had just culminated with the return of the Ayatollah. Prior to the Iranian revolution, Iran had been America's closest ally in the Persian Gulf ever since the CIA had helped overthrow populist Prime Minister Mohammed Mossadegh and replaced him with the Shah of Iran in 1953. From the years 1971–1977 alone, the United States sold Iran $12 billion dollars of high-grade military weaponry.[70] The Iranian population so resented the Shah and America's influence in their country they overthrew him in 1979 and replaced him with the rabidly anti-American Ayatollah Khomeini. Both the U.S. and Iraq's Hussein decided it was time to act on the opportunity the Iranian revolution had provided.

Iran and Iraq have long feuded over the border that divides the two countries at the center-tip of the Persian Gulf. Saddam Hussein wanted to reclaim the entire Shat al Arab River as the territory of Iraq, so, with the United State's blessing, he invaded Iran in 1980. The Iran-Iraq war lasted over eight bloody years and ended up costing the lives of over 250,000 Iraqis and 750,000 Iranians. The United States benefited politically from this war as it helped weaken the anti-American state of Iran and also generated healthy arms sales to Iraq while drawing Hussein closer to the United States. In fact, beginning in 1984, and continuing right up to Iraq's invasion of Kuwait in 1990, the United States government approved the sale of nearly $1.5 billion in American military technology to Iraq. This technology was approved even though the United States was fully aware that it was sold to help develop Iraq's biological, chemical, and nuclear capabilities. Moreover, when it was discovered that Hussein had deployed chemical agents during the war with Iran, then Vice-President Bush personally lobbied on Iraq's behalf to ensure that Hussein's use of gas would not interfere with Iraq's ability to secure international loans so he could continue to purchase American military products. As then Middle East section chief on the National Security Council, Geoffrey Kemp, stated: "We really weren't naive. We knew [Saddam] was an S.O.B., but he was our S.O.B."[71] Hence, by the time of Iraq's invasion of Kuwait, Saddam Hussein's regime was under the political influence of the United States government. So much so in fact, that he would never have invaded Kuwait without our permission—which we gave him in 1990.[72] Saddam Hussein felt justified in invading Kuwait for essentially four reasons: one, during the Iran-Iraq war Kuwait had over-produced oil beyond **OPEC** limits obstructing Iraq's ability to finance the war (a war in which the people of Iraq believed protected Kuwait as much as Iraq); two, Kuwait over-pumped an oil field which straddled the border between Iraq and Kuwait; three, the Kuwait government demanded instant repayment of its war loans to Iraq against the original terms of the agreement; and, four, Iraq has never recognized the existence of Kuwait.

Why would the United States allow Iraq to invade a neighboring country and then paint the invasion as a surprising outrage against international law and its leader as the next Hitler? Two political scientists who looked into this enigma concluded:

> Unless one espouses the conspiracy theory that the United States wanted Iraq to invade Kuwait as an excuse to crush Saddam Hussein, then surely the simplest explanation is that the Bush administration was trying to shove Kuwait into a more tractable

> posture with regard to the price of oil and possibly to the leasing of the two islands so desired by Iraq for the construction of a deep harbor in the Gulf. Iraq, after all, was a U.S. ally and already a serious trading partner. Nor would the Administration, strongly oriented to the oil lobby, have been at all averse to seeing a hike in prices, which had drifted in real terms below their 1973 level. By seizing the whole of Kuwait, Saddam Hussein overplayed the hand allowed by the United States.[73]

In other words, one explanation for why the United States orchestrated the 1991 Gulf War was not to keep the price of oil down, as popular conspiracy theorists like to claim, but rather to insure that oil prices would stay high.

Another explanation, posited by Howard Zinn in his superb book, *A People's History of the United States*, was that Bush had serious electoral concerns and hoped a successful war would carry him to reelection.[74] For example, in 1990 Elizabeth Drew of the *New Yorker* wrote: "[Chief presidential aide] John Sununu was telling people that a short successful war would be pure political gold for the president and would guarantee his reelection." The *Washington Post* contained the following headline on October 16, 1990, a few months before Desert Storm commenced: "Polls Show Plunge in Public Confidence: Bush's Ratings Plummet." A few weeks later, October 28, the *Washington Post* ran a follow-up story that contained this telling comment: "Some observers in his own party worry that the president will be forced to initiate combat to prevent further erosion of his support at home." Historian Jon Wiener concurs with Zinn's assessment: "Bush abandoned sanctions and chose war because his time frame was a political one set by the approaching 1992 presidential election." Given the aerial attacks on Iraq ordered by President Clinton in 1998, which just so happened to coincide with his impeachment vote in the House, it does not strain the reasonable mind to believe presidents may in fact undertake foreign policy actions for political reasons.

The Founders certainly would not find it unbelievable, which is why, as mentioned previously, they constitutionally prevented presidents from having the power to initiate military matters altogether. Of course, the most likely scenario for this troubling episode in American history is a combination of both explanations. Moreover, one must never underestimate the political power of the military-industrial complex and its interests in keeping America on a war footing.

In addition to the engagement in the Middle East, America found itself ensnared in two peacekeeping missions in the Balkans. Both situations are tied to the same historical contingencies. After World War II, Yugoslavia emerged as a communist nation-state under the authority of Marshal Josip Tito and quickly established its independence from the Soviet Union's influence. This political unity, however, masked deep religious and ethnic animosities, which simmered for decades just underneath the political surface. Two events proved the violent undoing of the old Yugoslavia—Tito's death in 1980 and the collapse of the Soviet Union in 1991. With these events, Yugoslavia began coming apart at the political seams. First, Slovenia and Croatia each declared independence in 1991, igniting primarily a religious war between the Catholic Croats and the Eastern Orthodox Serbs. The bitterness between these two groups goes back for centuries, most notoriously to WWII where the Ustashe Croats, who aligned themselves with the Nazi regime, committed atrocities against the Serbs that resulted in the deaths of tens of thousands, if not hundreds of thousands, of Serbs who resisted the Ustashe and their Nazi allies. This religious war spilled over into Bosnia when it declared its independence from Serbian-led Yugoslavia in 1992. The Bosnian majority is Muslim, having been converted to the faith by the Ottoman Turks who occupied the region from the 15th century until around 1878. The ensuing Bosnian war claimed the lives of over 100,000 people and lead to the placement of American ground troops there as peacekeepers in 1995. At the time, President Clinton assured the American people that the troops would serve no more than one year in the Balkans; however, as of this writing, not only are there still American troops deployed to Bosnia, American troops were committed to Kosovo as well.

Kosovo is a southern province of present-day Serbia, which was one of the two political republics that comprised the political unit of Serbia and Montenegro, until Montenegro voted for independence in April of 2006. About 90% of the population of Kosovo is Albanian, while the remaining 10% is primarily Serbian. Understandably, the Albanians want to follow the lead of their Croatian and Bosnian neighbors and declare independence from Serbia and Montenegro (formerly Yugoslavia). Adding to an already complex situation is the fact that Kosovo is considered the cultural heartland of Serbia, making the Serbians opposed to relinquishing sovereignty. In the 1990s, neither side was willing to compromise. So, the Albanian armed military secessionist movement, known as the Kosovo Liberation Army (KLA), began terrorizing the Serbian population in Kosovo while the Serbian military was ethnically cleansing the Albanians. All of this led President Clinton to authorize first, a U.S.-led NATO bombing campaign, and second, a commitment of American troops as part of a peacekeeping presence in Kosovo. Today, Kosovo is technically a independent nation-state; however, to this day, the Serbians do not accept its independence, and have warned of dire consequences should independence for Kosovo be maintained. Only history will tell if this whole enterprise was a wise use of American military power and foreign policy credibility.

Examples of covert activities of the 1990s would include attempts to undermine Saddam Hussein's regime plus covert support for the Taliban regime in Afghanistan (to be discussed in more detail below).

POST 9/11 AMERICAN FOREIGN POLICY: WAR ON TERRORISM

At 8:45 A.M. Eastern time, Flight 11 from Boston smashed into the north tower of the World Trade Center, and as mainstream story goes, this event with its attendant tragedies (three more hijackings, south tower struck, Pentagon struck, and doomed United Flight 93 crashing into the woods of Pennsylvania) changed American politics forever. Again, as the "conventional" story goes, these horrific events compelled a peaceful but sleeping giant to awaken from its internationally indifferent slumber to wage war against the enemies of freedom. The first stop on this war to rid the world of terrorists was to launch an all out war on the nest of these snakes, Afghanistan. This required that the U.S. military not only go after Osama bin Laden and his base (**Al-Qaeda**), but its supporting regime, the Taliban as well. Although this conflict was important, it was over in a relatively short time with Al-Qaeda generally destroyed and the Taliban routed. It all seemed so neat and tidy just like its political label "Operation Enduring Freedom."

The next phase of this War on Terrorism was to rid the world of the regime of Saddam Hussein once and for all—finish what the father had started. After all, according to the Bush administration, Saddam's regime had weapons of mass destruction, was willing to use them, and had close ties with the terrorist organization, Al-Qaeda. So after months of diplomacy, the U.S. was compelled to defend its own national security against this obvious global threat no matter that most of the world did not share our threat assessment of Saddam's Iraq. Nonetheless, the president did his duty, which is to protect the nation from imminent attack. Hence on March 20, 2003, the U.S. government, following years of aerial bombardment, invaded Iraq and within three weeks or so toppled one of history's worst dictators—Saddam Hussein. The U.S. troops were hailed as liberators and were ensured a quick return to America. The president himself celebrated the victory by flying by fighter jet to the aircraft carrier, the U.S.S. Abraham Lincoln, named after another great wartime Republican president. All of it seemed so perfectly choreographed, everything fitting just right, a lot like its operational name, "Iraqi Freedom." In New York City, on June 23, 2003, President Bush himself declared at one of his campaign fund raising events that "terrorists declared war on the United States of America, and war is what they got."[75] In short, the mainstream story—what Plato would call conventional wisdom—has it that the tragedy of 9/11/01 caused America to unleash her military might in what the Bush Administration referred to as battles in the larger War on Terrorism, and what the Obama Administration calls "Overseas Operational Contingencies."

However, as one looks into these situations with a more skeptical eye, one sees the wisdom of Plato's warnings to all political scholars in his masterwork, *The Republic*—beware of popular opinion or conventional wisdom, as it is only the product of those in authority for the purpose of solidifying injustice. As J.S. Mill warned in his masterpiece, *On Liberty*, the people tend to get it not only wrong but exactly backwards. If these political philosophers are correct, then we may find that 9/11 did not *cause* the wars in Afghanistan and Iraq, but rather the wars in Afghanistan and Iraq during the 1990s *caused* 9/11. Let us take a closer look at both situations and see if this is indeed the case.

We know that Osama bin Laden hates the United States due to what he perceives as an anti-Muslim foreign policy. These views are a reflection of his interpretation of the Sunni sect of Islam. What made Osama bin Laden the recognized leader of the new pan-Islamic movement? He got his reputation as a **mujahideen** (soldier of God) fighting against the godless Soviet occupiers of Afghanistan in the 1980s, supported of course by the U.S. government's Central Intelligence Agency (CIA). This was all done as a part of the Cold War, and the Soviet defeat in Afghanistan is rightly recognized as the last nail in the Soviet coffin. But after this successful confrontation in the Cold War, the U.S. paid little attention to Osama bin Laden and his hatred of the U.S., which he considered no better than the Soviet Union. In the meantime, the U.S. was, as previously mentioned, engaged in a total war to liberate Kuwait from Saddam Hussein.

While the U.S. military was driving the Iraqi forces out of Kuwait, America was also acquiring a permanent forward operating base in the Persian Gulf in Saudi Arabia, a nation that not only holds the world's largest and most accessible oil fields, but also conveniently borders Iraq. So, as the U.S. was preoccupied by the Gulf War in the early 1990s, Osama bin Laden was seething over the fact that "infidel" troops had been stationed in Islam's most holy ground—Saudi Arabia, home to Mecca and Medina. In the meantime, as post-Soviet Afghanistan degenerated into anarchy, a group of brutal Pashtun Muslim students, the Taliban (meaning religious students), began to take control to impose order in post Soviet Afghanistan. The Taliban was truly a nightmare regime, one that deserved to be overthrown if ever there was one. However, Osama bin Laden welcomed the coming of the Taliban, without ever knowing that the United States government welcomed them, too.[76] Professor William O. Beeman, of Brown University, who specializes in the Middle East and has done extensive research on Islamic Central Asia stated in 1997: "It is no secret, especially in the region, that the United States, Pakistan and Saudi Arabia have been supporting the fundamentalist Taliban in their war for control of Afghanistan for some time."[77]

Why did the United States covertly support the Taliban regime? Most investigative journalists and scholars who have looked into the situation believe American support for the Taliban was the result of U.S. geopolitical interests, namely, control of the energy reserves of the Caspian Sea region. Beeman argued that American support for the Taliban "ha[d] nothing to do with religion or ethnicity—but only with the economics of oil."[78] Specifically, the United States government thought that the Taliban would bring order to war-torn Afghanistan thereby facilitating the construction of various pipelines whose routes would travel through Afghanistan.[79] However, by the end of the 1990s, it became apparent to American officials that the Taliban would be incapable of providing the necessary security climate essential to the construction of the proposed energy projects.[80] The Taliban's inability to secure Afghanistan coupled with its support for Bin Laden during the Al-Qaeda bombing of American Embassies in Nairobi and Tanzania in 1998 forced the Clinton Administration to radically rethink its policy towards the Taliban regime. So, in 1998, President Clinton broke off contact with the Taliban regime and ordered cruise missiles strikes into Afghanistan (and Sudan) while imposing U.S. sanctions on Afghanistan followed by the United Nations imposing sanctions in 1999.[81] At that point it was clear that the Taliban no longer served American geopolitical interests and were thereby deemed expendable. In other words, the wars in Afghanistan prior to 9/11 created the conditions for the emergence of the brutal Taliban regime. The Taliban in turn nurtured Osama bin Laden's Al-Qaeda, whose main goal was to liberate the holy land from the American "infidels" after the first Gulf War left thousands of American troops in Saudi Arabia. These events lead, of course, to the tragic events of September 11, 2001, when Al-Qaeda launched their attacks against the United States. In response, the United States military quickly overthrows the Taliban and the American people celebrate their first victory of the War on Terrorism. This is where most Americans and the mainstream media, prompted by those in political authority, believed the story ended. However, the innocent Afghans destroyed by this war, along with the soldiers who continue to fight and die in Afghanistan, did not have the luxury of this political delusion. As of this writing, the Taliban is reemerging in Afghanistan, Al-Qaeda groups are stepping-up attacks on coalition soldiers, and President Obama has promised that his administration will put its focus back on the war in Afghanistan and has already committed thousands of more American troops to this conflict.

Remember, I am defending the thesis that the pre-9/11 wars in Afghanistan and Iraq created the situation that led to the 9/11 attacks. We now see that this is indeed the case, since there would have been no Osama bin Laden or his sponsoring regime, the Taliban, without first the Soviet War, plus the civil war that followed the defeat of the Soviets in Afghanistan. Recall as well, the first Gulf War created the very thing that so infuriated Osama bin Laden—U.S. troops in Saudi Arabia. Now we need to turn our attention to the war in Iraq.

The war in Iraq was launched by the United States because the American government believed Saddam Hussein had a stockpile of Weapons of Mass Destruction (WMDs) in the form of nuclear, chemical, and biological munitions; Saddam Hussein's Iraq constituted an imminent threat; Saddam Hussein had collaborated with Al-Qaeda during the September 11, 2001 terrorist attacks; and, the United States government wanted to introduce democracy to the Arab world. As of this writing, the whole story of the so-called intelligence about Iraq's alleged WMDs stockpiles has led not to discoveries of said weapons, but rather to political investigations in both the U.S. and Britain over the credibility of President Bush's and Prime Minister Tony Blair's "evidence" of such weapons. The distortions of intelligence were so numerous they need not be retold here (see chapter 5 for a fuller discussion of this event). Suffice it to say, we now know that both governments used forged documents, misleading the U.N. Security Council and their own people about Iraq's military capability and alleged cooperation with the 9/11 hijackers. The contemporary spin regarding the absence of WMDs in Iraq goes something like this: "Well, we may have been mistaken about our accusations of vast stores of WMDs, but that is all irrelevant now since we liberated the Iraqis from one of the worst dictators of all time." However, as conservative commentator, Republican George Will has written:

> Some say the war was justified even if WMDs are not found or their destruction explained because the world is "better off" without Saddam. Of course it is better off. But unless one is prepared to postulate a U.S. right, perhaps even a duty, to militarily dismantle any tyranny—on to Burma?—it is unacceptable to argue that Saddam's mass graves and torture chambers suffice as retrospective justifications for pre-emptive war. A long-term failure to validate the war's premise would unravel much of the president's policy and rhetoric.[82]

In other words, Bush's pre-emptive policy becomes a Pandora's Box under this fallacious reasoning because it excuses ignoring the professed reason for unleashing politics' greatest evil, necessary or otherwise, war, as long as the victorious state can find excuses for the exercise of military might after the fact.

Numerous critics of the war in Iraq and its pre-war justifications have argued that the Bush Administration's motivation to go to war had little, if anything, to do with WMDs, connections to Al-Qaeda, or any of the other various public pronouncements of why war in Iraq was necessary. Instead, they argue that the war was motivated by other less appealing interests. Some have argued the war was the result of the administration's thirst for control of Iraq's vast oil reserves; others have contended the war was initiated to provide a permanent forward operations base located in the heart of the oil-rich yet-volatile Middle East; while others have postulated that the war was a result of Saddam's professed desire to peg his oil exports to the Euro rather than the dollar; still others claim it was a result of a combination of these factors. No matter the reason why the war in Iraq was deemed necessary, it has lead to an American investment in both blood and treasure that will affect Americans and Iraqis for years, if not decades, to come—no matter what President Obama promises.

As mentioned at the beginning of this chapter, the president is the most influential actor when it comes to setting American foreign policy. President Obama campaigned on essentially two foreign policy themes. One, bring American troops out of Iraq, and two, refocus America's diplomatic and military efforts back on Afghanistan while taking the fight to neighboring Pakistan. Let me address each of these in turn. First to Afghanistan:

President Obama declared in March of 2009: "The United States of America did not choose to fight a war in Afghanistan. Nearly 3,000 of our people were killed on September 11, 2001, for doing nothing more than going about their daily lives. So let me be clear: Al-Qaeda and its allies—the terrorists who planned and supported the 9/11 attacks—are in Pakistan and Afghanistan. We have a clear and focused goal to disrupt, dismantle and defeat Al-Qaeda in Pakistan and Afghanistan, and to prevent their return to either country in the future."[83]

The Obama Administration is certainly right about one thing. The military and political situation has never been anywhere near being under control since the ouster of the Taliban regime in 2001—no matter that the media and the Bush Administration acted as if the war there was over long ago; however, Obama's policy is not to extricate American ground troops *from* Afghanistan, but rather to increase our military commitment *in* Afghanistan and Pakistan. There is an old axiom of political science that goes something like this: "Be careful what you wish for, as you might get it." Obama has already ordered thousands of additional American combat troops to Afghanistan with the promise of more thousands to come. Apparently, Obama wants to return American foreign policy vis-à-vis Afghanistan back to 2001 when the whole "War on Terror" commenced. This comes as no surprise given the fact that Obama, once elected, asked Bush's Secretary of Defense, Robert Gates, to stay on with his administration. So, what can we expect in the future? America's top general in Afghanistan recently stated the "we face a stalemate at best" in Afghanistan, and that "this will be a very difficult year for American troops in Afghanistan." There is agreement from all sectors of the American national security establishment that the United States has a very tough task ahead of it in Afghanistan.

In spring of 2009, America's allies in Afghanistan, Europe and Canada, rejected Obama's request for more combat troops to help America in its ramped up effort to turn the tide in Afghanistan. Also, a reporter who accompanied some very high level officials of the Obama Administration when they met with Afghanistan's Minister of the Interior, Hanif Atmar, in early April 2009, reported the following: "An illustration of how hard it will be to turn the war around comes in a security map displayed in Atmar's office. Districts where the insurgency poses a high threat are colored in red; those that are enemy-controlled are black. There is an arc of nearly unbroken red and black across the southern half of the country, where more than half the population lives." Later in his piece he states: "And Afghanistan isn't even the biggest worry for [the Americans]. What scares them more is the Taliban insurgency in neighboring Pakistan."[84]

What is of gravest concern is that Obama's foreign policy goals in Afghanistan and Pakistan are predicated on the hope that the war in Iraq is nearing its end, which will free up America's resources for its military escalation in Afghanistan. However, this hope is simply not supported by the facts on the ground in Iraq. First we need to clarify what Obama means when he says he will withdraw all American "combat" troops from Iraq by 2011. This does not mean there won't be thousands of American "contingency" troops still fighting and dying in Iraq. The top U.S. Commander in Iraq told a reporter that he "would like to see about 30,000 troops still there in 2014 or 2015." So the only difference between a "combat" troop and a "contingency" troop is a semantic one, and this play on words does nothing to change the reality that these terms are interchangeable.

Colonel Peter Mansor, who was executive officer in Iraq from 2006–2008 stated: "The United States has got to be willing to under write this effort for many, many years to come. I can't put it in any brighter colors than that." Another American military officer with years of combat experience in Iraq said this: "I don't think the civil war has been fought yet." Or as Colonel Michael Galloucis, the Military Police commander in Baghdad commented in 2007: "We've made a lot of deals with shady guys [that] is working. But is it sustainable?" As Thomas E. Ricks, a special military correspondent for the *Washington Post* and a senior fellow at the "Center for a New American Security," who has authored two of the most important books on the conflict in Iraq, *Fiasco* and *The Gamble*, wrote: "The quiet consensus emerging among many who have served in Iraq is that U.S. soldiers probably will be engaged in combat there until at least 2015, which puts us at about the midpoint of the conflict now [2009]."[85]

It seems the Obama Administration is going down the same road as the previous administration, only in opposite directions. Bush focused on Iraq while Afghanistan became America's "forgotten war"; now Obama is focusing on Afghanistan and Pakistan while hoping that Iraq simply goes away, or becomes American's new forgotten war. This foreign policy by wishful thinking seems to be working again with the American people as recent polling data confirms. A Gallup poll published in March 2009, found only 6% of Americans mentioned the Iraq war as the most important issues facing America today, while 80% of the respondents listed the economy as the most important issue. What this poll illustrates is Americans have still not grasped the fact that the state of the economy is a direct result of the trillions of dollars America is spending to fight both of these wars.

One last note: Remember all of this was supposed to be about defeating terrorism; particularly in the shape of Osama bin Laden and Al-Qaeda. However, as of this writing, not only does Osama bin Laden remain at large, but much that has occurred corresponds with some of the foreign policy goals for Al-Qaeda. Bin Laden wanted the U.S. troops out of Saudi Arabia—done. He wanted the regime of Saddam Hussein removed because of its secular foundations—done. He wanted a war between civilizations, Muslim versus Christian and Jew, East versus West. Well, America has invaded and occupied two Muslim countries and its government is now fighting on the borders of Syria while threatening Iran.

Osama bin Laden also expressed how he thought Al-Qaeda would win its war with America: "We are continuing this policy in bleeding America to the point of bankruptcy. Allah willing, and nothing is too great for Allah . . . [we did the same thing to the Soviet Union in Afghanistan] using guerrilla warfare and a war of attrition to fight tyrannical superpowers. We bled Russia for 10 years until it went bankrupt and was forced to withdraw in defeat."

For obvious reasons, there is no way to ascertain what covert activities the United States government has been up to during the present decade. For good or bad, to the scholar of American politics, it seems like one would only need to throw a dart at a map to chance upon American covert activity.

FINAL THOUGHTS

What this legacy of questionable United States' foreign policy (particularly since WWII) has cost, and will continue to cost the average American in both financial and moral capital is hard to even fathom; nonetheless, it is time for all of us to confront a fundamental question about our nation's place in the history of empires: Are we, the American people, content with history recording us as one of the greatest warrior nations ever to maintain a reign of terror over the globe? This may at first strike the reader as a bit exaggerated, but is it? Let me suggest a mind experiment that may help you see why this may in fact be an accurate rendition of the history (particularly recent history) of the American empire.

Imagine we are archeologists from the distant future attempting to explain what the culture was like in that long forgotten civilization known as America. In doing so, we have discovered the following salient facts: First, the history of the American people was one of constant warfare—from its beginning in armed rebellion against the

British to its removal of the Native Americans to its involvement in two World Wars, in Korea, in Vietnam, in Iraq, etc.; second, from the last half of the 20th century to the beginning of the 21st century, the Americans destroyed themselves under the weight of debt and domestic decay building and maintaining a military state capable of eliminating the very planet they were protecting; third, their universities, which at the time were the envy of the world, spent the majority of their resources, both economic and intellectual, on creating ever greater weapons of lethal capabilities; fourth, they entertained themselves with visions of human beings slaughtering other human beings at locations which may have been something like temples and were called either "movie theaters" or "video stores"; fifth, their children were left to amuse themselves by playing with war toys either in the form of plastic replications or on their primitive computer technology; sixth, there seems to be evidence that their communities' streets were battlefields, since America during the last part of the 20th to the beginning of the 21st century was a world leader in crimes against their own; lastly, toward the end of their reign, if any members of the community were to question this cultural obsession with conquest, they were considered socially suspect and labeled "un-American," or even worse, an "enemy of freedom." This must have been something terrible indeed, for, in the name of preventing this apparently horrible condition (a virus perhaps?) they destroyed themselves both morally and financially.

Would this not be an accurate picture of our community? If so, then what does this say about us and our democratic community? Of course, this is only a mind experiment and not the actual obituary of the American empire, so there is still time to rethink our place and purpose in the global community and adjust our foreign policy accordingly—but time *is* getting short.

NOTES

1. George Seldes, ed., *The Great Thoughts* (New York: Ballantine Books, 1985).
2. Lance Banning, *Jefferson and Madison: Three Conversations from the Founding* (Madison: Madison House, 1995), pp. 148–149.
3. The Old West: *The Soldiers* (New York: Time-Life Books, 1977), p. 28.
4. Renamed, "Defense," by the National Security Act of 1947.
5. Norman K. Risjord, *Jefferson's America: 1760–1815* (Madison: Madison House, 1991), p. 210.
6. Ronald Steel, *Pax Americana* (New York: Viking, 1967).
7. Robert Sherrill, *Why They Call It Politics: A Guide to America's Government* (New York: Harcourt Brace Jovanovich, 1990), p. 110.
8. Alexander Hamilton, *Federalist 69*.
9. Dean Rusk, who later became President Kennedy's and President Johnson's Secretary of State, made this comment in 1960. Quoted in Arthur M. Schlesinger, Jr., *The Imperial Presidency* (Boston: Houghton Mifflin, 1973).
10. Richard A. Watson and Norman C. Thomas, *The Politics of the Presidency*, 2nd ed. (Washington, D.C.: Congressional Quarterly Press, 1988), p. 478.
11. Ibid., p. 212.
12. Ibid., p. 459.
13. Sherrill, *Why They Call it Politics*, p. 74.

14. Quoted in Thomas E. Patterson, *The American Democracy*, 2nd ed. (New York: McGraw-Hill, Inc., 1994), p. 750.
15. General Douglas MacArthur, speech to Michigan State Legislature, May 15, 1952, quoted in Charles Yost, *The Conduct and Misconduct of Foreign Affairs* (New York: Random House, 1972).
16. Quoted in Sherrill, *Why They Call it Politics*, p. 104.
17. Molly Ivins, "WorldCom Joins War's Profiteers," *The Oregonian* (June 20, 2003) p. C7.
18. For a more thorough analysis of the Carlyle Group's influence see, Dan Briody, *The Iron Triangle: Inside the Secret World of the Carlyle Group*, April 2003.
19. www.thecarlylegroup.com/profile.html.
20. Speech before the American Society of Newspaper Editors, April 16, 1953, quoted in *The New York Times* (April 3, 1985).
21. For an excellent discussion of the war powers of Congress and the presidency see, Louis Fisher, *Constitutional Conflicts between Congress and the President* (Lawrence, Kansas: University Press of Kansas, 1991), and *Presidential War Power* (Lawrence, Kansas: University Press of Kansas, 1995).
22. W. A. Swanberg, *Citizen Hearst: A Biography of William Randolph Hearst* (New York: Charles Scribner's Sons, 1961).
23. For a more thorough discussion on this subject please see chapter 3 on public opinion.
24. See, for example, David Barstow, "Behind on TV Analysts, Pentagon's Hidden Hand," *The New York Times,* (April 20, 2008).
25. Colman McCarthy, "TV's Military 'Embeds,'" *Washington Post,* (April 19, 2003).
26. For an excellent discussion about all of this, see Frank Rich, *The Greatest Story Ever SOLD: The Decline and Fall of Truth in Bush's America,* (Penguin Books, New York) 2007.
27. Historian George Kennan, writing under an anonymous "X" byline, coined the term "containment" in 1947. See George F. Kennan, "The Sources of Soviet Conduct," *Foreign Affairs*, July 1947, Vol. XXV, 4.
28. This idea was also referred to as the "rotten apple" theory though this metaphor never quite caught on with the American public like the "domino theory." In any event, the "rotten apple" theory posits that if one nation goes commie, then eventually they all go communist. Hence, then Secretary of State, Dean Acheson could defend U.S. involvement in Greece by saying, "like apples in a barrel infected by a rotten one, the corruption of Greece would infect" Asia, Europe, and Africa. See Dean Acheson, *Present at the Creation: My Years in the State Department* (New York: WW Norton, 1969), p. 219.
29. Ronald Steele, *Imperialists and Other Heroes* (New York: Random House, 1871), pp. 21–22.
30. Sherrill, *Why they Call It Politics*, p. 112.
31. *The New York Times* (March 15, 1983).
32. Zbigniew Brzezinski, *The Grand Chessboard: American Primacy and its Geostrategic Imperatives* (New York: Basic Books, 1997). p. 124.
33. Ibid., p. 211.
34. See for example the web page www.copvcia.com for a thorough analysis of this issue.
35. See chapter 5 on the Media for a fuller discussion on the negligence of America's national security and intelligence services.
36. To access said document just punch in the acronym PNAC into any Internet search engine.
37. Ibid., p. 69.
38. Ibid., p. v.
39. Ibid., p. 2.
40. Ibid., p. 75.
41. Ibid., p. 23.
42. Ibid., p. 18.
43. Ibid., p. 18.
44. Ibid., p. 18.
45. Ibid., p. 18.

46. There is no more nebulous concept than the so-called "global economy." It is usually defined, if at all, with economically pretentious rhetoric sounding something like this: "The global economy is a result of advanced economic integration due to highly mobile capital and international financial uniformity," or "the global economy refers to the fact of growing international economic interdependence merged with fluid capital as well as a global work force." What all these pretentious explanations really boil down to is that the global economy refers to the fact that whatever serves the interests of global capital will happen and what does not, will not, end of definition. For a much more detailed explanation of this point, see Douglas Dowd, *U. S. Capitalism Since 1776: Of, By and for Which People?* (New York: M.E. Sharpe, 1993), William Greider's *One World Ready or Not: The Manic Logic of Global Capitalism* (New York: Simon & Schuster, 1997), and *Secrets of the Temple: How the Federal Reserve Runs the Country* (New York: Simon & Schuster, 1987). For a less critical analysis of the global economy see, Robert Kuttner's *Everything for Sale: The Virtues and Limits of Markets* (New York: Knopf, 1997).
47. John T. Rourke in, *International Politics on the World Stage*, 4th ed. (Guilford, CN: The Dushkin Publishing Group, Inc., 1993), from where most of the proceeding discussion on MNCs is drawn, writes on page 463, "between 1945 and 1968 direct private investment in international ventures increased 10% annually. Modern MNCs have become economic goliaths. . . . Now there are about 2,000 large MNCs (operating in six or more countries) and over 8,000 smaller MNCs."
48. Daniel S. Papp, *Contemporary International Relations: Frameworks for Understanding* (Macmillian, New York, 1994), p. 100.
49. Ibid., p. 104.
50. "Halliburton Iraq ties more than Cheney said," *NewsMax Wires*, United Press International (June 25, 2001).
51. Molly Ivins, "Cheney Has a Lot of Nerve Trash-Talking Iraq," *The Oregonian* (September 5, 2002), p. D13.
52. From wire reports, "Halliburton Settles Shareholder Suits," *The Oregonian*, (May 31, 2003) p. A2.
53. Warren Vieth and Elizabeth Douglass, "A Big Win for Big Oil," *The Oregonian* (March 14, 2003) p. A2.
54. Michael Liedtke, "The Contractor in Iraq," *The Oregonian* (April 22, 2003) p. A5.
55. Molly Ivins, "WorldCom Joins War's Profiteers," *The Oregonian* (June 20, 2003) p. C7.
56. Georgie Anne Geyer, "New Chapters Open in the Mystery behind the War," *Universal Press Syndicate* (March 13, 2003).
57. Molly Ivins, "WorldCom Joins War's Profiteers."
58. There is no substitute for reading history, and this chronology is not intended to be such a substitute. It is, however, intended to whet the interested reader's appetite.
59. Michael G. Roskin and Nicholas O. Berry, *IR: The New World of International Relations*, 2nd ed. (New Jersey: Prentice Hall, 1993), p. 178.
60. Robert McNamara, *In Retrospect* (New York: Random House, 1995).
61. During WWII, the French will maintain cosmetic administrative control under Japanese rule.
62. Howard Zinn, *A People's History of the United States: 1492–Present* (New York: HarperCollins, 1995) p. 469.
63. Seth Mydans, "Agent Orange Questions Continue," *The Oregonian* (May 16, 1999), p. A9.
64. Patterson, *The American Democracy*, pp. 733–734.
65. Howard Zinn, *A People's History of the United States: 1492–Present*, pp. 581–582.
66. Chris Mooney, "Did the United Nations Authorize 'No fly' Zones Over Iraq?," www.slate.com/?id =2074302, November 11, 2002.
67. "Morbidity and Mortality among Iraqi Children from 1980 to 1998: Assessing the Impact of the Gulf War and Economic Sanctions," A report commissioned by the Fourth Freedom Forum and The Joan B. Kroc Institute for International Peace Studies at the University of Notre Dame, March 1999. See David Cortright, *The Nation*, "A Hard Look at Sanctions," December 3, 2001 for Richard

Garfield's updated figures. This article also puts much of the blame for the humanitarian crisis on Saddam Hussein's regime. See also Seiji Yamada, *Znet*, "The Ongoing Assault: Sanctions and Child Mortality in Iraq," September 27, 2002, for even more updated figures by Garfield. The figure Garfield came up with was originally 227,000 deaths caused by the Gulf War and the sanctions, with three-fourths caused by the sanctions. Garfield subsequently updated his figures to 350,000 and then to 450,000, with the same ratio of Gulf War deaths to sanctions caused mortality.

68. Information and quotes from Geoff Simons, *The Scourging of Iraq: Sanctions, Law and Natural Justice*, 2nd ed. (New York: St. Martin's Press, Inc., 1998), pp. 17–20.
69. See, for example, Joy Gordon, "UN Oil for Food 'Scandal,'" *The Nation*, December 6, 2004.
70. Michael G. Roskin and Nicholas O. Berry, *IR: The New World of International Relations*, 3rd ed. (New Jersey: Prentice Hall, 1997), p. 147.
71. Christopher M. Jones, "American Prewar Technology Sales to Iraq: A Bureaucratic Politics Explanation," in *The Domestic Sources of American Foreign Policy: Insights and Evidence*, 2nd. ed., Eugene R. Wittkopf, ed. (New York: St. Martin's Press, Inc., 1994) pp. 279–282.
72. Michael G. Roskin and Nicholas O. Berry, *IR: The New World of International Relations*, 3rd ed., p. 154.
73. Douglass Kellner, *The Persian Gulf War* (Westview Press, Oxford, 1992) pp. 16–17.
74. The following quotes come from Howard Zinn, *A People's History of the United States: 1492–Present*, pp. 582–583.
75. Scott Lindlaw, "Bush Puts $4 Million More Into His Re-election Coffers," *The Oregonian*, (June 24, 2003) p. A4.
76. On July 12, 2000, the House Committee on International Relations conducted "Hearings on Global Terrorism and South Asia." During the hearing Republican Congressman Dana Rohrabacher asserts the following: "I have stated that I believe that there is a covert policy by [the Clinton Administration], a shameful covert policy of supporting the Taliban . . . it is clear that they discouraged all of the anti-Taliban supporters from supporting the efforts in Afghanistan to defeat the Taliban. . . . High ranking officials of the [Clinton] Administration, personally visited the region in order to discourage the Taliban's opposition from attacking the Taliban when they were vulnerable, and then going to neighboring countries to cut off any type of military assistance to the opponents of the Taliban. . . . One last note: Many people here understand that I have been in Afghanistan on numerous occasions and have close ties to people there. *And let me just say that some of my sources of information informed me of where bin Laden was, they told me they knew and could tell people where bin Laden could be located. And it took me three times before [the Clinton] administration responded . . . to even investigate that there might be someone who could give them the information. And when my contact was actually contacted, he said that the people who contacted him were half-hearted, did not follow through, did not appear to be that interested* . . . [emphasis added]." Moreover, on April 30, 2003, Congressman Rohrabacher gave a speech on the floor of the United States House of Representatives titled "American Foreign Policy," where he stated: "September 11, was the result of bad policy . . . And it was something that could have been averted had we had different policies. Yet, we had policies that led to 9/11 . . . I would submit that 9/11 need not to have happened. It started with our policy in Afghanistan . . . We helped the Afghans fight against the Soviet Army that occupied their country . . . [with our help] they drove the Soviets out . . . Yet the Afghans were left alone to fight each other in the rubble, with no assistance or help from the United States . . . So what ended up happening was that we simply left . . . Well, what emerged in Afghanistan was truly evil . . . But the Taliban . . . did not just emerge in power. It was there because the United States policy permitted it to be or . . . even supported the creation of the Taliban in agreement with Pakistan and Saudi Arabia . . . I was always so frustrated about this, because I knew that the United States Government had a policy of supporting . . . this monstrous regime . . . Well, what happened recently? About two months ago the foreign minister of Pakistan came to visit California and got up and publicly acknowledged that it was not just Pakistan and Saudi Arabia

that created the Taliban, but it was the United States . . . " To access the full speech just type in "Congressional Record" in any Internet search engine and when the site appears type in the page search area "page H3553" and it will appear in total.

77. See Nafeez Mosaddeq Ahmed, "Afghanistan, the Taliban and the United States: The Role of Human Rights in Western Foreign Policy," May 2, 2001, www.mediamonitors.net.
78. Ibid.
79. For a concise discussion on the matter see Larry Chin, "Unocal and the Afghanistan Pipeline," *Online Journal*, Centre for research on Globalisation, March 6, 2002, www.globalresearch.ca. For a more detailed analysis see Nafeez Mosaddeq Ahmed, "Afghanistan, the Taliban and the United States: The Role of Human Rights in Western Foreign Policy," May 2, 2001, www.mediamonitors.net.
80. Ibid.
81. Ibid.
82. George F. Will, *Washington Post Writers Group*, "Pre-Emptive Policy in Peril," *The Oregonian*, (June 22, 2003) p. F3.
83. Source, Foreign policy speech delivered on March 28, 2009.
84. David Ignatius, "A New Exercise in Strategic Listening," Washington Post Writer's Group, *The Oregonian*, (April 7, 2009) p. B5.
85. All of the above quotes come from an essay written by Thomas Ricks, titled, "We Fool Ourselves to Think We'll be Out Soon," Washington Post Writer's Group, *The Oregonian*, (February 22, 2009) p. B1.

Section III

National Institutions

CHAPTER 8
The Article I Branch: The Congress

"If there be any thing amiss . . . in the present state of our affairs . . . I ascribe it to the inattention of Congress to its duties, to their unwise dissipation and waste of the public contributions."
—Thomas Jefferson

"One should never see either sausage or laws being made"
—Otto von Bismarck

"The whole art of government consists in the art of being honest."
—Thomas Jefferson

INTRODUCTION

This chapter will examine the first branch of the federal government, the United States Congress. We will begin by reviewing the constitutional structure of Congress, spending some time looking at both the procedural and conceptual personality of the institution. In addition, we will detail the inherent duality of Congress, an institution that is both one entity (Congress) as well as two (the Senate and the House of Representatives). From there, we will focus on the present day workings of both houses to grasp their contemporary flavor. Next, we will articulate the three basic functions of Congress so as to gain a better comprehension of its purpose as well as its practice. Lastly, we will conclude with some final comments on Congress and its place in our representative scheme of government.

THE CONSTITUTIONAL CONGRESS

After the preamble, the Constitution begins with these words: "All legislative powers herein granted shall be vested in a Congress of the United States."[1] Immediately then, we see the first institution the Founders constructed via the Constitution was Congress; and for this reason alone, it is appropriate to call Congress the first branch of government. But, as we shall see shortly, there are more substantive reasons for its priority.

The Founders were well aware of the elementary political maxim that all governments have in essence three fundamental duties: They make law, they enforce law, and they resolve conflicts within the law. Furthermore, the Founders, much enamored with the Enlightenment political philosophy of their day, believed governing power could best be held in check by separating these three duties into different branches, thereby preventing any government from exercising too much authority.[2]

Unlike monarchical theory, which posited that kings had a "divine" right to perform all three tasks, republican theory demanded each function (lawmaking, enforcement, and adjudication) be performed by separate and distinct branches as a way to check the governing power of each. Hence, the Founders wove the theoretical principle of separation-of-powers into the fabric of the Constitution and created three distinct branches empowered to perform only one of these three functions. Moreover, since by necessity the function of lawmaking precedes the other two functions of government (government must, after all, make law before anything else can be done concerning it), it seemed only logical to place the legislative (lawmaking) branch first, followed in order by the executive (enforcement) and the judicial (adjudicatory) branches. Hence, Article 1 of the Constitution creates the legislative branch, Congress, while Article 2 creates the executive branch, consisting of the presidency and the bureaucracies, and, lastly, Article 3 creates the judicial branch, composed of the **Supreme Court** and all other federal courts—just as Enlightenment orthodoxy would have it. It was not only due to logical necessity, however, that the Founders listed Congress first in the Constitution. They believed the authority to make law to be the most powerful and dominant act of any government. As the chief architect of the Constitution, James Madison, himself stated: "In republican government the legislative authority, necessarily, predominates."[3] And, as one contemporary political scholar has written:

> The arguments at the Constitutional Convention assumed the doctrine of legislative supremacy . . . [and] the Constitution's measures fit the presumed background of legislative supremacy. Congress is given what might be called "shoot-out" power, the weapons for final showdown with both other branches. Suppose a President refuses to execute the laws passed by Congress. Congress has a resort: It can impeach the President. The President, unlike even limited or constitutional monarchs, cannot dissolve his parliament. He can veto; but if the Congress overrides, he has no further resort. The Supreme Court is in the same situation. It can declare a law passed by Congress unconstitutional. But Congress has further resort in the law: It can amend the Constitution on the contested point. Then the Court has no further say in the matter. Actually, Congress has a variety of weapons—it can impeach the justices; it can refuse to levy funds for enforcing the Court's decision; it can pass constitutional laws on related matters that make the Court's original declaration of unconstitutionality nugatory; it can change the makeup of the Court; it can amend the Constitution to deny judicial review. In all cases, the Court will have no further say in the matter. . . . The very structure of the Constitution, [therefore] . . . indicates the order of the branches both in logic and in scope.[4]

In short, Congress is considered the first branch of government because, not only did the Founders define it in Article 1 of the Constitution, they also knew Congress would be first in function as well as supreme in power. For reasons that will be discussed in more detail in the chapter on the executive branch, the notion of congressional supremacy strikes most Americans as an inaccurate picture of contemporary politics. Too many of us today see the president as the be all and end all of the governing establishment, relegating Congress to the sidelines of American politics. To be sure, Congresspersons themselves help facilitate this misconception so as to protect themselves from political accountability. Most contemporary congresspersons, in hopes of avoiding responsibility for the state of our political system today, seem only too willing to let the president take the spotlight, as well as the heat, of public scrutiny. In this way members of Congress can continue to run for reelection against the "lousy job government is doing" without ever worrying about the public recognizing it is they who are in fact the ones doing the lousy job. Nevertheless, Congress was designed, and, in practice, still is, the first branch of the federal government.

The Constitutional Duality of the Congress. As mentioned earlier, Article 1, Section 1 of the Constitution begins by creating "a Congress of the United States," however, these words are immediately followed by the clause, "which shall consist of a Senate and House of Representatives." As this language demonstrates, Congress is both one institution as well as two.[5] That is, there is an institutional duality to Congress; in some respects it is a single institution granted certain general powers, while it also consists of two distinct institutions with particular differences in qualifications, constituencies and duties. And, of course, the Constitution articulates this duality in both its structure and language, which we will now examine in more detail.

Congress as One Institution. Article 1 of the Constitution treats Congress as one institution for three general purposes. First, in Section 1, when granting both houses the general law making powers of the federal government. That is, the Constitution grants "Congress," and neither house in particular, the authority to write federal statutes, and, hence, both houses share this power. Second, it does so when listing the constitutional powers of Congress in Section 8. And, lastly, it does so when enumerating the limits on Congress' lawmaking power in Section 9. For example, Section 8 grants "Congress" in general the power "to lay and collect taxes," "to regulate commerce," and "to declare war." While Section 9 tells "Congress" that "the privilege of the writ of habeas corpus shall not be suspended," and that "no bill of attainder or ex post facto law shall be passed." In addition, Sections 5 and 6 also treat Congress as a single entity while stipulating, among other things, the self-governing nature of both houses and their compensation, respectively. On the other hand, Section 7 reflects the duality of Congress and serves as a nice segue to the next section, which deals with Congress as separate institutions, since it first states that only the House of Representatives can initiate "all bills for raising revenue," and then proceeds to treat Congress as one institution by granting both houses the general authority to override presidential vetoes.

Congress as Two Separate Institutions—The House of Representatives and the Senate. Before we detail the constitutional differences between the two houses, we first must review why the Founders thought it necessary to create separate houses within

Congress. The Founders did so for two reasons, one practical, and the other theoretical. The practical motivation was the result of the unique historical experience of the American founding. As most of us may recall, the American nation began as essentially thirteen independent communities, known first as colonies and later (after the Revolution) as states. Hence, when the colonies won independence from the British, the first political arrangement agreed upon was one of confederation (the constitution they adopted was called the *Articles of Confederation*). Under this arrangement, each state was loosely tied to the others, but for most intents and purposes, each state was free to govern its particular community as it saw fit.[6] After a brief period, there grew a demand for a stronger system of political association which led most of the states to send representatives to Philadelphia for a gathering to rethink the *Articles;* today, this gathering is referred to as the "Constitutional Convention." One of the first orders of business was to determine how each state should be represented in the new central legislature, which they labeled Congress. Predictably, the more populous and powerful states wanted Congress to reflect their political supremacy, and, of course, the less populous states were reluctant to agree to such a Congress as it would render them politically insignificant. After numerous debates, they settled on the so-called "Connecticut Compromise" and agreed to create two houses within Congress, with one favoring large states and one favoring the smaller states. Therefore, the House of Representatives is biased in favor of more populous states, as each state receives a number of representatives proportional to its population (for example, today Oregon has five, Minnesota eight whereas California is allotted 53), while the Senate is based on state equality, which favors smaller states, since each state gets two Senators regardless of population.

The theoretical reason the Founders created two institutions within the Congress was to check the power of the legislature. That is, the Founders, believing the legislature to be the supreme force in government, thought it would be wise to divide Congress in half to lessen its authority. Hence, under the principle of separation-of-powers, the Founders split the legislative branch in two so as to play one house against the other. This split personality between the House of Representatives and the Senate is manifested throughout Article 1, and to a much lesser extent, in Article 2. For example, Article 1, Section 2 declares that "the House of Representatives shall be composed of members chosen every second year by the people of the several states," and that "no person shall be a Representative who shall not have attained to the age of twenty-five years, and been seven years a citizen of the United States." Whereas, Section 3 stipulates, "the Senate of the United States shall be composed of two Senators from each state, chosen by the legislature thereof [later changed by the 17th Amendment], for six years," and that "no person shall be a Senator who shall not have attained to the age of thirty years, and been nine years a citizen of the United States." Furthermore, Article 1, Section 2 creates a "Speaker" of the House and demands that the House "shall have the sole power of Impeachment." Whereas, Article 1, Section 3 states, "the Vice-President of the United States shall be President of the Senate," and will cast the deciding vote if the Senate "be equally divided," and that "the Senate shall have the sole power to try all impeachments." Lastly, even the executive branch article, Article 2, treats the Senate and House as separate entities by granting, in Section 2, only the Senate the power to ratify treaties and confirm executive appointments. Therefore, as we proceed with our discussion, it is important to bear in mind the inherent duality of Congress, as this will require us to examine both its general nature as well as recognize the uniqueness of both its houses.

WORKING CONGRESS

Now that we have some sense of the constitutional personality of Congress, it is time to review its present day workings. Congress, like the country, and for better or for worse, has grown much beyond the wildest imaginations of the founding generation.[7] After all, what began in Philadelphia as a constitutional abstraction for a fledgling nation, and whose first Congress met in New York and consisted of 65 House members and 26 Senators, has grown into an institution totaling 535 members (435 Representatives and 100 Senators) which writes the laws for the most powerful government the world has ever known. And, coupled with this phenomenal growth, there have emerged some institutional developments which require our attention.[8] We will spend this section of the chapter detailing three specific developments which evolved, not from constitutional language, but from the actual practice of lawmaking—the rise of political parties, the development of the committee structure, and the emergence of the so-called "shadow" government.

The Rise of Political Parties. As noted in the chapter on political parties, the Founders warned against the dangers of "factions" and, hence, made no mention of political parties in the Constitution. However, as their own political experience taught them, it seems representative government is inherently "factious" and thereby requires some sort of official political organization, or, in short, political parties. In other words, even though the Founders argued against the evils of political parties in theory, almost immediately Congress became an institution permeated with party politics—and it has remained so ever since. For this reason, almost every action of the contemporary Congress is affected in some manner by partisan politics. The most obvious way in which party politics affects the workings of Congress is the fact that, except when overriding a presidential **veto**, all statutes are enacted by a simple majority vote, which of course favors the party with the majority of members.[9]

The rise of political parties has also drastically altered the leadership roles in both houses.[10] For example, the office of the Speaker, though constitutionally the leader of the whole House, has developed, with the emergence of parties, into a more partisan position since he or she is elected by a simple majority. Today the Speaker is more the Speaker of the majority party than **Speaker of the House**. The effect on the constitutional leadership of the Senate has been similar. For example, the constitutionally mandated leader of the Senate, the "President Pro Tempore," has been reduced to a mere ceremonial position (awarded the most senior member of the majority party), as its leadership role has been assumed by the non-constitutional position of Senate "**majority leader**." In addition, there has emerged within both institutions a full menu of leadership roles based entirely on the reality of partisan politics. For example, besides the Speaker, the majority party in the House now elects a "**majority leader**," who is second in command, as well as a "**majority whip**," whose main function is to "whip" the party members into agreement with the leadership. Furthermore, the minority party within both houses also has its leadership roles. Hence, there is a "**minority leader**" who is in charge of setting the legislative agenda of the minority party, a "**minority whip**," who serves the same function for the minority party as the **majority whip** does for his or her party.

Party politics also affects the committee structure of both houses of Congress. As we will see below, most of the actual legislative work takes place within the numerous committees that make up the actual organization of Congress. The committee structure of both houses is designed to ensure the party in power has a majority of members on every substantive committee. This, of course, guarantees the majority party control over legislation since almost all actions at the committee level are based on a simple majority vote. In short, understanding how Congress works depends, first and foremost, on recognizing how the rise and development of political parties has influenced, and will continue to influence, the very nature of the most representative branch of the American political system.

The Development of the Committee System. The single most striking organizational development in Congress has been the emergence of congressional committees. The first Congress had no permanent committees as legislative action took place entirely on the floor of each house.[11] However, in 1801 the House established the first committee structure in response to the nation's first partisan disagreement, which took place between Adams' Federalist Party and Jefferson's Anti-Federalist Party. Jefferson's party emerged victorious, winning both Congress and the presidency, and to help implement their political agenda they reconfigured the legislative process in the House. In doing so, Jefferson and his party colleagues (known as "Jefferson's Lieutenants" at the time) created the first committees in the House to help expedite the passage of their program. Though these first committees lacked a fixed jurisdiction, they proved so successful that by 1814 House committees not only were permanent and had fixed jurisdictions, they also, in the words of one political scientist, "had become the dominant force within the chamber," and have remained so today.[12]

The evolution of committees was slower in the Senate but no less irresistible. The committee structure evolved more slowly in the Senate due to its institutional peculiarities. As mentioned above, Congress is really two distinct institutions, each with a unique personality, and nowhere has this been this more evident than when it came to developing a committee system. The House, with its larger number of members and shorter terms, has developed into a much more rule-governed institution, whereas the Senate, with its exclusiveness and longer terms, has always granted much more autonomy to individual Senators. Hence, in the House, the leadership, starting with the Speaker, exercises more control over their membership than the leadership in the Senate exercises over theirs. For example, the House has strict rules regarding legislative debate, dictating what can be added to a bill, who can speak about the bill on the floor, and for how long, while each Senator has the privilege of filibuster (the right to speak on any bill for as long as they wish).[13] For this reason, up until the 1830s there was little impetus in the Senate to develop a formal committee structure, since this was viewed as encroaching upon the autonomy of each Senator. By the 1830s, however, the Senate, much like the country, could no longer ignore the moral outrage of slavery. Furthermore, given the state equality inherent in the Senate, it became the main political battleground over the issue since slave states and non-slave states were of equal political standing. The animosity between Northern and Southern Senators forced the Senate to substitute informal geniality with committee procedure and structure. In any event, by the beginning of the Civil War in 1861, the Senate had joined the House and placed permanent committees at the forefront of legislative activity.

Today, there are in essence four types of committees within both houses—**standing committees**, **select committees**, **joint committees**, and **conference committees**. Each type of committee has a unique purpose within the legislative process, hence, we will spend the rest of this section becoming more familiar with each, starting with the most important, the standing committees.

Standing committees get their name from the fact they are permanent committees, or, in other words, are left "standing" at the end of each session of Congress. Furthermore, there are two types of standing committees, **full committees** and **subcommittees**. Full committees and subcommittees differ in both number and scope. That is, there are only 20 full committees in the House and 16 in the Senate and they have a wider range of jurisdiction than subcommittees, which number over 100 in each house.[14] Where they are similar is in function; both full and subcommittees are the center of legislative activity and it is within these standing committees that the work of Congress is accomplished. As the authors of a text on American government have written:

> The standing committees and their subcommittees are the core of the congressional process. Votes on the floor of the Senate or House may finally determine the success or failure of a proposal, but the important decisions that determine its ultimate fate have normally been made in the committee that considered it.[15]

For example, the House has a full committee named "Ways and Means" which, along with the Senate's full "Finance" committee, drafts all the federal tax laws in America, while each house has an "Appropriations" committee which has jurisdiction over how this revenue will be spent. Needless to say, these are four of the most powerful committees in Congress and are considered plum assignments for any congressperson.[16] The only committees which rival these for influence would be both houses' "Budget" committees and the "Rules" committee in the House.[17] As the names imply, the first two committees have jurisdiction over the federal budget, while the Rules committee, among other important duties, sets the rules for debating and amending bills in the House when they come to floor for passage.

*These committees are very important & you never ever have to re-elected again

174 AMERICAN DEMOCRACY: PROMISE AND BETRAYAL

Standing Committees of the House and Senate

House **Senate**

Take decide where the money goes

Agriculture   Agriculture, Nutrition & Forestry
Appropriations *very important*   Appropriations Spending
Armed Services   Armed Services
Budget   Banking, Housing & Urban Affairs
Education and the Workforce   Budget
Energy and Commerce   Commerce, Science & Transportation
Financial Services   Energy and Natural Resources
Government Reform   Environment and Public Works
Homeland Security   Finance Taxation
House Administration   Foreign Relations
International Relations   Health, Education, Labor, and Pensions
Judiciary   Homeland Security & Government Affairs
Resources   Judiciary confirm fed juddice
Rules *Most important*   Rules and Administration
Science   Small Business and Entrepreneurship
Small Business   Veteran's Affairs
Standards of Official Conduct
Transportation and Infrastructure
Veteran's Affairs
Ways and Means Taxation committee

Select committees serve a more political function than a substantive one since, unlike standing committees, they lack the authority to write legislation. In other words, select committees perform such cosmetic duties as investigations, public hearings, and issuance of reports, but cannot propose any bill to address the concerns they voice. Examples of select committees are the Senate's select committees on ethics, Indian affairs, and intelligence, and the House's select committees on intelligence.

Joint committees are similar to select committees, as they also have no authority to propose legislation. The difference between the two is not in function but in membership. Joint committees, as the name implies, are composed of members of both houses, with the chair rotating between houses each year. In addition to the political cosmetics discussed above, joint committees also serve an advisory and coordination role for both houses. The best contemporary example of a joint committee is the Joint Economic Committee; other examples of joint committees are the Library, Printing, and Taxation committees. Conference committees, on the other hand, are special joint committees that perform a substantive role in the legislative process that will be discussed in much more detail later in the chapter.

The Growth of the Shadow Government. The last development of the working Congress we need to examine is the growth of the "**shadow government.**" The rather sinister phrase shadow government refers to the emergence and growth of congressional staffs.[18] The number of both committee staffs and personal staffs have grown much beyond what can be considered good for our representative scheme. As a group of political scientists have written:

> At the beginning of this century, representatives had no personal staff and senators had only thirty-nine personal assistants. [H]owever, the number of personal assistants allocated to members had mushroomed to more than eleven thousand. Although most of these assistants spend their time providing constituency service and casework, staffers also participate in the legislative process. Members of both the House and the Senate have come to rely heavily on their personal staff to conduct research, write questions to be posed to witnesses in committee hearings, write speeches, draft bills and amendments to bills, and prepare briefs on pending legislation. Moreover, much of the negotiation among members is conducted not by the members themselves but by the staff assistants. In addition to the personal staff, more than two thousand people are assigned to the various committees and subcommittees of Congress. With little responsibility for constituency service, committee staff are involved in drafting legislation and conducting committee investigations. Because they provide needed technical expertise, committee staffers often play a vital role in forming policy. In fact, committee staff often act as policy entrepreneurs, developing new initiatives and then persuading the committee to accept them.[19]

In other words, much of the work of Congress is now being performed by individuals who have never been elected and cannot be held accountable—hardly what we should expect from our "representative government."[20] Even some representatives are troubled by the growth of congressional staffs. For example, Senator Barry Goldwater, before leaving office in 1986, complained staff members "don't have anything to do, so they sit down and write amendments and bills. My god, the number of bills on the calendar every year is unbelievable."[21] Or, as former Senator Fritz Hollings of South Carolina remarked, "everybody is working for staff, staff, staff, driving you nutty, in fact. It has gotten to the point where the senators never actually sit down and learn from the experience of others and listen."[22] Congressman Christopher Shays, while ignoring the effect staff enlargement and entanglement has had on the representative nature of Congress, commented on the practical ramifications of this growth by stating, "we need to . . . reduce the committee staff by 50 percent. It would make Congress more efficient and save a small fortune."[23]

In addition to congressional staffs, there has also been a corresponding growth in the institutional support apparatus of Congress, as it has created four major agencies to furnish technical advice to its members. The Congressional Research Service, established in 1914 as an appendage to the Library of Congress, helps provide data and analysis for members of Congress. The Government Accountability Office, created in 1921, serves as Congress' auditing service, which helps the Congress perform its **oversight** responsibilities (to be discussed below). In 1972 Congress created the Office of Technology Assessment to perform evaluations of the various technologies which were, and still are, emerging. Lastly, in 1974 Congress created its own budgetary agency, the Congressional Budget Office, to provide it with budgetary information and analysis independent of the executive branch. Therefore, one of the most important developments of Congress since its first session in 1789 has been the enormous growth of its support personnel and agencies. So enormous in fact, that today "Congress boasts a support army of 30,000 people for 535 representatives" which can be detrimental to our political system by permitting too many nonelected personnel to perform the task of representation.[24]

FUNCTIONS OF CONGRESS

Now that we have a sense of the constitutional and working dimensions of Congress, it is time to articulate its basic functions or purposes. In the American political system there are in essence three primary functions to be performed by our federal representatives: First, they must make policy; second, they must represent their constituents; and, lastly, they must oversee the workings of the executive branch. We will now review each of these functions in turn.

Policy Making. As mentioned earlier, Congress is constitutionally charged with writing the **federal statutes** of the United States government. Today, congressional statutes are superior to all other laws in the American political system except for the Constitution itself. If a federal or state bureaucratic regulation conflicts with a federal statute, then the regulation must give way, for example. Additionally, no state constitution or statute may contradict any federal statute, for if they do, these state laws must also bow before the legal supremacy of the congressional statute. Hence, one of the main functions of Congress is writing the laws that set the most authoritative policies in the American political system. For example, there would not be a federal welfare program without a congressional statute creating one; there would be no military establishment without a series of authorizing statutes; and, there would be no federal environmental regulations at all without congressional permission. That is, most every policy of the federal government constitutionally requires at the outset an act of Congress for it to become a reality. The rest of this section will be dedicated to explaining the process by which Congress writes statutes or, in other words, makes policy.

As the accompanying graph illustrates, the legislative process is dominated by the standing committees of Congress and is basically similar in both houses. What the graph fails to articulate, however, is the reality that there is simply no single process a bill follows to become a law. To be sure, the graph does illustrate the most orthodox fashion in which a bill becomes a law, nonetheless, in many instances one house or the other will waver from standard procedure for political purposes. In any event, here is the most common way a bill becomes a law in Congress: First, a bill is introduced in both houses and assigned to a full committee which then sends it to a subcommittee for consideration. If approved by the subcommittee, it is then sent back to the full

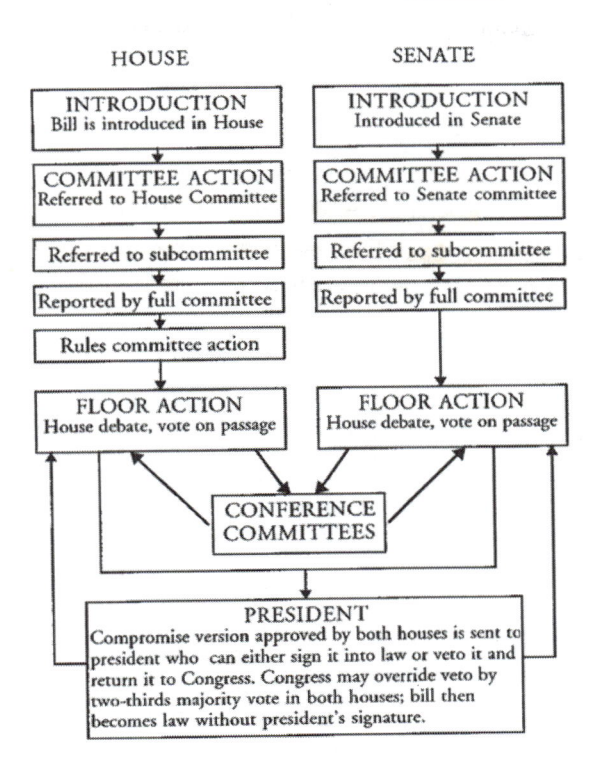

```
            HOUSE                    SENATE
      ┌─────────────────┐   ┌─────────────────┐
      │  INTRODUCTION   │   │  INTRODUCTION   │
      │Bill is introduced│   │Introduced in Senate│
      │    in House     │   │                 │
      └────────┬────────┘   └────────┬────────┘
               ▼                     ▼
      ┌─────────────────┐   ┌─────────────────┐
      │ COMMITTEE ACTION│   │COMMITTEE ACTION │
      │Referred to House│   │Referred to Senate│
      │   Committee     │   │   committee     │
      └────────┬────────┘   └────────┬────────┘
               ▼                     ▼
      ┌─────────────────┐   ┌─────────────────┐
      │Referred to      │   │Referred to      │
      │subcommittee     │   │subcommittee     │
      └────────┬────────┘   └────────┬────────┘
               ▼                     ▼
      ┌─────────────────┐   ┌─────────────────┐
      │Reported by full │   │Reported by full │
      │committee        │   │committee        │
      └────────┬────────┘   └────────┬────────┘
               ▼                     │
      ┌─────────────────┐            │
      │Rules committee  │            │
      │action           │            │
      └────────┬────────┘            ▼
               ▼                     
      ┌─────────────────┐   ┌─────────────────┐
      │  FLOOR ACTION   │   │  FLOOR ACTION   │
      │House debate,    │   │House debate,    │
      │vote on passage  │   │vote on passage  │
      └────────┬────────┘   └────────┬────────┘
               │                     │
               ▼                     ▼
              ┌───────────────────────┐
              │     CONFERENCE        │
              │     COMMITTEES        │
              └───────────┬───────────┘
                          ▼
           ┌────────────────────────────────┐
           │          PRESIDENT             │
           │Compromise version approved by  │
           │both houses is sent to president│
           │who can either sign it into law │
           │or veto it and return it to     │
           │Congress. Congress may override │
           │veto by two-thirds majority vote│
           │in both houses; bill then       │
           │becomes law without president's │
           │signature.                      │
           └────────────────────────────────┘
```

committee where, if approved, it is sent to the Rules Committee in the House or directly to the floor in the Senate. Hence, the only real procedural difference between the House and the Senate when it comes to the legislative process is the presence of the Rules Committee. The Rules Committee is so named because its members have the authority to set the "rules" of debate for all bills considered on the floor of the House. For example, the Rules Committee may, by issuing a closed rule, prohibit any amendments to a bill. It also sets the calendar of the House, determining when (or if) a bill comes to the floor for vote, as well as specifying the time allotted for debate and so forth. For these reasons, one of the most powerful committees in the House is the Rules Committee whose membership constitutes some of the most influential congresspersons in the House. Moreover, one of the most powerful tools at the Speaker's disposal is her authority to appoint the members of the Rules Committee, as the success of any given piece of legislation is very much in the hands of the Rules Committee. The absence of such a committee in the Senate helps demonstrate the different personality of both houses. As mentioned previously, the House is a much more rule-governed institution than the Senate, as is illustrated by the presence of a "rules" committee in one and not the other.

If a bill is fortunate enough to have survived the committee deliberations of both houses and has been approved by the majority of both houses in full (the floor), it, most likely, will then need to be sent to a conference committee. A conference committee is a committee made up of members of both houses who, having played a significant part in the proposed legislation, must now reconcile the two different versions of the same bill. That is, by the time a bill has completed the legislative process of both houses it very likely is identical in name only, since each house has probably added its own particular flavor to the proposed piece of legislation. To reconcile the two versions of the bill, the conference committee negotiates a single version of the bill that is then sent back to the floor of both houses, and if approved by majority vote of both, is then sent to the president. If the president signs the bill it becomes a federal statute; if he vetoes it, the Congress may override his veto with a two-thirds majority vote of both houses and enact the statute against the president's wishes.

As we can see, the legislative process is cumbersome indeed, and for this reason alone, is biased in favor of the status-quo.[25] Moreover, the conservative nature of the legislative process is further enhanced by the fact that bills can, and usually do, die at any stage of the legislative process. In fact the vast majority of bills never make it out of committee deliberations and, in the words of the authors of *American Government*, find their "final resting place" in committee.[26] In support of their contention, they quote Woodrow Wilson's description of a bill's fate in committee which bears repeating: "As a rule, a bill committed [to committee] is a bill doomed. When it goes from the clerk's desk to a committee room, it crosses a parliamentary bridge of sighs and dim dungeons of silence whence it will never return."[27]

Before moving on to the section on representation, I would be remiss if I failed to mention the more substantive and negative aspects of the legislative process.[28] As most of us are by now somewhat aware, the contemporary legislative process has been deeply contaminated by the enormous increase in special interest money, the growth of an army of big business professional lobbyists, and, most fundamentally, a lack of ethics on the part of too many congresspersons.[29] For example, one political scientist notes:

> Take the five U.S. senators who ran interference for a bankrupt savings and loan, delaying its seizure by federal bank regulators. Buying additional time permitted the owners to drain off liquid assets, adding considerably to the astonishing $2 billion cost of the eventual government bailout. Yet all five senators denied that their actions had been influenced by the more than $1 million in campaign contributions from the chairman of the S&L. They dismissed the episode as a routine constituent service. One of them went so far as to say, "I have done this kind of thing many, many times," and likened his actions to "helping the little old lady who didn't get her Social Security." The whole system of political finance that gives rise to these routine activities must be reformed if politicians are to develop a healthier sense of the public interest.[30]

Here are some more examples of federal lawmakers making policy that promotes the interests of their wealthy campaign contributors at the expense of the public good: In exchange for cable industry contributions amounting to almost $3 million, Congress passed the Telecommunications Act which has cost consumers $117 million a month in increased cable rates, while also generating billions of dollars of profit for these very same cable corporations; as a result of millions and millions of dollars in contributions from the so-called financial community, Congress deregulated the banking system that has led directly to America's dire financial situation; and, in return for their healthy campaign contributions, drug companies such as Searle & Co., and Glaxo Wellcome persuaded Congress to extend the patent on their most profitable medications preventing competition from less expensive generic drugs, resulting in billions of extra profits for these corporations at the expense of the consumer.[31] Is it any wonder William Greider, in his book *Who Will Tell the People,* likens the contemporary legislative process to a "grand bazaar" where the sacred ideal of participatory democracy has given way to a legislative culture in which congresspersons consider it standard operating procedure to auction off their vote to the highest bidder?[32] This provides an appropriate, though depressing, segue to our examination of the next function of Congress—representation.

Representation. The single most important function of any congressperson is representation. As noted throughout much of this book, the only source of moral authority behind the American government's coercive power is its claim to a representative character. In other words, the only thing that morally differentiates the American political system from, say, Nazi Germany, or Saddam's former regime in Iraq, is its representative constitutional structure. Let us not forget, however, the corollary is true as well: If our political system lacks a sufficient degree of representation, then it becomes no more morally defensible than the most evil regimes which have plagued mankind. This is no hyperbole; too many Americans have sacrificed their lives defending the representative principle for us, the contemporary Americans, to ignore its importance in our political system. For this reason, my concern for representation has permeated this entire book, and is the focus of an entire chapter (Chapter 11). Therefore, for present concerns, I would like to focus our attention primarily on one aspect of representation—namely, accountability. To this task we now turn.

The idea that the people, via elections, hold their representatives accountable for their actions is one of the bedrock principles of democracy. If the people agree with the policies adopted by their politicians, then they, the theory goes, will reward them with another term. If the people are not pleased, then they will elect someone else. Today, Congress increasingly attempts to sever the obvious connection between legislative policies and electoral success or failure by abdicating their responsibility, and, hence, their accountability. Explaining how congresspersons are avoiding responsibility for the policies of the federal government will constitute the rest of this section.

Too many representatives are so beholden to the financial elite that every policy they endorse must serve the interests of their wealthy masters. Yet in doing so, they necessarily harm the vast majority of Americans in the process. Therefore, to avoid accountability, contemporary congresspersons have learned to rely on extra-legislative commissions (usually referred to as "blue ribbon" commissions), which allow them to please their wealthy contributors while insulating them politically from the harm done to working families. Instead of authoring these policies themselves, congresspersons create "objective nonpartisan" commissions stocked with members of the corporate elite and let these commissions write the policies. This of course prevents them from being held accountable since, after all, they only enacted policies suggested by "experts" who are immune to party politics. In other words, Congress, to avoid responsibility for the policies of the federal legislature, in effect, sub-contract their representative responsibility to their wealthy contributors all under the guise of nonpartisan expert analysis. This was the tactic used to bail out the failing banking system on the backs of hard-working Americans. Congress asked members of the "financial community" to serve on a special commission to suggest "solutions" to the crisis. In the end, the commission decided that since the money lost by members of the very same "financial community" belonged to middle class Americans, it was only appropriate for working Americans to pay themselves back with an increase in their taxes—and Congress agreed; after all, they argued, this was too technical a matter for public deliberation.[33]

A good example of this political tactic was when a Republican Senator proposed that a "nonpartisan" commission reconfigure the so-called Consumer Price Index as a way to help balance the budget. In this way, he hoped to cut government spending by decreasing government aid to working Americans while still delivering tax cuts and more corporate welfare which so enrich his wealthy contributors.[34] So egregious was this move that one of the few responsible members of Congress, Peter DeFazio D-Ore., was compelled to write, "[t]hose who want to balance the budget on the backs of seniors and middle-income Americans shouldn't hide behind the dubious findings of a stacked commission. Let's . . . have our budget debates out in the open, without sham or pretense."[35] Let them indeed. Fred Wertheimer, then president of *Common Cause*, best summarized the whole sad state of contemporary representation when he observed:

> Washington has become an ethics swamp. Our nation's capital is addicted to special interest money, and members of Congress are benefiting professionally and personally from these funds. In the last six years, special interests have poured [millions of dollars into campaign contributions] along with millions in honoraria fees, and countless additional millions in illegal soft money and other payments into our system of government. These payments represent investments in government decision-making—investments which improperly and unfairly magnify voices of special interests at the expense of representative government. We've always experienced individual cases of corruption and impropriety in government. But today we have a system of institutionalized corruption. The rules themselves allow activities to take place legally that are improper and corrupting. Washington insiders argue that the American people don't really care about Washington's ethics mess. They're wrong. But what's happening is even more dangerous than what they perceive as indifference on the part of the American public. The American people are moving beyond outrage to a state of deep cynicism. They are reaching a state of "no expectations" about our government leaders. And in a democracy, that's a red flag alert. There cannot be a fundamental erosion of ethical values at the seat of government without grave consequences for the nation.[36]

Oversight. The third function of Congress we need to examine is its oversight duty. Congress is charged with the duty of monitoring the activities of the executive branch. That is, one of the primary functions of Congress is to make sure that the federal bureaucracies are performing their duties in accordance with congressional law. As mentioned previously, when Congress enacts a statute it creates a policy that must be administered by a bureaucracy. (In fact, no federal bureaucracy can even exist until Congress has seen fit to create it via statute.) Hence, one of the duties of our federal lawmakers is to monitor the activities of these bureaucracies so as to ensure their compliance with federal law. They do so in a variety of manners. Congress can perform hearings, as both houses, Intelligence and Armed Services committees are currently conducting investigations regarding the recent use of "enhanced interrogation techniques" during the Bush administration against suspected terrorists. They can also perform their oversight duties in a less spectacular, though more routine, manner by conducting audits requiring agencies to account for their spending, travel, and administrative habits.

One oversight device Congress is constitutionally prohibited from exercising is the so-called "legislative veto." What the term legislative veto refers to is Congress' ability to veto a specific bureaucratic rule (to be discussed more fully in the next chapter) it finds inappropriate. The Supreme Court ruled such action by Congress violates the principle of separation of powers and is thereby unconstitutional.[37] Nonetheless, Congress in fact continues to exercise such legislative vetoes,[38] demonstrating, I suppose, the difference between the law and politics. Additionally, much of the day-to-day oversight duties of Congress are now performed by the Government Accountability Office (GAO). In any event, one of the primary constitutional duties of Congress is overseeing the activities of the bureaucratic establishment.

In closing our discussion on oversight, I must make note of a less savory aspect of Congress' oversight performance. Many commentators have voiced concern with the way in which the oversight function has apparently mutated from its intended investigatory role and developed into a more incestuous relationship. They label this inbred relationship an "**iron triangle**." This triangle consists of a three-way arrangement between a bureaucratic agency, a committee of Congress, and a private corporation (see following figure). For example, imagine one corner of the triangle consists of the Department of Defense, while the other two consist of the Armed Services Committee and a private arms manufacturer. Now, instead of the Armed Services Committee monitoring the Pentagon in the

```
                    ┌──────────────────────┐
                    │   CONGRESSIONAL      │
                    │    COMMITTEES        │
                    │ Armed Service Committee │
                    └──────────────────────┘
                      ↗                  ↖
      Campaign contributions      Approval of higher
         and support              budget requests
              ↙                             ↘
         Legislation affecting
         Arms manufactures              Information
         and other members
         of the industry
                              
┌──────────────────┐   Support for    ┌──────────────────┐
│ PRIVATE INDUSTRY │   agency's budget │    BUREAUCRACY   │
│ Arms Manufacturers│→   requests     →│ Department of Defense │
│                  │   Rulings on Arms │                  │
│                  │←  productions and prices │          │
└──────────────────┘                   └──────────────────┘
```

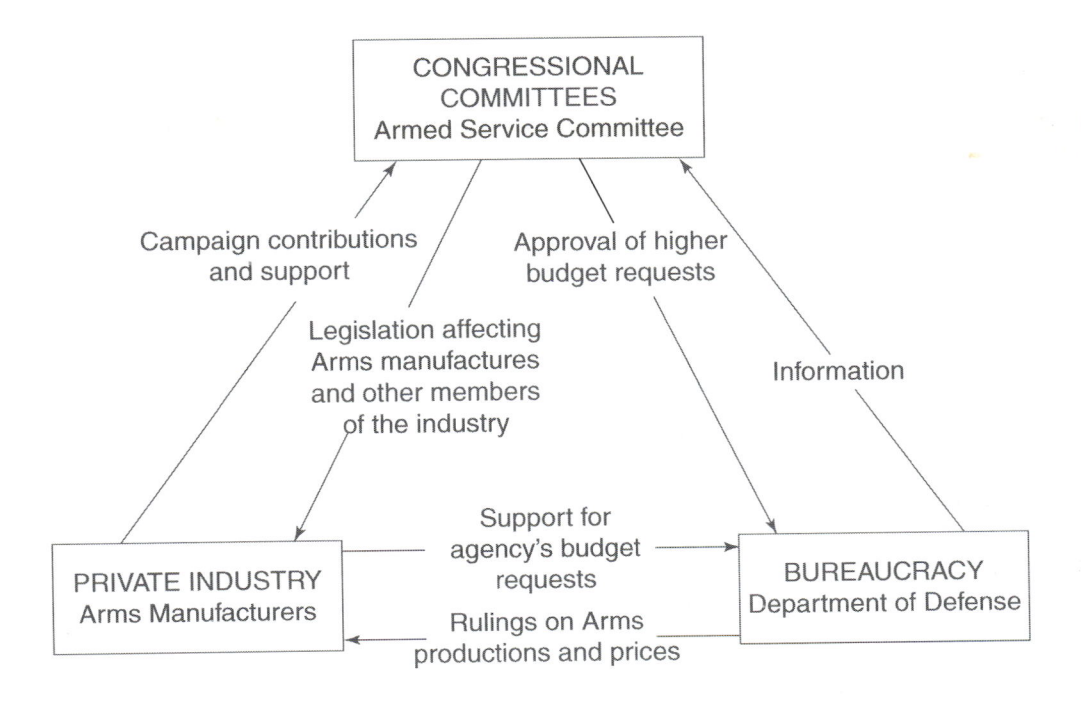

public interest, which in turn should regulate the private corporation, they work together to further their own particular interests. Here is how it works: The arms manufacturer wants public funding for its new Submergible Combat Assault Machine, or SCAM for short. Since SCAM will require congressional approval, the arms manufacturer contributes handsomely to the campaign chests of the members of the Armed Services Committee, while also guaranteeing high paying post military jobs to members of the Pentagon. The Pentagon in turn provides the necessary propaganda supporting the defense necessity of SCAM and in return Congress generously funds the Pentagon. Furthermore, the arms manufacturer lobbies the president (coupled with a campaign contribution) to ensure political appointments to the Pentagon for its high ranking executives and favored congresspersons who have done its bidding. Such an incestuous relationship takes place between all the standing committees, their respective bureaucracies, and their attendant private industries. For example, we have recently seen the iron triangle of the financial system allow the Banking Committees, the Department of Treasury, and the banking industry, authorize the financial bailout of the finance industry at the expense of American tax payers. These relationships are referred to as "iron" because they are so difficult to break, as all three players benefit from the arrangement. No matter who the players happen to be, it is easy to see that such iron triangles are simply not conducive to good representative government.

To summarize, let us review. Congress has three primary functions—policymaking, representation, and oversight. Moreover, each of these functions is interwoven with the other. That is, to make sound policy congresspersons must practice wise representation, which in turn requires them to perform their oversight duties responsibly. Of course the opposite is also true. If they refuse to practice appropriate oversight, then they have failed to represent us by making bad public policy.

FINAL THOUGHTS

Congress is the first branch of the federal government morally as well as conceptually and logically. For this reason alone there is no more important position in the entire American political system than that of an elected representative. How congresspersons perform their duties will go a long way in determining whether our American experiment in self-government is a success or failure. Therefore, the future of our democracy depends on the choices we make each and every congressional election—please choose wisely.

NOTES

1. U.S. Constitution, Article 1, section 1.
2. For a more thorough discussion on this point, see chapter 2 on the Constitution.
3. *The Federalist* #51.
4. Garry Wills, *Explaining America: The Federalist* (Garden City, New York: Doubleday & Company, Inc., 1981), pp. 127–29.
5. For an excellent discussion of this duality see, David C. Kozak, "House-Senate Differences: A Test Among Interview Data," in David C. Kozak and John D. Macartney, eds., *Congress and Public Policy,* 2nd ed. (New York: Dorsey Press, 1987), chapter 3.

6. For a deeper examination of this concept, see chapter 2 on the Constitution.
7. For an excellent discussion on the history of Congress, see Alvin M. Josephy, Jr., *On the Hill: A History of the American Congress from 1798 to the Present* (New York: Touchstone, 1980).
8. For a thorough comparison between Congress past and present see, Roger H. Davidson and Walter J. Oleszek, *Congress and Its Members*, 4th ed. (Washington D.C.: Congressional Quarterly Press, 1994).
9. Some of the other exceptions to the simple majority rule are votes to convict an impeached politician, to ratify treaties, and to close a filibuster, for example.
10. For two excellent discussions on congressional leadership, see John J. Kornacki, ed., *Leading Congress New Styles, New Strategies* (Washington, DC: Congressional Quarterly Press, 1990), and David W. Rohde, *Parties and Leaders in the Postreform Congress* (Chicago: University of Chicago Press, 1991).
11. Much of this discussion borrows from William Lyons, John M. Scheb II, and Lilliard E. Richardson, Jr., *American Government: Politics and Political Culture*, (St. Paul: West Publishing Co., 1995), pp. 347–351.
12. Ibid., p. 349, 5n.
13. The most notorious use of the filibuster in recent memory was when Southern senators used the privilege of unlimited debate to prevent civil rights legislation from passage in the 1950s. Today, a filibuster can be closed by a vote of 60 Senators.
14. For an excellent discussion on the effect committee growth has had on Congress see, Morris P. Fiorina, *Congress: Keystone of the Washington Establishment*, 2nd ed. (New Haven, CT: Yale University Press, 1989).
15. Robert A. Heineman, Steven A. Peterson, and Thomas H. Rasmussen, *American Government*, 2nd ed. (New York: McGraw-Hill, Inc., 1995), p. 158.
16. For an excellent discussion on committee assignments see, David A. Rhode and Kenneth A. Shepsle, "Democratic Committee Assignments in the House of Representatives: Strategic Aspects of a Social Choice Process," in Matthew D. McCubbins and Terry Sullivan, eds., *Congress: Structure and Policy* (New York: Cambridge University Press, 1987).
17. Two other committees which rival the above mentioned committees for influence are the Senate's Armed Services and Foreign Affairs Committees.
18. For example, see Edward S. Greenberg and Benjamin I. Page, *The Struggle for Democracy*, 2nd ed. (New York: HarperCollins College Publishers, 1995), p. 410.
19. Alan R. Gitelson, Robert L. Dudley, and Melvin J. Dubnick, *American Government*, 4th ed. (Boston: Houghton Mifflin Company, 1996), p. 287.
20. For an excellent discussion, see, Michael J. Malbin, *Unelected Representatives: Congressional Staff and the Future of Representation* (New York: Basic Books, 1980).
21. Quoted in *Time* (November 10, 1986) p. 25.
22. Gitelson, Dudley, and Dubnick, *American Government*, 4th ed., p. 288.
23. Martin L. Gross, *A Call for Revolution* (New York: Ballantine Books, 1993), p. 172.
24. Ibid., pp. 173–174.
25. For example, see Robert Bendiner, *Obstacle Course on Capital Hill* (New York: McGrawHill, 1964).
26. Alan R. Gitelson, Robert L. Dudley, and Melvin J. Dubnick, *American Government*, 4th ed., p. 290.
27. Ibid.
28. For an excellent discussion on this point, see Philip M. Stern, *The Best Congress Money Can Buy* (New York: Pantheon, 1988).
29. For an eye opening account on the nature of the contemporary legislative process see Dan Clawson, Alan Neutadtl, and Denise Scott, *Money Talks: Corporate PACs and Political Influence* (New York: Basic Books, 1992).
30. W. Lance Bennett, *The Governing Crisis: Media, Money, and Marketing in American Elections*, 2nd ed. (New York: St. Martin's Press, 1996), p. 231.

31. Staff Reports, "Think Big-Time Political Payoffs Don't Matter? Check Your Bank Account" *The Oregonian* (April 10, 1997), p. A12.
32. William Greider, *Who Will Tell the People? The Betrayal of American Democracy* (New York: Simon & Schuster, 1992).
33. Ibid., especially chapter 3.
34. Staff Reports, "Lott Wants Panel to Recommend Inflation Index Fix," *The Oregonian* (February 25, 1997), p. A4.
35. Staff Reports, "Economists Don't All Agree on the CPI Cut," *The Oregonian* (April 7, 1997), p. B9.
36. W. Lance Bennett, *The Governing Crisis: Media, Money, and Marketing in American Elections*, 2nd ed., pp. 231-232.
37. *Immigration & Naturalization Service v. Chadha*, 462 U.S. 919 (1983); for an excellent discussion of the impact of the Chadha decision in particular and the legislative veto in general see Louis Fisher, *Presidential War Power* (Lawrence, Kansas, University Press of Kansas, 1995), especially pp. 194–197.
38. See Louis Fisher, *American Constitutional Law,* (New York: McGraw-Hill, 1990), pp. 280–281.

CHAPTER 9
The Article II Branch: The Presidency

"His Highness the President of the United States and Protector of Their Liberties"
—*The first Senate's proposed title for the President*

"I was convinced that efficient, honest administration of the vast machine of the federal government would appeal to all citizens. I have since learned that efficient government does not interest the people as much as dramatics."
—*Herbert Hoover*

"I feel your pain."
—*Bill Clinton*

INTRODUCTION

This chapter will focus on the Executive branch of the federal government. In doing so, we will spend most of our inquiry detailing the office of **chief executive**, or in other words, the presidency. We will begin our inquiry with a look at the constitutional structure of the presidency. After that, we will discuss the dynamics of presidential power using the maxim, "less power than believed yet more power than before." To this end, we will analyze the historical nature of the presidency, while giving due attention to the constitutional parameters of the office. We will also discuss what political scientists label the "two presidencies," which refers to the fact the presidency is much weaker institutionally when dealing with domestic issues than when confronting foreign policy. Next, we will spend some time analyzing the nomination procedures (primaries and caucuses) and the mechanics of the Electoral College to gain a greater understanding of presidential campaign politics in addition to constitutional theory. Lastly, we will address the president's role as chief administrator over the federal bureaucracy.

PRESIDENTIAL POWER: PERCEPTIONS AND MISCONCEPTIONS

Before we begin looking at both the constitutional and practical dimensions of presidential authority, we first must dispel a misconception surrounding presidential power and gain a better appreciation for the historical character of the office in general. To improve our understanding of the presidency, I will ask each of you to please keep in mind the following maxim to help guide our perceptions of presidential authority: *"The President's political power is less than believed yet more than before."* That is to say, while the president's governing authority is nowhere near as powerful as most Americans believe, nonetheless, each succeeding president has more political power than his immediate predecessor.[1] Explaining what accounts for this phenomenon will be the primary point of this section. We can trace the first condition to two interrelated factors. One, Americans have an exaggerated sense of the presidency due to the media's obsessive interest in all things presidential, coupled with their indifference to the other aspects of the American political system. Two, this inflated sense of presidential authority is also fed by the exaggerated campaign rhetoric of presidential elections where both candidates attempt to surpass each other with political promises much beyond the reach of the executive branch. The second condition (that each successive president is more powerful than the one before him) is, as we shall see, the result of the inherent historical nature of the presidency. Simply stated, each president is permitted, due to constitutional ambiguities, to perform whatever activities prior presidents have engaged in, plus whatever additional activities he can muster. This, of course, sets a precedent for future presidents thereby perpetuating the aggrandizement of presidential power. We will now begin examining these two conditions in much more detail below.

"Less Power Than Believed"

There is no more recognizable figure in American politics than the president of the United States. He has become one of the most pervasive personalities of modern life, rivaling even the most popular movie and music stars for celebrity status. It seems his every move is shadowed by an ever-intrusive press breathlessly detailing his actions from the most important ("President commits troops to Iraq") to the most trivial ("Obama shoots hoop with national champions"). And, given the media's fascination with all things presidential, it should come as no surprise that there is a similar obsession among the public at large. It is no exaggeration to say that when most people think they are "discussing politics" they are more likely gossiping about the president. In other words, if one's political education consisted solely of information gleaned from the media and casual conversation (which is exactly where most Americans receive their political information) then one would surmise the entire American political system reduces to a single individual, namely, the president. Not only is this a gross distortion of political reality (the president is, after all, but one of millions of federal and state governing officials), it also creates a further and more disturbing misconception about the realities of the office of president. That is, given all this publicity, most people (the media as well as the public at large) believe that along with all this publicity must come an equal amount of political authority.[2]

Columnist George Will (a political scientist himself) made this very point to a group of media pundits as they discussed politics on the Sunday afternoon political show, *This Week*. After patiently listening to these media experts pontificate about what Clinton should do concerning one political issue after another, Will, finally fed up with their apparent ignorance, snapped, "it seems you all have mistaken prominence for power." He was referring to the mistaken assumption on the part of too many Americans that the president is simply the be all and end all of government since he is the be all and end all of public discussion. It seems people assume the president to be an all-powerful dictator able to solve any problem facing the community if he may be so inclined.

Though nothing could be further from the truth, this simplistic perception of presidential relevance and authority dominates most people's understanding of the American political system. For example, how often have you heard people say things like, "what's Obama going to do about the economy (or AIDS, or abortion, or terrorism, etc)?" Notice how statements such as this equate government with Obama, as if Obama *is* government rather than just one of millions of governmental actors. Think about it. What can Obama—*as president*—do about the economy other than make us feel better about it? To be sure, the president, (along with Congress, which, by the way, has the last word on fiscal policy), has an important role to play in the budgetary process; yet he still plays a very small part in affecting the economy one way or the other. Ponder this: What constitutes the "economy" anyway? The economy, if it is anything, must refer to the innumerable economic decisions made by the billions of consumers and producers throughout the global economy, which we collectively refer to as the "market." Now, ask yourself, how is the president going to affect the market in any, but the most trivial, way since he is but one (albeit a relatively more important one) of a seemingly infinite number of economic players? While we are at it, what can Obama do—*as president*—concerning AIDS? Wear a condom? He certainly cannot prevent it for the rest of us, only each and every sexual partner can; he cannot even spend public money on researching its causes and treatment, only Congress or state legislatures possess this authority. What about abortion? *As president,* he cannot declare abortion a right of all women; only the Supreme Court wields this power.

The media, as mentioned earlier, helps foster this exaggerated notion of presidential power by relentlessly reducing all political reporting to presidential gossip.[3] For example, notice how much of what constitutes "political news" consists solely of reporters following the president around and filming his daily activities. If the president gets off a plane, it's news; if he eats a cheeseburger, it's reported; if he drives a hay truck, well, roll the cameras. The only justification for this obsessive coverage would be if the president is some sort of dictator, which he is not. Yet the most meaningful acts of the other federal and state institutions starve for similar media attention. Apparently, too many political pundits fail to comprehend that governmental policy is not the result of presidential personality but of complex institutional procedures. In other words, competent political reporting demands monitoring the whole political *system* and not just spotlighting one *individual.* A good example of this presidential-centered reporting occurred during the federal elections of 2008. Throughout their election night coverage, all the networks pundits constantly referred to the elections as the "*presidential election* of 2008," forgetting the fact we were also electing all 435 members of the House as well as one-third of all Senators. There was no better example of this president-as-government bias than when Tom Brokaw, of NBC News, continually reported that the 1996 elections "would be the last election of the 20th century." When informed by knowledgeable viewers there would be congressional elections in 1998, he replied rather impatiently, "though some viewers have reminded me there will be another election before the 20th century, we're talking about the *presidential* race, so give it a rest." Implying, it seems, what really matters to Americans is who will be their next president and not such trivial issues as who will be their next federal lawmakers.

It is the very notion that the president is the government we need to avoid if we are to gain an accurate understanding of the presidency. As Harvard political scientist, Steven Kelman, writes:

> The power of the President appears awesome. It is symbolized by the finger the President has on the nuclear button. Compared with any other individual in the country, the President has powers that stand in a class by itself. Yet, if you assume that he "runs" the government . . . this impression is not nearly correct . . . The role of the President generally is limited to trying to *influence* decisions others have the *power* to make . . . It is crucial to remember that final decisions are generally made by others [emphasis original].[4]

The nature of presidential campaign politics also helps to foster an exaggerated sense of presidential power. Presidential candidates continually promise the American public they will solve any and all social ills if the public would only be so kind as to give them the chance. They do so because they have learned it is political suicide to respond to any question with the honest reply that the power of the presidency simply does not encompass that particular issue. Imagine an honest candidate responding to a question on, say, education by stating that, "well, under our constitutional system of separation of powers I, as president, simply couldn't do much at all to affect the educational system one way or the other." Or, a question on the economy, with this reply: "As president there's simply very little I can do other than to persuade Americans to feel confident about the economy in general." What are the chances this candidate would be elected? Particularly when his opponent is probably responding to these very same questions with either mind numbing detailed explanations or with references to some vague "plan" he will unveil right after getting elected. We, the American people, of course, also are to blame since we probably would not vote for any candidate who did not play this electoral lying game with us. In any event, the demands of presidential electoral politics also helps promote this president-as-government misconception among the public.

Hence, for the student of politics it is important to keep in mind the power differential between the president and the public at large versus the relative power between the presidency and other governing actors (Congress, bureaucracies, the courts, state governments, etc.). That is, the president is indeed much more politically powerful than the average citizen, yet he is nowhere near as powerful in comparison with the other institutions of government as people tend to believe. He cannot make federal law, only Congress can; he cannot enforce the law, only bureaucracies can; he cannot rule on constitutionality, only the Supreme Court can; and, lastly, when it comes to issues like crime, education, "welfare," and so forth, the president is further hampered by the fact that most of these policies are under the direct administrative control of state governments. To be sure, this in no way means the president is powerless in the American governmental system (later we will look at what power he does in fact have); what it does mean is the president is not nearly as powerful as the public tends to believe.[5]

In closing this section of the chapter, I think it appropriate to give the last word concerning the realities of presidential power to those select few who have held the job. For instance, President Truman, after serving two terms, was asked before leaving the White House what he thought his successor, General Eisenhower, would notice first about being president, here is what he said: "He'll sit here, and he'll say, 'Do this! Do that!' And nothing will happen. Poor Ike—it won't be a bit like the Army."[6] John Kennedy remarked after leaving the Congress and becoming the president that, "Congress looks more powerful sitting here than it did when I was there in the Congress."[7] And, lastly, Lyndon Johnson told Richard Nixon when Nixon was entering the White House, "before you get to be president, you think you're the most powerful leader since God. But when you get into that chair you'll find your hands tied."[8]

"More Power Than Before"

There is an old political science adage about presidential studies that states: "To understand the presidency is to understand its history." No institution in the American political system requires as thorough an understanding of history as the office of the president. Granted, no competent scholar of American politics can afford to be ignorant of history regardless of what they happen to study, be it Congress, the courts, bureaucracies, or what have you; nonetheless, the presidency, by design, requires a greater degree of historical analysis than any other aspect of the federal government. Unlike the legislative and judicial branches of government, the presidency was intentionally a constitutional abstraction. Whereas the Founders had a fairly keen sense of what they expected from Congress and the Supreme Court, they lacked any such definitive notion of what would constitute the character of the presidency. Hence, the Founders knowingly framed the presidency with as vague and general constitutional language as possible in Article II of the Constitution.[9] They did so, because they were really only sure of two things about the presidency: One, the president would perform such general duties as, "national leadership, statesmanship in foreign affairs, command in time of war or insurgency, [and] enforcement of the laws."[10] And, two, the first president would be George Washington.[11] Having only a vague idea of what the office would become, they decided to let history fill in the details—and it has. Therefore, given that the presidency was designed to allow the president to be, in the words of our 26th President, Theodore Roosevelt, "as big a man as he wants to be," any student of the presidency must begin and end his or her inquiry with history.[12]

The historical nature of the presidency is illustrated by the very first line of Article II, which creates the presidency: "The executive power shall be *vested in* a President of the United States of America. [italics added]" Now, compare that language with the following sentence which begins Article I of the Constitution, which creates the legislative branch: "All legislative powers *herein granted* shall be vested in a Congress of the United States . . . [italics added]" Notice how the phrase "herein granted," appears only in Article I and is not mentioned in Article II. The Founders, knowing exactly what they believed the powers of Congress should be, granted those powers *explicitly* herein the Constitution. On the other hand, they had only a nebulous notion of what the presidency would be, so they simply *vested* whatever the executive power was to become in the president. In other words, since the Founders had no clear idea of what powers a president should or should not have they decided to let the office gain substance via presidential performance. Therefore, much of what constitutes presidential power comes not from any constitutional grant, but rather through the actions of particular presidents. As two presidential scholars recently wrote: "[T]he essential constitutional framework of the presidential office remains as it was created almost two centuries ago. Most of the vast changes in the presidency since that time have arisen not from legal alterations in its structure but from informal political customs and precedents."[13]

Moreover, since the presidency is defined more through history than via the Constitution, it was inevitable that as each succeeding president performed his duties he would stretch the limits of presidential authority by doing something no previous president had attempted. For example, the first American president, George Washington, believed he could only veto acts of Congress which he thought were unconstitutional and not any bill he may personally find unwise. Later, Andrew Jackson expanded the president's veto authority for all future presidents by vetoing any bill of which he personally disapproved. Or as Harvard Law School professor Richard Fallon observes somewhat short-sighted, "all modern presidents since Nixon have staked out some executive power beyond their predecessor."[14] Furthermore, given the presidency's inherent historical nature, it should come as no surprise that we will encounter numerous examples throughout this chapter of presidential practice stretching the limits of executive power.

THE CONSTITUTIONAL PRESIDENCY

The Constitution articulates an office that has grown much beyond its original limits;[15] detailing this growth will be the primary point of much of this section. But before we begin examining the practical dimensions of presidential authority, we first need to gain a better understanding of the constitutional bedrock of the presidency. Let us review some basic constitutional facts about the office. The Constitution declares that any American who is a natural born citizen, has resided in the United States for at least 14 years prior to election, and has reached the age of 35 is eligible for the office of president.[16] The Constitution also creates a unique mechanism to elect the chief executive, something labeled the "electoral college," which was designed to ensure that neither the people nor Congress would actually elect the president (we will discuss the electoral college in much more detail later in the chapter).[17] Once elected, a president serves a four year term but is limited by the Constitution to serving no more than two terms.[18]

To remove a president before his term expires requires Congress to follow a two-step process outlined in the Constitution. The House of Representatives must first impeach the president (that is, formally charge him with a political crime)[19] and then the Senate must try him (with the Chief Justice of the Supreme Court presiding) and if two-thirds of the senators agree they can remove him from office.[20]

Though more a matter of congressional law than constitutional command,[21] this is as good a place as any to address briefly the issue of presidential succession. If the president is no longer able to execute his duties due to death, illness, or any other reason, the powers of the office, "shall devolve on the Vice President;" after the Vice President the line of succession in order is as follows: First, the Speaker of the House; second, the President Pro Tempore of the Senate; and then, the Secretaries of State, Treasury, and Defense and other Cabinet heads in order of their department's creation. Though eight presidents have died while in office (four via assassination and four by natural causes), there has never been a case where anyone but a sitting vice president has ever assumed the office of the presidency. In addition to these basic procedural matters, the Constitution also assigns three primary duties to the president: Chief Executive, Commander-in-Chief, and Chief Diplomat.[22] We will now briefly analyze each of these constitutional roles in more detail below.

Chief Executive: Article II, Section 1, of the Constitution states, "the executive power shall be vested in a President of the United States." This means that the president oversees the entire federal executive branch, including not only the White House but all other executive bureaucracies as well. To further cement the president's executive authority, the Constitution also empowers the president to appoint (with congressional approval in most cases) the top echelon of civil servants in the federal bureaucracies.[23] We will later see that his power to appoint is not as grand as it may appear at first glance, nonetheless, it centers bureaucratic control under the president. Lastly, the Constitution demands the president take an oath to "faithfully execute" all laws enacted by Congress as part of his duties as chief executive.[24] Recent presidents have interpreted the constitutional commandment to "faithfully execute" the laws in such a manner that one is left wondering if they understand what "faithfully" means. For example, Nixon "impounded" (refused to spend) money Congress had otherwise legally appropriated because he disagreed with their actions;[25] Reagan not only covertly (and illegally) funded some South American thugs known as the "contras" against the expressed wishes of Congress, he also created a so-called "council of competitiveness" centered in the vice-president's office which allowed the largest corporations to have laws they considered burdensome waived (this essentially ticket-fixing scheme continued under President Bush Sr. as well); and, Clinton's flagrant disregard for the federal campaign financing laws showed he had as little respect for the constitutional demand that he faithfully execute the laws as his predecessors. George W. Bush's so-called "signing statements" also demonstrated contempt for The Constitution's demand of faithfully executing the laws of Congress. Signing statements are when a president signs into a law a bill passed by Congress, but only after he has signed a statement explaining which parts of the law he intends to enforce and those he intends to ignore. Hence, as is the nature of the office, each of these presidents, by their actions, has increased the authority of future presidents to creatively (illiterately?) interpret the faithfully execute clause as they see fit.

Commander-in-Chief: There is no greater grant of presidential power than the constitutional language which declares that, "The President shall be Commander in Chief" of the Armed Services.[26] Though never meant to be a blank check regarding presidential war powers, in the age of nuclear technology, not to mention citizen apathy and neglect, it has evolved into just such an instrument. The Founders, in fact, spent much of their constitutional energy attempting to prevent the president from ever acquiring the expansive war powers all modern presidents take for granted. They did so, because as James Madison so prophetically stated: "The management of foreign relations appears to be the most susceptible to abuse of all the trusts committed to a government."[27] Hence, they empowered Congress, not the president, with the constitutional authority to declare war; to raise and spend money for war purposes; and to create, train and regulate the armed forces.[28] The Founders granted these powers to Congress to ensure that the president would have to share war powers with them as a coequal, if not inferior, partner. Nonetheless, the commander-in-chief clause of the Constitution has become the dominant source of contemporary presidential power whatever the Founders may have intended.

Chief Diplomat: Article II, Section 2, of the Constitution grants the president the power to make treaties (with the advice and consent of the Senate), to receive ambassadors from foreign nations, and to appoint ambassadors for the United States. That is, the president is the official representative of the United States government and is charged with the duty of recognizing foreign leaders, nation-states, and other important dignitaries as part of his ceremonial duties as head-of-state. Yet, given the Founders' fear of monarchy, the Founders did not intend for the president to exercise this authority alone. They meant the president, "should be the Senate's agent . . . [and] at the most, the president should be a joint participant in the field of foreign affairs, but not an equal one."[29] But, just like the commander-in-chief role, the president's chief diplomat role has also led to an increase in presidential power. For example, even though the president is constitutionally required to receive the advice and consent of the Senate (two-thirds must approve) for any treaty to become law, since 1978 ninety percent of all such agreements with foreign nations have never been approved or even reviewed by the Senate. Modern presidents have learned to circumvent the Senate by simply labeling their treaties with foreign nations "executive agreements."[30] Once again, the actions of specific presidents have enlarged the authority of the office much beyond the best constitutional intentions. It is now time to look at the contemporary character of the presidency as we keep in mind both the maxim regarding presidential power as well as its constitutional outline.

THE PRESIDENT IN PRACTICE: "THE TWO PRESIDENCIES"

To grasp the essential character of contemporary presidential authority we will need to divide the presidency in two, between a domestic policy president and a foreign policy president.³¹ And, in doing so, we will discover there are really two different presidencies each with its own measures of institutional power; in the arena of foreign affairs the president is unmatched in power, surpassing even the most powerful dictators, whereas, in the domestic sphere he is much more institutionally weak, limited to a mere pleading posture in the American political system. Explaining this phenomenon will be the central task of this section of the chapter.

The Foreign Policy President: As previously mentioned, the president has almost unlimited authority in the area of foreign policy given his position as commander-in-chief of the military establishment.³² And, as also previously noted, this was not the original intent of the Constitution but was the result of presidential practice, or, in other words, presidential history. Each succeeding president built upon the actions of prior presidents until it is now no exaggeration to say the world's existence is at the mercy of the president. The various explanations (some would say excuses) for this presidential evolution essentially boil down to two simple assertions. One, it is argued, given today's technology, there is simply no place for the constitutional limits on presidential war powers if the nation is to survive in a hostile world. Two, the president's increased authority was necessitated by the spread of (cue scary theme music) communism. Hence, even though the Constitution explicitly states Congress holds the sole power to declare war, this requirement has become nothing more than a constitutional anachronism since the end of World War II. To be sure, tracing the entire evolution of presidential war powers is much beyond the scope of this chapter, nonetheless, the mere fact that *not one war since that time has been declared by Congress,* even though these actions have cost more than 100,000 American lives, as well as the lives of millions of other people world wide, does more than enough to substantiate this trend. The magnitude of this constitutional change requires us to review a little post-WWII presidential history to make sense of how this occurred with so little reaction by the American people and their institutions of government.

As America emerged from the world's ashes as the undisputed super power after WWII, the United States government became increasingly entangled in world affairs, particularly as it became obsessed with stopping the spread of communism. And, just as George Washington, Thomas Jefferson and, indeed, the entire founding generation forewarned us, this led to the slow but constant erosion of any constitutional limit on the president's war powers. In conjunction with this military activity, the government also spent a good deal of tax payer money running a propaganda campaign designed to instill a fear of communism to such a degree, it not only continues today, it also encouraged the public to surrender their constitutional liberties in exchange for national security. Under the expressed purpose of fighting communism, the people and their representatives permitted President Truman to send American troops to Korea, in 1950, to fight what he called a United Nations "police action" without a constitutional declaration of war from Congress. In the 1960s and 70s, in a place called Vietnam, Presidents Kennedy, Johnson and Nixon were allowed to squander the lives of over 58,000 Americans without an overt declaration of war all in the name of stopping communism. And, like Truman, they avoided the constitutional necessity of asking Congress for permission by invoking such euphemisms as, "collective security," "sudden attack," and the "neutrality theory." To be sure, Congress did grant President Johnson a pseudo-declaration of war (known as the Tonkin Gulf Resolution), but it was issued only after Johnson had manufactured an incident with the Vietnamese which probably never even occurred. As further evidence of Johnson's disregard for the Constitution, his under Secretary of State, Nicholas Katzenbach, in 1964, told Congress their authority to declare war had become, "outmoded in the international arena."[33]

Armed with this presidential history, President Carter, in the late 1970s, authorized an invasion of Iran with eight helicopters, backed by three C-180 cargo planes without ever asking the people's representatives if it was okay to do so. What was Carter's explanation for this constitutional transgression? Well, he said, "I had planned on calling in a few members of the House and Senate . . . but I never got around to that."[34] In the 1980s, President Reagan involved Americans in military engagements in Nicaragua, Grenada, Lebanon, and Libya without once feeling it necessary to ask Congress if it was appropriate. And, of course, in the 1990s we were treated to George Herbert Walker Bush's "U.N. sanctioned engagement," in Iraq as well as Clinton's "peacekeeping exercises" in Bosnia and Kosovo, without either of them receiving proper constitutional approval.[35] As a matter of fact, Bush Sr., when asked if he had any regrets about his committing troops to the Gulf War, said, "you elect a president to make that decision,"[36] apparently forgetting that the Constitution explicitly states the American people elect Congress to make that decision. His son, George W. Bush, misled the country into a war that rages today, while President Obama has already stepped up America's combat presence in Afghanistan by adding thousands of additional American troops to that theatre of war.

This presidential duality between his authority in the domestic and foreign policy spheres helps explain why presidents, as they become more familiar with the character of the office, tend to focus their energy more and more in the area of foreign affairs. This, of course, comes as no surprise since it is in the arena of foreign policy the president has absolute authority. In short, when it comes to foreign policy the president is as powerful as he wants to be; there has simply been too little institutional or public reaction to prevent this from happening. And as each succeeding president builds upon the legacy of his predecessors, it becomes more and more difficult to even try—so goes the American constitutional experiment in restraining the war powers of a chief executive.

The Domestic Policy President: The authority of the president in domestic policy is as weak vis-a-vis other governmental institutions as it is strong in foreign policy. Unlike foreign policy, the president must rely on other institutions if he is to realize any of his domestic policy objectives. As mentioned earlier, on his own he is unable to address any of the major domestic policy areas, like crime, the economy, education, or welfare. For example, only Congress or state legislatures may write any law in the American political system, the president cannot; only the federal and state bureaucracies administer whatever programs their legislatures create, the president cannot; and, only state and federal courts may rule on the constitutionality of any given governmental activity, the president cannot. And these institutions have shown as much energy preserving their governmental authority in the domestic sphere as they have abdicated whatever authority they might have had in the foreign policy field. The president, of course, is not completely at the mercy of the other governmental entities when it comes to domestic policy. When attempting to influence domestic policy the president has three primary weapons: The veto, the budget, and the so-called "**bully pulpit**."

The Veto. As noted earlier the president has the constitutional authority to nullify any federal bill presented to him by Congress, though Congress is allowed to override (trump) any veto as long as two-thirds of the members of each house vote to do so. The Founders debated as to whether the president should have an unqualified veto (one that could not be over turned by Congress) or not. Some Founders believed the principle of "separation-of-powers" demanded that the chief executive be equipped with an absolute or unqualified veto. Benjamin Franklin opposed such a strong executive veto by arguing an absolute or unqualified veto would be used, "to extort money" from the legislature.[37] In the end, of course, they decided in favor of a legislative check on the president's veto power. Modern presidents (particularly FDR) have been much more likely to veto legislation than their 17th and 18th century predecessors. In any event, the veto power grants the president some reactive, if not proactive, authority in the area of domestic policy.

The Budget. In 1921, Congress, in an attempt to streamline the budgetary process, created a bureaucracy under the direct control of the president, named the Bureau of the Budget, charged with submitting a unified budget to Congress for their approval (prior to this, each federal bureaucracy would submit a separate operating budget to the appropriate **congressional committee**). This legal change allowed the president to begin initiating budgetary policy and thereby helped strengthen his standing in the domestic policy arena. In 1939, the Bureau of the Budget (in 1970, President Nixon changed its name to the Office of Management and Budget) was made part of the newly created Executive Office of the President (to be discussed below) which further solidified the president's control over the budgetary process. With these changes most people now view the president as the main player in the budgetary process; so much so, in fact, most people refer to the federal budget simply by the president's name, as in, "what do you think of Obama's budget?" Though close to the truth, this type of language much overstates his power since it is Congress and not the president which will have the final say over all matters relating to the federal budget. Nonetheless, the budget provides the president with a powerful tool in influencing domestic policy in the American political system.

The Bully Pulpit. The last and arguably most powerful instrument the president has at his disposal is his celebrity status.[38] That is, since the media is constantly reporting whatever it is the president has to say, he is in a unique position in the American political system to lobby on behalf of whatever causes he supports. President Theodore Roosevelt coined the phrase "bully pulpit" to refer to the president's ability to influence American politics by simply harping on any given subject. Much like a preacher at her pulpit delivering her Sunday sermon, the president stands at his media pulpit and strongly advocates for or against whatever issues he feels strongly about. Moreover, it is no exaggeration to say that whatever he talks about thereby becomes an important political issue simply because the president addressed it. In other words, though the president is in no position to actually enact domestic policy, he is most assuredly in the position to influence those who can. This is why one of the biggest windfalls for any given political group is convincing the president to mention their cause in any of his major speeches; it becomes an important political issue from that moment on. Presidents have used their bully pulpit to advocate for such important political issues as abolishing slavery, entering war, or eradicating America's poverty.

NOMINATING CANDIDATES FOR PRESIDENT: PRIMARIES AND CAUCUSES EXPLAINED

In the summer of every presidential election year, political parties in the United States typically conduct national conventions to choose their presidential candidates. At the conventions, the presidential candidates are selected by groups of **delegates** from each state. After a series of speeches and demonstrations in support of each candidate, the delegates begin to vote, state-by-state, for the candidate of their choice. The first candidate to receive a preset majority number of delegate votes becomes the party's presidential candidate. The candidate selected to run for president then selects a vice presidential candidate. Delegates to the national conventions are selected at the state level, according to rules and formulas determined by each political party's state committee. While these rules and formulas can change from state-to-state and from year-to-year, there remain two methods by which the states choose their delegates to the national conventions: the caucus and the primary.

The Primary

In states holding them, **presidential primary** elections are open to all registered voters. Just like in general elections, voting is done through a secret ballot. Voters may choose from among all registered candidates and write-ins are counted. There are two types of primaries, closed and open. In a closed primary, voters may vote only in the primary of the political party in which they registered. For example, a voter who registered as a Republican can only vote in the Republican primary. In an open primary, registered voters can vote in the primary of either party, but are allowed to vote in only one primary. Most states hold closed primaries. Primary elections also vary in what names appear on their ballots. Most states hold presidential preference primaries, in which the actual presidential candidates' names appear on the ballot. In other states, only the names of convention delegates appear on the ballot. Delegates may state their support for a candidate or declare themselves to be uncommitted. In some states, delegates are bound, or "pledged" to vote for the primary winner in voting at the national convention. In other states some or all delegates are "unpledged," and free to vote for any candidate they wish at the convention.

The Caucus

Caucuses are simply meetings, open to all registered voters of the party, at which delegates to the party's national convention are selected. When the caucus begins, the voters in attendance divide themselves into groups according to the candidate they support. The undecided voters congregate into their own group and prepare to be "courted" by supporters of other candidates. Voters in each group are then invited to give speeches supporting their candidate and trying to persuade others to join their group. At the end of the caucus, party organizers count the voters in each candidate's group and calculate how many delegates to the county convention each candidate has won. As in the primaries, the caucus process can produce both pledged and unpledged convention delegates, depending on the party rules of the various states.

How Delegates are Awarded

The Democratic and Republican parties use different methods for determining how many delegates are awarded to, or "pledged" to vote for the various candidates at their national conventions.

Democrats use a proportional method. Each candidate is awarded a number of delegates in proportion to their support in the state caucuses or the number of primary votes they won. For example, consider a state with 20 delegates at a democratic convention with three candidates. If candidate "A" received 70% of all caucus and primary votes, candidate "B" 20% and candidate "C" 10%, candidate "A" would get 14 delegates, candidate "B" would get 4 delegates and candidate "C" would get 2 delegates.

In the Republican Party, each state chooses either the proportional method or a "winner-take-all" method of awarding delegates. Under the winner-take-all method, the candidate getting the most votes from a state's caucus or primary, gets all of that state's delegates at the national convention.[39]

As you can see, each state and each party have their own particular way of nominating their candidates. So, feel free to contact your state's Secretary of State and/or each party's state organizations to find out the details of your state's nomination process. Nonetheless, each state and party will have at its core a primary—open or closed—or a caucus. Keep this in mind during the next **presidential nomination** cycle when you hear the media talk about the "New Hampshire primary" and the "Iowa Caucus." These two states are considered important for one simple reason: These states always hold their nomination process first, before any of the other states' nomination process. Why does that matter? Because the press believe that this gives an early indication of who is, and who is not, a viable candidate for the presidency. Recent presidential elections have proved that this is not the case, but the media continues to exaggerate their importance to justify its obsessive coverage of these relatively small and inconsequential states.

ELECTING THE PRESIDENT (THE ELECTORAL COLLEGE: A RELIC FROM AMERICA'S ANTIDEMOCRATIC PAST)

The electoral college is one of the most misunderstood creations of the Constitution. In addition to explaining the Founders' motivations for constructing the electoral college, we will also review not only how it works, but also why it is still with us and, most importantly, the political ramifications of all of this. In doing so, we will come to better understand the politics of presidential campaigns as well as the presidency in general. The concept "electoral college" refers to the rather cumbersome process by which the president of the United States is chosen. As noted earlier, it was designed by the Founders as a way to prevent the common people from electing the president, while also keeping the office independent from Congress. That is, most of the Founders believed the common people lacked the intelligence to elect a president and, therefore, were intent on creating a mechanism which would by-pass the common people and yet still prevent the president from becoming an entrenched monarch. For example, when James Madison, James Wilson and Gouverneur Morris suggested the people ought to elect their president, George Mason captured the prevailing sentiments of the remaining delegates when he remarked, "it would be as unnatural to refer the choice of a proper magistrate to the people as it would to refer a trial of colors to a blind man."[40] At the same time the majority of Founders also opposed allowing Congress to elect the chief executive as was presently the case in most of the states (that is, most states allowed the state legislators to elect their governor). They therefore compromised and created an institution for electing the president, which would remain independent of both Congress and the people—the so-called electoral college.

According to the original design of the electoral college, each state was granted the number of electors equal to their congressional representation and could choose them in whatever manner they deemed appropriate, provided no elector was currently a member of Congress or held any other national office. Once chosen, the electors gathered in their respective state capitals and cast two votes each for president; these votes were then sent to Washington, D.C., where they were counted during a joint session of Congress. Whoever received a majority of electoral votes was elected president. If no candidate received a majority of electoral votes, the House, with each state getting only one vote, then chose the president from amongst the five candidates with the most electoral votes. The candidate with the second highest number of votes was declared vice president unless there was a tie for second, in which the Senate picked the vice president from among the remaining four candidates. The electoral college has been modified somewhat since its inception, nonetheless, it remains essentially unchanged today. For example, in some fashion, all fifty states now require their electors to cast their votes in favor of whomever garners the majority of popular votes within their state. The Constitution also now demands the electors vote for a ticket (president and vice president) rather than having the second place finisher be the vice president (if this was still the case, McCain would be Obama's vice president, for instance). In addition, if no candidate attains a majority of electoral votes, the House now chooses from the top three candidates rather than the top five as the Constitution originally stated.⁴¹ And, lastly, Washington, D.C. is now treated as if it were a state during presidential elections and, hence, is awarded three electoral votes, which is equal to the representation it would receive in Congress if it were in fact a state (one representative and two senators).⁴²

The un-democratic nature of the electoral college is obvious once one realizes it is possible for a candidate to be elected without ever receiving a majority of popular votes. As mentioned above, the electoral college is made up of a number of electors equal to the total congressional representation of the states in Congress plus the District of Columbia. Therefore, since there are 535 members of Congress (435 representatives and 100 senators) plus 3 extra electors for Washington, D.C. (for a total of 538 electoral votes), a candidate needs to receive no more than 270 electoral votes to win the election *regardless of how many national popular votes any candidate receives.* Of course the 2000 presidential election provided a real world example of this theoretical imbalance. Officially, Gore received more total citizen votes than Bush nationwide (the so-called "popular vote,"); however, Bush won more state popular vote contests, 30 states to 20, and most importantly, enough electoral votes to garner the 270 electoral votes necessary to meet the Constitution's threshold for becoming president. Chapter 5 contains an analysis of the 2000 presidential election's less appealing side—the allegation that the State of Florida, (where the eventual winner's brother was executive authority over the branch that administers Florida's elections) a state which was absolutely necessary for Bush Jr. to win the electoral college contest by the slimmest of majorities and, hence, the presidency, may have, in fact, willfully corrupted the electoral process to ensure Bush's election. Suffice it to say at this point, the presidential election of 2000 reinforced the importance of a better understanding of the Electoral College by both the media and the American people.

To better understand how a candidate can lose an election in which he received more total votes than his opponent, one must keep in mind that the Electoral College has evolved into a mechanism that essentially has the majority of voters in the most populous states choose the president. To be sure, a candidate need not win all the big states to be president, as Obama demonstrated, but he better win at least two of the four—like, say, California and New York—if he is to reside in the White House, as Obama also illustrated. So, for example, a candidate may receive only one more popular vote than his or her opponent in the eleven most populous states but fail to receive a single vote from any other American in any other of the remaining 39 states and still win the election even though his or her opponent received millions more popular votes nationwide. Every state (except for Maine and Nebraska) grants all their electoral votes (votes cast by constitutional electors) to the candidate who receives at least one more popular vote (votes cast by the public) than any other candidate within their particular state. In other words, with the way the electoral college is designed, the popular vote only matters within a state and not as a total national count. Therefore, as long as most states maintain a winner-take-all system, a candidate need only muster enough votes to win a majority of popular votes within the eleven most populous states since those states, by virtue of their greater population, have a larger share of congressional delegates and, hence, presidential electors. Here is how our hypothetical election would look:

Winning Candidate

States won: California (54 electoral votes)

New York (33) plus Washington D.C.

Texas (32)

Florida (25)

Pennsylvania (23)

Illinois (22)

Ohio (21)

Michigan (18)

New Jersey (15)

North Carolina (14)

Georgia (13)

Total: 11 states won

(270 electoral votes)

Losing Candidate

States won: All 39 other states

Total: 39 states

(268 electoral votes)

As the above example illustrates, the electoral college is so severely biased in favor of the states with the highest population, any candidate who wishes to win the election must spend the vast majority of his or her time campaigning in those particular states. This is why during any presidential campaign the candidates always spend most of their time and money in states such as California, New York, Texas, Florida, etc.; if they do not win some of these states they simply have no chance of winning the general election. On the other hand, it is a rare sighting indeed to spot either candidate in such lesser states as Nevada, Alaska, or even Oregon. And, if they do happen to stop in one of the less populous states, these stops usually consist of a brief speech while the plane is refueled and then it is off to California, or Texas, or New York. Moreover, this also helps explain why even during non-election years presidents fall all over themselves coming up with excuses to provide various federal monies to the big states, particularly California (federal disaster relief ring a bell?); they do so, of course, in hopes that the voting public of those states will remember them come election time.

This begs the question: Why, during the constitutional convention, did the less populous states agree to a system which so disadvantages them? Because they believed very few candidates would ever receive enough electoral votes to win any election. For example, Madison, when asked how many elections he thought would be decided by an electoral vote, guessed it would be no more than one out of every twenty. And recall that any time a candidate fails to receive a majority of electoral votes, the House picks the president from the top three candidates, *but each state casts only one vote.* This the Founders thought was the perfect compromise: The more populous states would be favored when it came to picking the top three candidates, but the more numerous small states, given their voting equality for electoral concerns, would be advantaged when actually choosing the president from those three candidates offered by the bigger states. Or, in other words, the bigger states would choose who the candidates for president would be and the smaller states would choose the president from among those candidates. Needless to say, it has not worked out that way at all. Very few presidential elections have been determined by the House; the last part of this section will be dedicated to explaining why.

Why has the electoral college not performed as planned? That is, why has no election been decided by the House since John Q. Adams' victory over Andrew Jackson in 1824? There are two primary explanations for why the electoral college has not performed as expected. First, the emergence of a national two-party system has reduced the available electoral choices to only two candidates thereby guaranteeing one candidate will always receive a majority of electoral votes even if he fails to acquire a majority of popular votes, as has happened in both of Clinton's victories and Bush's 2000 victory.[43] (It is important to recall that the Founders never envisioned, and indeed warned against, political parties in general, so they had no way of predicting this "loophole" in the electoral college.) Second, the rise of a national electronic media has helped to cement further in the minds of the voting majority the belief that they are limited to only the choices offered by the two dominant political parties. Hence, by focusing all their presidential election coverage upon only the two major party candidates while, for all intents and purposes, ignoring all other possible candidates, the media ensures that no election will be contested in the House since there is no way one of the major party candidates will not get a majority of electoral votes.

In closing our discussion on the electoral college, it seems reasonably clear we, the modern Americans, will be saddled with this 18th century relic for many years to come. To replace the electoral college with a more democratic system would require two things to happen which seem highly unlikely in the near future. First, the majority of Americans would have to spend some time and energy learning how the present system actually works, which most, at least presently, show very little inclination to do. Second, it would require a constitutional amendment that must be ratified by some of the very states which currently benefit from the present system; and, since very few of their citizens are calling on them to change the system, it is doubtful they will initiate such a change on their own.

THE PRESIDENT AND THE BUREAUCRACY

The president is also constitutionally charged with overseeing the bureaucracies. Most federal bureaucracies are located in the executive branch because they perform the same basic function—they all enforce the laws written by Congress. And, since the president is the chief executive, he, therefore, technically controls almost all public bureaucratic institutions. We will see later that in reality he exercises very little authority over most bureaucracies, nonetheless, in theory he exercises complete control. In explaining why the president has so little actual authority over federal bureaucracies, we must first briefly outline the purpose and history of the federal bureaucratic establishment.

As mentioned above, bureaucracies, simply stated, administer the programs of government. In the American system of government the legislative branch formulates policy through its law making authority, while the executive branch enforces or implements these policies via the bureaucracies. Granted, the president has some role to play in the legislative process (for example, he can veto the law), but, as we have seen, his legislative function is at best reactionary and limited (for example, Congress can always override the president's veto). Therefore, the main purpose of any executive agency is to make real the wishes of Congress. In theory it works like this: First, Congress writes a law (technically, a federal statute) and then sends this statute to the appropriate federal bureaucracy for compliance or enforcement purposes. For example, if Congress writes a statute like, say, "the Clean Air Act," stipulating that industry will meet certain legal standards for pollution, this law would not be enforced by Congress but rather by the **Environmental Protection Agency**. The same would be true of any given federal statute; if the law addresses grazing rights on public lands, then it becomes the responsibility of the Department of the Interior; if the law deals with postal rates, then it becomes the province of the U.S. Postal Service; or, if it covers the workings of the stock market, then it becomes the duty of the Securities and Exchange Commission to ensure compliance.

For this reason, bureaucracies must generate immense amounts of governmental regulations, which are most often referred to as "**governmental red tape**."[44] Though these regulations (technically referred to as "regulatory rules") can be irritating to many citizens, they are, nonetheless, necessary to the functioning of government. Allow me to explain. Imagine, for example, we are employed as bureaucrats in a hypothetical "Parks and Recreation Department," and are charged with implementing the following federal statute: "No motor vehicles shall be allowed within any federal park." Though the statute itself is clear enough (and much simpler than actual statutes) it still requires us as bureaucrats to create numerous regulatory rules so we can enforce it in reality. For example, what happens if we see a parent and her child playing in the park with one of those remote controlled cars? Is this a violation since it is most certainly a motor vehicle and is definitely in the park? Whatever we decide will require us to stipulate, that is, write regulations, which will spell out exactly what the law is concerning remote controlled motor vehicles. Moreover, what if the citizens of a local community wish to place a tank in the park in memory of members of their community who have died to defend the country. Is this a violation? Again, whatever we decide will require us to write even more rules since this time we need to flesh out the regulations surrounding war memorials. Now, what about bicycles? They are in fact vehicles and the rider is in fact a motor, so is riding a bicycle in the park constitute a violation of the law? Or, does the motor have to be mechanical? What about emergency vehicles, are they allowed in the park? And, if so, then when? Only during specific times or during specific events (like softball games) or anytime? While we are at it, what about lawn mowers and other motorized maintenance tools? Will we only allow push mowers since, even though they are in fact motorized, they are not technically a vehicle? Or, does the fact they are motorized make them unsuitable for the park? By the way, what constitutes a "vehicle" anyway? As you can see by this example, even the simplest statute generates volumes of bureaucratic regulations or "governmental red tape," no matter how much we wish it otherwise.

In addition, this simple exercise also illustrates how important and how political the act of rule writing actually is. For example, if you happen to be in the bicycle selling business it matters greatly what the "Parks Department" rules concerning the legality of riding a bike in the park. If bureaucrats in the Parks Department decide it's illegal to ride bikes in the park, then sales will suffer accordingly. For this reason, it has always been a politically contentious issue over what qualifies someone to be a bureaucrat. Originally, most bureaucrats received their jobs simply because they were friends of a winning political candidate. Political scientists label such an administrative employment practice as either a "spoils system" or as "patronage." In either case, the essential element is that people receive government jobs because of who they know rather than what they know. On the positive side, the spoils system respects the democratic principle of electoral accountability since citizens are able to affect bureaucratic behavior simply by electing a different candidate. In other words, the spoils system allows the majority to affect bureaucratic practice by replacing one set of bureaucrats with another each election. Nevertheless, for all its apparent democratic spirit, the spoils system was ultimately rejected by Americans due to its inherent inadequacies.

As the American governing apparatus grew in both size and complexity, most Americans began to grow tired of a government stocked with unqualified administrators so there emerged a strong sentiment within the public for a more merit based system. The final push in the direction of a more professional civil service arrived in the form of an assassin's bullet. After a disgruntled federal job seeker assassinated President James A. Garfield in 1881 for refusing to appoint him to a federal post, the public demanded Congress do something about the spoils system. Hence, in 1883, Congress, with the enactment of The Pendleton Act, created the first merit based civil service. Though initially limited to only about 15% of all federal jobs, The Pendleton Act, nonetheless, required these bureaucrats to earn their jobs via competitive competency based exams—the so-called civil service exam. This proved so successful, that by 1952 over 90% of all federal bureaucrats were hired on the basis of merit rather than through patronage.[45] Unfortunately, a professional civil service turned out to be (as is the case in so much of politics) a double edged sword. To be sure, the merit system solved the problem of incompetent administration, however, it insulated bureaucrats from public accountability. Under the merit system bureaucrats were no longer beholden to the voting majority for their jobs since civil service reform made them immune from elected government officials. So, today most civil servants cannot be removed by any politician no matter how badly a politician's constituency demands it; they are, in effect, outside the reach of political accountability from both politicians and the public alike. This bureaucratic isolation and insulation from presidential authority led turn-of-the-century presidents to bemoan their lack of control over federal bureaucracies. Hence, Franklin D. Roosevelt was led to comment:

> The Treasury [Department] is so . . . ingrained in its practices that I find it impossible to get the actions and results I want. . . . But the Treasury is not to be compared with the State Department. You should go through the experience of trying to get any changes in the thinking, policy, and action of the career diplomats. . . . But both put together are nothing compared to the [Defense Department]. . . . To change anything in the [Defense Department] is like punching a feather bed. You punch it with your right and you punch it with your left until you are finally exhausted, and then you find the damn bed just as it was before you started punching.[46]

The problem became so acute for FDR that he lobbied Congress to create a special group of bureaucracies which would be more accountable to the president. So, in 1939, Congress agreed to address the problem by creating the Executive Office of the President.[47] Hence, the bureaucracies within the Executive Office of the President are, by design, under the direct control of the president. Presently, the Executive Office of the President contains 14 different agencies (see graph at end of chapter) of which the most important are The **White House Office**, the Office of Management and Budget, the Council of Economic Advisors, and the National Security Council.

The White House Office is comprised of the president's closest advisors and is in essence the command center for any president. The top aides of the White House Office owe absolute loyalty to the president as their job security depends on his; if he loses an election, then they lose their jobs. At the top of the administrative pyramid within the White House is the president's **Chief of Staff**. The Chief of Staff has authority over the most precious resource of any president—his time. That is, the Chief of Staff controls access to the president; if you want an appointment with the president, then you must go through the Chief of Staff. In addition to the Chief of Staff, the White House Office also contains the Office of the Vice-President as well as the staff for the First Lady. Moreover, it also houses various advisors and campaign strategists that serve only the president. In short, the White House Office is the closest thing a president has to a home away from home.

The Office of Management and Budget grew out of the Bureau of the Budget created in 1921. It contains a handful of political advisors in addition to over six hundred economic and budgetary experts who advise the president on matters of fiscal and domestic policy. The Council of Economic Advisors consists of three academic economists drawn from the most prestigious universities in America and was established in 1946 to provide expert economic advice to the president. Lastly, the National Security Council was created in 1947 to help streamline the president's foreign policy decision making. The NSC has evolved into the center of all American foreign policy with membership including every aspect of the foreign policy establishment. In short, the Executive Office of the President has worked as it was designed to—it provides the president with a group of bureaucrats who are both in tune with, and accountable to, the president. Now, we shall review the older and more insulated bureaucracies—The Cabinet, Government Corporations, and the Independent Agencies.

The Cabinet departments are the oldest bureaucracies in the federal system. The original Cabinet consisted of the Departments of State, Treasury and War (later renamed Defense) along with an Attorney General (who is now in charge of the Justice Department). And, even though there are now 14 different cabinet departments the most prestigious are still the original three (with the addition of the Justice Department). As a matter of fact, the Secretaries of State, Treasury and Defense are in this order the first non-elected officials in line to succeed the president in the case of his death or disability. As noted above, most members of all the cabinet departments are civil servants and, hence, acquire their jobs via merit exams.[48] However, the top executives (usually referred to as "Secretaries") receive their positions only after the president has nominated them and the Senate has confirmed their appointments by majority vote.

Government Corporations are bureaucracies designed essentially to run a nonprofit business. The most obvious example of a government corporation is the U.S. Postal Service. Other examples include Amtrak (American Train Company) which provides train service at a price most private carriers would not; the Federal Deposit Insurance Corporation (FDIC) which guarantees bank deposits up to $100,000; and the Tennessee Valley Authority (TVA) which helps provide inexpensive electricity to rural areas. For what it is worth, Congress previously disbanded a government corporation known as the Resolution Trust Corporation (RTC) after it was revealed it was plagued with "mismanagement." The RTC was designed to help mitigate the effects of Congress's misguided attempt to deregulate the savings and loan industry. Unfortunately, it was later discovered that the RTC did nothing to help relieve the S & L crisis but in fact increased by billions the amount tax payers have to spend to clean up the original mess. In any event, as is the case with Cabinet departments, most members of government corporations receive their jobs through civil service exams except for the high level executives who must be nominated by the president and confirmed by the Senate.

The last group of bureaucracies to examine are the Independent Agencies; so named because they are generally much more independent of the president than the other bureaucracies. Independent Agencies come in two types—independent regulatory agencies and establishments. Examples of the former include the Federal Reserve Board (FRB) which regulates monetary policy; the Securities and Exchange Commission (SEC) which regulates the stock market; and the Federal Communications Commission (FCC) which regulates the public airwaves. Examples of establishments are the Central Intelligence Agency (CIA) which houses the covert operations of the foreign policy establishment; the National Aeronautics and Space Administration (NASA) which manages the American nonmilitary space program; and the Environmental Protection Agency (EPA) which monitors air and water pollution. Most Independent Agencies, particularly the regulatory agencies, are designed so as to protect them from political pressure coming from the White House. Hence, even though the senior level executives of these agencies acquire their jobs via presidential appointment and Senate approval just like the administrators of both Cabinets and Government Corporations, they, unlike these other bosses, cannot be removed by the president and instead hold their offices for set terms.[49] In theory, this prevents these agencies from being pressured to manipulate regulatory policy in hopes of helping a president win reelection. For example, the Federal Reserve Board has been listed as a regulatory agency (which means its members cannot be removed by the president) so as to prevent the Fed from being pressured by a sitting president to flood the economy with paper money just prior to an election in hopes of ensuring an electoral victory. Of course it works the other way as well; there is no way for the public to demand the Fed change its policies to improve the economic conditions of most Americans since the Fed is immune to public pressure. In short, these bureaucracies are known as independent agencies because they are much more insulated from presidential pressure and public accountability.

In closing this section, we have seen that the president is theoretically in charge of the entire federal bureaucratic establishment, yet in reality he exercises very little control over the vast majority of bureaucratic agencies. This irony is due in no small part to the emergence of the civil service, a merit based system designed to provide for a more professional governmental administration but which has also created a more insulated one as well.

FINAL THOUGHTS

The presidency mirrors much of American political history. As the country grew much beyond even the grandest imaginations of the founding generation in both size and power, so has the presidency. As the country has become much more bureaucratic and superficial, so has the presidency. And, as the national government has emerged as the dominant player in most Americans' political lives, so has the presidency. In short, the presidency, much like America, is a dynamic and ever shifting entity, sometimes changing for the better, sometimes for the worse, but, nonetheless, always in motion. Where it will ultimately take us, is wherever we let it.

```
                    ┌─────────────────────┐
                    │   The President     │
                    │   Vice President    │
                    └──────────┬──────────┘
                               │
        ┌──────────────────────┼──────────────────────┐
        │                                             │
┌───────────────────┐                      ┌──────────────────────────┐
│     Cabinets      │                      │ Executive Office of the  │
│ Department of     │                      │         President        │
│ State, Treasury   │◄────────────────────►│  The White House Office  │
│ Department, Dept. │                      │ Office of Management &   │
│ of Defense, Dept. │                      │         Budget           │
│ of Justice, etc.  │                      │ National Security        │
└───────────────────┘                      │      Council, etc.       │
                                           └──────────────────────────┘

┌───────────────────────────┐              ┌──────────────────────────┐
│  Government Corporations  │              │   Independent Agencies   │
│ Post Office, Amtrak,      │◄────────────►│ Regulatory  Establishments│
│ F.D.I.C., etc.            │              │  F.R.B.       C.I.A.     │
└───────────────────────────┘              │  S.E.C.       N.A.S.A.   │
                                           │  F.C.C.       E.P.A.     │
                                           │ (Over 50 other           │
                                           │  Independent Agencies)   │
                                           └──────────────────────────┘
```

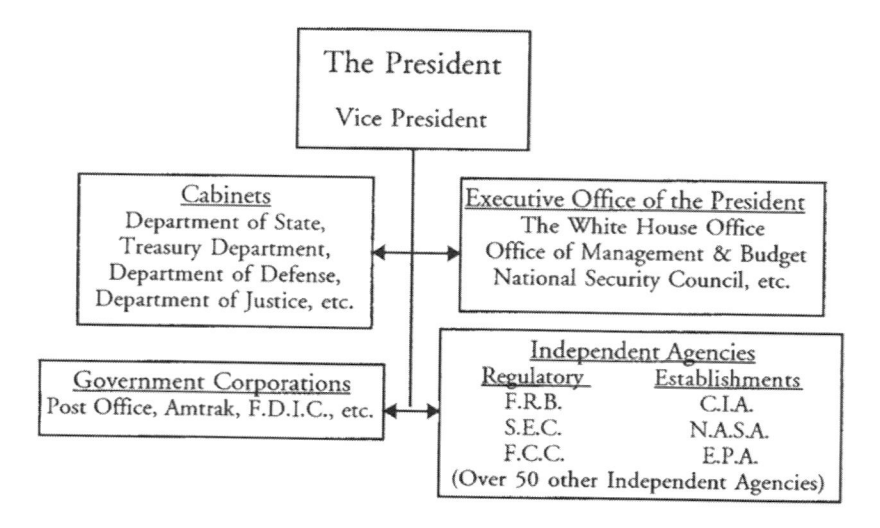

Organization of the Executive Branch

NOTES

1. For an excellent discussion on this point see, Bradley H. Patterson, Jr., *The Ring of Power: The White House Staff and its Expanding Role in Government* (New York: Basic Books, 1988).
2. See for example, George C. Edwards III, *The Public Presidency* (New York: St. Martin's Press, 1983), chapter 5.
3. For example, Stephen E. Frantzich and Stephen L. Percy, in *American Government: The Political Game* (Madison Wisconsin: Brown and Benchmark, 1994), p. 392, write: "Presidents are mentioned on evening news programs almost three times for every mention of the more complex and less visually orientated Congress." They graphically support this contention by noting that between 1975 and 1991 presidents were mentioned on the evening news anywhere from 2200 to 3500 times, whereas Congress during the same time frame was mentioned no more than 1200 times and as little as 300 times in any one year.
4. Steven Kelman, *American Democracy and the Public Good* (Fort Worth: Harcourt Brace, 1996), pp. 454–455.
5. For an excellent discussion on this point see Richard E. Neustadt, *Presidential Power and the Modern Presidents* (New York: Free Press, 1990).
6. Ibid, p. 10.
7. Quoted in Robert S. Hirschfield, ed., *The Power of the Presidency,* 2nd ed. (Chicago: Aldine, 1973), pp.141–142.
8. Quoted in Thomas E. Cronin, *The State of the Presidency,* 2nd ed. (Boston: Little Brown, 1980), p. 122.
9. For an excellent discussion on this point see James W. Davis, *The American Presidency* (New York: Harper & Row, 1987).
10. Thomas E. Patterson, *The American Democracy,* 2nd ed. (New York: McGraw-Hill, Inc., 1994), pp. 496–497.
11. For example see, Richard A. Watson and Norman C. Thomas, *The Politics of the Presidency,* 2nd ed. (Washington D.C.: Congressional Quarterly Press, 1988), p. 202.
12. Obviously, this chapter is no such history.
13. Richard A. Watson and Norman C. Thomas, *The Politics of the Presidency,* p. 204.
14. Quoted in *US News & World Report* (January 27, 1997).
15. On the creation of the presidency, see Donald L. Robinson, "To the Best of My Ability" (New York: Norton, 1987); and Thomas E. Cronin, ed., *Inventing the American Presidency* (Lawrence, Kan.: University Press of Kansas, 1989).
16. U.S. Constitution Article 2, Section 1.
17. U.S. Constitution Article 2, Section 1.
18. U.S. Constitution 22 Amendment.
19. U.S. Constitution Article 1, Section 2.
20. U.S. Constitution Article 1, Section 3.
21. See the Presidential Succession Act of 1947 (embodied within Title 3, chapter 1, Section d in particular which reads, "(d)(1) If, by reason of death, resignation, removal from office, inability, or failure to qualify, there is no President pro tempore to act as President under subsection (b) of this section, then the officer of the United States who is highest on the following list, and who is not under disability to discharge the powers and duties of the office of President shall act as president: Secretary of State, Secretary of the Treasury, Secretary of Defense, Attorney General, Secretary of the Interior, Secretary of Agriculture, Secretary of Commerce, Secretary of Labor, Secretary of Health and Human Services, Secretary of Housing and Urban Development, Secretary of Transportation, Secretary of Energy, Secretary of Education, Secretary of Veterans Affairs." However, the 20th and 25th Amendments to the U.S. Constitution do demand that the President fill any vacancy in the vice presidency subject to confirmation by a simple majority vote of both houses of Congress.
22. I am indebted to Stephen E. Frantzich and Stephen L. Percy, *American Government: The Political Game,* pp. 385–386, for these three constitutional roles.

23. U.S. Constitution Article 2, Section 2.
24. U.S. Constitution Article 2, Section 1.
25. For a full discussion see, Richard A. Watson and Norman C. Thomas, *The Politics of the Presidency*, 2nd ed., p. 302.
26. U.S. Constitution Article 2, Section 2.
27. Quoted in Robert Sherrill, *Why They Call it Politics: A Guide to America's Government*, 5th ed. (Harcourt Brace: San Diego, 1990), p. 70.
28. U.S. Constitution Article 1, Section 8.
29. Leonard W. Levy, *Original Intent and the Framers' Constitution* (New York: Macmillan, 1968), p. 30.
30. For a fuller discussion on this point see, Michael G. Roskin and Nicholas O. Berry, *The New World of International Relations*, 3rd ed. (New Jersey: Prentice-Hall, 1997), pp. 328–329.
31. See, Aaron Wildavsky, "The Two Presidencies," in Aaron Wildavsky, ed., *The Presidency* (Boston: Little, Brown, 1969). See also, Duane M. Oldfield and Aaron Wildavsky, "Reconsidering the Two Presidencies," in Steven A. Shull, ed. *The Two Presidencies: A Quarter Century Assessment* (Chicago: Nelson-Hall, 1991), pp. 181–190.
32. For a fuller discussion on this point see the chapter on foreign policy.
33. Quoted in Robert Sherrill, *Why They Call it Politics*, 5th ed., p. 75.
34. Ibid, p. 74.
35. For an excellent discussion on Clinton's disregard for the War Powers Resolution, see Louis Fisher's *Presidential War Power* (Lawrence, Kansas: University Press of Kansas, 1995).
36. Quoted in, *Parade Magazine* (December 1, 1996), p. 4.
37. Quoted in Karen O'Connor and Larry J. Sabato, *American Government: Roots and Reform* (New York: Macmillian, 1993), p. 232.
38. For an excellent discussion on the agenda setting power of the presidency, see John Kingdon, *Agendas, Alternatives, and Pubic Policies* (Boston: Little, Brown, 1984) and Paul C. Light, *The President's Agenda* (Baltimore: Johns Hopkins University Press, 1983).
39. Source: This section is taken verbatim from Robert Longley, "About the Primary—Caucus—Convention System: How Presidential Candidates are Chosen," About.com, US Government Information.
40. Quoted in, Richard A. Watson and Norman C. Thomas, *The Politics of the Presidency*, 2nd ed., p. 68.
41. This change was the result of the 12th Amendment to the U.S. Constitution.
42. This occurred in 1961 with the ratification of the 23rd Amendment to the U.S. Constitution.
43. This was the case, for example, in Lincoln's first term as president.
44. The phrase "red tape" originated from the fact that the French and British governments during their colonial empire days wrapped their administrative papers in red tape. In addition, see Herbert Kaufman, *Red Tape*, (Washington D.C.: The Brookings Institution, 1977), pp. 5-6.
45. Much of this history comes from William Lyons, John M. Scheb III, and Lilliard E. Richardson, Jr., *American Government: Politics and Public Culture* (St. Paul, Minnesota: West Publishing Company, 1995), pp. 449-452.
46. Quoted in M. S. Eccles, *Beckoning Frontiers* (New York: Knopf, 1951), p. 336.
47. See William A. Niskanen, Jr., *Bureaucracy and Representation* (Chicago: Aldine-Atherton, 1971).
48. For an excellent discussion of the backgrounds of Cabinet members see Jeffery E. Cohen, *The Politics of the U.S. Cabinet* (Pittsburgh: University of Pittsburgh Press, 1988).
49. *Wiener v. United States*, 357 U.S. 349 (1958).

CHAPTER 10
The Article III Branch: The Federal Judiciary

"[The Court] ought not be entrusted with the power to determine, instead of the people, what the people have the right to do in furthering social justice under the Constitution."
—*Theodore Roosevelt*

"To the ordinary citizen the United States Supreme Court is the embodiment of the majesty of the law, which makes all of us somewhat more willing to accept its edicts in good faith."
—*Robert Sherrill*

"The Court is in large part what people think it is . . . It is an 'image'."
—*Telford Taylor*

INTRODUCTION

This last chapter on institutions will focus on the **federal judiciary**. In doing so, we will spend most of our time articulating the nature and function of the Supreme Court. We will begin by reviewing its humble origins and constitutional character so as to help us grasp the Court's political and legal dimensions. From there, we will examine its function within the American political system and, in the process, address what one political scientist labels the "cult of the robe." Next, we will review the Court's present procedures for choosing and deciding the cases before it. Lastly, we will turn our attention to the other courts within the federal court system before concluding with some final thoughts on America's most mysterious branch of government.

The first session of the Supreme Court hardly got off to an auspicious start.[1] Only four of the original six justices named to the Court even made it to New York for its first session in 1790.[2] Those who did arrive gathered in the Exchange Building and found their duties were largely limited to qualifying attorneys to argue before them; consequently, the session lasted only ten days. The Court's second session proved even less noteworthy and lasted only two days. This led one historian to comment: "The first President immediately on taking office settled down to the pressing business of being

President. The first Congress enacted the first laws. The first Supreme Court adjourned."[3] Later that year, the United States Capitol moved from New York to Philadelphia and the Court moved with it. The Court reconvened in Independence Hall where they shared the courtroom with the Mayor's Court. In 1800 the Capitol, with the Supreme Court in tow, again moved, this time to its present day location, Washington D.C. For the next nine years the Court was compelled to meet in various rooms in the basement of the Capitol and for one year was even forced to hold its sessions in a local tavern while the Capitol underwent remodeling. In 1810 the Court finally was allotted its own room in the Capitol but this new luxury proved to be short-lived as the Capitol was burned by the British in 1814 during the War of 1812. This forced the Court to meet for the next two years in a rented house, Bell Tavern. They returned to the Capitol in 1817 and met in a small room in the basement until 1819 when their original courtroom was restored. A journalist at the time described the room:

> [The courtroom is] not in a style which comports with the dignity of [the Court], or which bears a comparison with the other Halls of the Capitol. In the first place, it is like going down a cellar to reach it. The room is on the basement story in an obscure part of the north wing. In arriving at it, you pass a labyrinth. . . . A stranger might traverse the dark avenues of the Capitol for a week, without finding the remote corner in which Justice is administered to the American Republic.[4]

In 1860 the Court relocated once again; this time moving upstairs in the Capitol to the old Senate Chamber. Finally, in 1935, the Court was provided with a building all their own in Washington D.C. where it still convenes today. Apparently making up for past insults, the Supreme Court Building was "designed as a replica of an ancient Greek temple, with the words 'Equal Justice under Law' carved above its massive bronze doors."[5] Nonetheless, as this very brief history illustrates, the Court was not held in high regard by the founding generation and was not granted the same esteem as the other two branches of the federal government. In fact, the first Chief Justice, John Jay, resigned his post to become envoy to England and later refused reappointment to the position by commenting that:

> [I am] not perfectly convinced that under a system so defective [the Court] would obtain the energy, weight and dignity which were essential to its affording due support for the National Government, nor acquire the public confidence and respect which, as the last resort of justice of the nation, it should possess.[6]

For many of the revolutionary generation, federal courts carried the stench of colonial rule and, hence, were viewed with suspicion by the majority of Americans. So, when the Founders met in Philadelphia to construct a new republic they were very much aware that only a relatively weak federal judiciary would be acceptable to the people of the several states on which ratification depended. At the same time, they were very much in agreement that a federal judiciary was necessary. Therefore, when they advocated passage of the new constitution, they assured Americans the newly proposed federal judiciary would be "the least dangerous branch." As Hamilton wrote in ***The Federalist Papers***:

> The executive not only dispenses the honors, but holds the sword of the community. The legislature not only commands the purse, but prescribes the rules by which the duties and rights of every citizen are to be regulated. The judiciary, on the con-

> trary, has no influence over either sword or the purse . . . [and will least likely be able to] annoy or injure [the basic constitutional rights since it can] take no active resolution whatever. It may truly be said to have neither FORCE nor WILL, but merely judgement. . . .[7]

This theoretical and historical reluctance to embrace national judicial power helps explain the experience of the early Court. American revolutionary political experience and theory simply did not square with a strong federal judiciary. Today, however, the Supreme Court's political influence has grown much beyond that of its earlier predecessors. As one historian has written:

> The United States Supreme Court, the most powerful court in the world, grew from humble origins. In the first decades of its existence, the Court was weak, and Americans held it in low esteem. In its first decade, the nation even had trouble finding citizens willing to take the job of Chief Justice of the Supreme Court. The job would have been a step down for most applicants.

> Today's Court little resembles that of 1789. In recent decades, our federal judiciary helped pry America away from racial segregation; granted the right to have an abortion; and, in the case United States v. Nixon, the Court proved instrumental in bringing down an American President. Now the Court regularly overturns federal and state laws and involves itself deeply in the nation's affairs.[8]

In other words, not only is the Supreme Court now a major player in American politics, arguably equal in standing to the other two branches of the federal government, it is also a thoroughly political institution which performs at the pinnacle of the American legal system. For this reason, political scientists consider it essential that Americans grasp its political nature and legal character if they are to acquire a meaningful political education, and the rest of this chapter will be dedicated to this purpose. To this end, we will now begin detailing its constitutional personality so as to help us better comprehend its political function.

CONSTITUTIONAL COURT

Article 3 of the Constitution begins by stating: "The judicial power of the United States, shall be vested in one Supreme Court, and in such inferior courts as the Congress may from time to time ordain and establish." Immediately we see that the Supreme Court is the only federal court explicitly named in the Constitution. All other federal courts are the result of congressional action. Today, as the graph at the end of the chapter illustrates, there has developed a very complex federal judicial system with **district courts**, circuit courts, administrative courts, and so forth.

Yet all of these courts, indeed every state court as well, is inferior to the Supreme Court. Nowhere in the Constitution, however, does it enumerate any substantive qualifications for a Supreme Court judge; the only requirement is procedural. That is, the only constitutional qualification for federal judgeship is that an individual be appointed by the president and confirmed by the Senate.[9] Unlike the offices of president or Congress, there are no age, citizenship, or residency conditions constitutionally imposed upon those serving on the federal bench. The Constitution also states that judges "shall hold their offices during good behavior"; in other words, federal judges, including Supreme Court justices, are not elected and cannot be removed except via impeachment once appointed. Of the 47 federal judges who have been threatened with impeachment only 13 faced trials and of those only seven were convicted. No Supreme Court justice has ever been removed from office via impeachment (although one justice was tried and acquitted while another had two unsuccessful impeachment resolutions drawn up against him), which led Jefferson to bemoan the fact that impeachment was a "mere scarecrow" over the federal judiciary.[10] Moreover, the Constitution does not stipulate how many judges shall sit on the Supreme Court. This decision is left up to Congress. Hence, the first Supreme Court created by the very first act of the first Congress in 1789 consisted of six judges;[11] in 1869 Congress changed its membership to nine judges where it has remained ever since. Hence, there is no constitutional reason Congress could not change the Court's membership in the future if it were so inclined. There are, however, political reasons for not doing so, as President Franklin Roosevelt and the "New Deal" Democratic Congress discovered in the 1930s. The New Deal Democrats had recently won a large electoral victory by promising to use the government's power to end the Depression.[12] So, as soon as the New Deal Democrats were in office, they enacted various so-called "alphabet soup" programs designed to improve the economy by putting Americans to work on governmental projects. Needless to say, these policies were very popular with the majority of Americans; however, many of these programs were declared unconstitutional by the Supreme Court and thereby rendered null and void. This infuriated the New Deal Democrats (FDR in particular) as their agenda was being stymied by a group of Supreme Court justices who were both wealthy economically and conservative ideologically.[13] Therefore, after their landslide victories in 1936, FDR and the Democrats in Congress came up with their so-called "court packing" plan to prevent any further interference by the Supreme Court. Aware that the Constitution granted Congress the power to decide the membership of the Court, the Democrats introduced legislation which would allow the president to appoint a new judge for every sitting Supreme Court justice who reaches the age of 70 (the most aggressive opponents of FDR's new deal policies just happened to be four justices who were all over 70).[14] Having had success with their political programs, the Democrats assumed their court packing legislation would be popular with the public—but they were wrong. The people may have in fact welcomed the policies of the New Deal as is evident by the electoral results of the era, but they were more beholden to their sacred Supreme Court. The public outcry over the Democrats' "scheme" was so intense that the people, who had elected FDR by a landslide and would do so two more times (he was never defeated and died in office), threatened to impeach the president for attempting to mess with their beloved Supreme Court, the very institution which was doing so much to prevent government from improving their economic lives. Needless to say, the chastised and humbled Democrats quietly and quickly revoked the plan. I will have more to say on the public's (blind?) acceptance of legal authority later. Suffice it to say at this point that 20th century politicians learned from FDR's experience that there is a big difference between what is constitutionally permitted and what is politically feasible when it comes to the Supreme Court.

The Constitution, in Article 3, Section 2, states: "The Judicial power shall extend to all cases, in law and equity, arising under this Constitution . . . " Today, this means in regards to adjudicating federal constitutional issues, the Supreme Court has jurisdiction (legal authority) over both state and federal criminal and civil law. Furthermore, later in Article 3, Section 2, it declares, "[i]n all cases affecting Ambassadors, other public ministers and consuls, and those in which a state shall be party, the Supreme Court shall have original jurisdiction. In all other cases before mentioned, the Supreme Court shall have appellate jurisdiction as to law and fact . . . " Hence, the Court is both an original jurisdiction court and an **appellate court** in which it has authority over both law and fact. To help better understand the Court and our legal system in general, we will now examine each of these concepts in more detail below.

State and Federal Law. The American political system is composed of 51 separate legal systems—50 state systems and one federal system. Each of these legal systems has a unique personality consisting of rules and procedures which would be foreign in any other. For this reason, before anyone is allowed to practice law within one of these jurisdictions, he or she must pass a "bar" exam covering the law of that particular legal system. For example, if you wish to practice law in, say, California, then you must pass the bar exam covering California law, and the same is true for all the other legal systems—each demands you pass its bar exam to practice law. The Constitution grants the Supreme Court appellate jurisdiction over "all cases" originating in any of these 51 jurisdictions. However, for the Court to hear a case coming from a state court, a federal constitutional issue must have been raised by an attorney during the original trial. Moreover, the Supreme Court has jurisdiction over both civil law as well as criminal law. The difference between the two is as follows: Punishment in criminal law extends to the loss of life, liberty, and property, whereas in civil law it can only extend to money or equity (to be discussed below); the government is always a party in a criminal case (the people of Oregon versus . . .), while in civil law each party to the litigation is private (Smith vs. Jones); criminal law is always statutory (based on a law written by a legislative body), whereas civil law can be either statutory or common law (law made by a judge); and, lastly, in criminal law the government picks up the cost of prosecution, while in a civil case each party is responsible for their own legal expense. In any event, the Supreme Court has authority over "all cases" in the American political system be they state or federal, criminal or civil.

Courts of Law and Equity. As we saw earlier, the Constitution also grants the Supreme Court jurisdiction over "all cases, in law and equity, arising under this Constitution." As this language illustrates, there are in essence two types of courts in the American legal system, law courts and equity courts, and, as the Constitution makes clear, the Supreme Court is both. The difference between the two types of courts concerns the remedies they may apply to any lawsuit which comes before them. Law courts are limited to granting money relief, whereas equity courts can "right the wrong." For example, if an individual seeks compensation for an alleged wrong, like, say, losing a leg in an automobile accident, it would behoove this individual to sue in a court of law as it could order monetary compensation, whereas a court of equity would be limited to ordering the leg be reattached which, at that point, is probably impossible. Hence, it is important for an attorney to sue in the right type of court as the above case illustrates. Nonetheless, the Supreme Court is constitutionally empowered to apply either remedy, money or equity. For example, in the school desegregation case, *Brown v. The Board of Education,* the attorney for the Browns, Thurgood Marshall (who later would be the first African-American appointed to the Court), asked the Supreme Court to act as a court of equity and right the wrong by ordering the desegregation of the school system of Topeka, Kansas. As noted above, a court of law would have been limited to providing merely money to compensate the Browns for the harm done to their children by Topeka's poor educational system for African-Americans.

Original Jurisdiction Courts and Appellate Courts. As noted above, the Constitution grants the Supreme Court original jurisdiction in some cases and "in all other cases . . . the Supreme Court shall have appellate jurisdiction." Hence, the Supreme Court is constitutionally both a trial court and a court of appeals. Though the Court's appellate jurisdiction is by far its most important contemporary function, we must articulate the difference between a trial court and an appellate court to fully grasp its political purpose. A trial court, as most of us have seen on some television show or another, is comprised of two parties, with legal representation, witnesses, a judge, and a jury. On the other hand, an appellate court consists only of the attorneys for both sides and a panel of judges; no juries or witnesses are present, just the officers of the court. The reason for their different composition is due to the procedural purposes of each. That is, an original jurisdiction court is, as the name suggests, where the case originated and, hence, is out to determine two fundamental things: First, what in fact happened? And, second, what does the law demand given the facts discovered? To the first end, lawyers for both sides will call witnesses to describe in the most favorable light possible for their clients what in fact happened. Yet, in the end, the only version of the facts which has any legal force are those of the jury (which is why the best witnesses are usually eyewitnesses as they are most likely to sway the jury). Therefore, the legal purpose of a jury is to determine what set of facts the law will enter into the legal record (which is why so much of contemporary litigation practice concerns itself with jury selection rather than justice *per se*). The judge's role in the trial is to act as an umpire to make certain the trial is conducted according to the law and is thereby fair. For example, if an attorney thinks a question asked by his or her adversary is unfair, or in other words, illegal, he or she will object and ask the judge, or umpire, to sustain him or her. If the judge agrees the question was unfair, then the judge will indeed sustain the objection, if the judge disagrees he or she will overrule the objection. At no time will the judge involve himself or herself in the factual issues of the proceedings, which brings us to the second purpose of any trial—deciding what the law requires given the legal facts. The judge's only legal duty is to rule on the law, while leaving the factual issues of the court to the jury. Therefore, when the jury renders its verdict (for example, did the defendant in fact commit murder?) the judge will then apply the law upon the verdict—"not guilty" and the defendant is released, "guilty" and the judge sentences according to law. As this discussion implies, notice how little truth itself comes into play in the American legal system. That is, nowhere during any trial does truth procedurally carry the day, the only issue at law is fairness. So, if a person gets convicted or acquitted, no matter how blatantly the truth speaks otherwise, courts are legally bound to accept the jury's version of the facts as the criminal trial involving O.J. Simpson sadly illustrates. To be sure, in the majority of cases the judgment of the court may very well reflect the truth, but, nonetheless, this is due more to luck than procedural intent. In any case, the purpose of an original jurisdiction court is to decide what in fact happened and then apply the law appropriately. And, when the Supreme Court convenes as an original jurisdiction court, it acts as both jury and judge determining both fact and law.

The purpose of an appellate court is different. The sole duty of an appeals court is to decide if the law was applied correctly during the original trial. Upon appeal, the only issues open to review are questions of law; there can be no debate as to the jury's version of the facts. In other words, the facts are considered, in the language of the law, "frozen" at the trial phase, and are not subject to further contest. Say an individual has been convicted of a crime in which facts discovered after the trial argue for his or her innocence, he or she is still limited legally to appealing only the legal aspects of the original court's proceedings. For this reason there are no juries or witnesses at the appeals phase of litigation since there is no question as to the facts concerning the case. The exception to this rule is the Supreme Court. The Constitution, as noted earlier, grants the Supreme Court when exercising its appellate powers "jurisdiction, both as to law and fact." Hence, if a case is fortunate enough to be heard on appeal by the Supreme Court, then the Court is free to retry the facts as well as the law. In closing this section of the chapter let us review: We have discovered the Constitution creates a Supreme Court by name but lets Congress determine the details of its make-up. We have seen the Constitution requires only that justices be appointed by the president and confirmed by the Senate, and that they hold their offices during good behavior. Moreover, we have learned the Supreme Court has constitutional jurisdiction over state and federal law as well as criminal and civil law. We have found it to be both a court of equity and a court of law in addition to being both a court of original jurisdiction and a court of appeals, yet with jurisdiction over both fact and law. In short, we have seen the Supreme Court is indeed the supreme court of the American political system.

THE POLITICAL FUNCTION OF THE SUPREME COURT—JUDICIAL REVIEW

The most important political duty of the Supreme Court is **judicial review**. The authors of *Constitutional Law: Cases in Context* define judicial review in the following manner:

> The power of judicial review is the ability of the Supreme Court to determine the constitutionality of acts of Congress, the executive, a state, or even a provision of a state constitution under the United States Constitution. Simply stated, it is the power to declare what the Constitution means . . . [In short] the power of judicial review gives a small group of nonelected justices authority to interpret the Constitution

and in the process to declare the meaning of and priorities among the fundamental principles of American constitutionalism. . . . [15]

Moreover, the authors of *Constitutional Law* write:

> [T]he U.S. Supreme Court's prestige and power . . . flows from its right of judicial review—the power to declare unconstitutional (1) laws of Congress and (2) of state governments, as well as (3) actions and regulations of the executive. This power gives to the Supreme Court glamour and a decisive weapon that allows it to compete on a plane of equality with the other and more active branches of government . . . [16]

As these excerpts attest, there is no greater power in a constitutional democracy than the ability to decide what the Constitution means. By definition a constitutional democracy depends first and foremost on an authoritative text which stipulates the fundamental priorities and legitimate functions of the government. Therefore, it is indeed a powerful institution which exercises the authority to decide what that constitution means as their opinions will determine the scope of all other political activity; and, of course, this institution in the American political system is the Supreme Court. Yet, "[t]he justification for [the Supreme Court's] power is neither easy nor obvious. Oddly, the Constitution does not explicitly call for judicial review."[17] That is, although judicial review is the primary duty and source of authority for the Supreme Court, nowhere in the Constitution does it actually grant them this power. As the authors of *American Constitutional Interpretation* write when discussing which of the three branches of the federal government should exercise judicial review: "There is not . . . a single word [in the Constitution] about whose views should prevail . . . "[18] In this context, the boldness with which the Supreme Court has exercised its authority of judicial review is startling. In exercising this power, the Supreme Court has, to mention but a few examples, in *Dred Scott v. Sanford* helped bring on the Civil War;[19] in *Korematsu v. United States* permitted the imprisonment of Japanese-Americans during World War II;[20] in cases such as *Plessy v. Ferguson, Brown v. Board of Education of Topeka (Brown I), and Brown v. Board of Education of Topeka (Brown II)* reconfigured the public standing of the black and white races;[21] in *Griswold v. Connecticut* created the right to privacy while addressing the relationship between physicians and their married patients when prescribing contraception;[22] in *United States v. Nixon* helped bring down one president,[23] and in *Youngstown Sheet and Tube Co. v. Sawyer* backed down another while he engaged America in an undeclared war;[24] in *Santa Clara County v. Southern Pacific Railroad* ruled that corporations were legal persons entitled to constitutional protection;[25] in *Lochner v. New York* prevented states from enacting minimum wage or maximum hour laws;[26] and, in *Miranda v. Arizona* regulated law enforcement policy for every police department in America.[27] Therefore, given that judicial review is a fundamental power which goes to the heart of the American constitutional democracy, we must explore how it was the Supreme Court assumed this authority—to this task we now turn.

The Supreme Court, simply stated, assumed the power of judicial review via the case **Marbury v. Madison** in 1803.[28] The case was precipitated by the election of 1800 when the newly created Jeffersonian Democratic-Republican party defeated the incumbent Federalist Party for both the Presidency and Congress.[29] The two parties disagreed fundamentally on whose interests governmental policy should promote. The Jeffersonians advocated on behalf of the people at large, while the Federalists supported policies which favored the economic elite. Given the results of the election, the Federalist party knew their only hope for influencing national policy was to stock the judiciary with partisan Federalist judges before Jefferson's party assumed control of Congress and the Presidency. To this end, they created numerous judgeships and began appointing Federalist judges. In this way the Federalist party hoped to affect national policy without actually having to win any elections. Needless to say, this infuriated Jefferson and his party. Upon taking office, Jefferson directed his new Secretary of State, James Madison, to refuse delivery of any more judicial commissions to those Federalist judges who had not yet received them. Hence, when William Marbury arrived in Washington to receive his commission Madison refused as directed. (Marbury waited until Jefferson's party had assumed power because in their haste to stock the bench the Federalist leaders forgot to inform him of his appointment.) Consequently, Marbury sued in the Supreme Court asking them to issue a writ of mandamus ordering Madison to hand over the commission—hence, the name of the case *Marbury v. Madison*. Somewhat ironically, the new Chief Justice of the Supreme Court, John Marshall, was not only a staunch Federalist and previous Secretary of State, he also happened to be Jefferson's cousin and avowed enemy. Nonetheless, Marshall was placed between a political rock and a hard place. If he ruled in favor of Marbury, he knew Jefferson would simply ignore the decision thereby leaving the Federalists in charge of an institution with no real political authority. On the other hand, if Marshall agreed with Jefferson and sided with Madison he would in effect be adding credence to Jefferson's claim that the Federalist judicial appointments were improper and, therefore, null and void. From this predicament, Marshall pulled political victory from the jaws of institutional defeat.

Marshall argued that the congressional statute, The Judiciary Act of 1789, which granted the Court original jurisdiction in this matter was itself unconstitutional. He reasoned that since the Constitution dictates the original jurisdiction of the Court, Congress could not, therefore, add to the Court's original jurisdiction via mere statute; rather, this would require a constitutional amendment. In effect what Marshall had done by allowing the Jeffersonians their symbolic victory (after all, Marbury never received his commission) was declare an act of Congress unconstitutional—a power, as mentioned above, not specifically granted to any branch of the government by the Constitution. To be sure, the Supreme Court was aware of its precarious position and did not overturn another act of Congress until the infamous Dred Scott case in 1857. Nonetheless, they had put in place the legal justification for this power and to this day cite it as proof of their unique constitutional authority to review the acts of all other governments in the American political system.

At a deeper level of analysis, the Court's real authority for exercising the awesome power of judicial review comes from the legitimacy the people grant it. That is, the Court's moral authority to interpret the Constitution comes from the fact the people believe they ought to. As FDR and his followers in Congress learned in the 1930s, the American people in the 20th century have an almost irrational respect for legal institutions and legal actors. I write irrational because though very few Americans know much at all about law or politics, they continue to bow before the mysteries of the Supreme Court in particular and the legal profession in general. The legal community is hardly unaware of the power they derive from the public's awe of legal ceremony, so they foster this reverence by playing up the mystical aspects of the law. For example, notice that all individuals must rise when the judge enters the courtroom and refer to him or her as "your honor." Furthermore, notice that attorneys dress as if in church, while judges wear robes similar in appearance to the gowns worn by the priestly class of the middle ages as they sit behind the most impressive desk in a cathedral like courtroom. And again much like church, those who come before the court not only may swear upon the Bible, they also dress and act as if they are in fact attending some religious service (notice how people whisper in a courtroom). This pomp and ceremony has proved so impressive that today the surest avenue to political success is a law degree, even though legal training does very little to prepare an individual for public service.[30] The original Supreme Court once even tried to bolster their reputation by wearing wigs in addition to the robes still worn by their contemporaries. However, 17th and 18th century Americans were less impressed with such pretensions as indicated by Jefferson's remark when he saw the justices in their English style wigs: "For Heaven's sake, discard the monstrous wigs which make [you] . . . look like rats peeping through bunches of oakum."[31] As you may recall, in *The Wizard of Oz* what transforms an ordinary human being into the "great and powerful Oz" is the edifice and pyrotechnics which surround him and not any special qualities of the man himself. Ironically, it took a dog to reveal the wizard for what he was—a mere mortal; and, if the dog had not, there is no telling how long the wizard would have exercised his unquestioned authority over his obedient subjects. One political scientist who studies the judicial process and its effect on the American political system labels this phenomenon "the cult of the robe."[32]

The biggest beneficiary of the people's blind faith in legal symbolism is the Supreme Court. This helps explain why no matter how much disdain the American people have for political institutions in general, they never waver in their respect for the Supreme Court. The Supreme Court goes to great lengths to protect its sacred place in the American collective conscience by avoiding the political spotlight and remaining a relative mystery to the American public. As one scholar noted:

> Knowing that the mystique of the Court is the source of much of their influence, members have done all they could possibly do to maintain an aura of majestic aloofness, of remoteness and secrecy. They may even believe it to be their patriotic duty to create this atmosphere as a way to help implement their decisions . . . [33]

In this way the Court hopes to perpetuate the myth that it is above politics and renders its decisions not according to political bias but pursuant to the high principles of the law. For example, cameras are not tolerated in the courtroom and the justices shy away from public scrutiny and political controversy. The Court further promotes its reputation as being above politics by avoiding politically controversial cases which would draw the Court into the political thicket and help expose its political essence. In doing so, the justices of the Supreme Court not only insulate themselves from political accountability, they also "cloak their political role in the mantle of law . . . "[34] For example, the Court may refuse to hear controversial cases by invoking the abstract legal concepts of "justiciability" and "standing." The principle of justiciability means the Court will only hear actual cases which deal with actual controversies but will not entertain contrived cases or issue advisory opinions.[35] In other words, the Court is reluctant to entangle itself in political controversy by weighing in with its opinion on, say, the constitutionality of the line-item veto, until someone has actually been harmed by the president's veto and has consequently sued in a court of law. In this way they avoid the attention such a political issue has at the moment and deal with it, if at all, much later in their closed courtroom when the issue has become, so to speak, yesterday's news. The rule of standing also provides legal cover for the Court. The rule of standing demands the Court hear only cases where both parties are recognized legal persons and meet the tests of "mootness" and "ripeness." For example, for much of American history neither African-Americans nor women were granted standing in most courts because they were not considered legal persons. Yet even if the parties are considered legal persons their case may still be denied a hearing on account of mootness or ripeness. Mootness refers to the fact the Court will not hear a case which has, in the eyes of the law, already worked itself out prior to legal adjudication. For example, say a white male sues under the equal protection clause of the 14th Amendment because he was denied admittance to a law school even though his scores were higher than some of the accepted applicants. Consequently, a local court grants him an injunction ordering the law school to admit him pending legal resolution of his claim. Now, suppose three years later his case is appealed to the Supreme Court. At this point, the Court could rule the case moot as the plaintiff has already finished law school.[36] Needless to say, this pleases the Court, as it shields it from the public scrutiny affirmative action cases entail. Ripeness is similar except it works from the other end of the time line. For example, say a white male has applied for a job as a professor at a state college but has heard through the grapevine the school is only considering female and minority applicants. Believing his constitutional right to equal protection of the laws will be violated, he asks the Court for redress but is denied on account of ripeness. In this case, the Court could argue the issue is not yet ripe since the plaintiff has not in fact been denied a job but only suspects he might be denied employment. Again, such rules help protect the Court from public scrutiny by empowering it to refuse to hear cases which may expose its political nature. If all else fails, the Court also has what it refers to as its "Political Questions" doctrine. This doctrine simply means the Supreme Court may refuse to hear any case it believes would be better resolved through the other branches of government. For example, some citizens during the Vietnam War asked the Court to rule on the constitutionality of the undeclared war. The Court wisely refused, arguing the best way for citizens to express their opinion regarding the war was through the ballot box and not through the court system. Nevertheless, not all people have been so quick to accept the authority of the Supreme Court to interpret the Constitution for the rest of us. As two scholars have noted:

> This power has troubled thinkers both on and off the bench. Why should nine lifetime appointees make such momentous decisions for a [democratic] society? Why should five justices be able to set aside the actions of a Congress and Presidency, who are responsible to the electorate?[37]

The political elites of early America seriously debated who should exercise the power of judicial review. There were in essence three different theories vying for recognition: The theory of judicial supremacy as we practice now; the theory of departmentalism as favored by such presidents as Jefferson, Jackson and Lincoln; and the theory of state nullification. Departmentalism, simply stated, is the belief that each branch of government has the right to judge the constitutionality of its own actions. Hence, Congress will only write laws it has deemed constitutional; the president will only enforce the law in a manner he considers constitutional; and, the Court will adjudicate the law according to its own constitutional standards. Jefferson wrote the following when explaining his theory of departmentalism to a proponent of judicial supremacy:

> You seem to think it devolved on the judges to decide on the validity of the . . . law. But nothing in the Constitution has given them a right to decide for the Executive, more than the Executive to decide for them. Both magistrates are equally independent in the sphere of action assigned to them. The judges, believing the law constitutional, [have] a right to pass a sentence. . . . But the executive, believing the law to be unconstitutional, were bound to remit execution of it because that power had been confined to them by the Constitution. That instrument meant that its coordinate branches should be checks on each other. But the opinion which gives to the judges the right to decide what laws are constitutional and what are not, not only for themselves in their own sphere of action, but for the legislature and executive also in their spheres, would make the judiciary a despotic branch.[38]

Madison in support of Jefferson's position added:

> There is not one Government . . . in the United States, in which provision is made for a particular authority to determine the limits of the constitutional division of power between the branches of the Government. In all systems, there are points which must be adjusted by the departments themselves, to which no one of them is competent.[39]

The theory of departmentalism, however, did not die along with the colonial generation. In 1832 President Andrew Jackson, when explaining a veto he had recently exercised, argued:

> The Congress, The Executive, and the Court must each for itself be guided by its own opinion of the Constitution. . . . It is as much the duty of the House of Representatives, of the Senate, and of the President to decide upon the constitutionality of any bill or resolution which may be presented to them for passage or approval as it is of the supreme judges when it may be brought before them for judicial decision. The opinion of the judges has no more authority over Congress than the opinion of Congress has over the judges, and on that point the President is independent of both.[40]

Abraham Lincoln expressed the deficiencies of judicial supremacy while defending his departmentalism in his first inaugural address in 1861. Here is what he said:

> At the same time the candid citizen must confess that if the policy of the government, upon vital questions, affecting the whole people, is to be irrevocably fixed by the decisions of the Supreme Court, the instant they are made, in ordinary litigation between parties, in personal actions, the people will have ceased, to be their own rulers, having, to that extent, practically resigned their government, into the hands of that eminent tribunal.[41]

As these quotes illustrate there was no shortage of American scholarship or notoriety supporting a different view of judicial review than we hold today. The belief each state could decide for itself the constitutionality of the laws within its borders was the other theory which competed with judicial supremacy. This theory became known as "nullification." Its most articulate spokesman was South Carolina's John C. Calhoun.[42] Here is an excerpt from one of his writings which nicely summarizes the theory:

> Now, as there is nothing in the Constitution which vests authority in the government of the United States, or any of its departments, to enforce its decision against that of the separate government of a state . . . it is manifest that there is nothing in the [Constitution], which can possibly give the judicial power authority to enforce the decision of the government of the United States, against that of a separate State. . . . How can [the notion of judicial supremacy] be reconciled with the admitted principle, that the federal government and those of the several states, are supreme in their respective spheres? Each, it is admitted, is supreme, as it regards the other, in its proper sphere; and, of course, as has been shown, coequal and coordinate.[43]

Nevertheless, for better or for worse, today all of this is a moot point. The Supreme Court is now recognized as the only institution which may legitimately exercise the power of judicial review. Therefore, the next section of this chapter will cover the procedures by which the Supreme Court chooses which cases to hear and how they go about deciding a case once selected.

THE WORKING SUPREME COURT

The Supreme Court begins each year's session on the first Monday in October and usually finishes toward the end of June. During this time, the Supreme Court can act as both an original or appellate court. Today, however, the Supreme Court spends the vast majority of its time and issues its most important decisions as an appellate court. About four-fifths of all the cases the Court hears on appeal come up through the federal court system; the other one-fifth come directly from **state supreme courts**.[44] Almost all of these cases arrive under a *writ of certiorari* (Latin for "made more certain") asking the Court to examine a lower court's ruling. Given the immensity of the American legal docket, it should come as no surprise that only 3% of all requests for appeal are granted by the Court.[45] The cases it does hear are chosen for one of the five following reasons:

1. **two federal courts of appeals have rendered conflicting decisions on a similar issue;**

2. **a federal court of appeals has rendered a decision which conflicts with a state supreme court;**

3. a federal court of appeals has acted in a legally unorthodox manner;

4. a state supreme court has issued a judgement which conflicts with either federal precedent or another state supreme court which has ruled on the same federal issue; or

5. the issue is in the judges view too important not to address.

At this point, it would behoove us to review the legal concept of **stare decisis** (Latin for "let the decision stand") which establishes a legal hierarchy within the American court system. Under the principle *stare decisis,* any decision made by a higher court controls the opinions of any lower court when dealing with a similar matter by setting what is referred to in legal circles as a "precedent." That is, if a lower court is deliberating on a case which is substantially similar to a case already ruled on by a higher court, then the higher court's opinion sets a precedent that the lower court is compelled to follow when issuing its decision. For this reason, most of the cases the Supreme Court agrees to hear are those which deal with conflicting precedents. Additionally, as is implied by the above, any decision the Supreme Court renders thereby sets a precedent for all other courts in the American legal system. When deciding which cases to hear on appeals the Court invokes the so-called "rule of four." In other words, if four of the nine judges agree to hear a case, then it is granted a hearing in front of the nation's highest tribunal. Once a case is granted a hearing, the case is placed on the docket and scheduled for oral argument (it usually takes about three months from the time the appeal is granted). During the hearing there are no witnesses or jury, only the two attorneys and the nine justices. Somewhat surprisingly, each attorney is allowed only a half hour to argue his or her case. Moreover, during each attorney's half hour the justices are free to interrupt and question the attorneys whenever they feel so inclined. After oral arguments, the justices will deliberate in secret, taking into consideration the parties' written briefs, their oral arguments, and what are known as *amicus curiae* or "friend of the court" briefs. *Amicus* briefs are written arguments from interested persons or groups which attempt to persuade the Court. For example, when, in 1989, the Court agreed to hear the abortion case *Webster v. Reproductive Health Services*[46] it received over 78 *amicus* briefs from over 400 different political organizations.[47] In any event, after deliberation, the justices take a vote with the party receiving at least five votes winning the case. The justices vote in a prescribed manner, with the Chief Justice voting first, followed in order from the most senior justice to the least senior justice.

Once the vote is final and the Court is ready to render a verdict, it issues a written opinion declaring which party won and detailing the reasons that party prevailed. Additionally, the Court's opinion is read out loud from the bench by the justice who authored it and is a major legal event, as this opinion will set a new precedent. The decision of the Court is known as the "majority opinion," and is written by the Chief Justice when he is in the majority or, when he is not, by the most senior justice among the majority (although in either case they may assign it to another justice within the majority). In addition to the majority opinion, there may also be concurring and/or dissenting opinions attached to the majority opinion. The former is an opinion written by one or more judges who agree with the verdict of the Court but for different reasons; the latter is an opinion written by one or more justices who disagree with the verdict. Before closing this section, it is important to note, once again, that these opinions are the only authoritative interpretation of what the Constitution means in practice. A former Supreme Court justice articulated it best when he stated: "We are under a Constitution but the Constitution is what the judges say it is. . . . "[48] Furthermore, these precedents will remain as such for as long as future justices of the Supreme Court refuse to overturn them. This highlights another aspect of the Court's supremacy—only the Supreme Court may overturn its own precedents and thereby reinterpret the Constitution. For this reason, years ago retired Chief Justice Warren Burger once responded to the question, "what does it take to change the Constitution?" with this concise and thoroughly accurate response: "Five votes."

THE FEDERAL COURT SYSTEM

This last section will focus on the other institutions which, along with the Supreme Court, constitute the federal court system.[49] In doing so, we will briefly detail the federal district courts, the **federal circuit courts**, and the state supreme courts, as well as some "speciality courts."

District Courts. The vast majority of Supreme Court cases bubble up from federal district courts. These are original jurisdiction or **trial courts** with no appellate jurisdiction. As trial courts, district courts perform the legal function of discovering the facts and then applying the law. Hence, they consist of a judge, lawyers for both sides, the parties themselves and usually a jury (in some cases the litigates may waive their right to a jury in which case the judge assumes jurisdiction over both fact and law). The jurisdiction of district courts covers such things as crimes against the United States; federal civil law; treaty law; and, whenever the parties to a lawsuit are citizens of different states. The number of district courts have increased along with the growth in litigation. For example, the Judiciary Act of 1789 created 13 district courts with 13 judges, whereas today there are 94 district courts employing nearly 650 judges with each state having at least one court. To help speed up the time it takes for a case to actually go to trial, Congress passed in 1974 The Speedy Trial Act which requires district court trials to begin within 100 days of the case being filed.

Federal Circuit Courts. Originally, individual Supreme Court justices were compelled to ride a "circuit" so as to hear appellate cases in various communities. This proved to be much too burdensome on the judges given their age and the road conditions of the time, so Congress created in 1891 the federal circuit as the first layer of review consisting of 9 courts staffed by 20 judges. Today, the circuit has grown to include 13 courts (11 regional and one each for the District of Columbia and the federal circuit) and 167 judges. Unlike district courts, circuit courts are appellate tribunals and, as discussed above, are limited to reviewing only questions of law. When doing so, they usually convene with three judges sitting as a panel while the attorneys for both sides present their arguments. Like district courts, the circuit docket has also grown by leaps and bounds. For example, in 1915 there were a total of 1,500 appellate cases argued at the circuit level, whereas in 1993 the circuit addressed a staggering 50,000 cases.

Speciality Courts. Speciality courts are tribunals designed to address unique or "special" areas of the law. For example, speciality courts include the U.S. Customs Court which deals with disputes over appraisals of imports; the U.S. Tax Court which deals with cases resulting from taxpayer disputes with the Internal Revenue Service; and, the Court of Military Appeals which resolves disputes originating in the martial courts of the Armed Forces. Additionally, speciality courts are designated either "Article I" or "Article III" courts depending on their authorization.[50] Courts like the above mentioned U.S. Customs Court are considered Article III courts because Congress creates them under its Article III authority to "ordain and establish" inferior courts. Other speciality courts like the other two courts mentioned above are created under Congress' Article I authority "to constitute tribunals inferior to the Supreme Court," and for this reason are considered Article I courts. However, the difference between the two is more than a matter of semantics. Judges who preside over Article III courts cannot be removed once appointed except via impeachment and their pay cannot be diminished during their tenure, whereas judges who serve on Article I courts sit for prescribed terms, must be reconfirmed once their term has expired and their pay is subject to congressional discretion.

State Supreme Courts. The last group of courts we need to examine are state supreme courts.[51] State supreme courts are the only state courts which are part of the federal system, as they serve as appellate courts to the Supreme Court when addressing federal questions. The Supreme Court will not, however, consider any case originating from within a state until that state's supreme court has ruled on the issue. Moreover, state supreme courts are, as the name implies, the court of last resort within their particular state and, as such, they exercise jurisdiction over all state legal issues and any federal question not reviewed by the Supreme Court. Hence, like the Supreme Court, each exercises judicial review over conflicts arising under its particular state's constitution. Furthermore, according to most estimates, state courts account for about 98% of all litigation in the United States, so they can hardly be considered junior partners with their federal counterparts.[52]

FINAL THOUGHTS

As we have seen, the Supreme Court has emerged as a major institutional player in American politics, holding the fundamental power of any constitutional democracy—the power to interpret the Constitution. Additionally, we have discovered the Court legitimately exercises this power primarily due to modern America's reverence for, and bewilderment by, the legal profession. Yet, as we have also seen, many earlier Americans were less accepting of the Court's authority to interpret the Constitution, as they had trouble reconciling judicial review with their concern for self-government. It is, of course, too late to turn back the clock and replay the debate over who may exercise constitutional review, as history has answered the issue emphatically in favor of the Supreme Court. Nevertheless, it is never too late to reacquaint ourselves with the passion for self-government which spawned the discussion to begin with. The Constitution does not, after all, acquire its meaning and moral authority from the writings of a legal tribunal, but from the dedicated hearts of committed patriots.

NOTES

1. This discussion borrows heavily from David M. O'Brien, *Storm Center: The Supreme Court in American Politics*, 3rd ed. (New York: W. W. Norton & Company, 1993), pp.142–147.
2. Robert Harrison resigned before the next session and John Rutledge resigned after riding circuit for a year when he was appointed Chief Justice of the South Carolina Supreme Court.
3. John Frank, *Marble Palace* (New York: Oxford University Press, 1968), p. 9.
4. O'Brien, *Storm Center: The Supreme Court in American Politics*, 3rd ed., p. 147.
5. Paul Light, *A Delicate Balance*, (St. Martin's Press: New York, 1997), p. 352.
6. O'Brien, *Storm Center: The Supreme Court in American Politics*, 3rd ed., p. 145.
7. Roy P. Fairfield, ed., *The Federalist Papers* (Baltimore: Johns Hopkins University Press, 1981), p. 227.
8. Thomas Woodhouse, "Two Centuries of U.S. Supreme Court History: An Historian's View," *Clackamas Collegiate Review*, Vol 1. No. 1, Winter 97, p. 41.
9. U.S. Constitution, Article 2, Section 2.
10. O'Brien, *Storm Center: The Supreme Court in American Politics*, 3rd ed., p.139.
11. See The Judiciary Act of 1789.
12. The academic basis for this change in attitude concerning the proper function of government within the economy is generally attributed to John Maynard Keynes' *General Theory of Employment, Interest and Money* published in 1936.
13. It is now generally accepted by most scholars that World War II did much more to bring America out of the so-called "Great Depression," than FDR's "New Deal" programs.
14. O'Brien, *Storm Center: The Supreme Court in American Politics*, pp. 92–94.
15. Susan M. Leeson and James C. Foster, *Constitutional Law: Cases in Conflict* (New York: St. Martin's Press, 1992), p. 4.
16. Malcolm M. Feeley and Samuel Krislov, *Constitutional Law* (Boston: Little Brown and Company,1985), p. 3.
17. Ibid., pp. 3–4.
18. Walter F. Murphy, James E. Fleming, and William F. Harris, II, *American Constitutional Interpretation* (New York: The Foundation Press, Inc., 1986), p.184.
19. 19 Howard 393 (1857).
20. 323 U.S. 214 (1944).
21. 163 U.S. 537 (1896); 347 U.S. 483 (1954); and, 349 U.S. 294 (1955).
22. 381 U.S. 479 (1965).
23. 418 U.S. 683 (1974).
24. 343 U.S. 579 (1952).
25. 118 U.S. 394 (1886).
26. 198 U.S. 45 (1905).
27. 384 U.S. 436 (1966).
28. 1 Cranch 137 (1803). Further support for those who assumed the Court's authority to interpret the Constitution was implied by the nature of the judicial function could be found in the practice of many state courts during colonial times, in addition to Hamilton's explicit argument in favor of such a theory in *Federalist* 78.

29. For an excellent discussion regarding the legal aspects of *Marbury v. Madison,* see Walter F. Dodd, *Cases On Constitutional Law,* 5th ed. (New York: West Publishing Co., 1954), pp. 1–17.
30. For a more thorough discussion on this point see chapter 11.
31. Quoted in David M. O'Brien, *Storm Center: The Supreme Court in American Politics,* p. 144.
32. Ibid., p. 65.
33. Robert Sherrill, *Why They Call it Politics: A Guide to America's Government,* 5th ed. (New York: Harcourt Brace Jovanovich, 1990), p. 236.
34. Leeson and Foster, *Constitutional Law: Cases in Context,* p. 5.
35. An advisory opinion is any opinion granted by a legal tribunal on a point of law independent of any particular law suit.
36. For an illustrative case see *DeFunis v. Odegard,* 416 U.S. 312 (1974); also, see *Regents of the University of California v. Bakke,* 438 U.S. 265 (1978) for an example of how Bakke's use of a class action lawsuit enabled him to avoid the mootness issue.
37. Feeley and Krislov, *Constitutional Law,* pp. 3–4.
38. Murphy, Fleming, and Harris, II, *American Constitutional Interpretation,* 190–191.
39. Ibid., p. 190.
40. Ibid., p. 225.
41. Ibid., p. 229.
42. The theory of nullification did not originate with Calhoun, however. Additionally, he, along with his contemporaries, most often referred to this idea as "interposition." This phraseology emerged from the first two proponents of interposition—Thomas Jefferson and James Madison. In the Kentucky and Virginia Resolutions of 1798 and 1799, Jefferson argued it was up to each state to decide if a federal law was, "unauthoritative, void, and of no force," while Madison argued that "nullification" was "the rightful remedy" as the states must "interpose" themselves between their citizens and unauthorized federal power. Nullification/interposition was such a recognized political position that it was hardly noteworthy at the time when Daniel Webster "criticized the War of 1812, suggesting that individual states could nullify a federal law by 'the solemn duty of the State Governments . . . to interpose between their citizens and arbitrary power.'" Margaret L. Coit, *The Life History of the United States: 1829–1849* (New York: Time-Life Books, 1975), pp. 12–15.
43. Murphy, Fleming, and Harris, *American Constitutional Interpretation,* p. 273.
44. Light, *A Delicate Balance,* p. 367.
45. Ibid., p. 368.
46. 492 U.S. 490 (1989).
47. Light, *A Delicate Balance,* p. 370.
48. Charles Evans Hughes quoted in, Leeson and Foster, *Constitutional Law: Cases in Context,* p 4.
49. For a nice discussion on the American judicial system see Robert A. Carp and Ronald Stidham, *Judicial Process in America,* 2nd ed. (Washington D.C.: Congressional Quarterly Press, 1993), especially chapter 2.
50. Some texts refer to Article I courts and Article III courts as "legislative" and "constitutional" courts respectively. I have not because strictly speaking these labels are misnomers, as all federal courts are constitutional whether created via Article I or Article III.
51. Today, somewhat surprisingly, there are actually 52 state supreme courts, as Oklahoma and Texas each have two, one civil, the other criminal. Additionally, there are a dozen rural states that have no intermediate appeals courts.
52. Light, *A Delicate Balance,* p. 358.

Section IV

Where Do We Go From Here?

CHAPTER 11
Representation: We the People

INTRODUCTION

This chapter will focus on arguably the most important concept in the American political system—representation. In doing so, we will discuss how restoring America's democracy begins with improving our understanding of what it means to represent someone politically and why so few politicians do so. Throughout the book we have discussed in detail the problems that need to be corrected to begin improving America's democracy. This chapter will address the question that has been implicit in all the previous chapters: How do we get our politicians to represent the majority of Americans? In answering this question, we will first need to look at how important the concept 'representation' is in our constitutional system. We will then articulate how the practice of modern politics fosters a political system skewed to represent only the interests of the most privileged Americans through four interrelated ways: One, through the cost of campaign financing; two, through electing business executives and lawyers who may be increasing this corruption; three, through being too easily influenced by information coming from those already benefiting by the system; and, four, through politicians' mastery of "spin-doctoring" tactics, which keeps ordinary Americans on the sidelines of politics and out of meaningful political participation.

REPRESENTATION: THE BACKBONE OF THE AMERICAN CONSTITUTIONAL SYSTEM

The whole purpose of the American Revolution was to remove an unrepresentative government and replace it with one that rested on the idea that the people are best able to secure the blessings of good government by electing representatives who will govern in their interests. Without a system of representation no government may claim to be democratic in even the most minimal sense of the word. This is why James Madison wrote that the United States government would be an improvement on all previous governments because it would be a "government in which the scheme of representation takes place."[1] It is no coincidence that the American Revolution was, first and foremost, a revolution over the lack of representation for Americans; as most of us learned in high school, the rallying cry of the Revolution was, "no taxation without representation."[2] Hence, the primary political legacy that emerges from America's revolutionary past is the belief in the principle that no person has a duty to obey a government unless that government represents him or her. As the *Declaration of Independence* affirms, a government is only legitimate if it derives its "just powers from the consent of the governed."

Moreover, the American idea of 'representation' assumes that all Americans will be represented equally; no one gets special treatment and everyone will play by the same rules. These ideals are the foundation on which the American government rests and generates its legitimacy. To ensure these ideals, the constitutional framers wrote into the Constitution an absolute rule that there shall be no titles of nobility granted in the United States.[3] Titles of nobility, or monarchy, such as "King," "Queen," "Prince," "Baron," and so forth, were outlawed by the Constitution for two very special reasons. One, individuals so named were not required to pay any taxes—that would be for the non-noble, working classes. Two, criminal law did not apply to individuals who were titled nobility. So, working class people were at the mercy of nobility, because the nobles were "above-the-law." It was this above-the-law status of certain individuals that the framers of America's democracy wanted to stomp out forever from the American experience, hence their prohibition of such titles in the Constitution.

It will be the thesis of this chapter that if the test of a government's legitimacy is its representative character, and the equality of its citizens before the law, then the contemporary American political system fails miserably on both these grounds.

To be sure, defenders of the status quo will respond that such an indictment is much too severe, since the present system is pregnant with representative elements. For example, they may point to the representative structure outlined in the federal Constitution and to frequent elections as proof of the government's representative legitimacy. But such an argument is as cosmetic as it is ignorant; it only defends the appearance of representation, while ignoring the fact of government's indifference to the concerns of the average American. In other words, governmental actions (policies) speak much louder than constitutional words when measuring the actual representative nature of a government. For instance, Saddam was elected, yet very few consider his former regime democratic, and as the experience of African-Americans clearly demonstrates, constitutional language can do as much to cement injustice as it can to secure liberty.[4]

Therefore, the only valid test of a government's representative legitimacy is not to be found in the speeches of politicians, but rather, it must be found in the actions of that government in promoting the interests of the majority of its citizens. And, it is here, in the realm of specific governmental action, where contemporary American politicians have revealed their betrayal of both the democratic words they speak, as well as the people they profess them to. It seems even the most disinterested American has some intuitive sense things are just not right with our political system. What is not so commonly understood is why this is the case and what can be done about it. William

Greider, in his monumental work, *Who Will Tell the People*,[5] best summarizes the nature of our political situation when he writes:

> The enduring question for democracy is how to revive and encourage the trusted representative. . . . Democracy does not require a representative system peopled with philosopher kings or saints, but it does need circumstances that encourage politicians to represent their constituents.[6]

It is a sad commentary indeed on the present state of our political system, that such an obvious condition of good representative government (that a representative should concern himself with the interests of those who elected him) has become more of a wish than a reality. The authors of the book, *America: What Went Wrong?*, conclude that the reason the political system is now so adverse to the interests of middle class Americans is because, "[s]omeone changed the rules. . . . Which means there is no one looking after the interests of the middle class."[7] Or, as another political scientist wrote when explaining why the middle class so often gets the short end of the political stick, "there are no longer any institutions that effectively represent their economic interests."[8] And, lastly, still another political scientist wrote:

> [P]erhaps the most troublesome development of the new politics is its role in reversing the very idea of elections and representation. Traditional assumptions about democracy describe a system in which representatives are sent back to the seat of government to push for ideas that won them votes in the last election . . . we are now approaching a system in which promises from the last election are routinely sacrificed to strategic calculations about how to win the next one.[9]

And, unfortunately, this usually means ignoring the concerns of the ordinary Americans who elected them to begin with.

REPRESENTATION OF THE MOST PRIVILEGED

There is one glaring puzzle within our political system when trying to identify why so few politicians represent average Americans: If democracy is a government where the majority rule, then why do most of the rules benefit the persons at the very top of America's social strata, who make up one of the smallest political minorities in America? That is, how do these politicians keep getting reelected to office by the very Americans they ignore once they secure their elected position? Greider sums up this democratic enigma nicely when he writes:

> Indeed, the classical case against democracy has always been a theoretical supposition that, sooner or later, the many would use their democratic control of government to violate the property rights of the few. The mob's insatiable appetites would be fed by unscrupulous politicians, who would use the tax system to confiscate the incomes and wealth of those who have more. This has not been the case in America, to put it mildly. On the contrary, during the past [twenty plus] years, monied interests and allied governing elites have used their political power to accomplish the opposite result: Federal tax burdens were steadily shifted from them to everyone else. Clearly, governing power does not reside with the people. . . . Nothing demonstrates the

atrophied condition of modern democracy more starkly than those facts. Behind all the confusion and complexity of the tax debate, democracy's natural inclinations were literally thrown into reverse—rewarding the few at the expense of the many.[10]

How do these elites, who are nowhere near as numerous as the middle class, so dominate a political system based on majority rule?[11] Answering this question, I would submit, is the central task of the modern patriot and citizen. Most casual critics of the American political system will respond that the reason the wealthy dominate the political system is because, "they have the financial wealth to do so!" To be sure, there is some truth to this claim, nonetheless, such a blanket and simplistic answer does very little to help improve the system since it neither explains why money matters or how having it furthers a political goal. It would be like someone thinking they have diagnosed the cause of cancer by exclaiming, "cancer is caused by being sick!" In short, we mistake the symptom for the disease. Therefore, the rest of this chapter will focus on explaining precisely how and why our democracy has turned away from its representative mandate while serving the political needs of the elite few.

It is time for us to begin taking concrete steps toward improving America's democracy. The rest of this chapter identifies four ways that modern politics fosters a system skewed to represent only the interests of the privileged few, and conversely, what the majority can do to combat these tactics so they can begin receiving the representation they deserve. I will be arguing below that Americans need to do four things to begin restoring America's democracy: One, we must address the politics of campaign financing; two, we must begin challenging our preconceived notions of who is best suited to be a representative (politician); three, we need to be much more skeptical of political information; and, four, we need to vastly enhance Americans' abilities to recognize and reject professional politicians' ability to "spin" information so that we are no longer susceptible to these tricks of the politician's trade.

1. Campaign Financing. Presently, campaigning for federal office in America requires an immense amount of money. Any person who intends on running for political office must accumulate a large sum of money to afford the high cost of campaigning in the media, hiring the necessary support staff, and traveling in person to spread one's message. If a citizen wishes to run for a meaningful political office, he or she must either be independently wealthy themselves (which may explain why so many of our contemporary candidates are themselves rich), or one must persuade the wealthy to bankroll his or her campaign. As Democratic campaign consultant Dane Strother stated, "the most important lesson we relearned is that money wins political campaigns."[12] So today any person interested in running for federal office is immediately required to plead at the feet of the elite if he or she stands any chance of electoral success. Which, needless to say, requires any "viable" candidate to adopt the political opinions of the elite as their own.

This electoral dependency on the super-rich not only helps explain why so many of the so-called "mainstream" candidates share the same political beliefs, it also helps to explain how the few are dominating the many under the guise of democratic government. Elections no longer serve their original political purpose, (which is to allow the majority to govern in their own interests by stocking the halls of government with politicians eager to do so), rather, they have become just another tool for allowing the privileged elite to get their way. The elite's domination of campaign financing is now so out of hand that one scholar of the subject describes modern elections, "as investment opportunities for organized interests, particularly big business."[13]

To be sure, there are federal laws limiting the amount of money any politician may personally accept or any one person may personally contribute; but these limits are in name only.[14] The politicians have become experts at finding ways around these limits (and remember, the politicians are the very same persons who write these laws to begin with). Politicians of both major parties, for example, can avoid the rigors of the law by utilizing so-called **527s** (named after their IRS tax code section). Federal election laws consider this money immune from campaign limits, since, it is argued, these organizations are not officially tied to the candidates campaign.[15] Hence, 527s are able to spend as much money as they want to influence the outcomes of our so-called democratic elections—and spend they have.

Many defenders of the status quo argue this infusion of 527s money into our electoral system is nothing to be worried about and is in fact a healthy symptom of a robust democracy—the more money involved, the more political opinions are being heard, they reason. Unfortunately, the claim that more money equates to a more diversified political dialogue does not stand up to scientific investigation.

This begs the question: why have we allowed campaign contributions in the form of 527s to skirt the law, even though any concerned American can see its negative affect on our democratic system? Or, why have we allowed our sacred democratic privilege of electing our politicians to be corrupted by the stench of money? Unfortunately, we have been convinced, by the very same groups who benefit from it, that it would be a violation of every American's right of free expression to limit the amount of money a person or 527 can spend to influence political opinion in the United States. We have been convinced that our constitutional right to free speech depends on letting them monopolize the electoral system—call it the "marketplace of ideas" defense. Of course, they have never adequately explained how it is that a monopoly over political debate helps foster competition in this marketplace of ideas. Of course, most of us have never thought to ask them. So, in short, since the elite know they will never be able to out vote the many (the middle class), they realize one way to control our democratic government is to simply decide who the majority votes for.

Now, ask yourself, how does allowing only the super-rich (or their cronies) to run for political office allow for the election of politicians who will represent the average American? And, does not such a system lead to a *de facto* monarchy, or a government by and for the new nobility? And, if we conclude (as we must) that such an electoral system makes a mockery of our representative framework, then what does this say about our moral duty to obey?

So how do we stop the influence money has on our electoral process? If we think of our political choices as analogous to our consumer choices at the mall, for example, we will begin to see how we can stop money from corrupting America's democracy. First we need to recognize what all this money is buying. Simply stated, this money is paying for political commercials that have an enormous impact on our electoral choices. Next, we need to think of voting for candidates as similar to buying any other product, and the best way a consumer can make sure they are buying the right product is to educate themselves about that product. So, to make us immune from the influence these campaign commercials have on average American voters we need not stop the money, we only need to reduce the political influence of these commercials. And how do we do that? We do it as any savvy consumer would—we educate ourselves politically so that we recognize these commercials for the nonsense that they are, and it is done.

2. Rethink who we are electing to office. Today there are two professions most American voters are convinced qualifies one to be elected to political office. These two professions are lawyers and business executives. One step to improving America's democracy is to rethink this assumption so that we stop electing lawyers and business people to political office instead of electing individuals with a rich political science education. Before we begin discussing the legal profession's traditional strangle hold on elected office, we first need to address America's recent infatuation with electing members of the business elite. To be sure, there have always been business people in the halls of government, however, lately the desire to "make government more like business" has reached such a fever pitch that there are almost as many CEOs in Congress as there are lawyers. What accounts for this situation? Aristotle, when analyzing why democracies are so prone to failure, concluded that in democracies people too often make the mistake of assuming someone is "superior in all things," simply because he or she happens to be "superior in one thing." That is, even though in a democracy the people elect their leaders, they have no real sense as to what constitutes the appropriate political training because very few of them have taken the time to educate themselves properly on the workings of their government. Hence, the majority winds up simply guessing at what qualifies any person to govern; and, because the voters themselves are preoccupied with making money, they make the mistaken assumption that just because a person is good at what Aristotle called the "art of money making" he or she must, therefore, be good at governing. If this seems like a reasonable assumption to you, then ask yourself this: Would a successful CEO make an acceptable surgeon, dentist, or carpenter, solely on the basis of his or her business training? And, if not, then why do so many of us assume it makes someone capable of governing wisely?

In other words, Aristotle believed the demise of all democracies was the public's misguided notion that just because an individual is superior in one thing (business) he or she must also be superior in all things (foremost among them, governing). If Aristotle is wrong, then what else could explain America's replaying of the historical tendency of democracies to surrender their government to wealthy business people? Or, to state it another way, what qualifies a CEO to govern? It certainly cannot be any sort of professional training members of the corporate elite are exposed to, since such training is hardly conducive to good government. Think about it. What is the sole function of any business enterprise? Simply stated, it is to turn a profit, period. So, how is it that anyone who has spent their entire professional lives focused solely on turning corporate action into *private* profit, suddenly going to be able to do just the opposite, which is to organize collective action into *public* gain? Moreover, given the business elite's indoctrination into a commercial world where all corporate action is to be for the benefit of the elite few at the top, is it any surprise that once elected they do all they can to further their own economic situations? Is this not what they have been trained to do?

In addition, Aristotle's dictum (superior in one thing, superior in all things) applies not only to the business elite but to the legal profession as well. That is, apparently, Americans also believe legal training somehow prepares one for public service even though very few would know since they have never been to law school themselves. As a matter of fact, the first political science department was created at Columbia University by a law professor unhappy with the fact so many students were graduating law school without the necessary training in statesmanship.[16] This law professor knew something about legal training that most of us do not: Law school is excellent training for anyone interested in being an attorney, but it is very poor training for anyone interested in doing anything else. Now, this may seem like a rather obvious and trivial point to make, but it is not. The legal profession, through its rhetorical skill, has convinced Americans they can do any political job available. For example, if government creates a commission to study, say, the salmon problem, it will most likely consist of lawyers. Or, if, for instance, there is a government panel charged with monitoring the health of our great national forests, then it will also be dominated by lawyers, even though very few law schools I know teach fly fishing or forestry as part of their curriculum. As one Stanford law professor stated in a book on legal history, "lawyers [are] in the midst of politics everywhere. . . . It [is] not so much the case that public office require[s] legal skill as that lawyers [are] skillful at getting elected and holding these offices."[17]

Unfortunately, this is not just a case of electing people who are simply not trained for the job; it is far more dangerous for our democracy. What we are doing is electing people who have been trained to perform at a high level advocating on behalf of whomever retains their services. Needless to say, this is the very opposite of what we should want from a public official. So it should come as no surprise that, once elected, lawyers tend to ignore the voting majority who sent them to office and, instead, do all they can to enact laws favorable to those who funded their campaigns. This is exactly what they have been trained to do—represent the interests of their clients regardless of the effect this may have on our democratic political system. Greider captures this condition superbly when he writes:

> "[C]lient" has a different meaning from "constituent" or "citizen," but the word accurately describes the common relationships that define contemporary politics. The representative structure has been transformed into something quite offensive to its original intent—a system in which it is nearly impossible to distinguish . . . if a political transaction was bribery or the normal daily business of Washington.[18]

And since lawyers are trained in the adversarial system of law they have little understanding about what is required of them as political representatives. In other words, they are experts only in the law and not in the practice of American politics. This may be why so many of them, once elected, seem to spend more time looking for campaign contributions or "clients" than they do serving their constituents. It may also explain why so many of these "lawyer-representatives" waste more energy looking for ways around the law for their wealthy clients than they will in attempting to make them obey it. And again, this is because legal training teaches lawyers to fight the enforcement of the law against their clients no matter what ramification this may have on the public at large. For example, one environmentalist bemoaned the election of corporately trained lawyers in politics by saying:

> Twenty years ago, we set out to eliminate sulfur dioxide from the air. Here we are twenty years later and more than 100 million Americans are still breathing air with unhealthful levels of sulfur dioxide. Why? Because the [lawyers] fight you when you try to pass a law. They fight you when you try to pass a second law. They fight you when you try to write the regulations. They fight you when you try to enforce the regulations. Nowhere do they ever stop and say: "Let's obey the law."[19]

In short, lawyers tend to be more concerned with protecting clients than they are in representing average Americans. So, if we find it disturbing that our contemporary politicians are too busy serving the interests of the wealthiest Americans and not concerned enough with promoting the interests of the majority, then we should stop electing members of the very professions which have been trained to do so.

3. Realize the power of political information, particularly propaganda, in shaping our opinions.
Another step toward improving our government is for Americans to become much more skeptical of information provided by those in political authority. One of the most effective ways of corrupting a democracy is when an elite few maintain a monopoly on information. The wealthy, in order to maintain a stranglehold on the minds of the voting majority, have created what might be described as an "information industry," made up of public relations firms, "blue ribbon" or expert laden commissions, and, above all else, "think tanks." These manufacturers of information provide the elites with the necessary factual ammunition required to dominate political debate in America. Therefore, anytime the majority of citizens begin to question the status quo, the elites will simply have their information industry spew forth all the necessary "facts" to demonstrate the "ignorance" of the middle class majority.

For example, how often have we heard that raising the minimum wage will only cost jobs and in no way help the working poor?[20] And, besides, we keep hearing that the majority of minimum wage workers are teenagers who come from well-to-do families, so there is no real need to raise it anyway. Of course none of this is actually true,[21] but in a democracy all it takes is to convince people it is true and you win—big. Now, ask yourself, where is this information coming from? This propaganda is generated by think tanks designed to convince working Americans that raising their wages would only hurt their economic situation—and it works. A think tank is a group of scholars who are paid by the economic elite to generate "objective" academic arguments that just so happen to agree always with the political interests of their wealthy supporters.[22] This is why one such think tank, The American Enterprise Institute, has consistently argued against the wisdom of increasing the minimum wage in America. As Greider has written:

> AEI has had quite a lot to say about minimum-wage laws and their supposedly deleterious effects. In recent years, AEI has published at least nine different scholarly reports arguing against the minimum wage. This position faithfully represents the interests of AEI's sponsoring patrons—the largest banks and corporations in America.[23]

In another example, a think tank called, The Cato Institute, released a study claiming that welfare families received benefits equivalent to $27,000 in income, and thus were doing much better than many working families. Given this "fact," they concluded, "if Congress or state governments are serious about reducing hard-core welfare dependence and rewarding work, the most promising reform is to cut benefit levels substantially." Not only was all their information wrong, it was so distorted that a journalist reporting on the subject concluded:

> A close reading of [the study] makes it difficult to avoid the conclusion that the errors and distortions in the Cato report were deliberate. Without doubt, they were destructive. . . . The Cato study was especially insidious in that it used poisoned data to pit two groups that are not doing well—welfare recipients and the working poor—against each other. The politicians who seized so gleefully on the study's conclusions have no interest in fairer economic treatment for either group.[24]

This is the oldest trick known to the ruling class—divide the peasants and keep them fighting amongst themselves.

In addition to think tanks, working Americans should also be wary of any propaganda that comes from public relations firms hired by the political elite. In chapter three we discussed some examples of how these "PR" firms help create political opinions that just so happen to support elite positions. For example, one scholar noted how PR firms were used to create fake letters from "soldiers in Iraq" writing their local papers to say how good things were going in Iraq:

> [T]he Gannett News Service discovered that scripted good news had some how been planted in the American press. At least eleven newspapers around the country had run identical letters from different soldiers 'describing their successes rebuilding Iraq,' at the precise moment when public opinion on the mission was going south . . . [when one soldier was asked about his letter] he said: "what Letter?"[25]

Lastly, Americans must also be wary of any information that comes from so-called "blue ribbon" commissions. These "expert" laden commissions are stocked with mouthpieces for the wealthy, who, under the guise of "expert analysis," always agree that what is best for America, is what is best for the rich, period. Presently, both major parties have agreed to a bi-partisan commission to study entitlement reform. Suffice it to say at this point, when this commission reports its results, Americans will find that their social security benefits need to be reduced; their social security taxes need to be increased; and, their retirement age will need to be pushed much beyond the age of 65.

4. Protect ourselves from the "spin doctoring" prowess of American politicians. The last and, I think, most important explanation for why the elite dominate the average American in our "democratic" government, is, simply stated, the political class has mastered the art of sophistry (making the weaker argument the stronger), also known as "spin doctoring." In other words, American politicians have become experts at "spinning" information in such a way that they trick the voters into electing persons, and endorsing policies, that are not in the voters' interests by using specific techniques. I know this is not a pleasant thing to hear; no one likes to hear they have been conned but, unfortunately, there is no other reasonable explanation. How else do you explain the present political situation? After teaching political science for nearly 19 years, I used to wonder why Americans (who can be some of the most sophisticated shoppers in the world) were so gullible when it comes to buying political propaganda until I realized that Americans never get a lesson in "spin doctoring 101"—until now.

The central message of this chapter (if not the entire book) has been to promote the idea that Americans need to be better educated in political science so that they are more critical and skeptical of the political information they receive. Granted, it is indeed sad we can no longer trust our politicians to do the job they are elected to do; nonetheless, if history is any guide, we need to trust our politicians less and question them more, if we are to restore America's democracy. This is not an academic point; the future of our communities resides with our ability to become more sophisticated thinkers when dealing with the rhetorical dexterity of contemporary politicians.

The rest of this section will be dedicated to helping us become more politically sophisticated by revealing some of the most common tricks politicians perform in order to con the American public. In short, we need to look at some basic spin doctoring techniques so that we don't keep getting fooled by these argumentative tricks every time we attempt to participate in politics.

The Ad Hominem Attack

This tactic is as effective as it is simple. When a career politician is confronted with an individual who is advocating for a position at odds with the politician's position, the professional politician will simply attack the person's reputation while dismissing whatever points that person is making. In short, if you can't kill the message, take out the messenger. During the 2008 elections Ron Paul's reputation was attacked, as was Dennis Kucinich's, because each of these men advocated for policies outside the accepted boundaries of both major political parties. When Paul talked about America becoming a police state he was dismissed as a "right wing nut." When Kucinich argued for a "Department of Peace" the establishment labeled him "UFO Kucinich." In both cases, these reformers were ad hominemed out of the presidential race.

Ralph Nader has lived with this ever since he began his career as a citizen activist 30 plus years ago. This writer has had his reputation smeared more than a few times by federal and state bureaucrats because of my desire to restore America's democracy and criticism of both major political parties.[26] So, if you hear a politician attacking a person's reputation instead of arguing with that person's opinion, then you know that person must be saying something important, so important in fact, that the system wants that person's reputation to be the focus of debate and not his or her opinions.

Straw Man Arguments

Another very effective yet simple spin doctoring tactic is the "straw man" approach to debate. When someone is straw manned those in power reduce a critic's political argument to an absurdity and, thereby, prevent that opinion from receiving any serious response. For example, when people questioned the wisdom of a war of choice in Iraq, their position was simply straw manned as "blame America first" or better yet "cut and runners". When many Americans voiced their concerns regarding the Obama administration's attempt to restrict Second Amendment rights, the mainstream dismissed them as "gun nuts" (ad hominem) and reduced their argument to the absurdity that "these people just want to run around the woods playing Rambo" (straw man). Once you are aware of these tactics not only will you recognize how often they are used, but also you will never have them played on you—welcome to the real world of politics.

The Fallacy of Composition

The fallacy of composition is when one conflates two or more things into one thing. For example, free speech is now the same as corporate campaign contributions. Saddam's secular regime in Iraq became the center of Islamic terrorism. Saddam is Bin Laden. Taxpayers bailing out billionaire bankers is equated with getting money in the hands of working Americans. Wall Street becomes synonymous with Main Street. Muslims are terrorists. The list can go on and on, unless we no longer fall for this simple but devastating trick.

The Fallacy of Division

The fallacy of division is the opposite of the fallacy of composition. This trick makes one thing seem like two or more things. How often have sales people sold people something they couldn't afford simply by focusing on how much something cost per month—this RV will cost you only $299 a month!—rather than the total cost of, say, $40,000. For example, we've been convinced there are two very different parties, the Republicans and Democrats. Or, that capital gains taxes are different than income taxes so they should be taxed at different rates. Think about it. When one gets paid (income) that is a capital gain. When someone gains capital, that's the same as money coming in (income). So, working Americans are taxed at nearly twice the rate of the super-rich all because of this simple divisional trick. Providing taxpayer supported health care is "socialistic" bailing out banks with taxpayer dollars is "responsible economics." And so it goes.

Judging a Book by Its Cover

Another trick politicians have learned is that as long as they title any policy or piece of legislation with a "feel-good" word or phrase, then they can get away with just about anything as long as they tuck it into the fine print of statutory language. In this way the politicians are able to appear as if they are governing in the interests of their constituents when in fact they are writing the rules to favor the economically privileged. Take, for example, the debate concerning "free trade" versus "protectionism." Notice that the policy that benefits the economic elite is labeled free trade, whereas, the policy which benefits the majority of Americans is labeled protectionism. Now, which sounds nicer, being for freedom or being for protectionism? Not only does this feel-good labeling tend to cut off the important political discussions necessary for any healthy democracy, it also distorts the issue fundamentally. In short, the debate has never been about free trade versus protectionism; it has always been about which Americans are protected.

Another example of this spin-doctoring tactic is naming a law the very opposite of what it actually does. For example, take the "Clean Air Act." Given the title, most Americans assume the law was intended to clean the air. Yet what the law actually does is extend the time allowed for corporations to continue polluting from the deadline set by the previous "Clean Air Act." That is, under the old law, corporations were ordered to reduce pollution by the year 2001; but under the new law, they have until 2010, or, for some heavy polluters, like the steel industry, until 2020. As Richard Ayers of the Clean Air Coalition said, "it's a nonlaw—making deadlines long enough so that they don't have meaning."[27]

An additional example of this tactic is to simply add the word "reform" to the title of whatever specific policy they are pursuing. Politicians, for instance, have learned that if they want to cut the taxes on the wealthy, while raising yours, all they need to do is title such legislation tax reform, and you will buy it—or in this case, pay for it. As the authors of *America: Who Really Pays the Taxes?* explain:

> Mellon [former Secretary of Treasury] . . . came up with a new strategy to enlist support for his cause—a more lofty motive than merely reducing taxes. The real problem, he said, "is not so much one of tax reduction as of tax reform." This was one of the first times—if not the very first—that the phrase "tax reform" was used to justify a tax cut for the affluent. It would not be the last. Other secretaries of the Treasury, other Presidents, other lawmakers, would adopt the same tactic . . . .Over time, much of the debate concerning tax rates would boil down to two phrases. Tax legislation that would increase the rate on the wealthy was called "class warfare." Tax legislation that would reduce the rate on the wealthy was called "tax reform."[28]

A recent example of this scheme is the so-called "Patriot Act," passed after the 9/11 attacks. What sounds like a freedom-loving American's dream law, in effect, eviscerates the very liberties the patriots, who's name it now carries, where trying to preserve when they fought for America's independence. Although a thorough analysis of the legal impact of "The Patriot Act" is much beyond the scope of this chapter, suffice it to say, it creates the legal grounds for the very police state its namesakes were fighting with their lives to prevent.

It seems apparent that if we, the people, are to ever realize the democratic possibilities of good government, we must ignore legislative titles and spend hours upon hours reviewing the minutiae of legislative policy, while, in whatever spare time we have left, also monitor the activity of government around the clock. If this seems impracticable, there is another more reasonable course. *We could always simply elect people with the integrity to do the job expected of a representative.* And, who are these wondrous people willing to give their political energy for the common good rather than for their own personal gain? Hopefully, they are we, the hard-working Americans, but only after we begin thoroughly educating ourselves in political science and ethics; however, if we cannot be bothered to take on that education, then America's democracy is lost.

False Choices: The Either/Or Alternatives

Another effective spin-doctoring technique is limiting the apparent menu of political choice to a set of either-or alternatives that leaves voters with no other option but to agree with what the spin-doctors want them to choose. That is, any time the middle class begins demanding some governmental action to address their problems, the political class will convince the voters that what they want is not at all in their interest, simply by giving the majority an either-or choice. For instance, say the middle class starts demanding higher wages, or a cleaner environment, or lower taxes. When this occurs, politicians simply set up the issue as a series of either-or choices to dissuade the middle class from demanding what they want. For example, they will respond that, "you can have either higher wages or a job." Or, "you can have either a cleaner environment or a car." And, "you can have either lower taxes or a safe America." In this way they trick you into believing that these are your only choices, as if you cannot have high wages and a healthy economy (and, ask yourself, could it be any other way?) And, why not employ people in green technology?

Moreover, how often is the entire menu of electoral choice reduced to this either-or alternative—either Republican or Democrat? Or, how about this one—either liberal or conservative?

This trick is also performed at a much deeper level. For example, how often are Americans tricked into limiting their thinking on some of our most troubling economic problems by politicians who skillfully frame these issues as an either-or choice between "either freedom or socialism?" In this way the politicians convince us we may "either stop poverty or live in freedom." Or, that the government can "either reform America's corrupt banking system or we can respect the free enterprise system." Or, they convince us we can "either reduce the influence of big money in our elections or respect the principle of free speech?" Or, that any citizen may "either question the war on terror or be a patriotic American." Needless to say, this type of thinking is not the way to run a democratic railroad. A recent example of this spin technique was how the political establishment framed the question of whether the U.S. should invade Iraq. Instead of presenting the matter with the respect and complexity it deserved, the American people were presented with a simple-minded either-or fallacy. That is, the issue was presented as either attacking Iraq or sitting by helplessly while Saddam planned for the next big terrorist attack. In short, either attack or be attacked. The present situation clearly shows that the numerous other options (continuing the U.N weapons inspections, for example) would have been much better policies than the one of two options chosen. In closing this section, I would like to leave you with a few either-or choices of my own. We, the contemporary Americans, must either start exercising our minds more or face exercising our liberties less; we must either be less eager to accept whatever the politicians tell us or be more eager to obey them; and, lastly, we must either be ready to intellectually defend our communities more or be ready to enjoy them less.

The Bait and Switch

Lastly, another spin-doctoring tactic that renders America's democracy less representative and healthy is what Greider calls the "bait and switch."[29] As you may be aware, the phrase originated in the advertising business and refers to the practice of advertising one object to attract a customer's attention (the bait) and then when he or she is in the store the salesperson replaces the item with a lesser one (the switch). For example, say we advertise a Cadillac for $10,000, but when the customers show up we inform them we are all out of Cadillacs, nonetheless, we would be more than happy to sell them any Yugo in stock for the same price. In this case, the Cadillac was the bait and the Yugo was the switch (oh, by the way, it is no longer legal to advertise any product using the bait and switch method, unless, of course, the product is political propaganda). Politicians have mastered the political bait and switch and employ it to facilitate the Elites' stranglehold on America's political system. This is why the political class baits Americans by advertising less government regulation and then switches it for a taxpayer bailout of America's financial system. Or, for example, politicians will advertise the benefits of fighting a war on terror and then switch it for an unnecessary war in Iraq.

One of the most politically destructive examples of this tactic occurs whenever the political class uses the bait of individual liberty to implement a more thorough system of corporate authority. That is, under the guise of deregulating the economy, they deliver a system of corporate tyranny that abridges individual liberty to a degree similar to an oligarchical regime. After all, the classical definition of an oligarchy is one in which the government is ruled by a few elites who govern solely in their own interests. And let us be aware: When the majority votes in favor of "deregulation," what they are really doing is not deregulating but reregulating; that is, they are reregulating from a system of democratic control, where the interests of the many are pursued, to a system of oligarchical control, where the interests of the few are paramount.[30] In other words, in the name of individual liberty, politicians are always demanding that government (the majority) get off the back of big business, and yet they never seem interested in getting big business off the backs of working Americans.

Another example of this tactic was the presidential election of 2008. Candidate Barack Obama baited Americans with a promise of "change we can believe in," and then, once elected, switched his administration into the second coming of the Clinton administration.

FINAL THOUGHTS

The next and final chapter will address the foundational remedies we need to achieve to make these four changes a reality for Americans. Suffice it to say at this point, I plead with you to think about the following: The next time you find yourself repeating something political, stop and ask yourself, how is it I have come to know this information, and whose political interests is it serving? Then, ask yourself this question, who do I know who can afford to pay for spreading this information? And, lastly, ask yourself, can my community, not to mention, our democracy, afford for me to repeat it?

NOTES

1. See *The Federalist* 10.
2. Winthrop D. Jordan and Leon F. Litwack, *The United States: Conquering a Continent, Volume One*, 7th ed. (New Jersey: Prentice Hall, 1991), p. 95 and beyond.
3. See U.S. Constitution, Article I, Sections 9 & 10.
4. For example, in Article 1, Section 2, the U.S. Constitution originally counted enslaved African-Americans as "three-fifths" a person. Additionally, prior to the ratification of the 13th Amendment and the North's victory in the Civil War, the Constitution declared: "No person held to service or labor. . . . shall . . . be discharged from such service or labor, but shall be delivered up on claim of the party to whom such service or labor may be due."
5. Much of this chapter borrows from the spirit of William Greider's, *Who Will Tell the People: The Betrayal of American Democracy* (New York: Simon and Schuster, 1992).
6. Ibid., p. 64.
7. Donald L. Barlett and James B. Steele, *America: What Went Wrong?* (Kansas City: Andrews and McMeel, 1992), p. xvi.
8. John J. Harrigan, *Empty Dreams, Empty Pockets: Class and Bias in American Politics* (New York: Macmillan Publishing Company, 1993), p. 17.
9. Lance Bennet, *The Governing Crisis* (New York: St. Martin's Press, 1996), p. 202.
10. Greider, *Who Will Tell the People,* p. 80–81.
11. For an eye-opening account of the vulgar character of contemporary "representation" see, David Stockman, *The Triumph of Politics* (New York: Harper & Row, 1992) and William Greider, "The Education of David Stockman," *Atlantic,* December 1981, 51.
12. Quoted in *Campaigns and Elections,* February edition, 1997, McInturff and Newhouse.
13. Bennet, *The Governing Crisis,* p. 18.
14. Ibid p. 91.

15. See the "Bipartisian Campaign Reform Act of 2002."
16. Lawrence M. Friedman, *A History of American Law* (New York: Simon and Schuster, 1973), p. 530.
17. Ibid., p. 560.
18. Greider, *Who Will Tell the People,* p. 26.
19. Ibid., p. 111.
20. Bill McCormick, "The First Rung on the Ladder has to be Low," *The Oregonian* (October 9, 1995), p. D7.
21. Bill Resnick, "Studies Refute Argument Wage Increase Costs Jobs," The Oregonian (October 25, 1995), p. B7; Peter T. Kilborn, "Even in Prosperous Days, Midwage Jobs Shrink, and No Job is Forever," *The Oregonian* (July 6, 1995), p. A12; Ellen Goodman, "Minimum Wage Increase May Even Have a Chance," *The Oregonian* (April 21, 1996), p. E3.
22. Greider, *Who Will Tell the People,* pp. 37, 48, 51, 52, 82, 187–88, 300, 338.
23. Ibid., p. 187.
24. Bob Herbert, "Welfare statistics Misuse Appears to be Deliberate," *The Oregonian* (April 23, 1996), p. B9.
25. Frank Rich, *The Greatest Story Ever SOLD* (New York: Penguin Books, 2007), p. 107.
26. Just Google my name and read all about my alleged "fake Ph.D." This smear campaign was so effective my graduate school had to shut down after bureaucrats cut its federal funding. One of these despicable individuals, by the name of Alan Contreras, was found guilty in federal court of violating constitutional rights and was also ordered to take remedial training in defamation law for these activities without ever discontinuing his baseless attacks on my reputation. Why he is still employed by the State of Oregon is beyond me.
27. Greider, *Who Will Tell the People,* p. 129.
28. Donald L. Barlett and James B. Steele, *America: Who Really Pays the Taxes?* (New York: Simon & Schuster, 1994), p. 65.
29. Greider, *Who Will Tell the People,* p. 300.
30. For an excellent discussion on this point see, Susan J. Tolchin and Martin J. Tolchin, *Dismantling America: The Rush to Deregulate* (New York: Oxford University Press, 1983).

CHAPTER 12
Remedies: Justice for All

At a time when democratic ideals seem ascendant abroad, there is reason to wonder whether we have lost possession of them at home. Our public life is rife with discontent. Americans do not believe they have much say in how they are governed and do not trust government to do the right thing. . . . [O]ur politics is beset with anxiety and frustration. The political parties, meanwhile, are unable to make sense of our condition . . . they do not [address] the two concerns that lie at the heart of democracy's discontent. One is the fear that, individually and collectively, we are losing control of the forces that govern our lives. The other is the sense that, from family to neighborhood to nation, the moral fabric of community is unraveling around us.[1]

These are the words which begin Harvard political theorist Michael J. Sandel's book, *Democracy's Discontent*, and they will also help to conclude my own. As doctors of the body politic, neither Sandel nor myself can ignore the dire condition of contemporary American politics; anymore than we can simply bemoan the sad state of things without providing some ideas on how we can improve our democratic practice. Therefore, following the lead of Sandel, the Founders, and many other political theorists, this chapter will articulate three possible remedies to America's political inadequacies. But, please be aware, these solutions are not quick fixes, not mere institutional tinkering, rather, they are remedies which go to the heart of any democracy's performance—the nature of our communities and the character of the people. We cannot improve our democratic institutions until we begin reforming our economics, improving our understanding of democratic principles, and, most importantly, cultivating within ourselves a much greater sense of what the Founders called civic virtue. Without these foundational remedies any institutional or procedural reforms will be merely treating the symptoms of democratic decay while ignoring the root causes of them.[2] It is an axiom of basic political science that a political system will only be as healthy as the community from which it springs. Hence, to cure our communities and improve the health of our democracy we need to go much beyond the mere "political" and venture into the realm of social and personal interaction. To this end, I will argue that what is required to begin real political change is the enactment of three republican ideals: One, we must address the growing economic inequality in America for civic and not merely economic reasons; two, we need to enrich our understanding of the role played by ethics in the health of any democracy; and, lastly, we need to strengthen our commitment to public education. As you read along, if you find yourself wondering if a healthy democracy is worth the "sacrifice" these remedies require, I suggest you visit any American military graveyard or hospital to help remind you what real sacrifice for democracy entails; after the experience the task ahead of us will seem slightly less burdensome, I assure you.

1. We Must Address the Growing Economic Inequality in Contemporary America.

Michael Sandel, in the book noted above, argues economic disparity has ramifications for self-government much beyond the mere material. That is, he rightly believes too much of the too few criticisms of recent economic trends have focused on merely the economic aspects of them, while ignoring the effect they have on the possibility of self-government. He writes:

> The [American] republican tradition teaches that severe inequality undermines freedom by corrupting the character of both rich and poor and destroying the commonality necessary to self-government. Aristotle held that persons of moderate means make the best citizens. The rich, distracted by luxury and prone to ambition, are unwilling to obey, while the poor, shackled by necessity and prone to envy, are ill suited to rule. A society of extremes lacks the "spirit of friendship" selfgovernment requires: "Community depends on friendship;" and when there is enmity instead of friendship, "men will not even share the same path." Rousseau argued, on similar grounds, that "no citizen should be so rich as to be capable of buying another citizen, and none so poor that he is forced to sell himself." Although absolute equality is impossible, a democratic state should "[t]olerate neither rich men nor beggars," for these two estates "are equally fatal to the common good."[3]

As proof of the relevance of this republican notion, one need only observe present social conditions to see how economic stratification has indeed created just such a reality in contemporary America; it has initiated a situation in which the wealthy few live in a condition of plenty, while the many exist in an ever more dangerous and desperate environment. And, again, American republican tradition warns against extreme divisions of wealth not for merely material purposes, but for democratic ones; the republican tradition views economic production not as an end in itself (as too many Americans believe today), but as a means to self-government. To the sincere advocate of self-government, it is simply wishful thinking to believe that people who are in no way equal economically are somehow so politically. Hence, Sandel, following this tradition, is not solely or even primarily concerned about the injustice of America's present economic distribution on economic grounds, but is deeply concerned about it due to its chilling effect on our democratic possibilities:

> More than a matter of money, the new inequality gives rise . . . to increasingly separate ways of life. Affluent professionals gradually secede from public life into "homogeneous enclaves" where they have little contact with those less fortunate than themselves. "As public parks and playgrounds deteriorate, there is a proliferation of private health clubs, golf clubs, tennis clubs, skating clubs," accessible only to paying members. As children of the prosperous enroll in private schools . . . urban schools are left to the poor. . . . As municipal services decline in urban areas, residents and businesses in upscale districts manage to insulate themselves from the

> effects by assessing themselves surtaxes to provide private garbage collection, street cleaning, and police protection unavailable to the city as a whole. More and more, the affluent evacuate public spaces, retreating to privatized communities defined largely by income level . . . [All of this] bears on the prospect of self-government. The secession of the affluent from the public sphere not only weakens the social fabric . . . it also erodes civic virtue more broadly conceived. . . . As affluent Americans increasingly buy their way out of reliance on public services, the formative, civic resources of American life diminish. . . . A more civic minded [philosophy] would seek communal provision less for the sake of [economic fairness] than for the sake of affirming the membership and forming the civic identity of rich and poor alike.[4]

The political principle Sandel is espousing is as old as political theory itself. For example, Plato, in *The Republic,* "provides only one general guideline: Philosopher rulers must, above all, guard against the emergence of extreme wealth and poverty."[5] Aristotle, as mentioned previously, also believed extremes in wealth and poverty sever the bonds of friendship on which all societies depend and quicken the demise of any democracy. These lessons were not lost on our founding generation as most of them were first-rate students of political philosophy. Jefferson resisted the rise of a corporately controlled economy because he thought such an economy would create a society of a few haves and many have nots in which, "dependence begets subservience and venality, suffocates the germ of virtue, and prepares fit tools for the designs of ambition."[6] For this reason, Sandel writes:

> Jefferson and his followers argued against large-scale manufactures primarily on moral and civic grounds . . . they feared that manufactures on a scale beyond that of a household or small workshop would create a propertyless class of impoverished workers, crowded into cities, incapable of exercising the independent judgment citizenship requires.[7]

Therefore, following both Jefferson and Sandel's lead, I will posit that the first step toward improving our democracy should be for Americans to rethink economics and its place in our representative scheme. And, in doing so, we need not look to radical ideologies for guidance but to our own traditional American philosophy. As Sandel writes:

> In Contemporary American politics, most of our economic arguments revolve around two considerations: prosperity and fairness. Whatever tax policies or budget proposals or regulatory schemes people may favor, they usually defend them on the grounds that they will contribute to economic growth or improve the distribution of income; they claim that their policy will increase the size of the economic pie, or distribute the pieces of the pie more fairly, or both. So familiar are these ways of justifying economic policy that they might seem to exhaust the possibilities. But our debates about economic policy have not always focused solely on the size and distribution of the national product. *Throughout much of American history they have also addressed a different question, namely, what economic arrangements are most hospitable to self-government? Along with prosperity and fairness, the civic consequences of economic policy have often loomed large in American political discourse* [emphasis added].[8]

Sandel is reminding us that the first question concerning economic policy for our community ought not to be, strictly speaking, about economics at all. The first question concerning economic policy should be, what is best for our democracy? In other words, the first step in improving the practice of our democracy requires us to relegate the distributive questions of how much? and to whom? to secondary standing. And in their place, the first question which should be asked about any economic policy is: What best promotes self-government? To be sure, this republican principle would require some radical changes in our present day economic policies but so much the better. Americans have never shied away from radical change whenever it served the needs of self-government—be it a revolutionary war with Great Britain, a civil war over slavery, or a world war against fascism. Now is not the time for Americans to start believing democracy is not worth the effort; for if we do, then all those who, in Lincoln's famous phrase, "gave the last full measure of devotion" will have most assuredly died in vain.

And what specific changes would a commitment to a democratic political economy entail? For starters, it would demand a thorough reworking of American monetary, fiscal, and trade policy. The democratic goal of these reforms should be to foster a community of relative political equals by creating some semblance of economic equality. For example, we could, as suggested in chapter 6, pursue a more debtor friendly monetary policy; enact a tax policy which taxes labor less and capital more; and, return to a trade policy which protects the living standards of Americans rather than the portfolios of the international financial community.

Nonetheless, these are only suggestions, we are free to design whatever economic system we, the people, think best, provided it addresses the growing inequality within the economy which renders it impossible to practice meaningful democracy.[9] In short, whatever economic reforms we initiate must be motivated, not by self-interest (whether rich or not), but by a genuine concern for our democracy, or in other words, the common good. And make no mistake, present economic policies are detrimental to the common good since they promote only the interests of a select few. The result of such policies is an emerging two-tiered society of haves and have nots which will only produce negative ramifications for our democracy. We must remember the words of our 16th president, Abraham Lincoln, who, during another moment of American crisis, cautioned: "A house divided against itself cannot stand."

Of course, I suppose, there are many Americans who may consider all of this theoretical nonsense, given the character of contemporary life. In support of this, they could point to the endemic selfishness inherent in American culture. They could remind us that, no matter how obvious it is that our political system is in serious need of a major overhaul, modern Americans are either too selfish or too preoccupied (or a little bit of both) to do much of anything about it. It seems there is no possible way to convince such minded people that much of the meaning in life comes, not from taking, but through giving; that any community, but particularly a democracy, requires for its health and vitality a sense of shared experience which can only be developed through communal engagement. In short, these pessimists could claim the idea of putting the common good before one's own is an idea as dead as the dinosaurs; besides, they could argue, it is simply not human nature to be motivated by concern for the public good. I wonder how many of the rest of us would agree with these sentiments? Nonetheless, can such a negative picture of human nature pass the test of experience? In other words, is it true people are so inherently selfish they cannot see how their own happiness depends on a healthy and democratic community? I think not.

If their claim is true, then what explains the brave Americans who gave their lives to ensure our liberty? It certainly could not have been on account of self-centered motives since they obviously had nothing personal to gain for giving their lives for ours. Moreover, what accounts for the tens of millions of American parents, past and present, who have sacrificed so their children could have a better tomorrow? What about the thousands upon thousands of instances in which Americans have lent a helping hand to a neighbor in need, be it a natural disaster, a death in the family, or some other calamity? Are these people simply psychotic individuals? Or, are they in fact proof of what Lincoln called the better angels of our nature? There is more at stake in this debate than our own interpersonal relations (although they alone should be enough to dissuade us from accepting this negative conception of human nature), the very future of our experiment in self-government resides in the balance. That is to say, if we as a community lack a sense of public virtue, defined by the Founders as putting the common good above our own,[10] then our experiment in self-government is doomed to failure. As the father of our Constitution, James Madison, himself stated so succinctly many generations ago:

> Is there no virtue among us? If there be not, we are in a wretched situation. No theoretical checks, no form of government, can render us secure. To suppose that any form of government will secure liberty or happiness without any virtue in the people, is a chimerical idea."[11]

The next remedy I suggest is one on which our entire community depends—namely, we need to cultivate within ourselves and our community a sense of public virtue.

2. We Must Cultivate within Ourselves a Higher Degree of Public Virtue. We, the contemporary Americans, have either forgotten, or more likely, have never been informed, of the first principle of self-government—without a thorough appreciation and practice of public virtue among the people, and most particularly among our representatives, no democracy will ever realize its awesome potential. As many theorists have argued, if the people themselves are not self-governed by concern for the public good, then they will most assuredly be governed by others. Benjamin Franklin once wrote, "[o]nly a virtuous people are capable of freedom. As nations become corrupt and vicious, they have more need of masters."[12] As mentioned in the introduction of this book, self-government requires more of each citizen than merely a vote now and then; it also requires each and every citizen to take seriously the job of governing. First and foremost, this demands that our politicians, as well as each member of the community (from which, after all, our politicians will emerge), recognize the primacy of public spiritedness, a spirit in which the political class puts the interests of the majority ahead of their own and their wealthy campaign contributors. How can we expect our government to function appropriately when our politicians have shown by their actions that they cannot be trusted to make it happen? How many scandals, improprieties, and outright violations of the law will it take before we realize that good government depends on good representatives?

And we must take the concept "good" in its most philosophical sense. That is, the concept "good" should not be considered synonymous with "clever." Too much of modern life is infused with the slogan espoused in a corporate ad campaign declaring "image is everything." Such disingenuous thinking may suit the needs of a marketing strategy but it spells doom for a democracy. A due respect for civic virtue means it is wrong to think a person is good simply because he or she appears to be; true goodness is measured by what one does when there is no audience and/or when your own self-interest argues for doing otherwise. What makes someone a good representative, in other words, is not *appearing* like one but actually *acting* as one. Unfortunately, our present crop of representatives are so preoccupied with their image, they spend more time being advised by spin doctors than by citizens. It seems our politicians have become so morally corrupt they invest more energy watching out for each other than they do watching over our communities. No wonder so much of public life (as well as tax money) is spent investigating apparent scandals or appointing special prosecutors. Apparently, even the political class is aware they cannot be trusted. In short, being a good representative does not imply granting privileges to the wealthy few in return for their patronage while, at the same time, tricking the people with rhetorical skill into supporting policies which any informed, civic minded individual knows will be detrimental to their happiness.

What does it mean to be good, or practice civic virtue? To begin, it means understanding that there is a higher reward for public service than mere wealth and privilege. The reason the public spirited individual should commit himself or herself to public service is for one simple yet profound reason—to see to it that the community is governed wisely. Think about it. Could the reason our political system is so corrupt be because our politicians are, if not solely, then primarily motivated by money? Is this why the political class constantly claims, "if you want good people, then you gotta pay 'em"? What would we think of a teacher, fireman, clergy member, or any other public servant who could only be motivated by greed? What definition of 'good' are they implying? It seems to me, if you have to pay someone to do what is right they cannot, therefore, qualify as good. Moreover, if they require more money in one year than most members of the community will ever earn in ten as motivation to act in an appropriate fashion, then they are motivated, not by public concern, but by private interest, which is the very antithesis of public virtue. Is it any wonder we have a political system rife with corruption, when we have so many politicians whose "integrity" is not merely for sale, but whose very identity is to find a buyer? And, as the above quote by James Madison illustrates, such a plea for a civic minded community is no new age touchy-feely psycho-babble, but was the primary ethic of our founding generation. Garry Wills, in his excellent book, *Explaining America: The Federalist*, sums this idea up nicely when he writes:

> [Theirs] was the world of the American Enlightenment—a world of the classical virtues reborn. . . . In that world, the concept of public virtue had a hard and clear meaning, a heft and weightiness of the real, no longer apparent to us. We do not even pretend that we choose our politicians for their virtue. That kind of talk would

> look sappy or insincere in our political discourse. But it was no such thing for Madison and his contemporaries. . . . Benjamin Franklin was often portrayed as a Roman senator. Jefferson wanted Houdon to sculpt Washington in a toga, as he had sculpted Voltaire. . . . It was the job of modern statesmen to play the role of a Brutus or a Cato; and yet the role playing was deadly serious. Men died to sustain their role—Joseph Warren himself at Bunker Hill, or Nathan Hale becoming Cato in his final moments. The public good—*res publica,* common weal—was a shining new ideal to those who swept away priestly and kingly power and put the people in command of their own fate. The French Revolution's cult of Rome appeared first in America. We gave the world its Cincinnatus. We not only admired Washington; we dared to think of him as the product of our new political science—the virtuous ruler serving not for private gain but out of pride in his own virtue; impartial; not consulting any interest but the "permanent and aggregate interests of the community." That is the vision of the [Founders]. . . . What kept [us] from falling back into monarchy, as France did after her great burst of revolutionary energy? Madison would not . . . hesitate one minute in answering that question. The public virtue kept us republican. It is the only thing that can.[13]

Wills is reminding modern Americans that the struggle for self-government did not die along side the patriots at Bunker Hill, Saratoga, or Yorktown, but instead requires the constant moral vigilance of every American generation to ensure its survival. In short, self-government, if it is to become a reality in the American experience, will require us to spend less time congratulating ourselves on the type of government we now have and more time working on the type of people we need to become. That is, republican self-government demands more of us than a simple Pavlovian response to some silly corporately sponsored "rock the vote" campaign every four years or so. What a genuine commitment to self-government does demand of us is a thorough understanding and respect for the duty of public virtue. Hence, Madison wrote, "republican government presupposes the existence of [public virtue] in a higher degree than any other form."[14] In addition, John Adams, on the eve of the American Revolution, declared:

> [P]ublic virtue is the only foundation of republics. . . . There must be a positive passion for the public good . . . established in the minds of the people, or there can be no republican government, nor any real liberty."[15]

Moreover, the practical ramifications of a commitment to civic virtue would be staggering. That is, if we actually instill amongst ourselves an appreciation for the practice of public virtue almost all of our political problems would vanish overnight. For example, we would no longer be in need of campaign finance reform since our representatives would never think to break the trust they hold with their communities no matter the monetary bribe. We would no longer need to enumerate a balanced budget amendment since a public spirited Congress would practice wise fiscal policy without needing a constitutional demand to do so. Furthermore, tax rates would plummet for three simple reasons. One, there would no longer be such an expensive (as well as expansive) governing system because a community endowed with public virtue would require less from government as it would address most social problems with voluntary action at the local level. Two, a representative system imbued with civic concern would not tolerate present fiscal policies which tax working Americans to death to fund the financing schemes of the privileged few. And, three, given our civic virtue, we would be able to cut "defense" spending drastically since we would no longer be financing corporate exploitation of foreign communities. Moreover, crime rates would drop astronomically since public virtue would eradicate the core causes of crime, namely, poverty and amorality. And, lastly, our quality of life in general would improve since a virtuous community would be less adversarial and mean spirited than is presently the case. Maybe this is why so many political philosophers from Aristotle to Jesus Christ to Madison have preached the wisdom of public virtue. They were aware it is the only thing which can guarantee good communities and thereby good government. In short, these political doctors thought it best to cure the disease of civic decay rather than simply being satisfied with treating the symptoms. Yet, as with all prescriptions, the doctor can only recommend the medicine, it is left to the patient to take it.

And, if we do decide to heed the advice of these philosophers and start appreciating the importance of public virtue, how would we go about it? That is, how does a community change its ways when they are found morally lacking? Can such a thing be done? It seems the answers to these questions lie again in our own history and political philosophy. American history is replete with examples of Americans radically changing the social fiber of the country for moral reasons. For example, when Americans came to believe it was no longer morally acceptable to serve a king, we revolted and created our own country centered on this belief. Additionally, when we thought it no longer morally justifiable to judge any individual on the basis of their skin color or gender we altered our public institutions accordingly. Now, of course, those who have a vested interest in maintaining the status quo will argue none of this would have occurred without the civil strife which accompanied them, while reminding us of the fact that there is still much work to be done in each of these areas. But such a response reveals an ignorance of the most basic sociology—real social change does not occur on account of bloodshed but only on account of education. What ultimately toppled the crown in America was not force but reason, not the musket but the pen, not might but right. In short, the death of monarchy in America was caused more by an idea than by an army. As John Adams stated: "The Revolution was effected before the war commenced. The revolution was in the minds and hearts of the people . . . [this] was the real American Revolution."[16] The same can be said of racism and sexism. The real victory over these ugly ideas also took place "in the minds and hearts" of Americans and not on any battle field or in any court of law. And, as each generation of Americans are educated to comprehend the intolerable nature of these ideas, they become less and less a part of the American social and political landscape. In short, once these rancid notions lost the battle of reason (as they most assuredly have), it is only a matter of time until the last vestiges of them die out in practice. Nonetheless, all of these monumental changes first required an educational mission dedicated to exposing Americans to the truth of our own political creed, a creed which tolerates neither inequality nor oppression for whatever reasons if we are to be truly committed to the democratic proposition that all persons "are created equal." Therefore, promoting a more civic minded public will require a similar educational effort dedicated to reminding Americans that their liberty and equality demands, first and foremost, a commitment to civic virtue instilled through public education.

3. We Need to Strengthen Our Commitment to, and Alter the Character of, Public Education. The last remedy I suggest to improve our democracy is strengthening our commitment to, and altering the character of, public education. And, just like the two previous remedies, this one is not motivated by some utopian fancy (or, for that matter, by the education establishment's never ending appetite for public funds) but is an essential part of classic American political philosophy. Merrill D. Peterson, in his biography *Thomas Jefferson & the New Nation,* writes:

> The backbone of Jefferson's republic was a system of public education. "If a nation expects to be ignorant and in a state of civilization, it expects what never was and never will be," he once observed. . . . Without the diffusion of knowledge through all the ranks of society . . . individuals could neither attend to their own happiness nor, as citizens, secure the freedom and welfare of the state. It was axiomatic with Jefferson that the people were the only depository of their rights and liberties, always provided, however, that they were adequately informed and instructed. Education was too important a matter to be left to chance. It must be planned and carried out as a paramount responsibility of republican government.[17]

America, of course, does appear to have a very strong (and expensive) commitment to public education in the 20th century, so it seems this remedy is moot at best. However, we must not confuse the funding source of education with its mission. In other words, just because we have publicly funded schools does not mean they are, therefore, focused on public issues and citizenship training. Instead, most public schools spend the vast amount of the public's money preparing students, not for public life, but for private employment; we are in effect publicly subsidizing private training under the guise of public education. Or to put it another way, the curriculum at most public schools is now geared almost exclusively toward churning out private sector employees rather than public minded citizens. To be sure, most public schools have some civics instruction as part of their curriculum, but these classes tend to consist more of simple minded platitudes celebrating American political processes rather than critical academic inquiries into present governmental practice. Hence, the first reform necessary to improve the public function of our public schools is to turn civic curriculum development and instruction over to political scientists who have been trained in democratic theory and practice. Too many people now teaching such courses are either not qualified to do so, or are not interested enough in critical inquiry, or both, to serve democratic purposes. The only legitimate end of civics training should be to teach citizenship, which, by definition, requires equipping students with critical reasoning skills and a healthy skepticism of authority, and not to instill mindless acceptance of the status quo. If this seems too radical, then this alone demonstrates the inadequate job public schools have done in the area of civic instruction. An adequate democratic education would have informed us that the Founders, after all, not only preached skepticism of authority they practiced it (as a quick read of the *Declaration of Independence* or any American history text will attest)—and hoped future Americans would never forget that liberty depends more on intellectual vigilance than military might.

For this reason, we must remove civic instruction from the present educational bureaucracies which currently exercise a stranglehold on curriculum. Too many educational bureaucrats are products of graduate schools in education which, frankly, poorly equip them to administer any area of the liberal arts, and most particularly political science. Political science in a democracy is, at its most basic level, about instructing citizens to understand their power and to exercise it democratically. This necessitates a tension between those who find themselves in positions of power and those citizens exercising their democratic responsibility of questioning power in whatever guise, be it a government official, a corporate donor, or an employer. School administrators lacking in political training tend to view such democratic action as irresponsible and unacceptable so they attempt (unconsciously or not) to neuter political education so that it is more user-friendly for those in positions of privilege (which makes sense as they themselves are in just such a position both economically and institutionally).[18] This, of course, helps explain the vacuous nature of most civics instruction, as well as why so few Americans become intellectually excited by the study of politics. Too many present teachers of civics act as mere apologists for the status quo, hence, students tend to find such instruction irrelevant at best since they are being instructed to accept their place as passive receptors of contemporary political reality. This not only detaches the study of politics from reality, it also distorts the very nature of democracy, which is for every generation to rethink their political present and adjust it accordingly.

Moreover, we need to remove political curriculum from the grasp of the education elite because they tend to align themselves much too closely to corporate power. This should come as no surprise since they a) lack a true understanding of democratic principles and b) are themselves members of the economically privileged. This attachment to economic power tends to encourage the present misconception that corporate power is complementary to democratic politics. As we have seen, political theorists from the Greeks to the Founders to the present have warned such relationships are unworkable; we simply cannot have a democracy in the political sphere when we are under the control of a corporate oligarchy in the economic sphere. This bias in favor of the economically privileged radically distorts the instruction of democratic citizenship; it does so by redefining democratic citizenship so that it reflects the obedience of a private sector employee. It seems the educational establishment has turned the relationship between economics and democracy on its head. That is, instead of equipping students with the intellectual tools to demand real economic change as required by American democratic theory, the educational elite are trying to reconfigure democratic theory to better fit the needs of corporate power. Is it any wonder so few Americans are involved in politics when they are being instructed to see their roles as citizens as equivalent to their passive subservient roles as employees? In short, if we keep indoctrinating Americans to see themselves as obedient employees of government, rather than correctly as citizens from which all political power flows, then we should not be surprised when they are reluctant to engage in politics. Think about it. When was the last time a corporation allowed the employees a vote in determining their economic futures or to otherwise have a real say in corporate management? It should not surprise us that citizens model this passivity when it comes to politics—have they not been taught to do so?

Lastly, how can such a corporate understanding of democracy encourage anyone to see the value in either of the first two remedies suggested in this chapter? The corporate mentality is, after all, what caused our present economic disparity in the first place, while public virtue is the very antithesis of the profit motive essential to corporate growth. A public instilled with a respect for civic virtue would necessarily place the common good above their own, which would be grand for our democracy but would spell bankruptcy for most corporations. Hence, the last thing the educational establishment can fathom is an active democratic citizenry no matter how much our political system depends on it. In short, the only thing the educational establishment really desires out of public education is not public engagement but rather collective obedience, which is, of course, the very thing so many of our fellow Americans gave their lives in the past to prevent. Therefore, public education for civic purposes demands civic training be divorced from the present educational bureaucrats and turned over to political scientists trained in democratic theory and practice. Moreover, this is no radical idea; almost all other training takes place under the supervision of experts in the field, be it medicine, sports, auto mechanics, or what have you, so we would only be extending this principle to the one area in which everyone already has an interest.

To realize the merits of public education we must also rethink who constitutes the public. That is, we need to stop being wedded to the idea that public education takes place only when we are young. The public is, after all, every one of us, and, hence, we need a much more inclusive model of public education. Furthermore, we need to much expand the scope of public instruction so it not only covers all citizens continually but is also required in order to be eligible to run for office, vote or otherwise engage in politics.[19] This is not as draconian as it sounds. We already compel citizens to perform many vital services necessary to the health of our democracy, be it drafting Americans to serve in times of war, taxing them to pay for public services, or requiring them to spend some time in school. Therefore, requiring people to give their academic attention to the duty of citizenship not only demonstrates respect for those who gave their lives for just such a privilege, it also is at least as important as compelling them to take, say, math, science, or computer classes designed to make them more likely to gain employment. Of course it could be argued math and science training is necessary to democracy since such instruction fosters the technological know-how necessary to protect our democracy from threats abroad. Ignoring for the present how an appropriate education in democratic citizenship would do much to obviate the need for such killing machines, political science is still at least as important in promoting liberty as math and science; math and science, after all, can only create the technologies which may defend freedom, whereas, political science allows us, as a people, to fully appreciate what liberty is and why it is worth protecting. To this end, we should create public discussion halls staffed with historians and political scientists who would be available night and day to instruct the public on political and historical matters, while remaining completely independent of the present public education system. Again, this separation would be necessary because the present system is geared to instill basic skills in children and adolescents while also being much too preoccupied with private sector training.[20]

To be sure, it could be argued such a commitment to a politically sophisticated public is, in theory, a fine idea, however, the cost of such a program makes it both impractical and undesirable. Yet such an argument is wholly ignorant of both the realities of public funding discussed earlier in the chapter on economic policy (bloated defense budget, corporate welfare, etc.), as well as of democratic theory and practice. Democratic self-government and, indeed, the entire American experience rests fundamentally on we, the people, exercising our political authority in a wise and appropriate manner. It seems elementary that to do so means we must acquire the education necessary to the task. How can it be argued such a challenge is not worth the price? In any event, it is nothing new in the American experience for citizens to be reluctant to put their money where their mouths are when it comes to promoting democracy. When an earlier friend of self-government encountered a similar resistance to an educational plan developed by Thomas Jefferson, Jefferson wrote to him and offered the following advice which is as pertinent today as it was generations ago:

> Preach, my dear Sir, a crusade against ignorance; establish and improve the law for educating the common people. . . . Let our countrymen know . . . that the tax which will be paid for this purpose is not more than the thousandth part of what will be paid to kings, priests and nobles who will rise up among us if we leave the people in ignorance.[21]

FINAL THOUGHTS

In conclusion, let me review my suggested remedies to America's democratic betrayal. Following traditional American political philosophy, I have advocated for a more equitable political economy for democratic purposes and not merely material ones; I have argued for a rekindling of America's tradition of civic virtue as the first principle of self-government; and, I have pleaded for a more truly public education system as both a means and an end to self-government. Yet, in the end, the future of our democratic promise rests with all of us. But, be aware, whatever we decide will most assuredly affect not only ourselves, but all those Americans who came before us and will succeed us. Therefore, if we decide it is not worth the effort to improve the actuality of our democratic promise, then we will guarantee all those earlier Americans who gave their lives for just such a promise did, indeed, die in vain, while also condemning our posterity to an even less democratic world than the one we currently inhabit. Such is the choice and task ahead of us. It is not always easy to be an American. No generation receives a free pass to liberty, all must give something in return; and, what is asked of the present generation is both the simplest and most confounding task of all—we must start believing (as Colonel Chamberlain asserted just prior to the bloodiest battle in the history of American freedom) that we all have value.[22] And, just because we are not members of the economic elite does not mean we are not worthy of equal representation, or, in short, equal concern and respect. It is time for us to demand that government—our government—recognize the lives of the majority are as valuable as those of the most privileged few. Or, to put it another way, who won the American Revolution anyway? Was not the primary purpose of the Revolution to ensure that never again would Americans be confronted with a government which taxes them without actually representing them? Was it not about denying the monarchical notion that the lives of the majority are only as valuable as their utility to the fortunate few? Yet to realize this American democratic promise will require us to become much more intellectually and morally vigilant. And, if we refuse to do so, then we, the modern Americans, will surrender by our intellectual and moral laziness what no king could take from our ancestors on the battlefield—our political liberty. Shame on us.

NOTES

1. In support of this claim Sandel cites the following evidence: A 1994 Gallup Poll (*Gallup Poll Monthly,* February 1994, p. 12) in which only 20% of Americans said they believe they can trust government to do what is right most of the time; a Gallup Poll (*Gallup Poll Monthly,* September 1992) which showed that 75% of Americans are dissatisfied with the way the political process is working; and a study (Alan F. Kay et al., "Steps for Democracy," *Americans Talk Issues,* March 25, 1994, p. 9), which demonstrated that three-quarters of Americans also believe that government is run by and for a few big corporations rather than for the public good. Cited in *Democracy's Discontent: America in Search of a Public Philosophy,* (Cambridge MA: Harvard University Press, 1996), p. 3. More recently, the Center on Policy Attitudes reported in January of 1999 that "an overwhelming majority believes that the government is not being run for the benefit of the public as a whole," and when asked "what percentage of the time Congress makes the same decisions the majority of Americans would make, only 18% of respondents picked a number over 50." Moreover, a 1999 poll for the National Association of Secretaries of State found nearly two-thirds of young people agreed with the statement that "government is run by a few big interests looking out for themselves, not for the benefit of all." David Broder, "Post-Trial State of U.S. Democracy: Not so Hot," *The Oregonian* (February 14, 1999) p. D5.
2. For this reason this chapter avoids promoting the present orthodox menu of political reforms consisting of such superficial ideas as amending the Constitution to compel Congress to balance the budget, invoking term limits, reconfiguring campaign funding legislation, and so forth.
3. Michael J, Sandel, *Democracy's Discontent: America in Search of a Public Philosophy,* p. 330.
4. Ibid, pp. 331–333.
5. Irving M. Zeitlin, *Plato's Vision* (New Jersey: Prentice Hall, 1993), p. 102.
6. Thomas Jefferson, *Notes on the State of Virginia* (Chapel Hill: University of North Carolina Press, 1996), pp. 290–291.
7. *Democracy's Discontent: America in Search of a Public Philosophy,* pp. 142–143.
8. Ibid, p. 124.
9. For example, in addition to the ideas mentioned, I would also suggest replacing our present single-member district electoral system with a proportional representation system which would help mitigate the wealthy's monopoly of present legislative office; community ownership in return for tax abatements; some form of plant closure legislation; stricter enforcement of anti-trust and wage and worker safety legislation; and, changing the legal standing of corporations.
10. See for an excellent discussion on this point, Garry Wills, *Explaining America: The Federalist* (New York: Doubleday & Company, Inc., 1981), in particular page 218.

11. Quoted in Michael J. Sandel, *Democracy's Discontent: America in Search of a Public Philosophy*, p. 132.
12. Ibid, p. 126.
13. New York: Doubleday & Company, 1981, pp. 268-269.
14. Ibid, p.188.
15. Quoted in Michael J. Sandel, *Democracy's Discontent: America in Search of a Public Philosophy*, p. 126.
16. Quoted in Dean Darris, *A View From Below: Lecture Notes from the Democratic Edge* (Fort Worth: Harcourt Brace, 1996), p. 5.
17. New York: Oxford University Press, 1970, p. 145.
18. See for an excellent discussion on a similar point, James E. Perley, "Tenure Remains Vital to Academic Freedom," *The Chronicle of Higher Education* (April 4, 1997), p. A48.
19. I have intentionally avoided spelling out the details of such a plan because self-government is best served by granting local communities the autonomy to flesh out the particular details of any educational reform.
20. This begs the question: Since "public" schools are now focusing more and more on private sector training, then should not the corporations who benefit from this "education" provide the lion's share of its funding. Instead, under the guise of "education reform" they sponsor tax revolts designed to reconfigure "public" education so the working American taxpayer bears more and more of the burden of paying for what amounts to employee training.
21. Quoted in Merrill D. Peterson, *Thomas Jefferson & the New Nation: A Biography* (New York: Oxford University Press, Inc., 1970), p. 151.
22. Michael Shaara, *The Killer Angels* (New York: Random House, 1974), p. 30.

APPENDIX

The Declaration of Independence

Action of Second Continental Congress, July 4, 1776

The unanimous Declaration of the thirteen United States of America

WHEN in the Course of human Events, it becomes necessary for one People to dissolve the Political Bands which have connected them with another, and to assume among the Powers of the Earth, the separate and equal Station to which the Laws of Nature and of Nature's God entitle them, a decent Respect to the Opinions of Mankind requires that they should declare the causes which impel them to the Separation.

WE hold these Truths to be self-evident, that all Men are created equal, that they are endowed by their Creator with certain unalienable Rights, that among these are Life, Liberty and the Pursuit of Happiness — That to secure these Rights, Governments are instituted among Men, deriving their just Powers from the Consent of the Governed, that whenever any Form of Government becomes destructive of these Ends, it is the Right of the People to alter or to abolish it, and to institute new Government, laying its Foundation on such Principles, and organizing its Powers in such Form, as to them shall seem most likely to effect their Safety and Happiness. Prudence, indeed, will dictate that Governments long established should not be changed for light and transient Causes; and accordingly all Experience hath shewn, that Mankind are more disposed to suffer, while Evils are sufferable, than to right themselves by abolishing the Forms to which they are accustomed. But when a long Train of Abuses and Usurpations, pursuing invariably the same Object, evinces a Design to reduce them under absolute Despotism, it is their Right, it is their Duty, to throw off such Government, and to provide new Guards for their future Security. Such has been the patient Sufferance of these Colonies; and such is now the Necessity which constrains them to alter their former Systems of Government. The History of the present King of Great- Britain is a History of repeated Injuries and Usurpations, all having in direct Object the Establishment of an absolute Tyranny over these States. To prove this, let Facts be submitted to a candid World.

HE has refused his Assent to Laws, the most wholesome and necessary for the public Good.

HE has forbidden his Governors to pass Laws of immediate and pressing Importance, unless suspended in their Operation till his Assent should be obtained; and when so suspended, he has utterly neglected to attend to them.

HE has refused to pass other Laws for the Accommodation of large Districts of People, unless those People would relinquish the Right of Representation in the Legislature, a Right inestimable to them, and formidable to Tyrants only.

HE has called together Legislative Bodies at Places unusual, uncomfortable, and distant from the Depository of their public Records, for the sole Purpose of fatiguing them into Compliance with his Measures.

HE has dissolved Representative Houses repeatedly, for opposing with manly Firmness his Invasions on the Rights of the People.

HE has refused for a long Time, after such Dissolutions, to cause others to be elected; whereby the Legislative Powers, incapable of the Annihilation, have returned to the People at large for their exercise; the State remaining in the mean time exposed to all the Dangers of Invasion from without, and the Convulsions within.

HE has endeavoured to prevent the Population of these States; for that Purpose obstructing the Laws for Naturalization of Foreigners; refusing to pass others to encourage their Migrations hither, and raising the Conditions of new Appropriations of Lands.

HE has obstructed the Administration of Justice, by refusing his Assent to Laws for establishing Judiciary Powers.

HE has made Judges dependent on his Will alone, for the Tenure of their Offices, and the Amount and Payment of their Salaries.

HE has erected a Multitude of new Offices, and sent hither Swarms of Officers to harrass our People, and eat out their Substance.

HE has kept among us, in Times of Peace, Standing Armies, without the consent of our Legislatures.

HE has affected to render the Military independent of and superior to the Civil Power.

HE has combined with others to subject us to a Jurisdiction foreign to our Constitution, and unacknowledged by our Laws; giving his Assent to their Acts of pretended Legislation:

FOR quartering large Bodies of Armed Troops among us;

FOR protecting them, by a mock Trial, from PUnishment for any Murders which they should commit on the Inhabitants of these States:

FOR cutting off our Trade with all Parts of the World:

FOR imposing Taxes on us without our Consent:

FOR depriving us, in many Cases, of the Benefits of Trial by Jury:

FOR transporting us beyond Seas to be tried for pretended Offences:

FOR abolishing the free System of English Laws in a neighbouring Province, establishing therein an arbitrary Government, and enlarging its Boundaries, so as to render it at once an Example and fit Instrument for introducing the same absolute Rules into these Colonies:

FOR taking away our Charters, abolishing our most valuable Laws, and altering fUndamentally the Forms of our Governments:

FOR suspending our own Legislatures, and declaring themselves invested with Power to legislate for us in all Cases whatsoever.

HE has abdicated Government here, by declaring us out of his Protection and waging War against us.

HE has plUndered our Seas, ravaged our Coasts, burnt our Towns, and destroyed the Lives of our People.

HE is, at this Time, transporting large Armies of foreign Mercenaries to compleat the Works of Death, Desolation, and Tyranny, already begUn with circumstances of Cruelty and Perfidy, scarcely paralleled in the most barbarous Ages, and totally unworthy the Head of a civilized Nation.

HE has constrained our fellow Citizens taken Captive on the high Seas to bear Arms against their Country, to become the Executioners of their Friends and Brethren, or to fall themselves by their Hands.

HE has excited domestic Insurrections amongst us, and has endeavoured to bring on the Inhabitants of our Frontiers, the merciless Indian Savages, whose known Rule of Warfare, is an undistinguished Destruction, of all Ages, Sexes and Conditions.

IN every stage of these Oppressions we have Petitioned for Redress in the most humble Terms: Our repeated Petitions have been answered only by repeated Injury. A Prince, whose Character is thus marked by every act which may define a Tyrant, is unfit to be the Ruler of a free People.

NOR have we been wanting in Attentions to our British Brethren. We have warned them from Time to Time of Attempts by their Legislature to extend an unwarrantable

Jurisdiction over us. We have reminded them of the Circumstances of our Emigration and Settlement here. We have appealed to their native Justice and Magnanimity, and we have conjured them by the Ties of our common Kindred to disavow these Usurpations, which, would inevitably interrupt our Connections and Correspondence. They too have been deaf to the Voice of Justice and of Consanguinity. We must, therefore, acquiesce in the Necessity, which denounces our Separation, and hold them, as we hold the rest of Mankind, Enemies in War, in Peace, Friends.

WE, therefore, the Representatives of the unITED STATES OF AMERICA, in GENERAL CONGRESS, Assembled, appealing to the Supreme Judge of the World for the Rectitude of our Intentions, do, in the Name, and by Authority of the good People of these Colonies, solemnly Publish and Declare, That these united Colonies are, and of Right ought to be, FREE AND INDEPENDENT STATES; that they are absolved from all Allegiance to the British Crown, and that all political Connection between them and the State of Great-Britain, is and ought to be totally dissolved; and that as FREE AND INDEPENDENT STATES, they have full Power to levy War, conclude Peace, contract Alliances, establish Commerce, and to do all other Acts and Things which INDEPENDENT STATES may of right do. And for the support of this Declaration, with a firm Reliance on the Protection of divine Providence, we mutually pledge to each other our Lives, our Fortunes, and our sacred Honor.

John Hancock. GEORGIA, Button Gwinnett, Lyman Hall, Geo. Walton. NORTH-CAROLINA, Wm. Hooper, Joseph Hewes, John Penn. SOUTH-CAROLINA, Edward Rutledge, Thos Heyward, Junr., Thomas Lynch, Junr., Arthur Middleton. MARYLAND, Samuel Chase, Wm. Paca, Thos. Stone, Charles Carroll, of Carrollton. VIRGINIA, George Wythe, Richard Henry Lee, Ths. Jefferson, Benja. Harrison, Thos. Nelson, Jr., Francis Lightfoot Lee, Carter Braxton. PENNSYLVANIA, Robt. Morris, Benjamin Rush, Benja. Franklin, John Morton, Geo. Clymer, Jas. Smith, Geo. Taylor, James Wilson, Geo. Ross. DELAWARE, Caesar Rodney, Geo. Read. NEW-YORK, Wm. Floyd, Phil. Livingston, Frank Lewis, Lewis Morris. NEW-JERSEY, Richd. Stockton, Jno. Witherspoon, Fras. Hopkinson, John Hart, Abra. Clark. NEW-HAMPSHIRE, Josiah Bartlett, Wm. Whipple, Matthew Thornton. MASSACHUSETTS-BAY, Saml. Adams, John Adams, Robt. Treat Paine, Elbridge Gerry. RHODE-ISLAND AND PROVIDENCE, C. Step. Hopkins, William Ellery. CONNECTICUT, Roger Sherman, Saml. Huntington, Wm. Williams, Oliver Wolcott.

The Articles of Confederation

Nov. 15, 1777

To all to whom these Presents shall come, we the undersigned Delegates of the States affixed to our Names send greeting.

Articles of Confederation and perpetual union between the states of New Hampshire, Massachusetts-bay Rhode Island and Providence Plantations, Connecticut, New York, New Jersey, Pennsylvania, Delaware, Maryland, Virginia, North Carolina, South Carolina and Georgia.

I. The Stile of this Confederacy shall be "The United States of America".

II. Each state retains its sovereignty, freedom, and independence, and every power, jurisdiction, and right, which is not by this Confederation expressly delegated to the United States, in Congress assembled.

III. The said States hereby severally enter into a firm league of friendship with each other, for their common defense, the security of their liberties, and their mutual and general welfare, binding themselves to assist each other, against all force offered to, or attacks made upon them, or any of them, on account of religion, sovereignty, trade, or any other pretense whatever.

IV. The better to secure and perpetuate mutual friendship and intercourse among the people of the different States in this union, the free inhabitants of each of these States, paupers, vagabonds, and fugitives from justice excepted, shall be entitled to all privileges and immUnities of free citizens in the several States; and the people of each State shall free ingress and regress to and from any other State, and shall enjoy therein all the privileges of trade and commerce, subject to the same duties, impositions, and restrictions as the inhabitants thereof respectively, provided that such restrictions shall not extend so far as to prevent the removal of property imported into any State, to any other State, of which the owner is an inhabitant; provided also that no imposition, duties or restriction shall be laid by any State, on the property of the United States, or either of them.

If any person guilty of, or charged with, treason, felony, or other high misdemeanor in any State, shall flee from justice, and be found in any of the United States, he shall, upon demand of the Governor or executive power of the State from which he fled, be delivered up and removed to the State having jurisdiction of his offense.

Full faith and credit shall be given in each of these States to the records, acts, and judicial proceedings of the courts and magistrates of every other State.

V. For the most convenient management of the general interests of the United States, delegates shall be annually appointed in such manner as the legislatures of each State shall direct, to meet in Congress on the first Monday in November, in every year, with a power reserved to each State to recall its delegates, or any of them, at any time within the year, and to send others in their stead for the remainder of the year.

No State shall be represented in Congress by less than two, nor more than seven members; and no person shall be capable of being a delegate for more than three years in any term of six years; nor shall any person, being a delegate, be capable of holding any office under the United States, for which he, or another for his benefit, receives any salary, fees or emolument of any kind.

Each State shall maintain its own delegates in a meeting of the States, and while they act as members of the committee of the States.

In determining questions in the United States in Congress assembled, each State shall have one vote.

Freedom of speech and debate in Congress shall not be impeached or questioned in any court or place out of Congress, and the members of Congress shall be protected in their persons from arrests or imprisonments, during the time of their going to and from, and attendence on Congress, except for treason, felony, or breach of the peace.

VI. No State, without the consent of the United States in Congress assembled, shall send any embassy to, or receive any embassy from, or enter into any conference, agreement, alliance or treaty with any King, Prince or State; nor shall any person holding any office of profit or trust under the United States, or any of them, accept any present, emolument, office or title of any kind whatever from any King, Prince or foreign State; nor shall the United States in Congress assembled, or any of them, grant any title of nobility.

No two or more States shall enter into any treaty, confederation or alliance whatever between them, without the consent of the United States in Congress assembled, specifying accurately the purposes for which the same is to be entered into, and how long it shall continue.

No State shall lay any imposts or duties, which may interfere with any stipulations in treaties, entered into by the United States in Congress assembled, with any King, Prince or State, in pursuance of any treaties already proposed by Congress, to the courts of France and Spain.

No vessel of war shall be kept up in time of peace by any State, except such number only, as shall be deemed necessary by the United States in Congress assembled, for the defense of such State, or its trade; nor shall any body of forces be kept up by any State in time of peace, except such number only, as in the judgement of the United States in Congress assembled, shall be deemed requisite to garrison the forts necessary for the defense of such State; but every State shall always keep up a well-regulated and disciplined militia, sufficiently armed and accoutered, and shall provide and constantly have ready for use, in public stores, a due number of filed pieces and tents, and a proper quantity of arms, ammUnition and camp equipage.

No State shall engage in any war without the consent of the United States in Congress assembled, unless such State be actually invaded by enemies, or shall have received certain advice of a resolution being formed by some nation of Indians to invade such State, and the danger is so imminent as not to admit of a delay till the United States in Congress assembled can be consulted; nor shall any State grant commissions to any ships or vessels of war, nor letters of marque or reprisal, except it be after a declaration of war by the United States in Congress assembled, and then only against the Kingdom or State and the subjects thereof, against which war has been so declared, and under such regulations as shall be established by the United States in Congress assembled, unless such State be infested by pirates, in which case vessels of war may be fitted out for that occasion, and kept so long as the danger shall continue, or until the United States in Congress assembled shall determine otherwise.

VII. When land forces are raised by any State for the common defense, all officers of or under the rank of colonel, shall be appointed by the legislature of each State respectively, by whom such forces shall be raised, or in such manner as such State shall direct, and all vacancies shall be filled up by the State which first made the appointment.

VIII. All charges of war, and all other expenses that shall be incurred for the common defense or general welfare, and allowed by the United States in Congress assembled, shall be defrayed out of a common treasury, which shall be supplied by the several States in proportion to the value of all land within each State, granted or surveyed for any person, as such land and the buildings and improvements thereon shall be estimated according to such mode as the United States in Congress assembled, shall from time to time direct and appoint.

The taxes for paying that proportion shall be laid and levied by the authority and direction of the legislatures of the several States within the time agreed upon by the United States in Congress assembled.

IX. The United States in Congress assembled, shall have the sole and exclusive right and power of determining on peace and war, except in the cases mentioned in the sixth article — of sending and receiving ambassadors — entering into treaties and alliances, provided that no treaty of commerce shall be made whereby the legislative power of the respective States shall be restrained from imposing such imposts and duties on foreigners, as their own people are subjected to, or from prohibiting the exportation or importation of any species of goods or commodities whatsoever — of establishing rules for deciding in all cases, what captures on land or water shall be legal, and in what manner prizes taken by land or naval forces in the service of the United States shall be divided or appropriated — of granting letters of marque and reprisal in times of peace — appointing courts for the trial of piracies and felonies commited on the high seas and establishing courts for receiving and determining finally appeals in all cases of captures, provided that no member of Congress shall be appointed a judge of any of the said courts.

The United States in Congress assembled shall also be the last resort on appeal in all disputes and differences now subsisting or that hereafter may arise between two or more States concerning boundary, jurisdiction or any other causes whatever; which authority shall always be exercised in the manner following. Whenever the legislative or executive authority or lawful agent of any State in controversy with another shall present a petition to Congress stating the matter in question and praying for a hearing, notice thereof shall be given by order of Congress to the legislative or executive authority of the other State in controversy, and a day assigned for the appearance of the parties by their lawful agents, who shall then be directed to appoint by joint consent, commissioners or judges to constitute a court for hearing and determining the matter in question: but if they cannot agree, Congress shall name three persons out of each of the United States, and from the list of such persons each party shall alternately strike out one, the petitioners beginning, until the number shall be reduced to thirteen; and from that number not less than seven, nor more than nine names as Congress shall direct, shall in the presence of Congress be drawn out by lot, and the persons whose names shall be so drawn or any five of them, shall be commissioners or judges, to hear and finally determine the controversy, so always as a major part of the judges who shall hear the cause shall agree in the determination: and if either party shall neglect to attend at the day appointed, without showing reasons, which Congress shall judge sufficient, or being present shall refuse to strike, the Congress shall proceed to nominate three persons out of each State, and the secretary of Congress shall strike in behalf of such party absent or refusing; and the judgement and sentence of the court to be appointed, in the manner before prescribed, shall be final and conclusive; and if any of the parties shall refuse to submit to the authority of such court, or to appear or defend their claim or cause, the court shall nevertheless proceed to pronounce sentence, or judgement, which shall in like manner be final and decisive, the judgement or sentence and other proceedings being in either case transmitted to Congress, and lodged among the acts of Congress for the security of the parties concerned: provided that every commissioner, before he sits in judgement, shall take an oath to be administered by one of the judges of the supreme or superior court of the State, where the cause shall be tried, 'well and truly to hear and determine the matter in question, according to the best of his judgement, without favor, affection or hope of reward': provided also, that no State shall be deprived of territory for the benefit of the United States.

All controversies concerning the private right of soil claimed under different grants of two or more States, whose jurisdictions as they may respect such lands, and the States which passed such grants are adjusted, the said grants or either of them being at the same time claimed to have originated antecedent to such settlement of jurisdiction, shall on the petition of either party to the Congress of the United States, be finally determined as near as may be in the same manner as is before presecribed for deciding disputes respecting territorial jurisdiction between different States.

The United States in Congress assembled shall also have the sole and exclusive right and power of regulating the alloy and value of coin struck by their own authority, or by that of the respective States — fixing the standards of weights and measures throughout the United States — regulating the trade and managing all affairs with the Indians, not members of any of the States, provided that the legislative right of any State within its own limits be not infringed or violated — establishing or regulating post offices from one State to another, throughout all the United States, and exacting such postage on the papers passing through the same as may be requisite to defray the expenses of the said office — appointing all officers of the land forces, in the service of the United States, excepting regimental officers — appointing all the officers of the naval forces, and commissioning all officers whatever in the service of the United States — making rules for the government and regulation of the said land and naval forces, and directing their operations.

The United States in Congress assembled shall have authority to appoint a committee, to sit in the recess of Congress, to be denominated 'A Committee of the States', and to consist of one delegate from each State; and to appoint such other committees and civil officers as may be necessary for managing the general affairs of the United States under their direction

— to appoint one of their members to preside, provided that no person be allowed to serve in the office of president more than one year in any term of three years; to ascertain the necessary sums of money to be raised for the service of the United States, and to appropriate and apply the same for defraying the public expenses — to borrow money, or emit bills on the credit of the United States, transmitting every half-year to the respective States an account of the sums of money so borrowed or emitted

— to build and equip a navy — to agree upon the number of land forces, and to make requisitions from each State for its quota, in proportion to the number of white inhabitants in such State; which requisition shall be binding, and thereupon the legislature of each State shall appoint the regimental officers, raise the men and cloath, arm and equip them in a solid-like manner, at the expense of the United States; and the officers and men so cloathed, armed and equipped shall march to the place appointed, and within the time agreed on by the United States in Congress assembled. But if the United States in Congress assembled shall, on consideration of circumstances judge proper that any State should not raise men, or should raise a smaller number of men than the quota thereof, such extra number shall be raised, officered, cloathed, armed and equipped in the same manner as the quota of each State, unless the legislature of such State shall judge that such extra number cannot be safely spread out in the same, in which case they shall raise, officer, cloath, arm and equip as many of such extra number as they judeg can be safely spared. And the officers and men so cloathed, armed, and equipped, shall march to the place appointed, and within the time agreed on by the United States in Congress assembled.

The United States in Congress assembled shall never engage in a war, nor grant letters of marque or reprisal in time of peace, nor enter into any treaties or alliances, nor coin money, nor regulate the value thereof, nor ascertain the sums and expenses necessary for the defense and welfare of the United States, or any of them, nor emit bills, nor borrow money on the credit of the United States, nor appropriate money, nor agree upon the number of vessels of war, to be built or purchased, or the number of land or sea forces to be raised, nor appoint a commander in chief of the army or navy, unless nine States assent to the same: nor shall a question on any other point, except for adjourning from day to day be determined, unless by the votes of the majority of the United States in Congress assembled.

The Congress of the United States shall have power to adjourn to any time within the year, and to any place within the United States, so that no period of adjournment be for a longer duration than the space of six months, and shall publish the journal of their proceedings monthly, except such parts thereof relating to treaties, alliances or military operations, as in their judgement require secrecy; and the yeas and nays of the delegates of each State on any question shall be entered on the journal, when it is desired by any delegates of a State, or any of them, at his or their request shall be furnished with a transcript of the said journal, except such parts as are above excepted, to lay before the legislatures of the several States.

X. The Committee of the States, or any nine of them, shall be authorized to execute, in the recess of Congress, such of the powers of Congress as the United States in Congress assembled, by the consent of the nine States, shall from time to time think expedient to vest them with; provided that no power be delegated to the said Committee, for the exercise of which, by the Articles of Confederation, the voice of nine States in the Congress of the United States assembled be requisite.

XI. Canada acceding to this confederation, and adjoining in the measures of the United States, shall be admitted into, and entitled to all the advantages of this union; but no other colony shall be admitted into the same, unless such admission be agreed to by nine States.

XII. All bills of credit emitted, monies borrowed, and debts contracted by, or under the authority of Congress, before the assembling of the United States, in pursuance of the present confederation, shall be deemed and considered as a charge against the United States, for payment and satisfaction whereof the said United States, and the public faith are hereby solemnly pleged.

XIII. Every State shall abide by the determination of the United States in Congress assembled, on all questions which by this confederation are submitted to them. And the Articles of this Confederation shall be inviolably observed by every State, and the union shall be perpetual; nor shall any alteration at any time hereafter be made in any of them; unless such alteration be agreed to in a Congress of the United States, and be afterwards confirmed by the legislatures of every State.

And Whereas it hath pleased the Great Governor of the World to incline the hearts of the legislatures we respectively represent in Congress, to approve of, and to authorize us to ratify the said Articles of Confederation and perpetual union. Know Ye that we the undersigned delegates, by virtue of the power and authority to us given for that purpose, do by these presents, in the name and in behalf of our respective constituents, fully and entirely ratify and confirm each and every of the said Articles of Confederation and perpetual union, and all and singular the matters and things therein contained: And we do further solemnly plight and engage the faith of our respective constituents, that they shall abide by the determinations of the United States in Congress assembled, on all questions, which by the said Confederation are submitted to them. And that the Articles thereof shall be inviolably observed by the States we respectively represent, and that the union shall be perpetual.

In Witness whereof we have here Unto set our hands in Congress. Done at Philadelphia in the State of Pennsylvania the ninth day of July in the Year of our Lord One Thousand Seven Hundred and Seventy-Eight, and in the Third Year of the independence of America.

Agreed to by Congress 15 November 1777

In force after ratification by Maryland, 1 March 1781

The Federalist No. 10

THE UNION AS A SAFEGUARD AGAINST DOMESTIC FACTION

James Madison
November 23, 1787.

To the People of the State of New York:

AMONG the numerous advantages promised by a wellconstructed union, none deserves to be more accurately developed than its tendency to break and control the violence of faction. The friend of popular governments never finds himself so much alarmed for their character and fate, as when he contemplates their propensity to this dangerous vice. He will not fail, therefore, to set a due value on any plan which, without violating the principles to which he is attached, provides a proper cure for it. The instability, injustice, and confusion introduced into the public councils, have, in truth, been the mortal diseases under which popular governments have everywhere perished; as they continue to be the favorite and fruitful topics from which the adversaries to liberty derive their most specious declamations. The valuable improvements made by the American constitutions on the popular models, both ancient and modern, cannot certainly be too much admired; but it would be an unwarrantable partiality, to contend that they have as effectually obviated the danger on this side, as was wished and expected. Complaints are everywhere heard from our most considerate and virtuous citizens, equally the friends of public and private faith, and of public and personal liberty, that our governments are too unstable, that the public good is disregarded in the conflicts of rival parties, and that measures are too often decided, not according to the rules of justice and the rights of the minor party, but by the superior force of an interested and overbearing majority. However anxiously we may wish that these complaints had no foundation, the evidence, of known facts will not permit us to deny that they are in some degree true. It will be found, indeed, on a candid review of our situation, that some of the distresses under which we labor have been erroneously charged on the operation of our governments; but it will be found, at the same time, that other causes will not alone account for many of our heaviest misfortunes; and, particularly, for that prevailing and increasing distrust of public engagements, and alarm for private rights, which are echoed from one end of the continent to the other. These must be chiefly, if not wholly, effects of the unsteadiness and injustice with which a factious spirit has tainted our public administrations.

By a faction, I understand a number of citizens, whether amounting to a majority or a minority of the whole, who are united and actuated by some common impulse of passion, or of interest, adversed to the rights of other citizens, or to the permanent and aggregate interests of the community.

There are two methods of curing the mischiefs of faction: the one, by removing its causes; the other, by controlling its effects.

There are again two methods of removing the causes of faction: the one, by destroying the liberty which is essential to its existence; the other, by giving to every citizen the same opinions, the same passions, and the same interests.

It could never be more truly said than of the first remedy, that it was worse than the disease. Liberty is to faction what air is to fire, an aliment without which it instantly expires. But it could not be less folly to abolish liberty, which is essential to political life, because it nourishes faction, than it would be to wish the annihilation of air, which is essential to animal life, because it imparts to fire its destructive agency.

The second expedient is as impracticable as the first would be unwise. As long as the reason of man continues fallible, and he is at liberty to exercise it, different opinions will be formed. As long as the connection subsists between his reason and his self-love, his opinions and his passions will have a reciprocal influence on each other; and the former will be objects to which the latter will attach themselves. The diversity in the faculties of men, from which the rights of property originate, is not less an insuperable obstacle to a uniformity of interests. The protection of these faculties is the first object of government. From the protection of different and unequal faculties of acquiring property, the possession of different degrees and kinds of property immediately results; and from the influence of these on the sentiments and views of the respective proprietors, ensues a division of the society into different interests and parties.

The latent causes of faction are thus sown in the nature of man; and we see them everywhere brought into different degrees of activity, according to the different circumstances of civil society. A zeal for different opinions concerning religion, concerning government, and many other points, as well of speculation as of practice; an attachment to different leaders ambitiously contending for pre-eminence and power; or to persons of other descriptions whose fortunes have been interesting to the human passions, have, in turn, divided mankind into parties, inflamed them with mutual animosity, and rendered them much more disposed to vex and oppress each other than to co-operate for their common good. So strong is this propensity of mankind to fall into mutual animosities, that where no substantial occasion presents itself, the most frivolous and fanciful distinctions have been sufficient to kindle their unfriendly passions and excite their most violent conflicts. But the most common and durable source of factions has been the various and unequal distribution of property. Those who hold and those who are without property have ever formed distinct interests in society. Those who are creditors, and those who are debtors, fall under a like discrimination. A landed interest, a manufacturing interest, a mercantile interest, a moneyed interest, with many lesser interests, grow up of necessity in civilized nations, and divide them into different classes, actuated by different sentiments and views. The regulation of these various and interfering interests forms the principal task of modern legislation, and involves the spirit of party and faction in the necessary and ordinary operations of the government.

No man is allowed to be a judge in his own cause, because his interest would certainly bias his judgment, and, not improbably, corrupt his integrity. With equal, nay with greater reason, a body of men are unfit to be both judges and parties at the same time; yet what are many of the most important acts of legislation, but so many judicial determinations, not indeed concerning the rights of single persons, but concerning the rights of large bodies of citizens? And what are the different classes of legislators but advocates and parties to the causes which they determine? Is a law proposed concerning private debts? It is a question to which the creditors are parties on one side and the debtors on the other. Justice ought to hold the balance between them. Yet the parties are, and must be, themselves the judges; and the most numerous party, or, in other words, the most powerful faction must be expected to prevail. Shall domestic manufactures be encouraged, and in what degree, by restrictions on foreign manufactures? are questions which would be differently decided by the landed and the manufacturing classes, and probably by neither with a sole regard to justice and the public good. The apportionment of taxes on the various descriptions of property is an act which seems to require the most exact impartiality; yet there is, perhaps, no legislative act in which greater opportunity and temptation are given to a predominant party to trample on the rules of justice. Every shilling with which they overburden the inferior number, is a shilling saved to their own pockets.

It is in vain to say that enlightened statesmen will be able to adjust these clashing interests, and render them all subservient to the public good. Enlightened statesmen will not always be at the helm. Nor, in many cases, can such an adjustment be made at all without taking into view indirect and remote considerations, which will rarely prevail over the immediate interest which one party may find in disregarding the rights of another or the good of the whole.

The inference to which we are brought is, that the CAUSES of faction cannot be removed, and that relief is only to be sought in the means of controlling its EFFECTS.

If a faction consists of less than a majority, relief is supplied by the republican principle, which enables the majority to defeat its sinister views by regular vote. It may clog the administration, it may convulse the society; but it will be unable to execute and mask its violence under the forms of the Constitution. When a majority is included in a faction, the form of popular government, on the other hand, enables it to sacrifice to its ruling passion or interest both the public good and the rights of other citizens. To secure the public good and private rights against the danger of such a faction, and at the same time to preserve the spirit and the form of popular government, is then the great object to which our inquiries are directed. Let me add that it is the great desideratum by which this form of government can be rescued from the opprobrium under which it has so long labored, and be recommended to the esteem and adoption of mankind.

By what means is this object attainable? Evidently by one of two only. Either the existence of the same passion or interest in a majority at the same time must be prevented, or the majority, having such coexistent passion or interest, must be rendered, by their number and local situation, unable to concert and carry into effect schemes of oppression. If the impulse and the opportunity be suffered to coincide, we well know that neither moral nor religious motives can be relied on as an adequate control. They are not found to be such on the injustice and violence of individuals, and lose their efficacy in proportion to the number combined together, that is, in proportion as their efficacy becomes needful.

From this view of the subject it may be concluded that a pure democracy, by which I mean a society consisting of a small number of citizens, who assemble and administer the government in person, can admit of no cure for the mischiefs of faction. A common passion or interest will, in almost every case, be felt by a majority of the whole; a communication and concert result from the form of government itself; and there is nothing to check the inducements to sacrifice the weaker party or an obnoxious individual. Hence it is that such democracies have ever been spectacles of turbulence and contention; have ever been found incompatible with personal security or the rights of property; and have in general been as short in their lives as they have been violent in their deaths. Theoretic politicians, who have patronized this species of government, have erroneously supposed that by reducing mankind to a perfect equality in their political rights, they would, at the same time, be perfectly equalized and assimilated in their possessions, their opinions, and their passions.

A republic, by which I mean a government in which the scheme of representation takes place, opens a different prospect, and promises the cure for which we are seeking. Let us examine the points in which it varies from pure democracy, and we shall comprehend both the nature of the cure and the efficacy which it must derive from the union.

The two great points of difference between a democracy and a republic are: first, the delegation of the government, in the latter, to a small number of citizens elected by the rest; secondly, the greater number of citizens, and greater sphere of country, over which the latter may be extended.

The effect of the first difference is, on the one hand, to refine and enlarge the public views, by passing them through the medium of a chosen body of citizens, whose wisdom may best discern the true interest of their country, and whose patriotism and love of justice will be least likely to sacrifice it to temporary or partial considerations. under such a regulation, it may well happen that the public voice, pronounced by the representatives of the people, will be more consonant to the public good than if pronounced by the people themselves, convened for the purpose. On the other hand, the effect may be inverted. Men of factious tempers, of local prejudices, or of sinister designs, may, by intrigue, by corruption, or by other means, first obtain the suffrages, and then betray the interests, of the people. The question resulting is, whether small or extensive republics are more favorable to the election of proper guardians of the public weal; and it is clearly decided in favor of the latter by two obvious considerations:

In the first place, it is to be remarked that, however small the republic may be, the representatives must be raised to a certain number, in order to guard against the cabals of a few; and that, however large it may be, they must be limited to a certain number, in order to guard against the confusion of a multitude. Hence, the number of representatives in the two cases not being in proportion to that of the two constituents, and being proportionally greater in the small republic, it follows that, if the proportion of fit characters be not less in the large than in the small republic, the former will present a greater option, and consequently a greater probability of a fit choice.

In the next place, as each representative will be chosen by a greater number of citizens in the large than in the small republic, it will be more difficult for unworthy candidates to practice with success the vicious arts by which elections are too often carried; and the suffrages of the people being more free, will be more likely to centre in men who possess the most attractive merit and the most diffusive and established characters.

It must be confessed that in this, as in most other cases, there is a mean, on both sides of which inconveniences will be found to lie. By enlarging too much the number of electors, you render the representatives too little acquainted with all their local circumstances and lesser interests; as by reducing it too much, you render him unduly attached to these, and too little fit to comprehend and pursue great and national objects. The federal Constitution forms a happy combination in this respect; the great and aggregate interests being referred to the national, the local and particular to the State legislatures.

The other point of difference is, the greater number of citizens and extent of territory which may be brought within the compass of republican than of democratic government; and it is this circumstance principally which renders factious combinations less to be dreaded in the former than in the latter. The smaller the society, the fewer probably will be the distinct parties and interests composing it; the fewer the distinct parties and interests, the more frequently will a majority be found of the same party; and the smaller the number of individuals composing a majority, and the smaller the compass within which they are placed, the more easily will they concert and execute their plans of oppression. Extend the sphere, and you take in a greater variety of parties and interests; you make it less probable that a majority of the whole will have a common motive to invade the rights of other citizens; or if such a common motive exists, it will be more difficult for all who feel it to discover their own strength, and to act in unison with each other. Besides other impediments, it may be remarked that, where there is a consciousness of unjust or dishonorable purposes, communication is always checked by distrust in proportion to the number whose concurrence is necessary.

Hence, it clearly appears, that the same advantage which a republic has over a democracy, in controlling the effects of faction, is enjoyed by a large over a small republic,—is enjoyed by the union over the States composing it. Does the advantage consist in the substitution of representatives whose enlightened views and virtuous sentiments render them superior to local prejudices and schemes of injustice? It will not be denied that the representation of the union will be most likely to possess these requisite endowments. Does it consist in the greater security afforded by a greater variety of parties, against the event of any one party being able to outnumber and oppress the rest? In an equal degree does the increased variety of parties comprised within the union, increase this security. Does it, in fine, consist in the greater obstacles opposed to the concert and accomplishment of the secret wishes of an unjust and interested majority? Here, again, the extent of the union gives it the most palpable advantage.

The influence of factious leaders may kindle a flame within their particular States, but will be unable to spread a general conflagration through the other States. A religious sect may degenerate into a political faction in a part of the Confederacy; but the variety of sects dispersed over the entire face of it must secure the national councils against any danger from that source. A rage for paper money, for an abolition of debts, for an equal division of property, or for any other improper or wicked project, will be less apt to pervade the whole body of the union than a particular member of it; in the same proportion as such a malady is more likely to taint a particular county or district, than an entire State.

In the extent and proper structure of the union, therefore, we behold a republican remedy for the diseases most incident to republican government. And according to the degree of pleasure and pride we feel in being republicans, ought to be our zeal in cherishing the spirit and supporting the character of Federalists.

PUBLIUS.

The Federalist No. 51

CHECKS AND BALANCES

James Madison
February 8, 1788.

To the People of the State of New York:

TO WHAT expedient, then, shall we finally resort, for maintaining in practice the necessary partition of power among the several departments, as laid down in the Constitution? The only answer that can be given is, that as all these exterior provisions are found to be inadequate, the defect must be supplied, by so contriving the interior structure of the government as that its several constituent parts may, by their mutual relations, be the means of keeping each other in their proper places. Without presuming to undertake a full development of this important idea, I will hazard a few general observations, which may perhaps place it in a clearer light, and enable us to form a more correct judgment of the principles and structure of the government planned by the convention.

In order to lay a due foundation for that separate and distinct exercise of the different powers of government, which to a certain extent is admitted on all hands to be essential to the preservation of liberty, it is evident that each department should have a will of its own; and consequently should be so constituted that the members of each should have as little agency as possible in the appointment of the members of the others. Were this principle rigorously adhered to, it would require that all the appointments for the supreme executive, legislative, and judiciary magistracies should be drawn from the same fountain of authority, the people, through channels having no communication whatever with one another. Perhaps such a plan of constructing the several departments would be less difficult in practice than it may in contemplation appear. Some difficulties, however, and some additional expense would attend the execution of it. Some deviations, therefore, from the principle must be admitted. In the constitution of the judiciary department in particular, it might be inexpedient to insist rigorously on the principle: first, because peculiar qualifications being essential in the members, the primary consideration ought to be to select that mode of choice which best secures these qualifications; secondly, because the permanent tenure by which the appointments are held in that department, must soon destroy all sense of dependence on the authority conferring them.

It is equally evident, that the members of each department should be as little dependent as possible on those of the others, for the emoluments annexed to their offices. Were the executive magistrate, or the judges, not independent of the legislature in this particular, their independence in every other would be merely nominal.

But the great security against a gradual concentration of the several powers in the same department, consists in giving to those who administer each department the necessary constitutional means and personal motives to resist encroachments of the others. The provision for defense must in this, as in all other cases, be made commensurate to the danger of attack. Ambition must be made to counteract ambition. The interest of the man must be connected with the constitutional rights of the place. It may be a reflection on human nature, that such devices should be necessary to control the abuses of government. But what is government itself, but the greatest of all reflections on human nature? If men were angels, no government would be necessary. If angels were to govern men, neither external nor internal controls on government would be necessary. In framing a government which is to be administered by men over men, the great difficulty lies in this: you must first enable the government to control the governed; and in the next place oblige it to control itself. A dependence on the people is, no doubt, the primary control on the government; but experience has taught mankind the necessity of auxiliary precautions.

This policy of supplying, by opposite and rival interests, the defect of better motives, might be traced through the whole system of human affairs, private as well as public. We see it particularly displayed in all the subordinate distributions of power, where the constant aim is to divide and arrange the several offices in such a manner as that each may be a check on the other that the private interest of every individual may be a sentinel over the public rights. These inventions of prudence cannot be less requisite in the distribution of the supreme powers of the State.

But it is not possible to give to each department an equal power of self-defense. In republican government, the legislative authority necessarily predominates. The remedy for this inconveniency is to divide the legislature into different branches; and to render them, by different modes of election and different principles of action, as little connected with each other as the nature of their common functions and their common dependence on the society will admit. It may even be necessary to guard against dangerous encroachments by still further precautions. As the weight of the legislative authority requires that it should be thus divided, the weakness of the executive may require, on the other hand, that it should be fortified. An absolute negative on the legislature appears, at first view, to be the natural defense with which the executive magistrate should be armed. But perhaps it would be neither altogether safe nor alone sufficient. On ordinary occasions it might not be exerted with the requisite firmness, and on extraordinary occasions it might be perfidiously abused. May not this defect of an absolute negative be supplied by some qualified connection between this weaker department and the weaker branch of the stronger department, by which the latter may be led to support the constitutional rights of the former, without being too much detached from the rights of its own department?

If the principles on which these observations are founded be just, as I persuade myself they are, and they be applied as a criterion to the several State constitutions, and to the federal Constitution it will be found that if the latter does not perfectly correspond with them, the former are infinitely less able to bear such a test.

There are, moreover, two considerations particularly applicable to the federal system of America, which place that system in a very interesting point of view.

First. In a single republic, all the power surrendered by the people is submitted to the administration of a single government; and the usurpations are guarded against by a division of the government into distinct and separate departments. In the compound republic of America, the power surrendered by the people is first divided between two distinct governments, and then the portion allotted to each subdivided among distinct and separate departments. Hence a double security arises to the rights of the people. The different governments will control each other, at the same time that each will be controlled by itself.

Second. It is of great importance in a republic not only to guard the society against the oppression of its rulers, but to guard one part of the society against the injustice of the other part. Different interests necessarily exist in different classes of citizens. If a majority be united by a common interest, the rights of the minority will be insecure. There are but two methods of providing against this evil: the one by creating a will in the community independent of the majority that is, of the society itself; the other, by comprehending in the society so many separate descriptions of citizens as will render an unjust combination of a majority of the whole very improbable, if not impracticable. The first method prevails in all governments possessing an hereditary or self-appointed authority. This, at best, is but a precarious security; because a power independent of the society may as well espouse the unjust views of the major, as the rightful interests of the minor party, and may possibly be turned against both parties. The second method will be exemplified in the federal republic of the United States. Whilst all authority in it will be derived from and dependent on the society, the society itself will be broken into so many parts, interests, and classes of citizens, that the rights of individuals, or of the minority, will be in little danger from interested combinations of the majority. In a free government the security for civil rights must be the same as that for religious rights. It consists in the one case in the multiplicity of interests, and in the other in the multiplicity of sects. The degree of security in both cases will depend on the number of interests and sects; and this may be presumed to depend on the extent of country and number of people comprehended under the same government. This view of the subject must particularly recommend a proper federal system to all the sincere and considerate friends of republican government, since it shows that in exact proportion as the territory of the union may be formed into more circumscribed Confederacies, or States oppressive combinations of a majority will be facilitated: the best security, under the republican forms, for the rights of every class of citizens, will be diminished: and consequently the stability and independence of some member of the government, the only other security, must be proportionately increased. Justice is the end of government. It is the end of civil society. It ever has been and ever will be pursued until it be obtained, or until liberty be lost in the pursuit. In a society under the forms of which the stronger faction can readily unite and oppress the weaker, anarchy may as truly be said to reign as in a state of nature, where the weaker individual is not secured against the violence of the stronger; and as, in the latter state, even the stronger individuals are prompted, by the uncertainty of their condition, to submit to a government which may protect the weak as well as themselves; so, in the former state, will the more powerful factions or parties be gradnally induced, by a like motive, to wish for a government which will protect all parties, the weaker as well as the more powerful. It can be little doubted that if the State of Rhode Island was separated from the Confederacy and left to itself, the insecurity of rights under the popular form of government within such narrow limits would be displayed by such reiterated oppressions of factious majorities that some power altogether independent of the people would soon be called for by the voice of the very factions whose misrule had proved the necessity of it. In the extended republic of the United States, and among the great variety of interests, parties, and sects which it embraces, a coalition of a majority of the whole society could seldom take place on any other principles than those of justice and the general good; whilst there being thus less danger to a minor from the will of a major party, there must be less pretext, also, to provide for the security of the former, by introducing into the government a will not dependent on the latter, or, in other words, a will independent of the society itself. It is no less certain than it is important, notwithstanding the contrary opinions which have been entertained, that the larger the society, provided it lie within a practical sphere, the more duly capable it will be of self-government. And happily for the REPUBLICAN CAUSE, the practicable sphere may be carried to a very great extent, by a judicious modification and mixture of the FEDERAL PRINCIPLE.

PUBLIUS.

The Constitution of the United States

THE UNITED STATES CONSTITUTION

We the People of the United States, in Order to form a more perfect Union, establish Justice, insure domestic Tranquility, provide for the common defence, promote the general Welfare, and secure the Blessings of Liberty to ourselves and our Posterity, do ordain and establish this Constitution for the United States of America.

ARTICLE I. *fed congress law maker*

don't need to remember exact section

Section 1. *law makers*

All legislative Powers herein granted shall be vested in a Congress of the United States, which shall consist of a Senate and House of Representatives.

Section 2.

CLAUSE 1: The House of Representatives shall be composed of Members chosen every second Year by the People of the several States, and the Electors in each State shall have the Qualifications requisite for Electors of the most numerous Branch of the State Legislature.

CLAUSE 2: No Person shall be a Representative who shall not have attained to the Age of twenty five Years *25+*, and been seven Years a Citizen of the United States, and who shall not, when elected, be an Inhabitant of that State in which he shall be chosen.

CLAUSE 3: Representatives and direct Taxes shall be apportioned among the several States which may be included within this Union, according to their respective Numbers, which shall be determined by adding to the whole Number of free Persons, including those bound to Service for a Term of Years, and excluding Indians not taxed, three fifths of all other Persons. The actual Enumeration *count* shall be made within three Years after the first Meeting of the Congress of the United States, and within every subsequent Term of ten Years, in such Manner as they shall by Law direct. The Number of

Representatives shall not exceed one for every thirty Thousand, but each State shall have at Least one Representative; and until such enumeration shall be made, the State of New Hampshire shall be entitled to choose three, Massachusetts eight, Rhode-Island and Providence Plantations one, Connecticut five, New-York six, New Jersey four, Pennsylvania eight, Delaware one, Maryland six, Virginia ten, North Carolina five, South Carolina five, and Georgia three.

CLAUSE 4: When vacancies happen in the Representation from any State, the Executive Authority thereof shall issue Writs of Election to fill such Vacancies.

[handwritten annotation: Governor is the representative of the state]

CLAUSE 5: The House of Representatives shall choose their Speaker and other Officers; and shall have the sole Power of Impeachment.

Section 3.

CLAUSE 1: The Senate of the United States shall be composed of two Senators from each State, chosen by the Legislature thereof, for six Years; and each Senator shall have one Vote.

CLAUSE 2: Immediately after they shall be assembled in Consequence of the first Election, they shall be divided as equally as may be into three Classes. The Seats of the Senators of the first Class shall be vacated at the Expiration of the second Year, of the second Class at the Expiration of the fourth Year, and of the third Class at the Expiration of the sixth Year, so that one third may be chosen every second Year; and if Vacancies happen by Resignation, or otherwise, during the Recess of the Legislature of any State, the Executive thereof may make temporary Appointments until the next Meeting of the Legislature, which shall then fill such Vacancies.

CLAUSE 3: No Person shall be a Senator who shall not have attained to the Age of thirty Years, and been nine Years a Citizen of the United States, and who shall not, when elected, be an Inhabitant of that State for which he shall be chosen.

CLAUSE 4: The Vice President of the United States shall be President of the Senate, but shall have no Vote, unless they be equally divided.

CLAUSE 5: The Senate shall choose their other Officers, and also a President pro tempore, in the Absence of the Vice President, or when he shall exercise the Office of President of the United States.

CLAUSE 6: The Senate shall have the sole Power to try all Impeachments. When sitting for that Purpose, they shall be on Oath or Affirmation. When the President of the United States is tried, the Chief Justice shall preside: And no Person shall be convicted without the Concurrence of two thirds of the Members present.

CLAUSE 7: Judgment in Cases of Impeachment shall not extend further than to removal from Office, and disqualification to hold and enjoy any Office of honor, Trust or Profit under the United States: but the Party convicted shall nevertheless be liable and subject to Indictment, Trial, Judgment and Punishment, according to Law.

Section 4.

Clause 1: The Times, Places and Manner of holding Elections for Senators and Representatives, shall be prescribed in each State by the Legislature thereof; but the Congress may at any time by Law make or alter such Regulations, except as to the Places of choosing Senators.

Clause 2: The Congress shall assemble at least once in every Year, and such Meeting shall be on the first Monday in December, unless they shall by Law appoint a different Day.

Section 5.

Clause 1: Each House shall be the Judge of the Elections, Returns and Qualifications of its own Members, and a Majority of each shall constitute a Quorum to do Business; but a smaller Number may adjourn from day to day, and may be authorized to compel the Attendance of absent Members, in such Manner, and under such Penalties as each House may provide.

Clause 2: Each House may determine the Rules of its Proceedings, punish its Members for disorderly Behaviour, and, with the Concurrence of two thirds, expel a Member.

Clause 3: Each House shall keep a Journal of its Proceedings, and from time to time publish the same, excepting such Parts as may in their Judgment require Secrecy; and the Yeas and Nays of the Members of either House on any question shall, at the Desire of one fifth of those Present, be entered on the Journal.

Clause 4: Neither House, during the Session of Congress, shall, without the Consent of the other, adjourn for more than three days, nor to any other Place than that in which the two Houses shall be sitting.

Section 6.

Clause 1: The Senators and Representatives shall receive a Compensation for their Services, to be ascertained by Law, and paid out of the Treasury of the United States. They shall in all Cases, except Treason, Felony and Breach of the Peace, be privileged from Arrest during their Attendance at the Session of their respective Houses, and in going to and returning from the same; and for any Speech or Debate in either House, they shall not be questioned in any other Place.

Clause 2: No Senator or Representative shall, during the Time for which he was elected, be appointed to any civil Office under the Authority of the United States, which shall have been created, or the Emoluments whereof shall have been encreased during such time; and no Person holding any Office under the United States, shall be a Member of either House during his Continuance in Office.

Section 7.

CLAUSE 1: All Bills for raising Revenue shall originate in the House of Representatives; but the Senate may propose or concur with Amendments as on other Bills.

CLAUSE 2: Every Bill which shall have passed the House of Representatives and the Senate, shall, before it become a Law, be presented to the President of the United States; If he approve he shall sign it, but if not he shall return it, with his Objections to that House in which it shall have originated, who shall enter the Objections at large on their Journal, and proceed to reconsider it. If after such Reconsideration two thirds of that House shall agree to pass the Bill, it shall be sent, together with the Objections, to the other House, by which it shall likewise be reconsidered, and if approved by two thirds of that House, it shall become a Law. But in all such Cases the Votes of both Houses shall be determined by yeas and Nays, and the Names of the Persons voting for and against the Bill shall be entered on the Journal of each House respectively. If any Bill shall not be returned by the President within ten Days (Sundays excepted) after it shall have been presented to him, the Same shall be a Law, in like Manner as if he had signed it, unless the Congress by their Adjournment prevent its Return, in which Case it shall not be a Law.

CLAUSE 3: Every Order, Resolution, or Vote to which the Concurrence of the Senate and House of Representatives may be necessary (except on a question of Adjournment) shall be presented to the President of the United States; and before the Same shall take Effect, shall be approved by him, or being disapproved by him, shall be repassed by two thirds of the Senate and House of Representatives, according to the Rules and Limitations prescribed in the Case of a Bill.

Section 8. Power of Congress

CLAUSE 1: The Congress shall have Power To lay and collect Taxes, Duties, Imposts and Excises, to pay the Debts and provide for the common Defence and general Welfare of the United States; but all Duties, Imposts and Excises shall be uniform throughout the United States;

CLAUSE 2: To borrow Money on the credit of the United States;

CLAUSE 3: To regulate Commerce with foreign Nations, and among the several States, and with the Indian Tribes;

CLAUSE 4: To establish an uniform Rule of Naturalization, and uniform Laws on the subject of Bankruptcies throughout the United States;

paper money is unconstitutional

CLAUSE 5: To coin Money, regulate the Value thereof, and of foreign Coin, and fix the Standard of Weights and Measures;

CLAUSE 6: To provide for the Punishment of counterfeiting the Securities and current Coin of the United States;

CLAUSE 7: To establish Post Offices and post Roads;

CLAUSE 8: To promote the Progress of Science and useful Arts, by securing for limited Times to Authors and Inventors the exclusive Right to their respective Writings and Discoveries;

CLAUSE 9: To constitute Tribunals inferior to the supreme Court;

CLAUSE 10: To define and punish Piracies and Felonies committed on the high Seas, and Offences against the Law of Nations;

CLAUSE 11: To declare War, grant Letters of Marque and Reprisal, and make Rules concerning Captures on Land and Water;

Spending

CLAUSE 12: To raise and support Armies, but no Appropriation of Money to that Use shall be for a longer Term than two Years;

CLAUSE 13: To provide and maintain a Navy; *to protect against attack*

CLAUSE 14: To make Rules for the Government and Regulation of the land and naval Forces;

CLAUSE 15: To provide for calling forth the Militia to execute the Laws of the Union, suppress Insurrections and repel Invasions; *UCMJ: Uniform code military*

CLAUSE 16: To provide for organizing, arming, and disciplining, the Militia, and for governing such Part of them as may be employed in the Service of the United States, reserving to the States respectively, the Appointment of the Officers, and the Authority of training the Militia according to the discipline prescribed by Congress;

CLAUSE 17: To exercise exclusive Legislation in all Cases whatsoever, over such District (not exceeding ten Miles square) as may, by Cession of particular States, and the Acceptance of Congress, become the Seat of the Government of the United States, and to exercise like Authority over all Places purchased by the Consent of the Legislature of the State in which the Same shall be, for the Erection of Forts, Magazines, Arsenals, dock-Yards, and other needful Buildings;—And

CLAUSE 18: To make all Laws which shall be necessary and proper for carrying into Execution the foregoing Powers, and all other Powers vested by this Constitution in the Government of the United States, or in any Department or Officer thereof.

→ Clause elastic (stretch)
→ Commerce clause
→ Necessary & proper clause (3 8 18)

3 great Freedoms: — Habeas Corpus
— No bill of Attainer
— No ex post Facto law

Section 9. *Limits of Congress*

CLAUSE 1: The Migration or Importation of such Persons as any of the States now existing shall think proper to admit, shall not be prohibited by the Congress prior to the Year one thousand eight hundred and eight, but a Tax or duty may be imposed on such Importation, not exceeding ten dollars for each Person.

CLAUSE 2: *judicial order* The Privilege of the Writ of Habeas Corpus shall not be suspended, unless when in Cases of Rebellion or Invasion the public Safety may require it.

CLAUSE 3: No Bill of Attainder or ex post facto Law shall be passed.

CLAUSE 4: No Capitation, or other direct, Tax shall be laid, unless in Proportion to the Census or Enumeration herein before directed to be taken.

CLAUSE 5: No Tax or Duty shall be laid on Articles exported from any State.

CLAUSE 6: No Preference shall be given by any Regulation of Commerce or Revenue to the Ports of one State over those of another: nor shall Vessels bound to, or from, one State, be obliged to enter, clear, or pay Duties in another.

CLAUSE 7: No Money shall be drawn from the Treasury, but in Consequence of Appropriations made by Law; and a regular Statement and Account of the Receipts and Expenditures of all public Money shall be published from time to time.

CLAUSE 8: No Title of Nobility shall be granted by the United States: And no Person holding any Office of Profit or Trust under them, shall, without the Consent of the Congress, accept of any present, Emolument, Office, or Title, of any kind whatever, from any King, Prince, or foreign State.

Section 10. *Limits the States*

CLAUSE 1: No State shall enter into any Treaty, Alliance, or Confederation; grant Letters of Marque and Reprisal; coin Money; emit Bills of Credit; make any Thing but gold and silver Coin a Tender in Payment of Debts; pass any Bill of Attainder, ex post facto Law, or Law impairing the Obligation of Contracts, or grant any Title of Nobility.

CLAUSE 2: No State shall, without the Consent of the Congress, lay any Imposts or Duties on Imports or Exports, except what may be absolutely necessary for executing it's inspection Laws: and the net Produce of all Duties and Imposts, laid by any State on Imports or Exports, shall be for the Use of the Treasury of the United States; and all such Laws shall be subject to the Revision and Controul of the Congress.

CLAUSE 3: No State shall, without the Consent of Congress, lay any Duty of Tonnage, keep Troops, or Ships of War in time of Peace, enter into any Agreement or Compact with another State, or with a foreign Power, or engage in War, unless actually invaded, or in such imminent Danger as will not admit of delay.

ARTICLE II. *President (Executive Chief)*

Section 1.

Clause 1: The executive Power shall be vested in a President of the United States of America. He shall hold his Office during the Term of four Years, and, together with the Vice President, chosen for the same Term, be elected, as follows

Clause 2: Each State shall appoint, in such Manner as the Legislature thereof may direct, a Number of Electors, equal to the whole Number of Senators and Representatives to which the State may be entitled in the Congress: but no Senator or Representative, or Person holding an Office of Trust or Profit under the United States, shall be appointed an Elector.

Clause 3: The Electors shall meet in their respective States, and vote by Ballot for two Persons, of whom one at least shall not be an Inhabitant of the same State with themselves. And they shall make a List of all the Persons voted for, and of the Number of Votes for each; which List they shall sign and certify, and transmit sealed to the Seat of the Government of the United States, directed to the President of the Senate. The President of the Senate shall, in the Presence of the Senate and House of Representatives, open all the Certificates, and the Votes shall then be counted. The Person having the greatest Number of Votes shall be the President, if such Number be a Majority of the whole Number of Electors appointed; and if there be more than one who have such Majority, and have an equal Number of Votes, then the House of Representatives shall immediately choose by Ballot one of them for President; and if no Person have a Majority, then from the five highest on the List the said House shall in like Manner choose the President. But in choosing the President, the Votes shall be taken by States, the Representation from each State having one Vote; A quorum for this Purpose shall consist of a Member or Members from two thirds of the States, and a Majority of all the States shall be necessary to a Choice. In every Case, after the Choice of the President, the Person having the greatest Number of Votes of the Electors shall be the Vice President. But if there should remain two or more who have equal Votes, the Senate shall choose from them by Ballot the Vice President.

Clause 4: The Congress may determine the Time of choosing the Electors, and the Day on which they shall give their Votes; which Day shall be the same throughout the United States.

Clause 5: No Person except a natural born Citizen, or a Citizen of the United States, at the time of the Adoption of this Constitution, shall be eligible to the Office of President; neither shall any Person be eligible to that Office who shall not have attained to the Age of thirty five Years, and been fourteen Years a Resident within the United States.

Clause 6: In Case of the Removal of the President from Office, or of his Death, Resignation, or Inability to discharge the Powers and Duties of the said Office, the Same shall devolve on the Vice President, and the Congress may by Law provide for the Case of Removal, Death, Resignation or Inability, both of the President and Vice President, declaring what Officer shall then act as President, and such Officer shall act accordingly, until the Disability be removed, or a President shall be elected.

Clause 7: The President shall, at stated Times, receive for his Services, a Compensation, which shall neither be encreased nor diminished during the Period for which he shall have been elected, and he shall not receive within that Period any other Emolument from the United States, or any of them.

Clause 8: Before he enter on the Execution of his Office, he shall take the following Oath or Affirmation:—"I do solemnly swear (or affirm) that I will faithfully execute the Office of President of the United States, and will to the best of my Ability, preserve, protect and defend the Constitution of the United States."

Section 2.

Clause 1: The President shall be Commander in Chief of the Army and Navy of the United States, and of the Militia of the several States, when called into the actual Service of the United States; he may require the Opinion, in writing, of the principal Officer in each of the executive Departments, upon any Subject relating to the Duties of their respective Offices, and he shall have Power to grant Reprieves and Pardons for Offences against the United States, except in Cases of Impeachment.

Clause 2: He shall have Power, by and with the Advice and Consent of the Senate, to make Treaties, provided two thirds of the Senators present concur; and he shall nominate, and by and with the Advice and Consent of the Senate, shall appoint Ambassadors, other public Ministers and Consuls, Judges of the supreme Court, and all other Officers of the United States, whose Appointments are not herein otherwise provided for, and which shall be established by Law: but the Congress may by Law vest the Appointment of such inferior Officers, as they think proper, in the President alone, in the Courts of Law, or in the Heads of Departments.

Clause 3: The President shall have Power to fill up all Vacancies that may happen during the Recess of the Senate, by granting Commissions which shall expire at the End of their next Session.

Section 3.

He shall from time to time give to the Congress Information of the State of the Union, and recommend to their Consideration such Measures as he shall judge necessary and expedient; he may, on extraordinary Occasions, convene both Houses, or either of them, and in Case of Disagreement between them, with Respect to the Time of Adjournment, he may adjourn them to such Time as he shall think proper; he shall receive Ambassadors and other public Ministers; he shall take Care that the Laws be faithfully executed, and shall Commission all the Officers of the United States.

Congress is Supreme branch

Section 4.

Executive Chief / enforce the law

The President, Vice President and all civil Officers of the United States, shall be removed from Office on Impeachment for, and Conviction of, Treason, Bribery, or other high Crimes and Misdemeanors.

by Congress
House of Representative can impeach · Senate can convict

ARTICLE III.

creates fed court

Section 1.

The judicial Power of the United States, shall be vested in one supreme Court, and in such inferior Courts as the Congress may from time to time ordain and establish. The Judges, both of the supreme and inferior Courts, shall hold their Offices during good Behaviour, and shall, at stated Times, receive for their Services, a Compensation, which shall not be diminished during their Continuance in Office.

Section 2.

to be a judge, nominate by President & confirm by ~~House~~ 2/3 of the Senate

CLAUSE 1: The judicial Power shall extend to all Cases, in Law and Equity, arising under this Constitution, the Laws of the United States, and Treaties made, or which shall be made, under their Authority;—to all Cases affecting Ambassadors, other public Ministers and Consuls;—to all Cases of admiralty and maritime Jurisdiction;—to Controversies to which the United States shall be a Party;—to Controversies between two or more States;—between a State and Citizens of another State;—between Citizens of different States,—between Citizens of the same State claiming Lands under Grants of different States, and between a State, or the Citizens thereof, and foreign States, Citizens or Subjects.

CLAUSE 2: In all Cases affecting Ambassadors, other public Ministers and Consuls, and those in which a State shall be Party, the supreme Court shall have original Jurisdiction. In all the other Cases before mentioned, the supreme Court shall have appellate Jurisdiction, both as to Law and Fact, with such Exceptions, and under such Regulations as the Congress shall make.

CLAUSE 3: The Trial of all Crimes, except in Cases of Impeachment, shall be by Jury; and such Trial shall be held in the State where the said Crimes shall have been committed; but when not committed within any State, the Trial shall be at such Place or Places as the Congress may by Law have directed.

Section 3.

CLAUSE 1: Treason against the United States, shall consist only in levying War against them, or in adhering to their Enemies, giving them Aid and Comfort. No Person shall be convicted of Treason unless on the Testimony of two Witnesses to the same overt Act, or on Confession in open Court.

CLAUSE 2: The Congress shall have Power to declare the Punishment of Treason, but no Attainder of Treason shall work Corruption of Blood, or Forfeiture except during the Life of the Person attainted.

ARTICLE IV. (contains full Faith & Credit)
Section 1. (most important 1) Gay Marriage is big controversy.
Full Faith and Credit shall be given in each State to the public Acts, Records, and judicial Proceedings of every other State. And the Congress may by general Laws prescribe the Manner in which such Acts, Records and Proceedings shall be proved, and the Effect thereof.

Section 2.

CLAUSE 1: The Citizens of each State shall be entitled to all Privileges and Immunities of Citizens in the several States.

CLAUSE 2: A Person charged in any State with Treason, Felony, or other Crime, who shall flee from Justice, and be found in another State, shall on Demand of the executive Authority of the State from which he fled, be delivered up, to be removed to the State having Jurisdiction of the Crime.

CLAUSE 3: No Person held to Service or Labour in one State, under the Laws thereof, escaping into another, shall, in Consequence of any Law or Regulation therein, be discharged from such Service or Labour, but shall be delivered up on Claim of the Party to whom such Service or Labour may be due.

Section 3.

CLAUSE 1: New States may be admitted by the Congress into this Union; but no new State shall be formed or erected within the Jurisdiction of any other State; nor any State be formed by the Junction of two or more States, or Parts of States, without the Consent of the Legislatures of the States concerned as well as of the Congress.

CLAUSE 2: The Congress shall have Power to dispose of and make all needful Rules and Regulations respecting the Territory or other Property belonging to the United States; and nothing in this Constitution shall be so construed as to Prejudice any Claims of the United States, or of any particular State.

Section 4.

The United States shall guarantee to every State in this Union a Republican Form of Government, and shall protect each of them against Invasion; and on Application of the Legislature, or of the Executive (when the Legislature cannot be convened) against domestic Violence.

ARTICLE V. *contain Amendment Process*

The Congress, whenever ==two thirds of both Houses sh==all deem it necessary, shall ==propose Amendments to this Constitution, or, on the Application of the Legislatures of two thirds of the several States,== shall call a Convention for proposing Amendments, which, in either Case, shall be valid to all Intents and Purposes, as Part of this Constitution, when ratified by the Legislatures of three fourths of the several States, or by Conventions in three fourths thereof, as the one or the other Mode of Ratification may be proposed by the Congress; Provided that no Amendment which may be made prior to the Year One thousand eight hundred and eight shall in any Manner affect the first and fourth Clauses in the Ninth Section of the first Article; and that no State, without its Consent, shall be deprived of its equal Suffrage in the Senate.

ARTICLE VI. *Assumption Clause*

CLAUSE 1: All Debts contracted and Engagements entered into, before the Adoption of this Constitution, shall be as valid against the United States under this Constitution, as under the Confederation.

CLAUSE 2: This Constitution, and the Laws of the United States which shall be made in Pursuance thereof; and all Treaties made, or which shall be made, under the Authority of the United States, shall be the ==supreme Law of the Land;== and the Judges in every State shall be bound thereby, any Thing in the Constitution or Laws of any State to the Contrary notwithstanding.

CLAUSE 3: The Senators and Representatives before mentioned, and the Members of the several State Legislatures, and all executive and judicial Officers, both of the United States and of the several States, shall be bound by Oath or Affirmation, to support this Constitution; but no religious Test shall ever be required as a Qualification to any Office or public Trust under the United States.

ARTICLE VII. *moot*

The ==Ratification of the Conventions of nine States,== shall be sufficient for the Establishment of this Constitution between the States so ratifying the Same.

AMENDMENTS TO THE CONSTITUTION

CONSTITUTION OF THE UNITED STATES ARTICLES IN ADDITION TO, AND AMENDMENT OF, THE CONSTITUTION OF THE UNITED STATES OF AMERICA, PROPOSED BY CONGRESS, AND RATIFIED BY THE LEGISLATURES OF THE SEVERAL STATES, PURSUANT TO THE FIFTH ARTICLE OF THE ORIGINAL CONSTITUTION

AMENDMENT I. (1791)

Congress shall make no law respecting an establishment of religion, or prohibiting the free exercise thereof; or abridging the freedom of speech, or of the press; or the right of the people peaceably to assemble, and to petition the Government for a redress of grievances.

AMENDMENT II. (1791)

A well regulated Militia, being necessary to the security of a free State, the right of the people to keep and bear Arms, shall not be infringed.

AMENDMENT III. (1791)

No Soldier shall, in time of peace be quartered in any house, without the consent of the Owner, nor in time of war, but in a manner to be prescribed by law.

AMENDMENT IV. (1791)

The right of the people to be secure in their persons, houses, papers, and effects, against unreasonable searches and seizures, shall not be violated, and no Warrants shall issue, but upon probable cause, supported by Oath or affirmation, and particularly describing the place to be searched, and the persons or things to be seized.

AMENDMENT V. (1791)

No person shall be held to answer for a capital, or otherwise infamous crime, unless on a presentment or indictment of a Grand Jury, except in cases arising in the land or naval forces, or in the Militia, when in actual service in time of War or public danger; nor shall any person be subject for the same offence to be twice put in jeopardy of life or limb; nor shall be compelled in any criminal case to be a witness against himself, nor be deprived of life, liberty, or property, without due process of law; nor shall private property be taken for public use, without just compensation.

AMENDMENT VI. (1791) Right to cancel

In all criminal prosecutions, the accused shall enjoy the right to a speedy and public trial, by an impartial jury of the State and district wherein the crime shall have been committed, which district shall have been previously ascertained by law, and to be informed of the nature and cause of the accusation; to be confronted with the witnesses against him; to have compulsory process for obtaining witnesses in his favor, and to have the Assistance of Counsel for his defence.

AMENDMENT VII. (1791)

In Suits at common law, where the value in controversy shall exceed twenty dollars, the right of trial by jury shall be preserved, and no fact tried by a jury, shall be otherwise re-examined in any Court of the United States, than according to the rules of the common law.

AMENDMENT VIII. (1791) Only play by fed, death penalty punishment

Excessive bail shall not be required, nor excessive fines imposed, nor cruel and unusual punishments inflicted. Cruel and unusual unConstitutional (if one is not applied) constitutional

AMENDMENT IX. (1791) Madison issurance policy

The enumeration in the Constitution, of certain rights, shall not be construed to deny or disparage others retained by the people. right of privacy

AMENDMENT X. (1791) State's Rights Amendment

The powers not delegated to the United States by the Constitution, nor prohibited by it to the States, are reserved to the States respectively, or to the people.

AMENDMENT XI. (1798)

The Judicial power of the United States shall not be construed to extend to any suit in law or equity, commenced or prosecuted against one of the United States by Citizens of another State, or by Citizens or Subjects of any Foreign State.

AMENDMENT XII. (1804) Sburr & Kill

The Electors shall meet in their respective states, and vote by ballot for President and Vice-President, one of whom, at least, shall not be an inhabitant of the same state with themselves; they shall name in their ballots the person voted for as President, and in distinct ballots the person voted for as Vice-President, and they shall make distinct lists of all persons voted for as President, and of all persons voted for as Vice-President, and of the number of votes for each, which lists they shall sign and certify, and transmit sealed to the seat of the government of the United States, directed to the President of the Senate;—The President of the Senate shall, in the presence of the Senate and House of Representatives, open all the certificates and the votes shall then be counted;—The person having the greatest number of votes for President, shall be the President, if such number be a majority of the whole number of Electors appointed; and if no person have such majority, then from the persons having the highest numbers not exceeding three on the list of those voted for as President, the House of Representatives shall choose immediately, by ballot, the President. But in choosing the President, the votes shall be taken by states, the representation from each state having one vote; a quorum for this purpose shall consist of a member or members from two-thirds of the states, and a majority of all the states shall be necessary to a choice. And if the House of Representatives shall not choose a President whenever the right of choice shall devolve upon them, before the fourth day of March next following, then the Vice-President shall act as President, as in the case of the death or other constitutional disability of the President.—The person having the greatest number of votes as Vice-President, shall be the Vice-President, if such number be a majority of the whole number of Electors appointed, and if no person have a majority, then from the two highest numbers on the list, the Senate shall choose the Vice-President; a quorum for the purpose shall consist of two-thirds of the whole number of Senators, and a majority of the whole number shall be necessary to a choice. But no person constitutionally ineligible to the office of President shall be eligible to that of Vice-President of the United States.

AMENDMENT XIII. (1865)

Section 1.

Neither slavery nor involuntary servitude, except as a punishment for crime whereof the party shall have been duly convicted, shall exist within the United States, or any place subject to their jurisdiction.

Section 2.

Congress shall have power to enforce this article by appropriate legislation.

AMENDMENT XIV. (1868)

Section 1.

All persons born or naturalized in the United States, and subject to the jurisdiction thereof, are citizens of the United States and of the State wherein they reside. No State

> *First due process is in Amendment 5, but int only applies to fed government*

shall make or enforce any law which shall abridge the privileges or immunities of citizens of the United States; nor shall any State deprive any person of life, liberty, or property, without ==due process of law;== nor deny to any person within its jurisdiction the ==equal protection of the laws.==

apply to 50 states

Section 2.

Representatives shall be apportioned among the several States according to their respective numbers, counting the whole number of persons in each State, excluding Indians not taxed. But when the right to vote at any election for the choice of electors for President and Vice President of the United States, Representatives in Congress, the Executive and Judicial officers of a State, or the members of the Legislature thereof, is denied to any of the male inhabitants of such State, being twenty-one years of age, and citizens of the United States, or in any way abridged, except for participation in rebellion, or other crime, the basis of representation therein shall be reduced in the proportion which the number of such male citizens shall bear to the whole number of male citizens twenty-one years of age in such State.

Section 3.

No person shall be a Senator or Representative in Congress, or elector of President and Vice President, or hold any office, civil or military, under the United States, or under any State, who, having previously taken an oath, as a member of Congress, or as an officer of the United States, or as a member of any State legislature, or as an executive or judicial officer of any State, to support the Constitution of the United States, shall have engaged in insurrection or rebellion against the same, or given aid or comfort to the enemies thereof. But Congress may by a vote of two-thirds of each House, remove such disability.

Section 4.

The validity of the public debt of the United States, authorized by law, including debts incurred for payment of pensions and bounties for services in suppressing insurrection or rebellion, shall not be questioned. But neither the United States nor any State shall assume or pay any debt or obligation incurred in aid of insurrection or rebellion against the United States, or any claim for the loss or emancipation of any slave; but all such debts, obligations and claims shall be held illegal and void.

Section 5.

The Congress shall have power to enforce, by appropriate legislation, the provisions of this article.

AMENDMENT XV. (1870)

Section 1.

The right of citizens of the United States to vote shall not be denied or abridged by the United States or by any State on account of race, color, or previous condition of servitude.

can't be denied base on these ground, but can be base on others

Section 2.

The Congress shall have power to enforce this article by appropriate legislation.

AMENDMENT XVI. (1913) *Add other power of Congress (Article 8)*

The Congress shall have power to lay and collect taxes on incomes, from whatever source derived, without apportionment among the several States, and without regard to any census or enumeration. *income tax amendment*

AMENDMENT XVII. (1913) *One has be able to vote for state senate can vote for fed senate (I don't c it → none of above*

The Senate of the United States shall be composed of two Senators from each State, elected by the people thereof, for six years; and each Senator shall have one vote. The electors in each State shall have the qualifications requisite for electors of the most numerous branch of the State legislatures.

When vacancies happen in the representation of any State in the Senate, the executive authority of such State shall issue writs of election to fill such vacancies: Provided, That the legislature of any State may empower the executive thereof to make temporary appointments until the people fill the vacancies by election as the legislature may direct. This amendment shall not be so construed as to affect the election or term of any Senator chosen before it becomes valid as part of the Constitution.

AMENDMENT XVIII. (1919)

Section 1. *Prohibit of alcohol in America*

After one year from the ratification of this article the manufacture, sale, or transportation of intoxicating liquors within, the importation thereof into, or the exportation thereof from the United States and all territory subject to the jurisdiction thereof for beverage purposes is hereby prohibited.

Section 2.

The Congress and the several States shall have concurrent power to enforce this article by appropriate legislation.

Section 3.

This article shall be inoperative unless it shall have been ratified as an amendment to the Constitution by the legislatures of the several States, as provided in the Constitution, within seven years from the date of the submission hereof to the States by the Congress.

AMENDMENT XIX. (1920)

The right of citizens of the United States to vote shall not be denied or abridged by the United States or by any State on account of sex.

Congress shall have power to enforce this article by appropriate legislation.

AMENDMENT XX. (1933)

Section 1.

The terms of the President and Vice President shall end at noon on the 20th day of January, and the terms of Senators and Representatives at noon on the 3d day of January, of the years in which such terms would have ended if this article had not been ratified; and the terms of their successors shall then begin.

Section 2.

The Congress shall assemble at least once in every year, and such meeting shall begin at noon on the 3d day of January, unless they shall by law appoint a different day.

Section 3.

If, at the time fixed for the beginning of the term of the President, the President elect shall have died, the Vice President elect shall become President. If a President shall not have been chosen before the time fixed for the beginning of his term, or if the President elect shall have failed to qualify, then the Vice President elect shall act as President until a President shall have qualified; and the Congress may by law provide for the case wherein neither a President elect nor a Vice President elect shall have qualified, declaring who shall then act as President, or the manner in which one who is to act shall be selected, and such person shall act accordingly until a President or Vice President shall have qualified.

Section 4.

The Congress may by law provide for the case of the death of any of the persons from whom the House of Representatives may choose a President whenever the right of choice shall have devolved upon them, and for the case of the death of any of the persons from whom the Senate may choose a Vice President whenever the right of choice shall have devolved upon them.

Section 5.

Sections 1 and 2 shall take effect on the 15th day of October following the ratification of this article.

Section 6.

This article shall be inoperative unless it shall have been ratified as an amendment to the Constitution by the legislatures of three-fourths of the several States within seven years from the date of its submission.

AMENDMENT XXI. (1933)

Section 1.

The eighteenth article of amendment to the Constitution of the United States is hereby repealed.

Section 2.

The transportation or importation into any State, Territory, or possession of the United States for delivery or use therein of intoxicating liquors, in violation of the laws thereof, is hereby prohibited.

Section 3.

This article shall be inoperative unless it shall have been ratified as an amendment to the Constitution by conventions in the several States, as provided in the Constitution, within seven years from the date of the submission hereof to the States by the Congress.

AMENDMENT XXII. (1951) *2 terms*

Section 1.

No person shall be elected to the office of the President more than twice, and no person who has held the office of President, or acted as President, for more than two years of a term to which some other person was elected President shall be elected to the office of the President more than once. But this Article shall not apply to any person holding the office of President when this Article was proposed by the Congress, and shall not prevent any person who may be holding the office of President, or acting as President, during the term within which this Article becomes operative from holding the office of President or acting as President during the remainder of such term.

Section 2.

This article shall be inoperative unless it shall have been ratified as an amendment to the Constitution by the legislatures of three-fourths of the several States within seven years from the date of its submission to the States by the Congress.

AMENDMENT XXIII. (1961)

[handwritten: allow ppl in D.C / 3 electial for DC]

Section 1.

The District constituting the seat of Government of the United States shall appoint in such manner as the Congress may direct:

A number of electors of President and Vice President equal to the whole number of Senators and Representatives in Congress to which the District would be entitled if it were a State, but in no event more than the least populous State; they shall be in addition to those appointed by the States, but they shall be considered, for the purposes of the election of President and Vice President, to be electors appointed by a State; and they shall meet in the District and perform such duties as provided by the twelfth article of amendment.

Section 2.

The Congress shall have power to enforce this article by appropriate legislation.

AMENDMENT XXIV. (1964)

[handwritten: No longer have to pay for vote]

Section 1.

The right of citizens of the United States to vote in any primary or other election for President or Vice President, for electors for President or Vice President, or for Senator or Representative in Congress, shall not be denied or abridged by the United States or any State by reason of failure to pay any poll tax or other tax.

Section 2.

The Congress shall have power to enforce this article by appropriate legislation.

AMENDMENT XXV. (1967)

Section 1.

In case of the removal of the President from office or of his death or resignation, the Vice President shall become President.

Section 2.

Whenever there is a vacancy in the office of the Vice President, the President shall nominate a Vice President who shall take office upon confirmation by a majority vote of both Houses of Congress.

Section 3.

Whenever the President transmits to the President pro tempore of the Senate and the Speaker of the House of Representatives his written declaration that he is unable to discharge the powers and duties of his office, and until he transmits to them a written declaration to the contrary, such powers and duties shall be discharged by the Vice President as Acting President.

Section 4.

Whenever the Vice President and a majority of either the principal officers of the executive departments or of such other body as Congress may by law provide, transmit to the President pro tempore of the Senate and the Speaker of the House of Representatives their written declaration that the President is unable to discharge the powers and duties of his office, the Vice President shall immediately assume the powers and duties of the office as Acting President.

Thereafter, when the President transmits to the President pro tempore of the Senate and the Speaker of the House of Representatives his written declaration that no inability exists, he shall resume the powers and duties of his office unless the Vice President and a majority of either the principal officers of the executive department or of such other body as Congress may by law provide, transmit within four days to the President pro tempore of the Senate and the Speaker of the House of Representatives their written declaration that the President is unable to discharge the powers and duties of his office. Thereupon Congress shall decide the issue, assembling within forty-eight hours for that purpose if not in session. If the Congress, within twenty-one days after receipt of the latter written declaration, or, if Congress is not in session, within twenty-one days after Congress is required to assemble, determines by two-thirds vote of both Houses that the President is unable to discharge the powers and duties of his office, the Vice President shall continue to discharge the same as Acting President; otherwise, the President shall resume the powers and duties of his office.

AMENDMENT XXVI. (1971)

Section 1.
The right of citizens of the United States, who are eighteen years of age or older, to vote shall not be denied or abridged by the United States or by any State on account of age.

Section 2.
The Congress shall have power to enforce this article by appropriate legislation.

AMENDMENT XXVII. (1992)

No law, varying the compensation for the services of the Senators and Representatives, shall take effect, until an election of Representatives shall have intervened.

Glossary

Glossary

527 527s are political organizations that can bypass the campaign finance regulations because they are not officially tied to any candidate. They get their name from the section of the IRS tax code (Section 527) that maintains their tax-exempt status.

Al-Qaeda Islamic terrorist organization. It literally means the "the Base."

Amendment A change in the Constitution. Currently there are 27 amendments to the Constitution.

Appellate Court A court that hears appeals from losers of a trial court.

Articles of Confederation The first American constitution. The present Constitution replaced it after the Revolution.

Bill of Attainder A legislative punishment. Congress and the states are forbidden to issue Bills of Attainder by the Constitution.

Bill of Rights The first 10 Amendments to the Constitution.

Bond Market The buyers and sellers of US treasury bonds.

Bully Pulpit Refers to one of the political powers of the presidency. The President can influence public policy by his ability to generate media attention through focusing on a particular issue, like, health care reform.

Bump and Run Reporting The tactic of the media where they avoid serious reporting of political wrong doing by lightly reporting incriminating facts and then moving on to less serious issues.

Bureaucracy Government institutions that enforce the law. Examples include the Internal Revenue Service, The State Department, The Post Office, The Environmental Protection Agency.

Capital Gains Income generated through the sell of stocks, bonds, and real estate.

Chief Executive The President of the United States.

Central Intelligence Agency (CIA) The chief spies of the US government. The CIA conducts secret (covert) activities on behalf of the US government. Among experts it is referred to as the "agency."

Cold War The conflict between the United States and the former Soviet Union begun after WWII and ending with the fall of the Soviet Union.

Communism Comes from the idea that people should hold material things in common and not privately. Usually refers to some form of Marxism, or Leninism, although there are many other types of communism.

Conference Committee A committee involved in the legislative process of Congress. The Conference Committee reconciles different versions of the same bill.

Congress The Article I branch of the Constitution. Congress enacts the federal statutes (laws) of the federal government.

Congressional Committees A smaller group of representatives in Congress who meet to consider specific bills that fall under its jurisdiction. All members of Congress belong to different committees that initiate legislation.

Connecticut Compromise The compromise that created the two houses of Congress—The House of Representatives and the Senate.

Conservative Most commonly understood as a member of the Republican Party. Conservatives tend to support corporate capitalism and a strong military establishment. Philosophically, it applies to any person who wants to conserve past traditions.

Constitution The Supreme Law of the United States.

Consumer Price Index (CPI) The tracking of the cost of goods through a specific amount of time.

Declaration of Independence The document that the founding generation sent to Great Britain to formally inform the King and Parliament that the 13 colonies consider themselves free and independent countries. It officially started the Revolutionary War.

Delegate A type of representation where the "delegate" does what those who voted for them tell them to do.

Democracy A form of government that has at its core the idea that the majority of average people should govern. Comes from the Greek word for rule of the many poor.

District Courts The United States trial courts. The first stage of the judicial process in the federal court system.

Domino Theory (a.k.a Containment Doctrine) The idea that dominated US foreign policy during the Cold War. It argued that if one country falls to communism then another will fall then another, like a bunch of dominos. This idea led to the Korean War and the Vietnam War.

Economy The activity of society that produces goods and consumes goods.

Electoral College The mechanism that elects the President. Created in Article II of the Constitution.

Environmental Protection Agency (EPA) A federal bureaucracy that enforces the environmental laws enacted by Congress.

Ex Post Facto A law that criminalizes an act after it was performed. Ex post facto laws are prohibited by the Constitution.

Federal Circuit Courts US courts of appeal.

Federal Judge An individual who has been nominated by the President and confirmed by the Senate to serve as a judge in a federal court.

Federal Judiciary The US Court system.

Federal Reserve Board Seven individuals appointed to oversee America's monetary policy.

Federal Statute A law enacted by Congress.

Federalism The idea that the United States has 51 different governments—the 50 states and the federal government.

Fiscal Debt The total amount that the US government owes its creditors. The sum of all previous deficits.

Fiscal Deficit The amount the US government has spent beyond its revenues for that fiscal year alone.

Fiscal Policy The US government's tax and spend policy, spelled out in the government's budget.

Flat Tax A tax code that taxes all incomes at the same rate or percentage.

Federal Open Market Committee (FOMC) A hybrid committee of the Federal Reserve System that influences interest rates by buying and selling treasury bonds.

Foreign Policy The US government's activities and goals that deal with matters outside the domestic borders of the United States.

Founders The generation that declared independence from Great Britain, fought the Revolutionary War, and created the Constitution.

Free Trade An economic policy that removes all tariffs (taxes) on imports and exports, as well as, eliminating all non-tariff trade barriers.

Full Committee A standing committee in Congress.

General Agreement on Tariffs and Trade (GATT) An international treaty that controls America's trade policy with other countries.

Geopolitics A concept in political science that refers to how a country's location greatly affects its political situation.

GOP (Grand Old Party) Another name for the Republican Party.

Great Depression The economic collapse that began in 1929 and ended with the onset of WWII.

Green Party A progressive/liberal political party.

House of Representatives One of the two law-making institutions that make up Congress.

Inflation An economic situation where there is too much money trying to buy too few goods.

Interest Rates The price of money one pays when borrowing money from a creditor.

Iron Triangle A concept that refers to the detrimental relationship between a committee of Congress, a federal bureaucracy, and a private industry. Each of these entities constitutes a corner of the triangle.

Joint Committee A committee that has members from both houses of Congress.

Judicial Review What the Supreme Court does in the American political system. It refers to the Court's authority to hear a case and determine if any law violates the Constitution.

Korean War A conflict between the United States and North Korea and the Chinese. America's first non-declared war of the 20th Century.

Legislation A statute (law) written by Congress or a State Legislature.

Legislator A member of Congress or a state legislature. Literally means a "lawmaker."

Levelers The term applied to Americans who wanted more equal distribution of wealth in the United States right after the Revolution. It was the wealthy American's fear of these "levelers" that led to the suppression of Shay's Rebellion and the creation of the Constitution.

Liberal Usually applied to a member of the Democratic Party. Liberals tend to support social welfare and a less militaristic foreign policy. Philosophically it refers to any one who believes every individual should be free from institutional authority, particularly in the guise of church or state.

Majority Leader One of the leaders of the majority party in both houses of Congress.

Majority Whip A leadership position in both Houses of Congress.

Marbury v. Madison The case that created the Supreme Court's power of Judicial Review.

Means Testing The idea that government benefits like welfare, Medicare, and Social Security, should only go to those who actually need them and not to everyone as is presently the case.

Media Those institutions that present information to the public. Examples are TV, Radio, Newspapers, and the Internet.

Military-Industrial Complex A term coined by President Eisenhower. It refers to the dangerous situation when corporations make most, if not all, of their profits because of America's foreign policy.

Minority Leader A leadership position in both houses of Congress that is given to a member of the political party not holding the majority in that chamber of Congress.

Minority Whip A leadership position in both houses of Congress. It is the second highest position for a member of the minority party.

Monarchy A form of government where absolute power resides in a King or Queen who inherits their authority from their parents.

Monetary Policy One of the three areas that make up economic policy. Monetary policy deals with the amount of liquidity (money) circulating in the economy in relation to the amount of goods (commodities) available in the economy.

Mujahideen Arabic for "Soldier of God"; the phrase was coined by the CIA to motivate the Islamic resistance to the Soviet Union's occupation of Afghanistan in the 1980s.

Multinational Corporations (MNCs) Any business enterprise that has subsidiaries in more than one country. Also known as transnational corporations.

NAFTA (North American Free Trade Agreement) A treaty that promotes free trade between the United States, Canada, and Mexico.

National Security Counsel (NSC) The primary bureaucracy in forming America's foreign policy. Congress created it when it enacted the "National Security Act" of 1947.

Natural Rights The political theory that individuals have rights that predate the establishment of any government and, hence, all governments are only legitimate when they protect an individual's natural rights. The idea is most closely associated with the political philosopher, John Locke, and served as the theoretical basis of the American Revolution.

New Deal The term President Franklin D. Roosevelt used to describe his domestic programs to counter the Great Depression. Also known as the "alphabet soup" programs.

Non-tariff Trade Barriers Any regulation that does not employ a tax to prevent a good from being imported or exported.

OPEC (Oil Producing Exporting Countries) An international governmental organization whose members are some of the most oil-rich countries in the world.

Pentagon The building where the Department of Defense is located. Also used to refer to the US military high command.

Political Ideology A set of political beliefs that explains the political world, evaluates it, orientates individuals on how to see themselves politically, and provides a specific governmental program to realize its goals.

Political Party Any organization that is fundamentally about winning elections.

Political Spectrum A diagram that places political parties and ideologies in relationship to other parties and ideologies. Think of it as a political map that locates a person based on their political beliefs.

Popular Opinion The political opinion of the general public not to be confused with public opinion.

Presidential Caucus A process employed by some states so political parties can nominate candidates for the presidential election.

Presidential Primary A process employed by some states so political parties can nominate candidates for the presidential election. A slightly more democratic process than caucuses.

Progressive Tax A tax code that increases the percentage of income taxed as an individual income increases—the more one makes the higher the percentage one pays.

Project for a New American Century (PNAC) A group of politically powerful neo-conservatives who issue policy statements regarding America's foreign policy. The PNAC ideas were the essence of President George W. Bush's foreign policy.

Propaganda Any form of political information intended to promote a specific agenda.

Proportional Representation A system of representation where the representative seats are allotted based on how many votes a specific political party received. This system is used in the vast majority of democracies in the world; however, the United States does not, and instead uses a single-member district plan.

Protectionism Any trade policy geared to protecting a country's manufacturing base and domestic wages.

Public Opinion The opinion of experts about what is best for the "people"; not to be confused with popular opinion.

Pundit Any individual whose political opinions are promulgated by the media. Not necessarily an expert, but rather someone who gets his or her opinions amplified by a media source.

Recession An economic situation where there is too few dollars trying to buy too many goods.

Reform Party A political party that resides somewhere between the Democratic and Republican Parties. Its founder was Ross Perot.

Regressive Tax A tax code that increase the percentage of income taxed the less income an individual has—the less you have the higher the tax rate.

Republicanism A form of government based on the principles of constitutionalism, representation, rule of law, balance between economic classes, and separation of powers.

Roe v. Wade A Supreme Court case that ruled women have a constitutional right to abortion in the first trimester of pregnancy.

Running to Authority Reporting A media tactic that protects those in power by asking those accused of wrongdoing if the claims against them are true.

Securities A title to debt. Holders of US Securities are the people, entities, or countries that the federal debt (plus interest) is owed to.

Select Committee A congressional committee that serves for a specific time frame and concerns itself with a specific issue. Unlike other congressional committees, Select Committees have no legislative powers.

Senate One of the two houses of Congress.

Shadow Government A term political scientists apply to the massive number of non-elected staff members in Congress.

Shays' Rebellion A rebellion of farmers (debtors) led by a Revolutionary War veteran, Daniel Shays, against banks (creditors) that prompted the well-off to call for the constitutional convention.

Single Member District A system of representation where only one individual represents a specific region (district) as long as that representative received more votes than any other candidate in that district. One does not need to receive a majority of votes in a single-member representative scheme, just more than any other candidate.

Social Contract Theory of Government A theory of government that stipulates that all governments and their authority come from a constitution (contract) that the people have consented to.

Socialism A political philosophy that believes people should have some semblance of equality of property so that people can share in human happiness.

Speaker of the House An office created by the Constitution. The Speaker is the most powerful member of the House of Representative. The majority party elects the Speaker of the House.

Straw Poll A non-scientific political poll. They were invented as a way to sell magazines.

Supreme Court Created by the Constitution. It is the most powerful court in the United States.

Taliban Afghanistan insurgents who US troops are fighting presently. They are devout Muslims and are ethnically Pashtun. Taliban is Pashtun for "religious students."

Tariffs Taxes imposed on imports or exports.

The Federalist Papers A series of newspaper articles written primarily by James Madison and Alexander Hamilton urging the state of New York to ratify the Constitution. Today, they are seen as the best analysis of the purpose and theory behind the Constitution.

Trade Deficit The difference between what a country sells (exports) and what a country buys (imports). A trade deficit occurs when a country spends more money on imports than it makes selling exports.

Trade Policy The regulation of imports and exports.

Treasury Bonds The securities or notes that an individual, entity, or country receives as proof that it has lent the United States government money to help it finance its debt. Treasury bonds are redeemable with interests.

United Nations An international governmental agency created at the end of WWII to help resolve international disputes. Its primary institutions are the General Assembly, The Security Council, and the International Court of Justice.

US Constitution Party A very conservative American political party.

Veto The president's authority to stop legislation written and approved by Congress. All vetoes are subject to congressional override.

Veto Override When Congress nullifies a presidential veto by passing the legislation with at least two-thirds of the members of both houses of Congress after the president has vetoed that bill.

Vietnam War The war between the United States and the North Vietnamese and the Viet Cong in Southeast Asia from 1956-1973.

War on Terrorism The term coined by President George W. Bush's administration to cover all of its military engagements, especially those in Iraq and Afghanistan.

White House Office Any president's closest advisors. The White House Office includes the Chief of Staff, the Press Secretary, Council of Economic Advisors, The White House Counsel, and many other experts that serve at the pleasure of the president.

World Trade Organization (WTO) The international governmental agency that regulates the dictates of GATT and ensures compliance from all member countries.

Index

Index

527s, use in campaign financing, 233

A

ABC News, 138

Abortion, 92–93

Absolute power, 7

Academics, foreign policy and, 138–143

Acheson, Dean, 139

ACLU, 55

Adams, John, 3, 17, 50, 172, 200, 252

Adams, John Quincy, 41

Adams, Sam, 17

Ad Hominem attack, 238–239

Afghanistan, 54, 65, 79, 130, 135, 138

African-Americans, 20–21, 40, 79, 87, 214, 219, 230

Agent Orange, 148

Albania, 153

Albright, David, 81

"Alphabet soup" programs, 212

Al-Qaeda, 154, 155–159

Amendments to Constitution, 14, 294–303
    1st, 28, 78
    2nd, 28
    3rd, 28
    4th, 28
    5th, 24, 26, 28
    6th, 28
    7th, 28
    8th, 28
    9th, 28
    10th, 28
    12th, 28
    13th, 28
    14th, 28, 219
    15th, 28
    16th, 68, 112
    17th, 28, 170
    18th, 28–29
    19th, 29
    21st, 28, 29
    26th, 29

American Association of University Women, 93–94

American Constitutional Interpretation, 216

American Enterprise Institute, 237

American Government, 178

American Revolution, 15, 229–230, 252

American Socialist Party, 67

America: What Went Wrong?, 231

America: Who Really Pays the Taxes?, 115, 240

Amicus curiae, 222

Appellate court, 213

Appomattox Court House, 131
Arbuthnot, John, 49
Aristotle, 4, 37, 234, 235, 247
Armed Forces, 132
Articles of Confederation, 14–17, 170, 265–271
Associated Press, 144
Atmar, Hanif, 158
Attorney General, 205
Ayers, Richard, 240

B

Baer, Robert, 81
Baghdad, 136
Bait and switch tactic, 242
Baker, James, III, 135
Balkans, 149
Barry, Dave, 86–87
Bay of Pigs, 146–147
Bearden, Milt, 81
Bebel, August, 49
Bechtel Corporation, 144
Beeman, William O., 155
Best Democracy Money Can Buy (Palast), 78
Bible, the, 13, 218
Bill of attainder, 23–24
Bill of Rights, 21–22, 27–28
Bismarck, Otto von, 167
Blair, Tony, 84, 156

Bosnia, 149, 153
Brady, John, 82
Brandeis, Louis D., 77
Bremer, Paul, 145
Britain, 149
Broder, David, 53, 117
Brokaw, Tom, 188
Brown & Root, 144
Brown University, 155
Brown v. Board of Education of Topeka (Brown I), 214, 216
Brown v. Board of Education of Topeka (Brown II), 216
Brzezinski, Zbigniew, 139–140
Buchanan, Patrick, 7, 71, 121
Bully pulpit, 195–196
"Bump and run" reporting, 83, 85
Bureaucracy, 119, 201–206
Bureau of the Budget, 204
Burger, Warren, 223
Burr, Aaron, 28
Bush Administration, 44, 116, 157
Bush family, 7
Bush, George H.W., 43, 149, 191–192
Bush, George W., 54, 55, 56, 78, 154, 191–192, 199
Bush, Jeb, 79, 141

C

Cabinet, 204–205
Calhoun, John C., 221

Campaign financing, 64–65, 232–234

Capital gains, 107

Capitalism, 60

Capitalists, 59

Carlucci, Frank, 135

Carlyle Group, 135

Cato Institute, 237

Caucus, 197

CBS Network, 79, 80, 138

Central American Free Trade Agreement (CAFTA), 16

Central Intelligence Agency (CIA), 55, 81, 146, 149, 154, 205

Chairman of the Joint Chiefs of Staff, 133

Chamberlain, Colonel, 7–8

Cheney, Dick, 79, 82, 141, 143–144

Chief Diplomat (president), 192

Chief Executive (president), 185, 191–192

Chief of Staff, 204

China, 123–124

"Christian Communists," 72

Citizenship, responsible, 5

Civil law, 213

Civil War, 7, 27, 51, 131, 173

Civil War Amendments (to Constitution), 28

Clay, Henry, 41

Clean Air Act, 240

Clean Air Act Coalition, 240

Clinton Administration, 149, 155

Clinton, Bill, 44, 53, 56, 65, 73–74, 103, 152, 185, 191–192

Clinton family, 7

Clinton, Hillary, 55, 86, 87–88

CNN, 56, 122, 137, 138

CNN/Opinion Research Group poll, 39

Cold War, 98, 131, 133, 134

Columbia University, 235

Commander-in-Chief (president), 192

Commercial banks and credit unions, 104

Common Cause, 180

Common Sense (Paine), 69

Communism, 139

Conference committees, congressional, 173

Congress, 15, 136, 167–182

Congressional Budget Office, 176

Congressional committees, 172–173, 195

Connecticut Compromise, 20, 170

Conservatism, 59–60

Conservative, 49, 58, 73

Constitutional Congress, 167–171

Constitutional Convention, 170

Constitutional Law: Cases in Context, 215–216

Constitution party, 68, 71–72

Constitution, U.S., 5, 13–14, 17–30, 283–303

Consumer Price Index (CPI), 120

Containment doctrine (domino theory), 139

Continental Congress, 14

Contras, 133

Contreras, Alan, 239

Cost of living adjustment (COLA), 108

Council of Economic Advisors, 204

Court of Military Appeals, 224

Courts of appellate jurisdiction, 214

Courts of equity, 213

Courts of law, 213

Criminal law, 213

Croatia, 152–153

Crossley, Archibald, 41

Cuba, 137, 146–147

D

"Dan Rather Syndrome," 138

Darman, Richard, 135

Davis, Martin S., 121

Dean, John, 82

Declaration of Independence, 13, 17, 29, 69, 147, 230, 253, 261–264

De facto monarchy, 233

DeFazio, Peter, 116, 125

Defense, collective, 60

Delegates, 196, 197

Democracy, 3–4

Democracy's Discontent, 245

Democratic Party, 49–66

Democratic-Republican Party, 50, 51, 72–74

Democrats, 50, 62

Departments of State, 205

Deregulation, 15

Desert Fox, 149

Desert Storm, 137

Dewey, Thomas, 42

Dickinson, John, 18

Director of National Intelligence, 133

Discount Rate, 110

District courts, 211, 223

Diversity, 61, 62

"Divine Rights of Kings" (Locke), 25

Dobbs, Lou, 56, 122

Domestic policy, presidential role in, 194–195

Dow Chemical Company, 121

Dred Scott v. Sanford, 216

Drew, Elizabeth, 152

"Due process" of law, 24

"Dumbing down" (of political thought), 45, 86

Dutch East India Trading Company, 143

E

Economic inequality, 245, 246–249

Economic policy, 103–125

Economy, American, 15

Eddington, Patrick, 82

Education, public, 245–246, 253–256

Eisenhower, Dwight D., 37, 134, 135, 136, 189

Elections, 196–197

Elections, and public opinion, 39–41

Electoral College, 28, 185, 198–201

Electoral system, 62–63

Energy-industrial complex, 144

Enlightenment philosophy, 22–23, 168

Environmental Protection Agency (EPA), 202, 205

E pluribus unum, 13

Equity courts, 213

Ethics, public virtue, 245, 249–253

Executive branch of government, 24, 168

Explaining America: The Federalist, 250–251

Exporting America: Why Corporate Greed is Shipping American Jobs Overseas (Dobbs), 122–123

Ex post facto laws, 23–24

F

Fallacy of composition, 239

Fallacy of division, 239

Fallon, Richard, 190

Family values, 60

Federal and state law, 213

Federal circuit courts, 223–224

Federal Communications Commission (FCC), 205

Federal Court System, 223–224

Federal funds rate, 110

Federalism, 23, 27

Federalist No. 10, 272–278

Federalist No. 51, 279–282

Federalist Papers, 210

Federalist Party, 50, 172

Federalists, 217

Federal Judiciary, 209–225

Federal Open Market Committee (FOMC), 104

Federal Reserve Act of 1913, 104

Federal Reserve Banks, 104

Federal Reserve Board (The "Fed"), 104, 206

Federal Reserve System, 6, 104, 105–107, 109–110

Federal statutes, 176

Fey, Tina, 90

Financial bailout, 57

Financing, campaign, 64–65

Fiscal policy, 111–118

Fitsimmons, Ron, 93

Flat tax, 112

Ford, Henry, 103, 105

Foreign policy, 45, 129–159

Foreign policy, presidential role in, 193–194

Founders, *Articles of Confederation*, 16

Fox News, 138

France, 149

Franklin, Benjamin, 18, 195, 249

Freeman, Chris, 82

Free trade, 16, 54, 57, 68, 121–125

Free trade versus protectionism debate, 240

Full committees, congressional, 173

Fuller, Graham, 82

G

Galloucis, Michael, 158

Gallup, George, 41

Garfield, James A., 203

Garfield, Richard, 149

Garner, Jay M., 145

Geopolitics, 139

General Agreement on Tariffs and Trade (GATT), 119, 120, 146

Gerstacker, Carl A., 121

Gettysburg, 7

Geyer, Georgie Anne, 145

Glass, Carter, 104

Global economy, 143

Goldwater, Barry, 175

Goodman, Mel, 82

Gore, Al, 57

Governmental red tape, 202

Government Corporations, 204–205

Grand Chessboard: American Primacy and Its Geostrategic Imperatives (Brzezinski), 139–140

Grant, Ulysses S., 131

Great depression (1929–1930s), 52, 212

Greenback party, 51–52

Greenberg & Page, 59

Green party, 63, 68, 71

Greider, William, 7, 56, 104, 107, 109, 119–120, 179, 230–231, 237

Grenada, 148

Griswold v. Connecticut, 216

Gulf and Western, 121

H

Halliburton, 79, 143–144

Halliday, Denis, 150

Hamilton, Alexander, 17, 18, 28, 38, 121, 210

Hancock, John, 17

Hanks, Tom, 5

Harrisburg Pennsylvanian, 41

Harris, Catherine, 79

Harrison, William Henry, 103

Harvard, 141

Harvard University, 149, 190

Hearst, William Randolph, 137

Henry, Patrick, 17

Hill & Knowlton (H&K), 43

Hollings, Fritz, 175

Hoover, Herbert, 185

Hoskyns, Eric, 149

House of Representatives, 20, 25, 168

Hussein, Saddam, 44, 81, 82, 83, 85, 130, 144, 149, 150, 154, 155, 156, 230

I

Ideologies, political, 49–74, 61, 69

Immigration, 51, 66

Import/export regulations, 119–120

Inalienable rights, 26

Independent Agencies, 204, 205–206

Indian Wars, 131

Individualism, 60

Inflation, 92, 105, 107–111

Interest rates, 105

Internal Revenue Service (IRS), 68, 224

Internet, 97–98

Iowa Caucus, 197

Iran-Contra Affair, 133

Iraq, 54, 55, 57, 65, 79, 130, 135, 137, 146, 149

Iraqi Freedom, 154

"Iron triangle," 181

Ivins, Molly, 55

J

Jackson, Andrew, 41, 121, 190, 200, 220

Jay, John, 210

Jeffersonians, 217

Jefferson, Thomas, 17, 21, 28, 50, 77, 103, 105, 121, 129, 130, 167, 172, 212, 218, 220, 247, 256

Jesus Christ, 25, 67, 72

Johns Hopkins Universities, 141

Johnson, Lyndon, 139, 189

Johnston, David Cay, 56

Joint committees, congressional, 173

Judicial branch of government, 24, 168

Judicial review, 215–221

Judiciary Act of 1789, 223

Justice Department, 205

K

Kelman, Steven, 188

Kemp, Geoffrey, 151

Kennan, George F., 139

Kennedy family, 7

Kennedy, John F., 146, 189

Khomeini, Ayatollah, 151

Klein, Naomi, 145

Know-Nothing Party, 51

Knox, Henry, 17

Koppel, Ted, 138

Korea, 139

Korematsu v. United States, 216

Kosovo, 137, 149, 153

Kosovo Liberation Army (KLA), 153

Kucinich, Dennis, 63, 238

Kuwait, 43, 137, 149, 151, 155

Kwintkowski, Karen, 82

L

Laden, Osama bin, 91, 154–159

Lang, Patrick, 82

LA Times-Washington Post, 144

Law courts, 213

Lee, Richard Henry, 17

Lee, Robert E., 131

"Left" in political parties, 53

Legislation, 54

Legislative branch of government, 24, 168

Legislative process, 176–182

"Levelers" (rebels), 17

Liberal, 49, 58–59, 61, 73

Liberalism, 61

Libertarians, 62, 66–67, 70

Lincoln, Abraham, 3, 37, 51, 120, 121, 129, 220, 220–221, 248

Lineberry, Edwards & Wattenberg, 61

Lippmann, Walter, 37

Lochner v. New York, 216

Locke, John, 25–26

Los Angeles Times, 145

M

MacArthur, Douglas, 134–135, 135

MacMichael, David C., 82

Madison, James, 4, 16, 17, 21, 29, 77, 83, 121, 130, 168, 198, 200, 217, 220, 229, 249, 272–282

Major, John, 135

Majority leader, 172

Majority whip, 172

Mansor, Peter, 158

Marbury v. Madison, 216–217

Marbury, William, 217

Marshall, Thurgood, 214

Marx, Karl, 25, 67, 71

Mason, George, 17, 198

McCain, John, 54, 72, 198

McGovern, Ray, 82

Means testing, for tax reform, 113

Media, 42, 64, 77–99

Media, affect on foreign policy, 137–138

Media, class bias and, 91–92

Media, liberal *vs.* conservative biases in, 92–98

Media Reform Information Center, 96

Microsoft, 121

Middle East, 149–152, 155, 157

Military-industrial complex, 57, 133–136

Mill, John Stuart, 4, 154

Minarik, Joseph J., 107

Minh, Ho Chi, 129

Minority leader, 172

Minority whip, 172

Miranda v. Arizona, 216

Mixed (or balanced) government, 24–25

Monarchy, 14, 18, 23

Monetary conservatives, 105

Monetary liberals, 105

Monetary policy, 52, 104

Money process, in American economics, 104

Money supply, regulation of U.S., 105

Montesquieu, 24

Moore, Michael, 57

Morris, Gouverneur, 17, 198

Morris, Robert, 17

Mujahideen (soldier of God), 154

Multinational corporations (MNCs), 143–146

N

Nader, Ralph, 7, 55, 71, 119, 239

National Aeronautics and Space Administration (NASA), 205

National Coalition of Abortion Providers, 93

National Defense University, 141

National Security Advisor, 133

National Security Council (NSC), 133, 151

Natural rights, 23, 26

NBC Network, 98, 138, 188

NCR, 121

Net worth, changes in average household 1983–98, 9

New Deal, 52, 212

New Hampshire primary, 197

New Yorker, 152

New York Times, 55, 56, 80, 98, 123, 138

New York Times News Service, 116

Nicaragua, 133

Nike, 122

Nixon, Richard, 189, 191–192

Nomination, presidential, 197

Nonprofit, 205

Non-tariff trade barriers, 120

Noriega, Manuel, 149

North American Free Trade Agreement (NAFTA), 16, 122, 146

North Korea, 130, 141–143

North, Oliver, 133, 149

Nuclear arms, 134

O

Obama Administration, 43, 154, 157

Obama, Barack, 54, 55, 63, 64, 65, 72–73, 74, 80, 87, 90, 117–118, 141, 156, 157, 187, 198, 243

Obama, Michelle, 80

O'Connor & Sabato, 59, 60

Office of Management and Budget, 204

Oil industry, 143–144, 151–152

On Liberty (Mill), 154

OPEC, 151

Operation Enduring Freedom, 154

Orwell, George, 49

Overseas Operational Contingencies, 154

Oversight responsibilities, congressional, 176, 180–182

P

Paine, Thomas, 69

Palast, Greg, 78, 79, 80

Palin, Sarah, 90

Patriot Act, 241

Paul, Ron, 238

Pendleton Act, 203

Pentagon, 79, 153

People's History of the United States (Zinn), 152

People's Republic of China, 142

Perfectly Legal (Johnston), 56

Perle, Richard, 145
Perot, Henry Ross, 52
Persian Gulf, 151, 155
Peterson, Merrill D., 253
Phillips, Kevin, 7, 56
Pinckney, Cotesworth Charles, 18
Plato, 4, 25, 67, 154, 247
Plessy v. Ferguson, 216
POGS (or Armchair Rangers), 45
Policy making, congressional, 176
Political parties, 6, 49–74, 171–172
Political ideology, 61
Political party, defined, 50
Political process, 5
Political spectrum, 49–74
Political system, state of, 245–257
Polling techniques, 41
Polls, and public opinion, 41–46
Polls, problems with, 42–46
Popular opinion, 4
Populous party, 52
Presidency, 185–206
Presidency, role in foreign policy, 131–145
Presidential nomination, 197
Primary, presidential, 196
Progressive era (1900–1916), 52
Progressive tax, 112
Project for the New American Century, 141

Propaganda, 63, 236
Proportional representation, in political campaigns, 54
Protectionism, 97
Protestant Reformation, 59
Public education, 245–246, 253–256
Public, influence in foreign policy, 136–137
Public opinion, 37–46
Public vs. popular opinion, 38–39
Pundit, 55

Q
Quayle, Dan, 141

R
Racism, 42
Ratification, of Constitution, 21
Raudalen, Magne, 150
Reagan Revolution, 53
Reagan, Ronald, 139, 191–192
Rebuilding America's Defenses: Strategy, Forces and Resources for a New Century, 140–141
Recession, 105
Reform Party (Perot's party), 68, 73–74
Regressive tax code, 91
Reich, Robert, 121
Religion, media bias and, 94–95

Religious groups, voting and, 51

"Religious liberalism," 59

Religious Right, 59, 61, 68

Representation, 23, 179–180, 229–243

Republicanism, 18, 23–25

Republican party, 49–66

Republicans, 50, 62

Republic, The (Plato), 154, 247

Ricks, Thomas E., 158

"Right" in political parties, 53

Ritter, Scott, 82

Rivera, Geraldo, 138

Rockefeller family, 7, 43

Romney, Mitt, 86

Roosevelt, Franklin D., 41, 52, 135, 195, 204, 212

Roosevelt, Theodore, 120, 121, 132, 189, 195, 209

Roper, Elmo, 41

Rule of law, 23–24

Rumsfeld, Donald, 141, 145

"Running to authority" reporting, 79

Rush, Benjamin, 16

Rutledge, John, 18

S

Sandel, Michael J., 245, 246

Santa Clara County v. Southern Pacific Railroad, 216

Satterthwaite, Margaret, 55

Savile, George, 49

Saving Private Ryan, 5

Secretary of Defense, 133, 205

Secretary of State, 133, 205

Secretary of the Treasury, 133, 205

Securities, 110–111

Securities and Exchange Commission (SEC), 205

Select committees, congressional, 173

Self-government, 5, 14

Senate, 25, 168

Separation of powers, 24

September 11, 2001, 44, 80–81, 140

Serbs, 153

Shadow government, 175

Shah of Iran, 151

Shays, Christopher, 175

Shays, Daniel, 17

Shays' Rebellion, 16–17

Sherrill, Robert, 209

Simpson, O.J., 215

Single-member districts, in electoral system, 62

Slavery, 20–21, 51, 173

Social contract theory (of government), 25–26

Social security, 52

Socialism, 67

"Socialist intent," 67

Socialists, 52, 62, 67–68, 70–71
Socrates, 103
Soviet Union, 131, 152
Spanish-American War, 137
Speaker of the House, 170, 171
Specialty courts, 224
Speedy Trial Act (1974), 223
"Spin-doctor" tactic, 80, 238
Sponek, Hans von, 150
Standing committees, congressional, 173, 174
Stare decisis, 222
State and federal law, 213
State supreme courts, 221, 224
Statistics, 112–113
Stocks, funds, retirement accounts 1998, 10
Straw man argument, 239
Straw polls, 41
Strother, Dane, 232
Sununu, John, 152
Supreme Allied Commander, 134
Supreme Court, 168, 209–225
Supreme Court Building, 210
System, political, 49

T

Taliban, 130, 153, 154, 155
Tariff, 51, 120
Tax, 112, 113, 180
Taylor, Telford, 209
Telecommunications Act, 178
This Week, 186
Thomas Jefferson & the New Nation, 253
Times of India, 121
Tito, Marshal Josip, 152
Tocqueville, Alexis de, 4
Trade deficit, 123, 124–125
Trade policy, 104, 118–125
Trade regulations, 120–121
Treasury and War (Defense) department, 205
Treasury Bonds, 115
Trial courts, 223
Truman, Harry, 42, 139, 189
Twain, Mark, 112
Tweedledee and Tweedledum political view, 55, 57
Two-party system, 54, 57, 62–66

U

U.N. General Assembly, 15
Union Carbide, 121
United Nations Oil-for-Food Program, 150
United Nations Security Council, 44, 149, 150, 156
United Nations (UN), 14, 21, 149
United States v. Nixon, 216
Universal Press Syndicate, 145
UNOCOL pipeline, 140

U.S. Bureau of Labor, 120

U.S. Customs Court, 224

U.S. Department of Defense, 116

U.S. Space Forces, 141

U.S. Tax Court, 224

U.S. Treasury debt, 115–116

Ustashe Croats, 153

V

Veto, 171, 195

Vietnam, 139, 146

Vietnam War, 40, 147–148

Voter apathy, factors in, 40–41

Voter participation, 40

Voting, 50–51

Voting, corruption in process, 199

W

Wall Street Journal, 55, 58

War on Terrorism, 38, 54, 135, 137, 139, 153–159

Warren, Rick, 74

Washington, DC, 210

Washington, George, 3, 18, 50, 121, 129, 130, 189, 190

Washington Post, 53, 117, 138, 143, 152

Ways and Means committee, 173

Wealth, distribution of U.S., 8

Wealth, top one percent of household 1922–98, 9

Weapons of Mass Destruction (WMD), 81, 154, 156–157

Webster's Dictionary, 62

Webster v. Reproductive Health Services, 222

Welfare, 53

Wertheimer, Fred, 180

Whig party, 51

"Whiskey Rebellion," 18

White House Office, 204

Who Will Tell the People? (Greider), 179, 230–231

Will, George, 87, 156, 186

Williams, Brian, 138

Williamson, Gilbert, 121

Wills, Garry, 250–251

Wilson, James, 17, 198

Wilson, Joseph, 82

Wilson, Woodrow, 104, 178

Wolfowitz, Paul, 141

Women, and voting, 40

World Trade Center, 153

World Trade Organization (WTO), 54, 119, 120

World War II, 131, 134, 143, 146

Wright, Mary Ann, 82

Writ of certiorari, 221

Y

Yale, 141

Youngstown Sheet and Tube Company v. Sawyer, 216

Yugoslavia, 152

Z

Zimmerman, Peter, 83

Zinn, Howard, 152

ABOUT THE AUTHOR

Dean Darris received his Ph.D. in government from Berne University, International Graduate School, in addition to earning a master's degree in public law and political theory and a bachelor's degree in political science from Portland State University. He is currently a professor of political science at Clackamas Community College in Oregon City, Oregon, where he is consistently recognized by the student body for his outstanding teaching. He has also taught political science at Chemeketa Community College in Salem, Oregon, and Marylhurst College in Marylhurst, Oregon, as well as serving as a graduate assistant in political science at Portland State University. Prior to teaching, Dean Darris worked as a law clerk for the State of Oregon, Building Codes Agency. Before attending college, he enlisted in the United States Air Force and served as a security policeman. He lives with his wife, Tara, and son, Jordan.